LESSONS AND LEGACIES V

LESSONS AND LEGACIES V

The Holocaust and Justice

Edited and with an introduction
by Ronald Smelser

NORTHWESTERN UNIVERSITY PRESS   EVANSTON, ILLINOIS

Northwestern University Press
Evanston, Illinois 60208-4210

Copyright © 2002 by Northwestern University Press. Published 2002.
All rights reserved.

Printed in the United States of America

10 9 8 7 6 5 4 3 2 1

ISBN 0-8101-1915-3 (cloth)
ISBN 0-8101-1916-1 (paper)

Library of Congress Cataloging-in-Publication Data
Lessons and Legacies V: the Holocaust and justice / edited and with an introduction by Ronald Smelser
    p. cm.
    ISBN 0-8101-1915-3—ISBN 0-8101-1916-1 (pbk.)
    1. Holocaust, Jewish (1939–1945)—Congresses. 2. Holocaust, Jewish (1939–1945)—Historiography—Congresses. 3. Holocaust, Jewish (1939–1945)—Influence—Congresses. I. Smelser, Ronald.
D810.J4L4 1991
940.53'18—dc20

                                                                    91-14707
                                                                        CIP

The paper used in this publication meets the minimum requirements of the
American National Standard for Information Sciences—Permanence of Paper for
Printed Library Materials, ANSI Z39.48-1984.

In memory of our beloved parents and grandparents
Albert and Goldie Stone
Joseph and Sylvia Good

—Howard and Ferne Stone and family

Contents

Theodore Zev Weiss

Foreword

THIS IS THE FIFTH VOLUME OF SCHOLARLY PAPERS PUBLISHED AS AN outgrowth of the Lessons and Legacies Conferences that the Holocaust Educational Foundation sponsors in partnership with major centers of higher learning. These conferences have become a tradition. The two Northwestern University conferences of 1990 and 1992 were followed by others at Dartmouth College in 1994 and Notre Dame University in 1996. We are pleased to acknowledge Florida Atlantic University for hosting Lessons and Legacies V in 1998. We are very grateful to Professor Alan Berger for all his help in preparing a successful conference.

The successful Lessons and Legacies Conference is only one area in which the Holocaust Educational Foundation has made gratifying strides in recent years. The number of colleges and universities teaching courses on the Holocaust with the foundation's help has grown from twenty at the beginning of the 1990s to more than two hundred. Moreover, the foundation has established the biannual summer seminar trip to Holocaust sites in Central and Eastern Europe, enabling some one hundred fifty scholars who teach courses on the Holocaust to acquaint themselves firsthand with the "topography of terror" that the Nazi regime established. Finally, by establishing the annual Summer Institute on the Holocaust and Jewish Civilization held at Northwestern University, the foundation has begun a program of educating current and future college and university professors about the history, faith, and culture of the Jewish people, whom Nazism targeted for extinction. To date, more than two hundred fifty professors and doctoral candidates have been fellows of the institute. All these efforts have brought us into ever more fulfilling contact with a growing "family" of decent and dedicated academicians who share our conviction that learning remains the best antidote to humanity's most inhumane impulses.

I want to express my deep gratitude to the board members who have contributed so generously to the foundation's work and who made all this possible.

My personal thanks and appreciation to Professor Christopher Browning for chairing the conference and for his personal devotion to the foundation and its work and to all the scholars who participated and contributed so greatly to the success of the Lessons and Legacies Conference.

Finally, as always, my strongest sense of gratitude is to my wife, Alice, and my children, Deborah and Gabriel and Danny, who have encouraged the work of the foundation at every juncture and replenished my energies at every step.

Ronald Smelser

Introduction

THIS VOLUME IS THE RESULT OF THE FIFTH LESSONS AND LEGACIES Conference held in Boca Raton, Florida, November 7–9, 1998. The conference focused on the theme of "Law, Evidence, and Context" and represented an attempt to wrestle with the complex and often contradictory question of the Holocaust and justice. Is justice possible for such a horrendous crime as the Holocaust? If so, what kind of justice? In the courts? Before the bar of history? Retrospective as well as contemporary? Divine?

These essays, then, written by a number of distinguished scholars, represent attempts to deal with the question of achieving justice in a number of venues and contexts, while recognizing the very problematic nature of such an attempt. In constructing these essays, the authors have raised as many questions as they have answered, and we leave it to the readers of this volume to continue the process that the conference and its resulting papers began.

The initial focus, as in any judicial proceeding, is on the perpetrators. Who were they? This is not always an easy question to answer. What were their motivations? This, too, is a complex question. In what context did they function? What was the complex interplay between individual and institutional perpetrator?

These considerations, in turn, take us into the courtroom, where the attempt to achieve justice is played out. What kinds of trials have been launched, and what kind of "justice" was the result? What kinds of evidence is it possible to adduce, particularly in proceedings decades after the event? What problems are involved in documentary evidence? In eyewitness testimony? In survivor memory? How does ideology play into the judicial process? What purpose do the trials have? Punishment? How does any punishment accord with the enormity of the crime? Retribution? Didactic lessons for history? What, if any, role do historians have in legal proceedings? For, after all, attorneys and scholars have very different agendas.

What do establishing historical perspective and drawing on memory have to do with contributing to justice in its larger sense, that is, to the verdict of the future on the past as reflected in history, literature, societal discourse, and retrospective memory? How has the Holocaust been presented to date in textbooks? How will it be presented to future generations in various countries in the differing contexts, which the evolution of the human experience will establish? The Holocaust was once barely visible in broad histories of World War II. Will this once again be the case in future decades?

Within the context of Holocaust and justice, how do those who are profoundly but indirectly affected by that tragedy—the children and grandchildren of the victims, including survivors—contribute to our understanding of the Holocaust through their own attempts at coming to grips with what happened to their relatives? By writing literature, making films, and re-creating experience with imagination and empathy, they become "character witnesses" for the plaintiffs in the larger courtroom of history.

Two authors set the context for the others. Omer Bartov picks up the quasi-religious theme in setting a larger context for the Holocaust: that of people's age-old attempts to create the utopian society—one which is harmonious, clean, healthy, salubrious, and beautiful. These attempts involved establishing boundaries, the most lethal of which were between humanity and those placed outside of humanity by whatever criteria. Once established, the boundary allows people to lay the most grandiose plans for the in-group and the most destructive ones for those on the out, whose very existence poses a lethal threat to the ins and their plans.

What has made utopian planning so dangerous in the twentieth century, Bartov suggests, has been the wedding of the utopian spirit to modern scientific and social planning, harnessed, in turn, to advanced technology and the power of the modern state.

Keynote speaker Saul Friedländer focused on the immediate context of the crucial period in the summer and fall of 1941, during which—probably in mid-October—the decision to kill all the Jews of Europe was made by Adolf Hitler. Friedländer reemphasizes the role of ideology in Hitler's motivation, underscoring "redemptive anti-Semitism," a chiliastic, millennial, quasi-religious belief system, reinforced by racial science, which Hitler, the self-appointed messiah, embraced and made the core of his life's work. It was his initiatives—setting guidelines for the genocide against the Jews—which were decisive in turning apocalyptic ideology into wartime social policy. Friedländer places emphasis on Hitler's words and on the context in which he uttered them. Hitler gave the signals. The Nazi Party, ideological protector of National Socialism, received the charge. Other agencies, government and military, already to a degree anti-Semitic and certainly violently anti-Bolshevik, allowed the Hitlerian combination of "Jewish-Bolshevism" to enlist their complicity in the Final Solution. Mass indifference to the fate of Jews plus mass faith in Hitler completed the necessary prerequisites for genocide.

It is these contexts—broad and narrow—in which the perpetrators functioned. The section on the perpetrators raises important questions about the who and the why. Our contributors examine the broad range of perpetrators, individual and institutional, and their motivation. They shed light on individuals who operated within the machinery of death and explore the complex relationships between individual motivation and institutional involvement. How were the perpetrators governed by considerations such as ideology, career advancement, peer pressure, proximity to crimes, attitudes toward authority, desire to avoid combat assignments, and other factors? The range of perpetrators is very broad and includes not only Nazi Party and SS/police but also the military, the diplomatic corps, the corporate world, and foreign countries.

Alvin Rosenfeld problematizes the perpetrators by suggesting that we think we know who the killers are—at the top and at the bottom of the process—but what we know does not satisfy. Much remains inaccessible to us, and what we do know leaves us uneasy. What we know changes constantly; how we receive knowledge varies tremendously, much of it not coming from didactic sources. Much of it, in fact, is presented in such a way as to create the opposite effect as that intended: not enlightenment but titillation. We know much more about the victims, he suggests, than about the perpetrators, who remain shadowy stereotypes. More daunting yet is the question of how we gain access to the perpetrators as human beings when they are so bound up in the killing machinery, in the process of genocide, in the impersonal bureaucracy of mass murder. Problematic too is the fact that today we meet the perpetrators in the courtrooms as undistinguished, often ill, old men; we do not meet them in the vigor of their destructive youth.

Rosenfeld also underscores the importance of art and popular literature in conveying images of the killers; but this carries the risk of focus on social deviancy and disturbed minds—not the condition of most killers. In these remarks, Rosenfeld points to some of the difficulties of identifying and understanding the perpetrators, particularly for the general public in today's world—over a half century after the events of the Holocaust.

Several contributors wrestle with these questions specifically. Peter Black sheds light on the social typology of the top leadership of the RSHA (*Reichssicherheitshauptamt,* or Reich Central Office for Security), the SS police empire, men, it turns out, who were solid, middle-class, well-educated individuals—anything but the sociopaths the public often assumes these men to be. Henry Friedlander looks at middle-level managers and discovers that, very often, rather mundane concerns drove these men. They were for the most part career men, who largely accepted most of the tenets of Nazi ideology but were not particularly fanatic in their beliefs. Coming from somewhat lower social and educational levels than the RSHA leaders, these men joined the SS for upward mobility. Frequently they were involved in brutality and corruption, occasionally they were even disciplined, especially if their behavior impaired the functioning of the system. By contrast, Michael Allen in his study of the engineers in the SS economic empire finds a large degree of ideological commitment. These were not soulless technocrats but men who shaped their activity along the lines of Nazi ideology.

Hannes Heer examines the Wehrmacht as perpetrator organization. He reveals what historians have known for years but which only came to the attention of a larger audience, especially in Germany, in conjunction with the traveling exhibit on the crimes of the Wehrmacht: that Hitler's military was deeply implicated in the crimes of the regime. Heer examines the formative influences on German soldiers prior to the war; the war experience itself; and the way in which the soldiers, under the impact of propaganda, interpreted that experience to legitimize their participation in the darker side of the conflict.

Peter Hayes examines the process by which corporate executives gradually became complicit in the crimes of the regime. Analyzing the experience of executives from the Degussa company, he reveals that their involvement was not precipitous but rather a long, slippery slope at each stage of which they undertook steps that seemed in context simply to be to the advantage of the company. Ultimately, without full realization of what they were doing, they crossed a fatal Rubicon.

Sybil Milton recasts the role of the Swiss government during the period of the Holocaust from that of "neutral" country to "silent partner" of the Nazis, particularly in providing valuable services such as laundering money and fencing stolen goods.

Gitta Sereny brings us back full circle to the thoughts of Alvin Rosenfeld: How do we get at the identity of the perpetrators? As an author who has assumed the role of journalist/interviewer/amateur psychologist in her many in-depth interviews of perpetrators such as Franz Stangl, commandant of Auschwitz, Sereny here tries to understand and convey the motivation of Albert Speer, Hitler's personal architect and confidant as well as mobilizer of the Nazi war economy.

Two authors introduce the section on courts by problematizing the process of trying to achieve justice through judicial process. Michael Marrus notes that justice has been sought not only before the bar of history, never mind divine judgment, but more typically through the courts. Marrus briefly analyzes six kinds of trials: the International Military Tribunal, which tried the major Nazi war criminals immediately after the war; the "successor trials" such as that of the doctors and the *Einsatzgruppen;* trials in formerly occupied countries; trials before German courts; trials of collaborators, Jewish and other; and finally, the recent libel trials of deniers in civil court. Using these various trials as examples, Marrus points out the pitfalls of courtroom trials, in particular, the attempt to use them either as didactic devices or as historical sources. Lawyers, he points out, do not do what historians do.

Robert Paxton specifically focuses on the pitfalls of the trials of Vichy officials. He points out the great unevenness that appears in the treatment of various groups of defendants. Those with a paper trail were punished severely, while those who had been more discreet in covering their tracks or whose efforts were needed in rebuilding got off more leniently. Moreover, the way in which Vichy officials were dealt with for their treatment and deportation of the Jews was misleading. The trials focused on activities that could be deemed "treasonous," that is, collaborating with and acting under the aegis of the Germans. Situations in which Vichy officials actually took the initiative were given short shrift and were only brought to light decades later. Vichy's own legal responsibility for crimes against the Jews was most convincingly demonstrated only in the recent Papon trial.

Three other contributions in this section focus more specifically both on the reliability of human memory as testimony and on the ways in which evidence has come to be "tainted" by being refracted through ideology and cultural bias or simply by the passage of time. Therkel Straede joins the debate over whether there can be a recoverable past by examining the question of how useful survivor testimonies can be to history or to the judicial process. He concludes that, despite the often problematic role of human memory and ex post facto testimony, one can, in fact, recover the past in ways that can be useful not only in court but also before the bar of history.

Insa Eschebach looks at East German trials, not so much for what they reveal about perpetration as about prevailing depictions of the perpetrators as they are revealed in the trial records. She depicts how East German courts, animated by propaganda opportunity and gender prejudice as much as by the quest for justice, portrayed female perpetrators. The women in the docket, she reveals, were, in contrast to male defendants, judged not so much for their actual deeds as for their very stereotyped identities, either as young "innocent dupes" or as older "beautiful but cruel gun molls."

Andrew Ezergailis, examining Soviet Latvia, demonstrates how trials there during the Khrushchev era were not primarily designed to bring Holocaust perpetrators, especially German ones, to justice but rather to get at Latvian nationalists.

Human memory in historical perspective represents the next theme. Donald Schilling points out that changing times bring different perspectives. This is, in a sense, a truism, but he puts it firmly into the framework of the question of why the Holocaust against the Jews is missing from virtually all history textbooks on World War II published during the two decades after the war. He responds to that question by advancing a number of reasons, including anti-Semitism, or at least widespread ignorance of Jewish history; the tendency to put the war into the narrow framework of military history; lack of adequate sources; and bewilderment at the enormity of the crime. In recent studies, by contrast, the Holocaust has been much more successfully integrated into the history of World War II, in part owing to the pioneering work of Gerhard Weinberg and others.

Renée Poznanski addresses historical perspective from a somewhat different angle: How does the long tradition of anti-Semitism in France relate to the fate of the Jews? She analyzes the behavior of the French at two specific times and places during the war: Paris early in the occupation and southern France during the time of the roundups. Though she identifies indifference as the main attitude of most French people, she indicates that this view must be refined to explain why three-quarters of French Jews escaped the fate intended for them. In Paris, initial general public support of discriminatory measures initiated by the Vichy government indicated a widespread anti-Semitism and acceptance of the idea of a "Jewish problem," while widespread individual expressions of sympathy can to some degree reflect resentment at the presence of German occupiers. Later, in the south, after summer 1942, mass roundups provoked public indignation, and, as the legitimacy of Vichy waned, so did the respectability of its anti-Semitic measures.

David Bankier takes us to a rather forlorn group—German anti-Nazi exiles in London, including Social Democrats, Conservatives, and Communists—and analyzes their plans for the Jews in a postwar Germany. To a remarkable degree these people, already marginalized by Hitler's victory in Germany and his hold on most of Europe, remained largely untouched by these dramatic events in their attitudes toward the Jews and adhered to older positions, which the exiles now reaffirmed. Most of them set terms by which the Jews, then largely perishing in the Holocaust, might achieve integration back into German society. Like the earlier Bourbons in France, these exiles showed that they had forgotten nothing and learned nothing. Only the Communists responded with some flexibility, contemplating the possibility of a Jewish state as well as reintegration, but this was the result of Stalin's political tactics, not their own initiatives.

Vojtech Blodig gives us an illustration of how ideology and political expediency can be used to color the memory of the Holocaust by demonstrating how the Communist regime in Czechoslovakia used the memorial at Terezín (Theresienstadt) as a vehicle for anti-Semitic, later anti-Zionist, ideology.

Three of the four essays in the final section, which deals with the second generation—the children of survivors—represent a dialogue

of sorts among the authors. As Alan Berger puts it, the second generation has the combined responsibility of "mourning a past that they
never knew but which shapes their lives while, at the same time, they
seek to shape this elusive memory for their own children and for
future generations." Some of the discussion revolves around the concept of *tikkun,* a Hebrew word meaning to mend, to repair, to reha-
bilitate, to redeem, and suggests that one larger aspect of the Holocaust and justice is, in a sense, to make a fragmented universe whole
again.

In his contribution, Berger observes one person, writer Helen
Epstein, as she "works through" the Holocaust therapeutically in her
literary texts with the intent of first "repairing herself" and then, by
gaining access to ever larger communities, "creat[ing] a family." She
eventually completes her journey by connecting with Judaism. This,
says Berger, is a prime illustration of how the Shoah has provided an
entry (or reentry) in Jewish identity to secularized Jews.

Rachel Feldhay Brenner notes, however, that expression is not
easy; a tension arises out of the fact that the overpowering need to tell
is often constricted by the fear of not being able to—thus leading to
muteness. Added to this is the problem of finding the words to explain to the uninitiated about the "other planet" of the Holocaust.
She points out, on the basis of Berger's work, how problematic a task
it is to achieve *tikkun.* The Shoah has come dangerously close to placing the world beyond the possibility of redemption; has distorted all
previous conceptions of humanism. One dare not forget, but in not
forgetting, one cannot totally mend, for to mend implies reestablishing ties to continuity, yet doing so in a world made random and capri-
cious by the Holocaust is extremely difficult.

The children of survivors have not just served memory by writing about the Holocaust, they have also made films about it in their
attempt at working through the experience, including films in which
they interview their parent survivors. In these films, the children are
at once recorders and participants, and they function as mediators between the surviving parents and contemporaries. They are "biography and autobiography intertwined." For all of this, though, Sara
Horowitz concludes in the penultimate essay, the films demonstrate
the impossibility of children "knowing" their parents' past. She also
concludes that films, like literature, "implicate the Holocaust in the
construction of postwar Jewish identity."

Finally, Robert Melson tells his own story of interviewing his parents, portraying them as three-dimensional human beings—warts and all—always striving for fidelity to the truth. In doing so, he sees himself as a witness at a trial. And here we come full circle in the volume, from contemplating the possibility of "justice," in any sense of the word in the wake of the Holocaust, to the real judicial processes of the postwar period, to the bench of history, and to the confrontation of each individual with his or her own memory and sense of justice.

LESSONS AND LEGACIES V

I. C·O·N·T·E·X·T

Omer Bartov

Utopia and Violence
Visions of Perfection and Practices of Purification

You cannot make an omelette without breaking eggs.
    —*Modern revolutionary motto*

FROM THE EARLIEST RECORDS OF HUMAN CIVILIZATION TO OUR OWN century, people have been fascinated by the notion of remaking humanity—molding individuals and societies in accordance with the laws of God or nature, history or science, into more perfect entities. But this quest for perfection has often been accompanied by an urge to unmake the present and erase the heritage of the past. Hence the path to utopia is strewn with shattered edifices and mounds of corpses. Because by definition it must always remain a goal, utopia engenders fantasies about a future whose imagined fabric draws heavily on myths about the past; fabricating a future earthly paradise is predicated on the imagery of a lost Garden of Eden. Such links between mythology and vision make for mechanisms of remembrance and prediction, fiction and representation, repression and categorization, which are at the core of humanity's self-perception and sense of identity. Materially nowhere, utopia fills the mind; a site of infinite fantasy, it can also trigger limitless destruction.

BOUNDARIES AND TRANSGRESSIONS

Life as an idea is dead. This may be the beginning of a great new era, a redemption from suffering. . . . Only one crime remains: cursed be he who creates life. I cremate life. That is modern humanitarianism—the sole salvation from the future.[1]

Utopia begins by setting up boundaries: between reality and vision, the desirable and the undesirable, the intimate and the alien. It banishes the disruptive in the name of harmony, the eccentric in favor of the collective. Whether it is predicated on metaphysical dogmas, political principles, social ideals, or biological determinants, utopia cannot tolerate dissent. It is thus defined by what it excludes. Yet once the boundaries are set up, transgressions are bound to follow.[2]

Historically we can speak of several types of boundaries, based on ethnic, religious, geographical, political, and social categories, as well as on gender and generational differences, although individual identity will normally be determined by belonging to more than one such category. Boundaries can produce a sense of security and stability but at same time may be the cause of tension and competition, oppression and submission. As long as they are accepted by the majority, boundaries can therefore make for an appearance of harmony; for this very reason, any transgression will be seen as posing a threat of disintegration and chaos. Conversely, transgression of established boundaries can also be presented as a step toward greater harmony. Indeed, perfect, universal utopia assumes the ultimate eradication of boundaries, between sexes or races, classes or faiths, the present and the future. Nevertheless, the idea of utopia is predicated on a fundamental rift between conventional, sordid reality and the ideal toward which one ought to strive. Hence it is a harmony based on difference.[3]

Antiquity recognized boundaries between civilization and barbarism. Barbarian conquest of Greek, Roman, or Chinese civilization led in turn to the emergence of new boundaries between an idyllic, remote past, and a more recent, decadent period, seen as the cause of destruction, occupation, and the erasure of previously established boundaries associated with cultural superiority and traditional privilege. But utopian visions were also informed by the image of a purer barbaric invader as yet uncorrupted by the social and moral ills of degenerate civilization, who could serve as a model of ancient ideals. Hence the boundaries between civilization and barbarism, reality and utopia, constantly shifted even as they asserted eternal immutability.[4]

In medieval and early modern Europe, the predominant utopia was Heaven, whose essential attributes were similar across denominations and estates. But aside from this purely religious utopia, wherein the boundary between life and death had to be negotiated and traversed, other utopias focused on transforming the world of the living. Here one group's utopia was another's nightmare, whether it involved redeeming the Holy Land or unshackling the serfs, the "reconquest" of Spain or the Islamization of Christendom, the rise of Protestantism or the messianism of Shabbetai Zevi. If the gates of Heaven could open only after the outrage of death, then earthly paradise could be accomplished only by the violent overthrow of established regimes and religions, the massacre of dissidents, the conquest of land. Europe's emergence from the Middle Ages was followed by centuries of political and military expansion, invariably accompanied by the exclusion, expulsion, and murder of those perceived as obstructing the realization of religious and secular utopias and the redefinition of identity within newly drawn boundaries.[5]

This was especially noticeable in the course of European colonialism, which perforce made for encounters with hitherto unknown cultures and religions, customs and norms, races and ethnicities. Here the most fundamental boundary established was that between men and savages, or human and nonhuman. The European discourse on the humanity of colonized peoples largely determined both the fate of the indigenous populations in the colonies and the self-perception of Europeans and their increasing predilection to differentiate between, and rank, types and degrees of humanity according to physical, mental, and cultural criteria. Modern Western utopias now included the same split we have noted in antiquity, between a romanticized view of nature and its "noble savages," on the one hand, and the dehumanization of other, "lower" races and cultures, on the other. But both the notion of "returning" to nature and that of Europe's "civilizing mission" involved a great deal of violence, exacerbated by rapidly improved technologies of killing. Thus utopian societies established far from civilization's corrupting reach could simultaneously assume the eradication or enslavement of indigenous populations while schemes for social justice, liberty, and equality could at the same time be predicated on the exclusion or annihilation of those no longer recognized as members of humanity.[6]

Cultural differentiation extended also to distinctions between societies with and without history, increasingly seen as the basic criterion of civilization following the decline of religion and the concomitant recognition of non-Christian civilizations in Asia and antiquity. If modern utopian visions aimed to reach a point where history would come to a standstill and humanity achieve a condition of perfect rest, this was a process to be accomplished *through* history rather than by avoiding it altogether, just as the true saint would emerge from the valley of sin or classless society from a bitter struggle with a historically necessary phase of ruthless capitalism. The innocence of the original, prehistorical paradise was derived from an absence of history; this naïveté would now have to be replaced by an awareness of history as a precondition for the posthistorical utopia. And while some sites of presumed innocence were still to be found in the shrinking white areas of European cartography, the utopias discovered there had to be unmade and then remade again so as to fit the needs and dreams of modernity's refugees.[7]

Utopia was not perceived as a natural development but as planned and controlled nature, whose boundaries were determined, set, and guarded by man, not by the whims of climate and biology. Nature was the site in which utopia would be built, but nature was also the transgressor par excellence and thus had to be kept under strict control and supervision. Utopia was a garden society, where chance and mutation, disorder and catastrophe could not to be allowed to disrupt the orderly development of man-made environment. This quest for domination over nature characterized most civilizations, both ancient and modern. Its most recent manifestations are related to the industrialization of the nineteenth century and can be found in fascist rhetoric and planning, liberal suburban schemes and garden cities, and postwar "green" ideologies. The contemporary discourse on ecology, whose roots go back at least two centuries, is especially pertinent in this context, since it involves the relationship between categories of people and types of environment, nature preservation and human habitation, transgressing the laws of biology and setting limits to reproduction.[8]

Boundaries can also be set between species; nature prevents most interspecies procreation, and civilization makes such transgressions strictly taboo. Yet modern science has been preoccupied with evolution, genetics, and cloning, while nineteenth- and early-twentieth-century ideologies have popularized the ideas of social Darwinism, eugenics, and scientific racism. If civilization has for millennia do-

mesticated plants and bred animals, the modern utopia of a perfect
humanity has included the idea of breeding pure races of human beings. This is the great temptation of purging physical deformities,
mental handicaps, and foreign races, of manipulating nature to fit desirable aesthetic and intellectual criteria, and of eradicating so-called
life unworthy of life or categories of people deemed detrimental to society's health and progress. Here conventional taboos against tam-
pering with humanity are transgressed, while the boundaries between
humans and animals tend to disappear: superhumans are put above
the rest of humanity, subhumans are considered less worthy of life
and often more pernicious than domestic animals. Nor should we
think of this phenomenon as being limited to such extreme manifestations as Nazism, for the modern discourse on links between biology
and society, science and ethics, nature and nurture, is the necessary
context for such radical policies as racial genocide.[9]

PLANS AND INEVITABILITIES

*Man models himself on earth, earth on heaven, heaven on the
way. And the way on that which is naturally so.*

—Lao Tzu

Utopias can be the products of ordering the past, planning the future,
and controlling nature—both people's and their environment's. But
utopias may also be perceived as the inevitable outcome of a divinely
ordained apocalypse or of the immutable laws of nature and history.
God or the *Weltgeist,* evolution or the class struggle, racial war or genetic destiny may all be cited as potential agents in humanity's journey to utopia.

Apocalypse by divine decree and by human action are the two divergent paths to the end of history. The former entrusts the future to
the metaphysical, the latter is determined to establish rational control
over the universe. Both are at the very root of civilization across a vast
array of cultures and societies, and both retain great relevance today,
at a time of religious revival and a simultaneous faith in science.
Whatever the specific path they have chosen, various religious and
secular, ancient and modern, European and extra-European utopian
notions have constructed a notion of inevitability. It is this idea which

is the basis of both apocalyptic theology and planned society, geared as they are either to keep the anticipated catastrophe at bay or to exploit it for political purposes. It is thus also at the center of any discourse on the relationship between creativity and destruction, hope and despair, and is crucial to understanding how societies have come to terms with uncertainty and fear. At the same time, apocalypse is often seen as bearing utopian consequences; it is thus both an end and a beginning, feared and anticipated, accompanied by social violence and creative change. Precisely when secularized and incorporated into modern ideologies, apocalyptic reasoning and fantasies have fueled a paroxysm of unprecedented destruction.[10]

Human agency is of course a crucial feature both in planning utopia and in contemplating its place within God's scheme or the logic of history. The modern era has become especially preoccupied with the idea of remaking people and society, nature and the environment, according to a precisely laid out plan which, at the same time, would remain in accordance with natural and inevitable progression. Hence too the perceived need to eradicate resistance to such plans, which by definition is regressive, reactionary, degenerate, or abnormal. For the link between healing and killing, creating and destroying life is derived from a modern utopianism that postulates the need to tamper with nature or change the course of history while simultaneously asserting compliance with its laws. All that is called for is merely an acceleration of such inevitable natural processes as selection, evolution, and mutation or of such inevitable social developments as the disappearance of one class and the hegemony of another. In other words, such utopias will either seek to ensure the survival of the fittest, or push toward the end of history, both of which are certain to happen yet also seem to be threatened by unnatural intervention or a lack of understanding. Those who do not fit into nature's plan, or the unfolding of history—as interpreted by human beings— must be eliminated as so much genetic waste, or will be discarded, thrown into the dustbin of history or ground to dust by the wheels of the revolution. In this context, conventional moral arguments are seen as fundamentally immoral, for they obstruct the higher morality expressed in the course of nature or history and thus prevent humanity from reaching utopia by implementing plans based on objective biological determinants or the science of history. The destruction of those who stand in the way is therefore a moral imperative, and individual existence must be subordinated to the good of humanity as a whole.[11]

It should be pointed out that notions of social engineering, economic planning, and inevitable historical processes played some role in many parts of the world throughout the twentieth century. If Communist regimes hoped to realize the proletarian paradise by means of planned economies and the destruction of feudal leftovers and capitalist ventures, liberal capitalism set out on a pursuit of universal happiness by combining trust in the "invisible hand" of market forces with state intervention during times of domestic social turmoil and international conflict. While imperialism legitimized itself by asserting both the West's "natural" superiority and its beneficial impact on indigenous populations, decolonization was also presented as a natural, inevitable process, yet one in which new nations were cast by persecuting minorities, suppressing public opinion, and seeking to reach a more "civilized" condition through molding and controlling social, political, and economic forces. Moreover, the clash between the defenders of natural procreation, whether religious or nationalist, and the promoters of family planning and demographic control has been at the root of a variety of crucial discussions over the nature of and divisions within humanity. The utopian urge in human civilization can thus be seen in debates over the definition of life and the right to end or prevent it; in arguments for and against state intervention in the privacy of the individual; in struggles over relations between the sexes and between poor and rich countries or classes; and in disputes on the role of religion or science in our perception of humanity and the option of remaking it in accordance with theological or ideological schemes. Indeed, assertions about the inevitable forces of nature or history, whose relentless logic induces either domination and submission or rebellion and planned intervention, combine with the modern predilection toward biological and psychological imperatives. Explaining individual and collective behavior by reference to innate or essential predispositions also leads to projects of genetic engineering that would remake humanity according to particular behavioral, moral, and aesthetic criteria, so as to better "fit" it into a predetermined plan or ideal. In this technological and moral utopia, humanity's environment must also be reordered, whether to return it to its perceived natural, primeval state or to better serve the interests of civilization.[12]

MEMORY AND ERASURE

However this war may end, we have won the war against you;
none of you will be left to bear witness, but even if someone were
to survive, the world will not believe him . . . people will say that
the events you describe are too monstrous to be believed. . . . We
will be the ones to dictate the history of the Lagers.[13]

Utopian visions combine hopes for an idyllic future with recollections of a mythical past; they are also about wiping out the reality and memory of the present in order to facilitate the creation of a new world no longer haunted by ancient nightmares and lingering nostalgia. The construction of utopia requires radical mental and physical measures, geared not only toward the future but also to a reorganization of the past. Holy war or social revolution, for instance, even while they strive to change present reality, derive their image of an ideal future from a selective representation of history, where both that which should be restored and that which must be destroyed are to be found. This in turn makes for the centrality of historical records, their keepers and interpreters. To be sure, memory and erasure are not only the outcome of conscious and willed acts of people but also of chance and nature. Yet the discourse of utopia often refers to precisely those past events whose disastrous consequences had ensured the destruction of their records, leaving behind only scattered remains and traumatic recollections. Thus if utopia is about radically changing the past, it does so both by material eradication and by erasure of memory; it therefore suffers from both chronic and self-induced amnesia while legitimizing and sustaining itself by means of vivid, but highly selective, memories.[14]

Such memories are contained not only in historical documents and personal recollections but also in collections of artifacts. For utopia's ambivalent relationship with the past concerns both a desire to overcome it and a need to retain a link to it, if only to manifest its own superiority. But this competition between past and future cannot avoid a measure of nostalgia, since the collected remnants of the past are by their very nature the last symbols of a lost world, acting as the agents provocateurs of a forbidden longing for preutopian existence. Yet utopias cannot desist from collecting and presenting such relics, even when they serve as evidence of the present's murderous roots. Thus the Nazis began collecting material for a museum of Judaica even as the Holocaust was in progress so as to document their triumph over Germany's most evil, repulsive enemy; precisely because the Jews were to wiped off the face of the earth, the public had to be provided with the Nazi version of their past existence.[15] Similarly, Goebbels arranged for an exhibit of "degenerate art" before stowing away some of Germany's greatest modernist works. In this manner, Germans were shown one last time what would never be seen again, reminded, that is, of what must no longer be remembered: that so-called Nazi art was a cultural throwback made possible by massive erasure, just as Jewish life in Eastern Europe had been so thoroughly erased that its only surviving echo remains in Polish ethnic museums representing a long forgotten and exotic people that had once inhabited the land.[16]

Collections of remnants of the past have served many other regimes to glorify their own accomplishments and demonstrate their greater proximity to current ideals while simultaneously provoking nostalgia for a mythical past. Communists often resorted to an arsenal of nationalist sentiments in periods of crises. Thus Stalin encouraged references to holy Russia's medieval wars against the Teutonic order during the early phases of what was significantly called the Great Patriotic War of 1941–45, even if the Bolshevik revolution's main slogan had been "destroy the old world and build up the new." Nor could aesthetic sensibilities always entirely dismiss the great works of the past. The British and the French, for their part, filled vast museums with the riches of ancient empires looted from their colonies, even as they claimed to bring civilization to the "natives" and show them the path to Western utopia. The same Europeans who carried the "white man's burden" thus became fascinated with African "primitivism," "japonisme," Chinese, Indian, Near Eastern and pre-Columbian art and expressed a longing to a presumed state of primeval harmony which they were in the process of destroying.[17]

For utopia, the selective memory and erasure of past or competing utopias is crucial not least because attempts to create a perfect humanity often generate conflict, violence, and victims, and therefore also potential counternarratives by witnesses and chroniclers. The memory of utopia is predicated on perspective, for in the process of carving out a place for itself in a world that denies it a site, utopia may resort to a violent overthrow of existing structures. Hence those who inhabit the newly created utopian space will necessarily perceive reality differently from those who had been eliminated from it. In this sense, one person's utopia is another person's hell. In our own twentieth century in particular, this mechanism created a crisis of testimony and evidence, confronted as we are with a multiplicity of contradictory documents and memories all vying for attention with the kind of urgency and desperation characteristic of the extremity of the events they recall. Hence too the crisis experienced by historians, who find themselves torn between a hankering for the alleged objectivity of archival records and a sense that however hard they toil, their reconstruction of the past will be dismissed or rejected by those whose perspective of the events cannot allow for the balanced narrative demanded by modern historiography. This, in turn, has led to the emergence of radical skepticism and historical relativity, for if the historian's utopia is to tell the past as it really happened, the reaction to this utopia's perceived failure is the assertion that the past can never be told, that it is, so to speak, not only a foreign country but a vast Tower of Babel in which each individual or group experiences the world through the prism of its own unique and untranslatable tongue.[18]

The historian is therefore actively, albeit not always consciously, engaged in the creation of utopia, for it is the historian's authority— dating back in some civilizations to early antiquity—that provides a picture of the past as a model for the future; it is the historian's selection of episodes and personages from both a documented and a mythical past that determines what will be remembered and what will recede forever into oblivion, erased without a trace from the written annals of historical time. And while this is surely the case when we ponder the remote past, our own time too contains gaping black holes, the consequence of material destruction, tormented and distorted memories, or events whose nature defies representation and comprehension by means of conventional scholarship and fiction, art and philosophy. Thus individual, often inarticulate, inexpressible, and unstable memories are ultimately erased through the biological extinction of their carriers, without ever having been molded into a transmittable, even if selective, narrative. Paradoxically, it is precisely thanks to the haphazard but unrelenting erasure of these memories that future utopias can be woven, whose fundamental outlines do not differ in any essential sense from those that had produced the necessary space of material and mental erasure on which they are built. And yet, if our current civilization has recently become so concerned with memory, it is because the shattered utopias of the past have profoundly undermined hope; and in order to dream of the future, we need to remember the past.[19]

FINAL SOLUTIONS

We have exterminated a bacterium because we do not want in the end to be infected by the bacterium and die of it. . . . All in all, we can say that we have fulfilled this most difficult duty for the love of our people. And our spirit, our soul, our character has not suffered from it . . .[20]

Utopias propose final solutions to perennial questions of human existence and social organization. Utopian society permanently eliminates irksome problems that had never been resolved before. Such attempts to eradicate the inherent ills of civilization or human biology often generate violence, whose perceived legitimacy in view of the noble goal it serves greatly enhances its ferocity.

Both the nature of utopia and the type and scope of its violence reflect the societies and cultures that produce it. Religious utopias must be understood within the context of the established religious doctrine, social organization, and power structure they hope to reform or overthrow. Here the first step to utopia is made by adopting a new or reformed faith, even if eventually the inevitable institutional, hierarchical, and social organization of this new creed tends to divert its followers from the path on which it had originally set out. Moreover, since numerous religions associate utopia with death, the afterlife, or reincarnation, earthly existence maintains an ambivalent relationship with its final destination, goal, and purpose.[21]

Modern utopias reflect the growing predominance of science and technology, mass politics and state control, secularization and alienation. Hence the longing to achieve greater proximity to nature and thereby also social harmony in an increasingly industrialized and atomized environment, while harnessing modern science and techniques of social organization for that purpose. If the vast expanses of colonial empires seemed to offer the best opportunity to realize such schemes, it soon transpired that modern utopias of this genre create a relationship of subjugation and control vis-à-vis their human environment, even as they brought the newcomers closer to the natural setting. Indeed, the evident links between utopia and violence in the European colonies demonstrate that imperialism is one crucial root of modern utopian thinking, whose most distinct and devastating outcome in the twentieth century was the totalitarian state.[22]

The nineteenth century produced an array of utopian visions. Some, such as the Hegelian *Weltgeist*'s curious culmination in Prussia and Mazzini's optimistic fraternity of national liberation movements, were directly related to the emerging nation-state. Others, such as the British trust in improvement and the French enchantment with positivism, as well as Saint-Simon's republic of technocrats, were rooted in the new religion of scientific discovery and progress. Conversely, such grand utopian schemes as Fourier's phalanx and Marx's classless society expressed a reaction to the impoverishment and alienation that came in the wake of industrialization, urbanization, and secularization. But totalitarian utopia was finally propelled into existence by the event of total, industrial war, which combined modern science and technology, universal mobilization of soldiers and workers, and an elaborate surveillance apparatus geared to control and mold the conduct and mind of the public. Totalitarianism evolved from the crises it claimed to resolve, offering a final solution to humanity's ills predicated on the proven ability to eradicate everything that could not or would not be suppressed, healed, or transformed. For here the goal was not mere control but rather making control altogether unnecessary by re-creating humanity in a manner that would ensure its acceptance of and active participation in the new society. Totalitarianism is modern utopia par excellence; obsessed with mobilizing mass society and employing the most sophisticated technological means and administrative practices to establish its rule, it simultaneously strives to put an end to history and to prevent any movement beyond what it perceives as the utopian phase. Once the ideal has been achieved, nothing should be allowed to undermine it; once the undesirable classes have been eliminated, the polluting races exterminated, the old elites smashed, the history and memory of past events erased or rewritten, time must come to a standstill. From this point on, change can only spell subversion.[23]

But just as in Aristotelian physics, this ideal point of absolute rest can never be reached, its closest approximation being a circle, which in the case of modern utopia is a vicious circle of constant striving toward perfection in a violent process of remaking and unmaking humanity. The totalitarian state insists on being defined as such precisely because it can recognize no limits to its unrelenting march toward utopia. But totalitarianism is only the most extreme expression of a widespread, if at times more benign, urge whose roots stretch back to the beginning of civilization and whose modern manifestations are distinguished by unprecedented technological and organizational capacities unaccompanied by a matching expansion of either wisdom or moral sensibilities. This is the urge to seize control over time, matter, and mind, to gain the power to make and unmake, to arrest or accelerate the drift of history and to challenge whichever natural or divine laws may rule it. Since the utopia of controlling the universe is both the consequence and the cause of domestic and international conflict, its wars are all the more absolutist in their goals and execution, geared as they are toward final solutions to problems and final removal of obstacles by means of total annihilation. For while war is always about destruction, the most destructive armies are those motivated by utopian theologies or ideologies. And the vast conscript armies of total war—raised and supported by mass modern societies—have released unparalleled annihilatory energies, not least because the tremendous exertion and suffering that modern warfare demands of citizen-soldiers can only be justified by reference to abstract utopian goals, be they eternal peace or social justice, freedom from hunger or universal liberation from oppression, world empire and endless living spaces, or total eradication of racial and ideological foes.[24]

Modern war and totalitarianism therefore necessitate and devise final solutions in which humanity is perceived as a mass of matter to be molded, controlled, moved, purged, and annihilated. This conceptualization of the world biologizes society and sociologizes biology; humanity becomes an organism in need of radical surgery or a social construct in need of extreme sociological reordering. Hence the vast population transfers, brutal operations of ethnic cleansing, eradication of whole social classes, and ultimately outright genocide, the most final solution of all. For while the modern world has learned how to extend life, it has also come to think of death as the absolute end of existence. Once the afterworld has been discarded and both paradise and hell have become mere metaphors to describe (or serve as a model for creating) conditions in our own world, death has assumed a more important function than ever before, and mass murder can be seen as both an achievable goal and a perfect means for resolving previously insoluble problems.[25]

Final solutions are of inherent interest to historians not only because of their potential to transform them into antiquarians by putting a stop to history but because in the process of working toward utopia, they mobilize the past and exploit the tools and sources of the historian, albeit with the goal of ultimately undermining the raison d'être of the historical profession. In the modern era, final solutions are predicated on bureaucratic structures, which in turn depend on archives, documentation, and experts in all areas relevant to organizing society and ordering the past. Moreover, final solutions require techniques that will facilitate their task of identifying the enemy, mobilizing perpetrators, and ensuring the collaboration or passivity of bystanders, all within the context of mass society. Identity, whether biologically, sociologically, or historically constructed, is a crucial component in motivating genocide and defining its parameters, just as it is a requisite element in delineating the future utopia whose creation will have been made possible by mass murder. Here, of course, not only the social sciences are involved but also the medical and legal professions, whose role in legitimizing and organizing genocide as a necessary step on the path to utopia is obviously indispensable. Hence utopian violence in the twentieth century reflects the complexity of modern identity, the ambiguities of its historical and institutional roots, and the perilous potentials of its future aspirations.[26]

Scholarly rumination and scientific innovation, studies of the past and investigations of nature have all played a role in planning, legitimizing, and enacting violent final solutions to the contradictions of human existence.[27] And yet, despite some important but ultimately marginal exceptions—mostly incorporated into the conventional disciplinary and intellectual discourse—the prestige and status of the social and natural sciences have, by and large, not diminished, and their basic assumptions have escaped fundamental critique and revision in view of their impact on society in the context of modern war and genocide.[28] In all major cases of state-organized murder in the twentieth century, the rhetoric of the past legitimized the horror of the present, technology facilitated mass killing, war provided a convenient psychological and organizational context. Moreover, in all these instances, either religion or science (and at times a mix thereof) claimed a monopoly over truth, knowledge, and visions of a utopian future: by asserting divine sanction to purge the infidel, linking ethnicity to faith, or mobilizing the moral authority of religious leaders—as in the Armenian, Rwandan, and Bosnian genocides; by claiming to obey the allegedly immutable if also ruthless laws history—as in the "scientific" Marxism of the Soviet Union, China, and Cambodia; or by making biology into destiny and asserting the need for eugenic policies of breeding, selection and eradication—as in the case of Nazi "scientific" racism, "racial hygiene," "euthanasia," and racial genocide.[29]

At the end of the second millennium, modernism, nationalism, indeed history itself, have again been questioned even as they served to fan new utopias and further violence. The fall of the Berlin Wall, the disintegration of Communism, the "victory" of capitalism, the exile of war to parts of the world that rarely concern us, and the ongoing project of genetic mapping, to name just some of the most important recent developments, have induced some to argue that we are either at the end of history or on the threshold of a utopian future. Yet growing poverty, economic exploitation, raging new viruses, global warming, and, not least, the threat of biological, chemical, and nuclear terrorism, may similarly indicate that our world is about to plunge into another apocalypse. It is thus more than likely that the twenty-first century will be no less afflicted by utopian and apocalyptic visions and by attempts to reshape humanity in their image than the century of violence that has finally come to a close.

REMAKING AND UNMAKING HUMANITY

The subterranean stream of Western history has finally come to the surface and usurped the dignity of our tradition. . . . And this is why all efforts to escape from the grimness of the present into nostalgia for a still intact past, or into the anticipated oblivion of a better future, are vain.[30]

Exposed and vulnerable, humanity itself can die. It is at the mercy of men, and most especially of those who consider themselves as its emissaries or as the executors of its great designs. The notion of crimes against humanity is the legal evidence of this realization.[31]

Humanity has always been haunted by the idea of its own making and unmaking. This is both an exhilarating and a frightening notion; it encompasses creation and destruction, social organization and religious doctrine, cultural upheaval and biological determinants. It has generated visions of universal happiness and of apocalyptic annihilation. Hence the optimism of progress and evolution is often accompanied by fear of the unknown, resentment of the unfit, and an impatient urge to wipe the slate clean once and for all.

The modern era has been especially plagued by tension between social improvement, scientific discovery, and technological innovation, on the one hand, and social disintegration, abuse of nature, and technological devastation, on the other. And while the notion of the end of an era has often been associated both with nostalgia for the vanishing past and with hopes for a better future, what the modern age has added to this is the capacity to bring about far more radical and rapid change. Time, space, and human sentiment have been revolutionized; within the span of a single individual's lifetime, the world has changed several times over, destroyed and rebuilt and destroyed again with such thoroughness and speed that the meaning of nostalgia and the vision of the future have been transformed almost beyond recognition.

The twentieth century, moreover, cast doubt on the very definition of the "human."[32] The fragility, nay, the mortality of humanity, has been posited as being situated in the definitive historical legacies of our time: genocide and the Holocaust, imperialism and postcolonialism, Enlightenment traditions leading to both industrial capitalism and industrial killing.[33] Hence the creation, extinction, erasure, and remaking of the "human" must be understood within the context of the twentieth century's tremendous efforts to remold humanity through indoctrination and education, population transfers and resettlement, ethnic cleansing and urban planning, policies of natalism, eugenics, and genetics, the redrawing of maps and frontiers, redefinitions of individual and collective identities, and, not least, mass murder. Both universalist and particularistic utopian ideologies, allied with the administrative, technological, and bureaucratic powers of the modern state, have wrought vast changes on the human condition in a continuing process of annihilation and reconstruction, demographic restructuring and exterminatory outbursts. Hence the predilection of some to abandon claims to universality altogether and thus to defy the very possibility of a history and a reality of "humanity," all-encompassing theories about which have caused so much suffering and bloodshed. Hence too, however, the insistence of others to retain the Enlightenment conceptualization of humanity as a conglomerate of individuals endowed with inalienable rights to life and justice as the only bulwark against the genocidal tendencies and capacities of our time.[34]

Such transformations in our perception of humanity may be cited as evidence of fragmentation, dissolution, and anarchy, or, conversely, as the beginning of a liberatory narrative and the emergence of new, hitherto neglected or ignored "humanities." Similarly, the public and scholarly fascination with genocide and destruction, erasure and commemoration, can be viewed as indicating a deep cultural pessimism at the end of the millennium or as sign of a new willingness to face up to and confront the devastating legacy of the past. Current struggles over the historical agents of humanity are also deeply implicated in questions of inclusion and exclusion, identity and enemies, utopian dreams of rebirth and renewal and apocalyptic visions of war and extermination. At the end of the millennium, civilization seemed to be both exhausted by, and yet endlessly obsessed with, its bloody chronicles of happy futures.[35] We know the history of those "republics of virtue" and "brave new worlds," the "workers' paradise" and the "racial community"; what we fear is their future. For while the history of remaking and unmaking of humanity is about the actions and perceptions of individuals and collectives in search of the "human," it is just as much about the marginalization, confinement, or destruction of the "un-" or "subhuman," the socially, physically, or culturally "unfit." The "human" has been variously defined as that which was created in the image of God or as that which has self-consciousness; it has been identified as possessing the ability to distinguish good from evil and as such has been endowed with the inalienable right to life and happiness. But since we know that civilization has often divided humanity into categories and degrees, we should beware of toying with the notion of social, cultural, and genetic engineering, whether its goal is to make for greater uniformity or to produce controlled diversity.[36]

NOTES

This essay was published as part of chapter 4 of Omer Bartov, *Mirrors of Destruction: War, Genocide, and Modern Identity* (Oxford, 2000).

1. R. Hochhuth, *The Deputy* (New York, 1964), p. 248.

2. See, e.g., T. Todorov, *On Human Diversity: Nationalism, Racism, and Exoticism in French Thought* (Cambridge, Mass., 1993); A. Memmi, *Le racisme* (Paris, 1982); P. Sahlins, *Boundaries: The Making of France and Spain in the Pyrenees* (Berkeley, Calif., 1989).

3. On boundaries between epochs, see, e.g., R. Heilbronner, *Visions of the Future: The Distant Past, Yesterday, Today, and Tomorrow* (New York, 1995); between reality and the mind: P. Loewenberg, *Fantasy and Reality in History* (New York, 1995); between genders: J. W. Scott, *Feminism and History* (New York, 1996). On modern technological utopias, see, e.g., S. Kern, *The Culture of Time and Space, 1880–1918* (Cambridge, Mass., 1983); A. Rabinbach, *The Human Motor: Energy, Fatigue, and the Origins of Modernity* (Berkeley, Calif., 1990).

4. Nostalgia for a mythical past in antiquity is the leitmotiv of Livy's *The Early History of Rome*, while making the (Germanic) barbarians into models of lost purity is at the core of Tacitus's *The Annals of Imperial Rome*. Nostalgia for a mythical past in ancient China characterizes Ssu-ma Ch'ien's *Records of the Historian* (New York, 1958). See also D. Lowenthal, *The Past is a Foreign Country* (Cambridge, 1985).

5. See, e.g., W. H. McNeill, *The Pursuit of Power: Technology, Armed Force, and Society since A.D. 1000* (Oxford, 1983); B. M. Downing, *The Military Revolution and Political Change: Origins of Democracy and Autocracy in Early Modern Europe* (Princeton, N.J., 1992); B. Moore Jr., *Social Origins of Dictatorship and Democracy: Lord and Peasant in the Making of the Modern World* (Boston, 1967); B. Z. Kedar, "Expulsion as a Problem in World History," *Alpayim* 13 (1996): 9–22 [in Hebrew].

6. M. Adas, *Machines as the Measure of Men: Science, Technology, and Ideologies of Western Dominance* (Ithaca, N.Y., 1989); M. Ferro, *Colonization: A Global History* (London, 1997); V. G. Kiernan, *European Empires from Conquest to Collapse, 1815–1960* (Bungay, Suffolk, 1982); D. B. Ralston, *Importing the European Army: The Introduction of European Military Techniques and Institutions into the Extra-European World, 1600–1914* (Chicago, 1990); D. Pick, *Faces of Degeneration: A European Disorder, c. 1848–c.1918* (Cambridge, 1989); I. Hannford, *Race: The History of an Idea in the West* (Baltimore, Md., 1996); E. Barkan, *The Retreat of Scientific Racism: Changing Concepts of Race in Britain and the United States between the World Wars* (Cambridge, 1992). See also C. Lévi-Strauss, *The Savage Mind* (London, 1966), and Lévi-Strauss, *Tristes Tropiques* (New York, 1976).

7. See, e.g., C. Essner, *Deutsche Afrikareisende im neunzenten Jahr-hundert: Zur Sozialgeschichte des Reisens* (Stuttgart, 1985); S. Friedrichs-meyer et al., eds., *The Imperialist Imagination: German Colonialism and Its Legacy* (Ann Arbor, Mich., 1998); R. Aldrich, *Greater France: A History of French Overseas Expansion* (New York, 1996); M. K. Matsuda, *The Memory of the Modern* (New York, 1996), chap. 7; L. Lowe, *Critical Terrains: French and British Orientalisms* (Ithaca, N.Y., 1991); E. W. Said, *Orientalism* (New York, 1979).

8. For the German case and the links between the "gardening society," ecological thinking, "ethnic landscapes," and genocide, see Z. Bauman, *Modernity and the Holocaust* (Ithaca, N.Y., 1991); J. Wolschke-Bulmahn, "Nature and Ideology: The Search for Identity and Nationalism in Early 20th-Century German Landscape Architecture," *American Institute for Contemporary German Studies* 17 (February 1996): 1–31; G. Gröning and J. Wolschke-Bulmahn, "Politics, Planning and the Protection of Nature: Political Abuse of Early Ecological Ideas in Germany, 1933–45," *Planning Perspectives* 2 (1987): 127–48; D. Inkelas, "Landscape Planning and the Development of SS Policy in Annexed Poland, 1939–1942" (unpublished paper, 1996); D. Dwork and R. Jan van Pelt, *Auschwitz: 1270 to the Present* (New York, 1996), part 1. On Chinese gardens and utopian thought, see J. Stuart, "A Scholar's Garden in Ming China: Dream and Reality," in *Asian Art* 3, no. 4 (fall 1990): 31–51, and literature cited therein; W. Bauer, *China and the Search for Happiness* (New York, 1976).

9. P. Crook, *Darwinism, War and History: The Debate Over the Biology of War from the "Origin of Species" to the First World War* (Cambridge, 1994); L. L. Clark, *Social Darwinism in France* (Alabama, 1984); E. Conte and C. Essner, *La quête de la race: Une anthropologie du Nazisme* (Paris, 1995); J. M. Effron, *Defenders of the Race: Jewish Doctors and Race Science in Fin-de-Siècle Europe* (New Haven, Conn., 1994); P. Weindling, *Health, Race and German Politics between National Unification and Nazism, 1870–1945* (Cambridge, 1989); R. N. Proctor, *Racial Hygiene: Medicine under the Nazis* (Cambridge, Mass., 1988); G. Aly et al., *Cleansing the Fatherland: Nazi Medicine and Racial Hygiene* (Baltimore, Md., 1994); M. Burleigh, *Death and Deliverance: "Euthanasia" in Germany, 1900–1945* (Cambridge, 1994). Some of the literature on recent debates on these issues is cited in O. Bartov, *Murder in Our Midst: The Holocaust, Industrial Killing, and Representation* (New York, 1996), p. 3, n. 2.

10. See, e.g., T. Head and R. Landes, eds., *The Peace of God: Social Violence and Religious Response around the Year 1000* (Ithaca, N.Y., 1992); T. J. J. Altizer, *History as Apocalypse* (Albany, N.Y., 1985); D. G. Roskies, ed., *The Literature of Destruction: Jewish Responses to Catastrophe* (Philadelphia, 1989); S. E. Aschheim, *Culture and Catastrophe: German and Jewish*

Confrontations with National Socialism and Other Crises (New York, 1996); T. W. Adorno, *Negative Dialectics* (New York, 1973), esp. part 3, chaps. 2–3; H. Arendt, *Between Past and Future: Eight Exercises in Political Thought*, rev. ed. (New York, 1968), esp. chap. 3; R. J. B. Bosworth, *Explaining Auschwitz and Hiroshima: History Writing and the Second World War, 1945–1990* (London, 1993); R. J. Lifton and E. Markusen, *The Genocidal Mentality: Nazi Holocaust and Nuclear Threat* (New York, 1990).

11. See, e.g., H. Arendt, *The Origins of Totalitarianism* (New York, 1951); F. Furet, *Le Passé d'une illusion* (Paris, 1995); M. Burleigh and W. Wippermann, *The Racial State: Germany 1933–1945* (Cambridge, 1991); R. J. Lifton, *The Nazi Doctors: Medical Killing and the Psychology of Genocide* (New York, 1986). See also E. Hobsbawm, *The Age of Extremes: A History of the World, 1914–1991* (New York, 1995); M. Mazower, *Dark Continent: Europe's Twentieth Century* (New York, 1999).

12. On the Soviet Union, see esp. M. Lewin, *Russia/USSR/Russia: The Drive and Drift of a Superstate* (New York, 1995); G. Hosking, *The First Socialist Society: A History of the Soviet Union from Within*, 2d ed. (Cambridge, Mass., 1993); S. Kotkin, *Magnetic Mountain: Stalinism as a Civilization* (Berkeley, Calif., 1995); R. Conquest, *The Great Terror: A Reassessment* (New York, 1990); and R. Conquest, *The Harvest of Sorrow: Soviet Collectivization and the Terror-Famine* (New York, 1986). On capitalism in crisis, see. e.g., B. Moore Jr., *Injustice: The Social Bases of Obedience and Revolt* (Stamford, Conn., 1978); C. S. Maier, *Recasting Bourgeois Europe: Stabilization in France, Germany, and Italy in the Decade after World War I* (Princeton, N.J., 1975). On demography, see M. S. Quine, *Population Politics in Twentieth-Century Europe* (London, 1996); J. M. Winter, *The Great War and the British People* (Cambridge, Mass., 1986). On gender, see M. R. Higonnet et al., eds., *Behind the Lines: Gender and the Two World Wars* (New Haven, Conn., 1987); M. L. Roberts, *Civilization without Sexes: Reconstructing Gender in Postwar France, 1917–1927* (Chicago, 1994); R. Bridenthal et al., *When Biology Became Destiny: Women in Weimar and Nazi Germany* (New York, 1984). On empire and decolonization, see, E. J. Hobsbawm, *Industry and Empire: From 1750 to the Present Day* (London, 1968); F. Fanon, *The Wretched of the Earth* (London, 1965); R. Girardet, *L'Idée coloniale en France* (Paris, 1972); J.-P. Rioux, ed., *La Guerre d'Algérie et les français* (Paris, 1990). See also G. Kolko, *Century of War: Politics, Conflicts, and Society since 1914* (New York, 1994); J. L. Talmon, *The Age of Violence* (Tel Aviv, 1974) [in Hebrew].

13. Speech by an SS-man as cited by Simon Wiesenthal, in P. Levi, *The Drowned and the Saved* (New York, 1988), pp. 11–12.

14. For some suggestive works on this theme, see J. McConkey, *The Anatomy of Memory: An Anthology* (New York, 1996); F. A. Yates, *The Art*

of Memory (Chicago, 1966); P. H. Hutton, *History as an Art of Memory* (Hanover, N.H., 1993); M. Halbwachs, *On Collective Memory* (Chicago, 1992); J. Le Goff, *Histoire et mémoire* (Paris, 1988); P. Nora, ed., *Les Lieux de mémoire,* 3 vols., paperback edition (Paris, 1997); J. R. Gillis, ed., *Commemorations: The Politics of National Identity* (Princeton, N.J., 1994).

15. In this context, see O. Bartov, "'Seit die Juden weg sind. . .': Germany, History, and Representations of Absence," in *A User's Guide to German Cultural Studies,* ed. S. Denham et al. (Ann Arbor, Mich., 1997), pp. 209–26.

16. On collecting and nostalgia, see W. Benjamin, "Unpacking My Library: A Talk about Book Collecting," in Benjamin, *Illuminations,* ed. H. Arendt (New York, 1969), pp. 59–67. For an example from China, see W. Li, "The Collector, the Connoisseur, and Late-Ming Sensibility," *T'oung Pao* 81 (1995): 269–302. On the aesthetics, politics, and theft of art in Nazi Germany, see B. Hinz, *Art in the Third Reich* (New York, 1979); J. Petropoulos, *Art as Politics in the Third Reich* (Chapel Hill, N.C., 1996); A. E. Steinweis, *Art, Ideology, and Economics in Nazi Germany* (Chapel Hill, N.C., 1993); L. H. Nicholas, *The Rape of Europe: The Fate of Europe's Treasures in the Third Reich and the Second World War* (New York, 1994). For Polish museums see, e.g., S. Markowski, *Krakowski Kazimierz: Dzielnica zydowska, 1870–1988* (Kraców, 1992).

17. On the USSR, see R. Stites, ed., *Culture and Entertainment in Wartime Russia* (Bloomington, Ind., 1995), esp. on Sergei Eisenstein's film *Alexander Nevskii* (1938), pp. 65–66; D. Bordwell, *The Cinema of Eisenstein* (Cambridge, Mass., 1993); P. Kenez, *Cinema and Soviet Society, 1917–1953* (Cambridge, Mass., 1992). See also J. Hay, *Popular Film Culture in Fascist Italy: The Passing of the Rex* (Bloomington, Ind., 1987), chap. 5; R. A. Rosenstone, ed., *Revisioning History: Film and the Construction of a New Past* (Princeton, N.J., 1995). A good introduction to European art at the turn of the century, including the impact of colonialism, technology, and war, is R. Hughes, *The Shock of the New: Art and the Century of Change* (London, 1980). On the links between French national identity and colonial artifacts, see H. Lebovics, *True France: The Wars over Cultural Identity, 1900–1945* (Ithaca, N.Y., 1992). See also the extraordinary catalog of the 1986 Vienna Exhibition, J. Claire (ed.), *Vienne 1880–1938: L'Apocalypse Joyeuse* (Paris, 1986). Paris also hosted an exhibition on "japonisme," or the impact of Japanese prints on French art.

18. For some discussion of the nature, purpose, and crisis of modern historiography, see W. Dilthey, *Selected Works,* vol. 1, *Introduction to the Human Sciences* (Princeton, N.J., 1989); R. A. Makkreel, *Dilthey: Philosopher of the Human Sciences* (Princeton, 1975); J. Ortega y Gasset, *History as a System and Other Essays toward a Philosophy of History* (New York, 1941);

N. Chiaromonte, *The Paradox of History*, rev. ed. (Philadelphia, 1985); R. Koselleck, *Futures Past: On the Semantics of Historical Time* (Cambridge, Mass., 1985); H. White, *The Content of the Form: Narrative Discourse and Historical Representation* (Baltimore, Md., 1987); L. Gossman, *Between History and Literature* (Cambridge, Mass., 1990).

19. On the Jewish idea of history, see Y. H. Yerushalmi, *Zakhor: Jewish History and Jewish Memory* (New York, 1989). On German historiography, see G. G. Iggers, *The German Conception of History: The National Tradition of Historical Thought from Herder to the Present*, rev. ed. (Hanover, N.H., 1988). On the historian's authority in ancient China, see W. Li, "The Idea of Authority in the Shih chi (Records of the Historian)," *Journal of Asian Studies* 54, no. 2 (December 1994): 345–405. On the memory, testimony, and representation of trauma, see L. L. Langer, *Holocaust Testimonies: The Ruins of Memory* (New Haven, Conn., 1991); G. H. Hartman, ed., *Holocaust Remembrance: The Shapes of Memory* (Oxford, 1994); W. von Bredow, *Tükische Geschichte: Kollektive Erinnerung an den Holocaust* (Stuttgart, 1996); S. Felman and D. Laub, *Testimony: Crises of Witnessing in Literature, Psychoanalysis, and History* (New York, 1992); M. Blanchot, *The Writing of the Disaster* (Lincoln, Neb., 1986); S. Friedländer, ed., *Probing the Limits of Representation: Nazism and the "Final Solution"* (Cambridge, Mass., 1992).

20. From Heinrich Himmler's speech to SS leaders on October 4, 1943, in Posen. Cited in J. Noakes and G. Pridham, *Nazism 1919–1945*, vol. 3 (Exeter, 1988), pp. 1199–200.

21. For some examples, see M. Eliade, *The Myth of the Eternal Return or Cosmos and History* (Princeton, N.J., 1954), and Eliade, *The Sacred and the Profane: The Nature of Religion* (New York, 1959); J. Campbell, ed., *Man and Time: Papers from the Eranos Yearbooks* (Princeton, N.J., 1957). On Jewish mysticism and preoccupation with mending the world, see G. Scholem, *Kabbalah* (New York, 1974); F. Rosenzweig, *The Star of Redemption* (Notre Dame, 1970); E. L. Fackenheim, *To Mend the World: Foundations of Post-Holocaust Jewish Thought* (Bloomington, 1982); E. Levinas, *Difficult Freedom: Essays on Judaism* (Baltimore, Md., 1990). On religious and secular communal or communist utopias, see I. Oved, *Two Hundred Years of American Communes* (New Brunswick, N.J., 1988); Y. Gorni et al., eds., *Communal Life: An International Perspective* (New Brunswick, N.J., 1987).

22. On colonial atrocities and links to later events in Europe, see S. Lindqvist, *"Exterminate All the Brutes"* (New York, 1996); J. Walston, "History and Memory in the Italian Concentration Camps," *Harvard Journal of Asiatic Studies* 10, no. 1 (1997); I. Hull, "Military Culture and the Production of 'Final Solutions' in the Colonies: The Example of Wil-

helmine Germany" (1998, photocopy; part of a larger project to be published in book form); C. Essner, "Zwischen Vernunft und Gefühl: Die Reichstagsdebatten von 1912 um koloniale 'Rassenmischehe' und 'Sexualität,'" *Zeitschrift für Geschichte* 6 (1997): 503–19; M. Levene and P. Roberts, eds., *The Massacre in History* (forthcoming), esp. the chapter on the massacre of the Herero (Dedering). See also V. N. Dadrian, *German Responsibility in the Armenian Genocide : A Review of the Historical Evidence of German Complicity* (Watertown, Mass., 1996).

23. On Nationalism see, e.g., B. Anderson, *Imagined Communities: Reflections on the Origin and Spread of Nationalism,* rev. ed. (London, 1991); E. J. Hobsbawm, *Nations and Nationalism since 1780: Programme, Myth, Reality,* rev. ed. (Cambridge, 1993); L. Greenfeld, *Nationalism: Five Roads to Modernity* (Cambridge, Mass., 1992); E. Gellner, *Nations and Nationalism* (Ithaca, N.Y., 1983); G. Eley and R. G. Suny, eds., *Becoming National: A Reader* (New York, 1996). See also J. L. Talmon, *Political Messianism: The Romantic Phase* (Boulder, Colo., 1985), and *Talmon, The Origins of Totalitarian Democracy* (Boulder, 1985). On the links between modernity, total war, and genocide, see D. Pick, *War Machine: The Rationalisation of Slaughter in the Modern Age* (New Haven, Conn., 1993); J. J. Reid, "Total War, the Annihilation Ethic and the Armenian Genocide," in *The Armenian Genocide: History, Politics, Ethics,* ed. R. G. Hovannisian (New York, 1992); R. G. Hovannisian, ed., *The Armenian Genocide in Perspective* (New Brunswick, N.J, 1986); V. N. Dadrian, *The History of the Armenian Genocide: Ethnic Conflict from the Balkans to Anatolia to the Caucasus* (Providence, R.I., 1995); Bartov, *Murder in Our Midst.* On the emergence of the surveillance state, see P. Holquist, "'Information Is the Alpha and Omega of Our Work': Bolshevik Surveillance in Its Pan-European Context," *Journal of Modern History* 69 (September 1997): 415–50.

24. The links between modern warfare and genocide can be gleaned from any major study of the latter. See, e.g., H. Hirsch, *Genocide and the Politics of Memory: Studying Death to Preserve Life* (Chapel Hill, N.C., 1995); L. Kuper, *Genocide: Its Political Use in the Twentieth Century* (New Haven, Conn., 1981); S. Totten et al., eds., *Century of Genocide: Eyewitness Accounts and Critical Views* (New York, 1997); R. J. Rummel, *Death by Government* (New Brunswick, N.J., 1994). On genocide as combined cleansing of racial pollution and asocial behavior, see M. Zimmermann, *Rassenutopie und Genozid: Die nationalsozialistische "Lösung der Zigeunerfrage"* (Hamburg, 1996); and as combined ethnic and class war, see B. Kiernan, ed., "The Ethnic Element in the Cambodian Genocide" (paper delivered at "Lessons and Legacies: Laws, Evidence, and Context," Florida Atlantic University, November 6 to 9, 1998). On ideological soldiers and war crimes, see O. Bartov, *Hitler's Army: Soldiers, Nazis, and War* (New

York, 1991); H. Heer and K. Naumann, eds., *Vernichtungskrieg: Verbrechen der Wehrmacht 1941–1944* (Hamburg, 1995); M. von Hagen, *Soldiers in the Proletarian Dictatorship: The Red Army and the Soviet Socialist State, 1917–1930* (Ithaca, N.Y., 1990).

25. For comparisons between Soviet and Nazi sociologically or racially motivated policies of population transfers and mass murder, see, e.g., S. Wheatcroft, "The Scale and Nature of German and Soviet Repressions and Mass Killings," *Europe-Asia Studies* 48, no. 8 (1996); N. Naimark, "Ethnic Cleansing between War and Peace in the USSR" (in Amir Weiner, ed., *Landscaping the Human Garden* [Stanford, Calif., forthcoming]); P. Holquist, "State Violence as Technique: The Logic of Violence in Soviet Totalitarianism" (in Amir Weiner, ed., *Landscaping the Human Garden* [Stanford, Calif., forthcoming]); A. Weiner, "Delineating the Soviet Body national in the Age of Socialism: Ukrainians, Jews and the Myth of the Second World War," (in Amir Weiner, ed., *Landscaping the Human Garden* [Stanford, Calif., forthcoming]); A. Bullock, *Hitler and Stalin: Parallel Lives* (New York, 1992); B. Wegner, ed., *From Peace to War: Germany, Soviet Russia and the World, 1939–1941* (Providence, R.I., 1997); I. Kershaw and M. Lewin, eds., *Stalinism and Nazism: Dictatorships in Comparison* (Cambridge, 1997). On other links and comparisons, see R. F. Melson, *Revolution and Genocide: On the Origins of the Armenian Genocide and the Holocaust* (Chicago, 1992); R. Secher, *Juifs et Vendéens: d'un génocide à l'autre* (Paris, 1991); E. Malet, ed., *Résistance et mémoire: D'Auschwitz à Sarajevo* (Paris, 1993).

26. On the bureaucratic nature of the Nazi genocide of the Jews, see R. Hilberg, *The Destruction of the European Jews*, 3 vols. (New York, 1985); H. Mommsen, *From Weimar to Auschwitz* (Princeton, 1991), esp. chap. 11. On technocrats and genocide, see G. Aly and S. Heim, *Vordenker der Vernichtung: Auschwitz und die deutschen Pläne für eine neue europäische Ordnung* (Frankfurt am Main, 1993); G. Aly, *Endlösung: Völkerverschiebung und der Mord an den europäischen Juden* (Frankfurt am Main, 1995). On Historians and Nazism, see G. Aly, *Macht-Geist-Wahn: Kontinuitäten deutschen Denkens* (Berlin, 1997); P. Schöttler, ed., *Geschichtsschreibung als Legitimationswissenschaft 1918–1945* (Frankfurt am Main, 1997); K. Schönwälder, "'Taking Their Place in the Front-Line'(?): German Historians during Nazism and War," *Tel Aviver Jahrbuch fuer deutsche geschichte* 25 (1996): 205–17; O. Heilbronner, "'. . . aber das "Reich" lebt in uns.' Katholische Historiker unter dem Nationalsozialismus," *Tel Aviver Jahrbuch für deutsche Geschichte* 25 (1996): 219–31; S. Heim, "'Überbevölkerung' und 'Rassenkampf': Werner Conze und Gunther Ipsen" (unpublished paper, 1997); B. Mrozek, "Hitlers willige Wissenschaftler?" *Die Weltwoche*, 3 July 3 1997; M. Kröger and R. Thimme, *Die Geschichtsbilder des Historikers Karl Diet-*

rich Erdmann: Vom Dritten Reich zur Bundesrepublik (Munich, 1996); W. Oberkrome, *Volksgeschichte: Methodische Innovation und völkische Ideologisierung in der deutschen Geschichtswissenschaft 1918–1945* (Göttingen, 1993); K.-H. Roth and A. Ebbinghaus, "Vorläufer des 'Generalplan Ost': Eine Dokumentation über Theodor Schieders Polendenkschrift," *Zeitschrift fuer* 21 (1992). On lawyers and judges, see I. Müller, *Hitler's Justice: The Courts of the Third Reich* (Cambridge, Mass., 1991). On physicians, see M. Kater, *Doctors under Hitler* (Chapel Hill, N.C., 1989); H. Friedlander, *The Origins of Nazi Genocide: From Euthanasia to the Final Solution* (Chapel Hill, N.C., 1995); G. Cocks, *Psychotherapy in the Third Reich: The Göring Institute,* rev. ed. (New Brunswick, N.J., 1997).

27. See, e.g., H. Sluga, *Heidegger's Crisis: Philosophy and Politics in Nazi Germany* (Cambridge, Mass., 1993); A. D. Beyerchen, *Scientists under Hitler: Politics and the Physics Community in the Third Reich* (New Haven, Conn., 1977); T. Powers, *Heisenberg's War: The Secret Story of the German Bomb* (New York, 1993).

28. The most sustained criticism is M. Foucault, *The Order of Things: An Archeology of the Human Sciences* (London, 1970). Bauman, *Modernity and the Holocaust,* is a critique of the sociological profession. D. J. K. Peukert, "The Genesis of the 'Final Solution' from the Spirit of Science," in *Reevaluating the Third Reich,* ed. T. Childers and J. Caplan (New York, 1993) criticizes modern science; see, most recently, A. Beyerchen, "Rational Means and Irrational Ends: Thoughts on the Technology of Racism in the Third Reich," *Central European History* 30/3 (1997): 386–402. B. Lang, *Act and Idea in the Nazi Genocide* (Chicago, 1990), is a philosophical critique, as is, of course, Adorno, *Negative Dialectics.* H. Kaplan, *Conscience and Memory: Meditations in a Museum of the Holocaust* (Chicago, 1994), is a critique of modern political ethics. D. LaCapra, *Representing the Holocaust: History, Theory, and Trauma* (Ithaca, N.Y., 1994), and LaCapra, *History and Memory after Auschwitz* (Ithaca, N.Y., 1998) are critiques of the historiography and representation of the Holocaust. Yet by and large, the academic disciplines have continued their nineteenth-century traditions without seeing twentieth-century utopias and genocides as anything more than a series of road accidents on the path to a better future, deeper understanding, and expanding knowledge, on the basis of the old and "proven" frameworks of learning, conceptualization, and progress.

29. Omer Bartov, *Mirrors of Destruction: War, Genocide, and Modern Identity* (New York, 2000), chapter 3, notes 109–17.

30. Arendt, *Origins of Totalitarianism,* p. ix.

31. A. Finkielkraut, *Remembering in Vain: The Klaus Barbie Trial and Crimes against Humanity* (New York, 1992), p. 31.

32. See, e.g., L. Ferry and A. Renaut, *Système et critique: Essais sur la*

critique de la raison dans la philosophie contemporaine (Brussels, 1984); J.-F. Lyotard, *The Inhuman: Reflections on Time* (Stanford, Calif., 1991); D. J. Haraway, *Primate Visions: Gender, Race, and Nature in the World of Modern Science* (New York, 1989).

33. M. Horkheimer and T. W. Adorno, *Dialectic of Enlightenment* (New York, 1991); A. Finkielkraut, *The Defeat of the Mind* (New York, 1995); Finkielkraut, *Remembering in Vain;* Bauman, *Modernity and the Holocaust;* Arendt, *Origins of Totalitarianism;* Bartov, *Murder in Our Midst.*

34. For examples of the consequent realignment and reconceptualization of history and historiography, see D. LaCapra, *Rethinking Intellectual History: Texts, Contents, Language* (Ithaca, 1983); S. Cohen, *Historical Culture: On the Recoding of an Academic Discipline* (Berkeley, Calif., 1986); J. W. Scott, *Gender and the Politics of History* (New York, 1988); L. Hunt, ed., *The New Cultural History* (Berkeley, 1989); R. Cohen, ed., *Studies in Historical Change* (Charlottesville, Va., 1992); J. Appelby et al., eds., *Knowledge and Postmodernism in Historical Perspective* (New York, 1996); P. Hamilton, *Historicism* (London, 1996). See also D. Harvey, *The Condition of Postmodernity: An Enquiry into the Origins of Cultural Change* (Oxford, 1989).

35. On coming to terms with inhumanity in the twentieth century, see, e.g., G. M. Kren and L. Rappoport, *The Holocaust and the Crisis of Human Behavior,* rev. ed. (New York, 1994); G. E. Markle, *Meditations of a Holocaust Traveler* (New York, 1995); J. K. Roth and M. Berenbaum, eds., *Holocaust: Religious and Philosophical Implications* (New York, 1989); T. Des Pres, *Writing into the World: Essays, 1973–1987* (New York, 1991); J. E. Dimsdale, ed., *Survivors, Victims, and Perpetrators: Essays on the Nazi Holocaust* (Washington, 1980); R. Moses, ed., *Persistent Shadows of the Holocaust: The Meaning to Those Not Directly Affected* (Madison, Conn., 1993). On pain and torture, see J. Améry, *At the Mind's Limits: Contemplations by a Survivor on Auschwitz and Its Realities* (New York, 1986), esp. the chapter "Torture"; E. Scarry, *The Body in Pain: The Making and Unmaking of the World* (New York, 1985); E. Peters, *Torture,* expanded ed. (Philadelphia, 1996). See also J. Baudrillard, *The Transparency of Evil: Essays on Extreme Phenomena* (London, 1993).

36. In this context, it is important to note that Primo Levi's memoir, known in its English translation as *Survival in Auschwitz* (New York, 1961), is called in the original Italian *Se questo è un uomo* (Is this a man?), carrying the obvious association of the Christian *Ecce Homo.* See also Levi, *Drowned and Saved,* for further and more pessimistic ruminations on the humanity of man in inhuman circumstances.

Saul Friedländer

Ideology and Extermination
The Immediate Origins of the Final Solution

ON OCTOBER 2, 1941, OPERATION TYPHOON, THE FINAL GERMAN assault on Moscow, was launched. In his order of the day to the millions of soldiers poised for what was supposed to be "the last of the great decisive battles of the year . . . the last powerful blow that will shatter this enemy before the onset of the winter," Hitler made quite clear what was the true identity of the "horrendous, beast-like" enemy that had been about to "annihilate not only Germany, but the whole of Europe." The carriers of the system, in which Bolshevism was but the other face of the vilest capitalism, he proclaimed, were in both cases the same: "Jews and only Jews! (*Juden und nur Juden*!)."[1]

As a new phase of the war started with the attack against the Soviet Union, a radical escalation of "the war against the Jews" unfolded on Russian territory. Within this new phase, early or mid-October 1941 appears as another fateful turning point. It was probably between mid-October and mid-December 1941 that the final decision regarding the murder of the whole of European Jewry was made.

As we consider these events from a distance of six decades, their historical place still remains undetermined. Was this the horrendous finale of an anti-Jewish tradition embedded in the evolution of Christianity and that of the Western world? Was it the murderous end phase of the age of ideology? Does it demonstrate the deadly potential of modernity? Or, could one define the annihilation of European Jewry as the result of an entirely unforeseeable convergence of these three historical developments within a specific German context?

This text will mainly concentrate on the fall months of 1941 that have probably been more systematically scrutinized than any other phase of these events. I will not uncover any new facts; rather, I wish to reemphasize, against the grain of present-day historiography, the importance of Hitler's initiatives and of his ideology in the context of the anti-Jewish crusade. I shall stress the pseudoreligious dimensions of this ideology—redemptive anti-Semitism—and its integrative and mobilizing function within a system including party, state, and society, with which the Nazi leader constantly interacted. More generally, I shall attempt to point to the conflation of the three historical processes mentioned earlier with the immediate circumstances that triggered the onset of the most extreme enterprise of sustained, systematic mass extermination in modern history.

"REDEMPTIVE ANTI-SEMITISM"

"Redemptive anti-Semitism" is the most radical form of anti-Jewish hatred: the convergence of racial anti-Semitism, on the one hand, *and* of a religious or pseudoreligious ideology of redemption (or perdition), on the other. Whereas racial anti-Semitism in general was but one element within a wider racial worldview, redemptive anti-Semitism constituted an all-encompassing belief system in which race rationalized the struggle against the Jews but was not the foundation of it. Moreover, in redemptive anti-Semitism the struggle against the Jews took on an apocalyptic dimension. The redemption of the *Volk,* the race, or Aryan humanity would be achieved only by the elimination of the Jews. The victory of the Jews remained a possibility: it would mean the end of the *Volk,* the race, or Aryan humanity. This apocalyptic ideology found its first systematic expression in the writings of the Bayreuth Circle and particularly in Houston Stewart Chamberlain's *Foundations of the Nineteenth Century.* It strongly influenced Dietrich Eckart's anti-Jewish message and found its ultimate form in the faith of Adolf Hitler. In its characteristics and in its historical origins, redemptive anti-Semitism was a German ideology.

Shortly after the beginning of his political career, Hitler came to see himself as the messianic figure chosen by Providence to lead Germany in this fateful battle. According to his own words in *Mein Kampf,* in defending himself against the Jew, he was fighting for the work of the Lord.

Very tentatively and only a priori at this stage, one could suggest the following link between "redemptive anti-Semitism," the Christian tradition, the era of ideology, and modernity. In the final stage of the era of ideology, the two hegemonically oriented worldviews of the century, Nazism and Communism, surged on the world scene as pseudoscientific constructs *and* as millenarian utopias. These political religions mobilized the deepest fears and hopes of the Christian tradition, particularly its apocalyptic dimension: the vision of a struggle against a demonic force that, in Nazism, became "the Jew." But, whereas a concept such as "redemptive anti-Semitism" is easily included in a synthesis of twentieth-century ideology and deep-rooted millenarianism, it seems ill suited to an approach that identifies Nazism with modernity. Are we thus facing two incompatible and basically opposed interpretive approaches?

According to the leading thesis that links Nazi exterminations and modernity, the Final Solution was born from "the spirit of science," as an aspect of rationally pursued "social therapies" generated at the end of the nineteenth century, which led to more extreme corollaries in the 1920s, in the wake of war and crisis, and assumed their most radical form under the Nazi regime. From this perspective, the anti-Jewish measures of the Nazis become part of a general biological-racial selection plan. After the beginning of the war, these policies were integrated by various, often competing, Nazi agencies in a systematic program of ethnic population relocation and elimination embracing the whole of Eastern Europe, in order to strengthen the Germanic racial core. According to this interpretation, the extermination of the Jews was mainly the outcome of biological and demographic-economic planning, similarly directed against the mentally ill, the Gypsies, and, potentially, other groups defined as "asocials" or racially inferior by Nazi criteria. In the longer run, this kind of rationality could have led to the mass transfer and killing of entire populations all over Eastern Europe, as outlined in the *Generalplan Ost* (General Plan for the East). Thus explicated, Nazi exterminations were essentially the product of a "pitiless instrumental rationality" in terms of racial-demographic plans or, for that matter, in line with more immediate military needs.

Thus, for example, the extermination of the Jews on Soviet territory did possibly accelerate as a result of food supply problems of the Wehrmacht; the annihilation in the Warthegau may have been triggered by the overfilling of the ghettos and the need to resettle incoming ethnic Germans; the general concept of mass liquidation of Jews in the Eastern territories may have been indirectly influenced by some Nazi demographic/economic planning for the entire area. Yet, neither these explanations nor any other schemes based on the same type of "instrumental rationality" apply to the deportations of the Jews from Western Europe that immediately followed the beginning of total extermination in the East or to the deportations from Norway, or from Saloniki, or from the island of Rhodes.

It has also become common to equate Nazism and its crimes with *basic utopias of modernity* beyond "the spirit of science" as such. More specifically, the goal supposedly pursued by the Nazis was "the utopian aim of transforming society in the image of perfection" or, in other terms, the realization of "a social homogeneity and social identity endemic to the Western ideal of a rational society."[2] This identification of Nazi goals with quintessential visions of modernity is highly questionable. By definition these goals should have applied to the domain of the *Volksgemeinschaft* ([German] people's community) only. And, indeed, no attempt was made to kill the mentally sick or to jail the "asocials" in the occupied countries. This racial "sanitation" was concentrated in Germany only and in the areas annexed to Germany. Only one group was hounded all over the continent, to the very last individual, to the very last day of German presence: the Jews. These diverging policies against various groups of victims suffice to indicate that the war against the Jews was only indirectly related to the transformation of the *Volksgemeinschaft* in the image of perfection.

Finally, the equation of Nazism and modernity is based on an ongoing confusion between the "modernist" utopias of middle-range Nazi racial theorists, scientists, bureaucrats, and intellectuals of various brands and a political religion identifying the Jews as the enemy of humankind, preached by the ultimate bearer of all authority: Adolf Hitler. His message may not have been shared by all, but *his* were the guidelines for the policies of total extermination.

Thus we are brought back to a peculiar brand of apocalyptic anti-Semitism, the extraordinary virulence of which remains the only way of explaining both the physical onslaught against *all* Jews living within German reach *and* against any part of human culture created by Jews or showing any trace of the Jewish spirit.

Physically separating Jews from Aryans may have fitted into a racial or biological vision of humanity, but separating Jewish authors from Aryan ones, or Jewish from Aryan science, Jewish from Aryan music, and the like belongs to a different kind of obsession. The evolution of Nazi euthanasia may explain how the methods and the "specialized" personnel for the killing of the mentally ill were utilized in the extermination of the Jews, but the connection between these logistics of mass murder and the elimination of librettos written by Jewish authors from operas performed in the Reich or the identification of Heinrich Heine as an "unknown poet" demands a different historical framework. *What is ultimately so difficult to grasp in National Socialism is precisely the fact that the Jewish issue was at its ideological core.* Victor Klemperer, the Jewish diarist, living in Dresden, expressed this idea unequivocally when he wrote on April 16, 1941: "Once I would have said: I do not judge as a Jew. . . . Now: Yes, I judge as a Jew, because as such I am particularly affected by the Jewish business in Hitlerism, and because it is central to the whole structure, to the whole character of National Socialism and is uncharacteristic of everything else."[3]

In other words, Hitler's goals, mainly his vision of an apocalyptic final struggle against the Jews, were metapolitical. This vision invested the core of his movement with the fervor of a crusading sect. But, as we shall see, the Nazi leader knew how to "translate" his metapolitical aims into modern politics, modern organization, modern concepts. Far more than in Communism, this peculiar fusion of seemingly distinct worlds gave to the regime both its fanaticism and its deadly efficiency.

HITLER'S RHETORIC AND THE ONSET OF THE FINAL SOLUTION

Notwithstanding the growing difficulties encountered by the Wehrmacht on the Russian front, when Operation Typhoon started, Hitler was convinced that the Soviet capital would fall before the onset of the winter. By mid-October, however, Goebbels's diaries indicated growing pessimism regarding the possibility of a rapid victory in the East. Simultaneously, the U.S. Congress had agreed to the arming of American vessels. This, in Goebbels's (and Hitler's) eyes, meant "a further [American] step towards war."[4] And, yet another threat was lurking: On October 20, the German commander of the French city of Nantes was shot. Armed internal resistance was beginning even in occupied Western Europe. The German situation grew worse as weeks went by. Then, in early December, as the United States was pulled into the war, the Red Army counterattacked in front of Moscow.

During the same period, the murder of the Jews on Soviet territory expanded rapidly. Throughout the first two months of the campaign, the victims were mainly Jewish men. From mid-August onward, the extermination engulfed the entire Jewish population. In mid-September, the wearing of the Star of David was imposed upon the Jews of the Reich. Simultaneously, Hitler ordered the deportation of most of the Jews of Germany and the Protectorate to the ghettos of the East. From October 17 onward, the first transports of Jews left for Kovno, Riga, Minsk, and Lodz. Many of these Jews were shot on arrival. In October, as well, the construction of Belzec, the first extermination camp, started near Lublin and, at the end of the month, all Jewish emigration from Europe was forbidden "in view of the forthcoming final solution of the Jewish question." It was also in October that some 7,000 Jews were executed by the Wehrmacht in Serbia and that mass killings of Jews took place in Eastern Galicia. In early December, a killing site started operating in Chelmno, near Lodz. The first victims came from the Lodz region.

Most of the historians who study the origins of the Final Solution agree that the immediate process leading to the total extermination of European Jewry started at some point between the launching of the German attack on the Soviet Union and the end of 1941. Some scholars have argued that a decision (indirectly expressed in Göring's letter to Heydrich of July 31, 1941, ordering him to start the preparations for the "Final Solution of the Jewish Question in Europe") was made early on, in the euphoria of German victories; the order for concrete implementation may have been issued a few months later, sometime in the early fall, probably in October. Others, pointing to the absence of any new plan regarding the Jews in Hitler's comments during the summer months, mainly in his talks with Goebbels, have located the decision for total extermination sometime in the early fall of 1941. Yet others have emphasized the chaotic aspects of the Nazi anti-Jewish measures of this entire period and argued against the notion of a single order regarding the extermination; instead, they have stressed the unfolding of increasingly more radical measures at various local levels; step-by-step, these measures coalesced into a general extermination plan.

Finally, the discovery of Himmler's appointments calendar and, in it, the entry of December 18, 1941, and the related interpretation of Hitler's address to the Gauleiters on December 12, to both of which I shall return, have brought up the argument that Hitler ordered the total extermination of the Jews following the entry of the United States into the war. It is in the context of these events that we shall now replace Hitler's declarations about the Jews and interpret their possible significance, first in relation to the onset of the Final Solution and its interpretations and then in terms of the wider ideological framework that has been previously outlined.

Hitler's apocalyptic anti-Jewish faith was not instrumental, but he was a master at transforming his obsessions into an effective political instrument. Thus, an analysis of the varying intensity of his anti-Jewish declarations and of the changing emphasis placed on specific anti-Jewish themes in a particular context may shed light, as we shall see, on intentions and policies otherwise not clearly apparent.

On the Bavarian scene of his political beginnings and during the reconstruction period of the Nazi Party, after 1925, anti-Semitic fury was a perfect propaganda tool. It became less functional after 1930, once Hitler had to don a statesmanly garb, and it could have been a liability during the first years of the regime. Thus, between 1930 and 1935, Hitler maintained, in public at least, a measure of restraint in regard to the Jews. That restraint disappeared in the atmosphere of ideological confrontation and mobilization that dominated the Reich and engulfed Europe between 1936 and the beginning of the war. Hitler's murderous anti-Jewish Reichstag speech of January 1939 was both an outburst of rage at foreign reactions to the pogrom of the previous November and an attempt to frighten the "Jewish warmongers" in Paris, London, and Washington, who, he believed, dictated the policies of the Western democracies.

After the beginning of the war, in the period from September 1939 to the victory over France, public anti-Jewish pronouncements were more subdued, as befitted the Nazi leader's hope of reaching a compromise peace with Great Britain. Once it had become clear that the British would continue fighting and once the decision to attack the Soviet Union had been made, the threatening anti-Jewish prophecy of January 1939 resounded again in the Reichstag speech of January 1941. The ensuing rhetorical lull that lasted until the fall of that year, notwithstanding the onset of the Russian campaign, is more difficult to explain.

Hitler's "proclamation to the German people" on June 22, 1941, the day of the attack against the Soviet Union, used only such consecrated formulas as a plot between "Jews, Democrats and Reactionaries" or "the Judeo-Bolshevik power center in Moscow."[5] The speeches that followed, until early October, either contained no references to the Jews or merely reiterated those standard formulas. The only partially significant *nonpublic* exceptions are two conversations between Hitler and Goebbels on August 18 and 19 and the Nazi leader's statements to a Croatian visitor in July. During the two meetings with Goebbels, Hitler allowed his propaganda minister to introduce the "Jewish star" to be worn by all Jews over the age of six in the Greater Reich and the Protectorate of Bohemia and Moravia and promised that *immediately after the end of the Russian campaign,* the Jews of the Reich—and first and foremost the Jews of Berlin—would be deported to the East: "There, under a much harder climate, they would be taken in hand."[6] Hitler mentioned the same plans (Madagascar or Siberia) in his conversation with the Croatian Marshall Sladko Kvarternik on July 22. They did not indicate a total change of course.

In line with the general paucity of public anti-Jewish statements, in Hitler's "Table Talks," the Jews are hardly mentioned between July (when the "Table Talks" were first recorded) and mid-October of 1941. Given the all-out ideological nature of the Eastern campaign, such "silence" is puzzling. It may be that during the first months of the campaign, Hitler was so sure of an imminent victory that he did not see the need to evoke the sinister power of the Jews. In October, however, a sudden change occurred. In Hitler's private and public repertory, the Jews were again moved to center stage.

The strange "order of the day," let us recall, was dated October 2. It was a first signal. A few days later, Hitler launched his first massive attack against the Jews in his "Table Talks": Jesus was not a Jew; the Jew Paul had falsified Jesus' teaching in order to undermine the Roman Empire. . . . The Jew's aim was to destroy the nations by destroying their racial core. In Russia, he argued, the Jews deported hundreds of thousands of men in order to leave the abandoned women to males imported from other regions. They organized miscegenation on a huge scale. The Jews continued to torture people in the name of Bolshevism, just as Christianity, the offshoot of Judaism, had tortured its opponents in the Middle Ages. "Saul became Saint Paul; Mordechai became Karl Marx." Then came the notorious finale: *"In exterminating this pest, we render a service to humanity that our soldiers cannot imagine.*"[7] The most rabid themes of the early speeches, of the dialogue with Dietrich Eckart and especially of *Mein Kampf,* had returned, sometimes in almost identical words.

At the end of October , in the presence of Himmler and Heydrich, Hitler was even more explicit, reminding his guests—as if they needed to be reminded—of his notorious "prophecy": "I prophesied to Jewry," Hitler declared, "that the Jew would disappear from Europe if the war could not be avoided. This race of criminals carries the guilt of the two millions of dead of the World War and now already that of hundreds of thousands. Nobody should come and tell me that one cannot drive them into the marshes in the East! Who thinks of our men? It is not bad, moreover, that public rumor attributes to us the intention of exterminating the Jews. Terror is a salutary thing."[8] The last two sentences are unusual. I shall return to them further on.

At the beginning of the following month, another long historical-political tirade against the Jews took place in the presence of two other SS guests, commanders Blaschke and Richter. Once the Europeans discovered the nature of the Jew, Hitler stated, they would also understand the solidarity that tied them together. The Jew was the obstacle to this solidarity. He lived only because European solidarity did not exist.[9]

The first of Hitler's two major public anti-Jewish speeches of those weeks was the address to the Party "old fighters" on November 8, 1941, the annual commemoration date of the aborted Munich putsch of 1923. A year before, on the same occasion, the Jews had not been mentioned at all. This time, the Nazi leader launched into one of the most vicious and massive anti-Jewish tirades of his career. Many of his themes merely reiterated his former rantings, those of 1936 and 1937 in particular but also the outpourings of the previous three or four weeks. Hitler pointed to "the international Jew" as "the one behind this war" and called him "world arsonist" (*Weltbrandstifter*). "I wouldn't be a National Socialist any more," he yelled, "if I distanced myself from this finding." After attacking Jewish exploitation of the war, he turned to the Jews' enslavement of the Soviet Union: "The man who is temporarily the master of that state [Stalin] is nothing else but an instrument in the hands of omnipotent Jewry. . . . When Stalin is on the scene, in front of the curtain, Kaganowitsch [Stalin's Jewish son-in-law] stands behind him" . . . and so on. In between these anti-

Jewish insults and threats, the Nazi leader gave clear expression to the apocalyptic dimension of the ongoing struggle: "This struggle, my old Party comrades, has really become not only a struggle for Germany, but for the whole of Europe, a struggle [that will decide] between existence and annihilation!"[10] In this same speech Hitler again reminded his audience that he had often been a prophet in his life, but this time the prophecy did not relate to the extermination of the Jews, implicit in his entire speech, but to a closely related theme: November 1918, when Germany was stabbed in the back, would never occur again. "Everything is imaginable," he exclaimed, "except one thing, that Germany will ever capitulate!"[11]

In a notorious article in *Das Reich* entitled "The Jews are guilty" (*Die Juden sind schuld*), Goebbels echoed his master's voice. He reminded his readers of Hitler's prophecy that the Jews would be exterminated in case of war and added: "We are experiencing now the consummation of this prophecy; the fate of the Jews that is being fulfilled is harsh, but more than deserved. Pity or regret is completely out of place here."[12] Within the limits imposed by the occasion, Hitler returned to his anti-Jewish tirades when, on November 28, he received the Great Mufti of Jerusalem.[13]

On December 11, in the wake of Japan's attack on Pearl Harbor, Hitler announced to the Reichstag that Germany was declaring war on the United States. From the outset, the messianic theme was present: "If Providence wanted that this struggle should not spare the German people, then I am grateful that [Providence] entrusted me with the leadership of this historical confrontation, a confrontation that will decisively mold not only the history of our Germany but that of Europe, actually that of the entire world for the next five hundred or one thousand years."[14] Hitler finally turned his fury against Roosevelt. The Jews, according to the Nazi leader, were planning to use the American tool in order to prepare "a second Purim to the European nations that were becoming increasingly antisemitic. . . . It was the Jew, in his full satanic vileness who gathered around this man [Roosevelt], but also to whom this man reached out."[15] This was total, uncontrolled rage: for Hitler, America and Roosevelt were completely in the hands of the Jews. It may explain the otherwise puzzling German declaration of war on the United States. Hitler would not wait for the initiative to come from Roosevelt and the Jews.

The next day, Hitler addressed the Reichsleiter and Gauleiter in a secret speech summed up by Goebbels in his diary: "In regard to the Jewish question the Führer is determined to wipe the table clean (*reinen Tisch zu machen*). He prophesied to the Jews that if they once more brought about a world war, they would be annihilated. It was not a mere declaration. The world war is here, the extermination of the Jews must be its necessary consequence. This matter has to be envisaged without any sentimentality. We are not here to have compassion for the Jews, but to have compassion for our German people. As the German people have once again sacrificed some 160,000 dead in the Eastern campaign, those responsible for this bloody conflict will have to pay for it with their lives."[16]

Finally—according to the already mentioned entry in Himmler's appointment calender, discovered in Moscow and recently published by a group of young German historians—in a meeting with Himmler on December 18, Hitler gave the following instruction: "Jewish question | exterminate as partisans."[17] The vertical line remains unexplained. The identification of the Jews as "partisans" obviously did not refer to the Jews on Soviet territory who were being exterminated for the last six months but rather to the deadly internal enemy who, by treasonously plotting in Germany and German-occupied Europe, could, as in November 1918, stab the Reich in the back.

Thus, after ten months of relative public silence about the Jewish issue, Hitler suddenly addressed it with unusual frequency and growing fury between mid-October and mid-December 1941. Over the course of these two months, the Nazi leader explicitly mentioned the extermination of the Jews on October 19, October 25, December 12, and December 18 and was indirectly quoted to that effect by Goebbels, Alfred Rosenberg, and Hans Frank between December 12 and 16. Nothing of the kind had ever happened before in Hitler's declarations. It was a sign of radical change. Indeed, the fact that four out of six of these exterminatory statements were made within a few days in December could be seen as an explicitly ominous message conveying that a final decision had been made, probably as a result of the American entry into the war. Let us briefly consider the October-to-December period again.

By mid-October 1941, Hitler had certainly become aware of the threatening convergence of external and internal dangers: The war in the East could not be won before the winter, the United States was coming ever closer to military intervention, and, in occupied Europe, behind the German lines, armed resistance was starting. In Hitlerian logic, these threats were necessarily the work of the Jews, those behind the Bolsheviks, behind Roosevelt, those who were also the "partisans." November 1918, let us recall, would never happen again. As the deportation of all European Jews to Siberia was impossible, as local Nazi chieftains were clamoring for solutions to the overfilling of the ghettos, as the regional massacres were extending to Jews outside of Soviet territory, it seems plausible that the outburst of anti-Jewish statements in mid-October coincided with *the beginning of a process that could lead to total extermination.* But, nothing indicates that a decision was already made. No uniform way of handling the Jews deported from the Reich was apparent, and the setting up of both Belzec and Chelmno could still have been local initiatives. Moreover, let us recall the sentences of October 25: "It is not bad that public opinion attributes to us the intention of exterminating the Jews. Terror is a salutary thing." Which public opinion had to be frightened? American opinion, most plausibly. As in January 1939, Hitler probably still hoped to avoid a confrontation with the United States by letting the American Jews believe that such a war would spell the end of their brethren in Europe. *The American entry into the war occurred nonetheless, and so did the Russian counterattack on the Moscow front.* In a context in which total extermination was an ever closer possibility, the decision probably fell. Instructions were given to Himmler on December 18, but Hitler's declarations in December were in themselves sufficient and made any further order superfluous.

On the eve of the meeting with Himmler, Hitler had once more raised the Jewish issue with Goebbels. According to the propaganda minister, "the Führer is determined to proceed consistently in this matter [the Jewish question] and not be stopped by bourgeois sentimentality." Hitler and his minister discussed the evacuation of the Jews from the Reich, but it seems that subsequently the Jewish issue in general was addressed: "All the Jews have to be transferred to the East. What happens to them there, cannot be of great interest to us. They have asked for this fate; they brought about the war, now they must also pay the bill." Then Goebbels adds: "It is comforting that despite the burden of military responsibility the Führer still finds the time . . . for these matters and mainly has a clear view about them. He alone is in the position to solve this problem definitively, with the necessary hardness."[18]

In Hitler's anti-Jewish tirades of October to December 1941, the overall argument, many times repeated, was clear: on the one side of the battle line was Europe, its ancient culture and its true religion: Aryan Christianity; on the other side were the Jew Paul and the Jew Marx, the Jews' tools Stalin, Roosevelt, and all those Jews to whom he referred twice as "satanic" beings, beings who were preparing a "second Purim" for the European nations. The battle, as the Nazi leader proclaimed, was about "existence or annihilation." Providence had chosen him to lead Germany and Europe in this ultimate confrontation. As he had already declared in *Mein Kampf*, "there is no making pacts with Jews, there can only be the hard either-or."[19]

There is no need to dwell any further upon the convergence of some sort of messianic faith and the most extreme ideological statements in Hitler's declarations against Bolshevism and plutocracy, those twin bases of the forces of evil, "the Jews." Two main concepts linked this metapolitical level with the spirit of "scientific modernity": "race," obviously, and, less obviously so, "Europe."

From the outset, the notion of race was part and parcel of Hitler's worldview. As we know, it could be understood in biological terms, but also as a biological-cultural concept or as a quasi-metaphysical category. By switching from one level to the other, Hitler could use race in any circumstance and accommodate any audience. In his November 8, 1941, speech to the "old fighters," for example, he wanted to assure his audience that his apocalyptic vision was based upon scientific certainty: "We have followed his [the Jew's] traces during so many years and for the first time in this Reich we have clarified the problem forever (*für alle Zeiten*) in a scientifically planned way; thereby we have in fact followed the words of a great Jew [Disraeli] according to whom race was the key to world history."[20]

As for the notion of "Europe," it was newer and gained significance first after the victory in the West but mainly after the attack against the Soviet Union and the declaration of war against the United States. Like "race," it has different meanings: mystical, cultural-racial, economic-demographic. Hitler was reasserting what the party planners had known since 1940: the European *Grossraumord-*

nung was closely linked to the overall ideological crusade, that is to the overall crusade against the Jews, the obstacles to European solidarity.

IDEOLOGY, SOCIETY, AND MASS MURDER UNDER NATIONAL SOCIALISM

The hard core of the National Socialist Party probably shared Hitler's redemptive anti-Semitism. What is certain is that the anti-Jewish campaign was carried out under the responsibility of Hitler's ideological guard: the party. In his closing speech at the 1935 party rally, in which he proclaimed the anti-Jewish racial laws, Hitler had declared that if the Jewish problem "should yet again prove insoluble [it] would have to be assigned by law to the National Socialist Party for a definitive solution."[21] Since 1938, the Jewish issue had been mainly in the hands of the National Socialist Party; at the end of 1941, the party was put in charge of the Final Solution.

The ideologically motivated plans of various party agencies and the power struggles that they reflected were not determined only by anti-Jewish goals; however, they tied in with the anti-Jewish policies once decisions were made, and this not only at the general "racial" or "European" levels. Mass resettlement of ethnic Germans, for example, demanded, in Nazi eyes, the expulsion and, eventually, the extermination of part of East European Jewry; such partial plans could easily become part of a general plan of total extermination. In other terms, sectorial party interests were always subordinated to Hitler's goals. Once the decision about the fate of European Jewry had been taken, all party agencies became the support and implementation system which, from the end of 1941, made the anti-Jewish extermination crusade its absolute priority. The enormous amount of loot that fell into the hands of party members, high and low, certainly bolstered their ideological commitment.

It is difficult to estimate how deeply Hitler's brand of anti-Semitism penetrated nonparty agencies and particularly the Wehrmacht. The extreme anti-Jewish proclamations of Field Marshalls Walter von Reichenau, Erich von Manstein, and some others among the highest-ranking officers do not seem typical. Yet, the "barbarisation of warfare" and the "ideologisation of warfare," mainly on the Eastern Front and in the Balkans, are hard to disentangle. After the

invasion of Poland, General Johannes Blaskowitz had sent a complaint about the murder operations of the SS; but after the invasion
of the Soviet Union, the Wehrmacht became an active auxiliary in
many of the anti-Jewish murder operations. In Western Europe, it
even initiated some of the anti-Jewish measures during the second
half of 1940 and almost always cooperated in their implementation.[22] In his order of the day of October 2, 1941, Hitler would probably not have declared that behind all of Germany's enemies stood
"the Jews and only the Jews" if he had not known or sensed that
among hundreds of thousands of soldiers such a radical anti-Jewish
outburst would find some echo. At officer rank, in any case, traditional conservative anti-Semitism and violent anti-Bolshevism were
the ready ideological ground for the anti-Jewish crusade. The same is
true for other state agencies and for the economic sector. Here too the
immense material advantages resulting from the persecution and the
extermination of the Jews bolstered the readiness to accept the most
radical measures.

There remains the much-debated issue of the attitudes and reactions of the wider German population to Hitler's anti-Jewish dia-
tribes and to the anti-Jewish policies of the regime. Recent inquiries
indicate that there was more day-to-day anti-Jewish violence among
the German populace than previously assumed and that later possibly
up to one third of the population was aware that mass killings of Jews
were taking place in the East, although the full extent and details of
the Final Solution may possibly not have been known to most of
these Germans.

In August 1941, outrage among the population and the churches
had put an end to the murder of the mentally ill, at least in part; later,
the Aryan wives of a group of Jewish men about to be deported from
Berlin forced their release. Thus, at times, popular reactions were
taken into account by the regime. But, the Berlin demonstration—
and it was a very limited and peculiar one—was the only popular
protest regarding the fate of the Jews. In general terms, the population's indifference to persecution of the Jews during the 1930s continued as indifference to mass murder during the war. Churches often expelled Christian members who wore the Jewish star, and
intellectuals in various domains (including future luminaries of West
German historiography) enthusiastically joined the anti-Semitic
campaign, adding studies and theories of their own. Even opposition

circles adhered to their traditional anti-Jewish stances, notwithstanding their knowledge of the extermination. Moreover, as Frank Bajohr has shown, tens of thousands of Germans were purchasing for next to nothing belongings transported from all over occupied Europe in the *Judenmärkte* (Jewish markets) of major German cities,[23] and hundreds of thousands of *Volksgenossen* (racial comrades) were now living in Jewish homes.

From 1933 to 1939, widespread indifference to the fate of the Jews may have been fueled by *traditional anti-Semitism,* as well as by the primacy of the "führer cult" and the enthusiasm for "national revival." In 1940 and early 1941, the immense surge of nationalist pride triggered by German victories may have bolstered even further the support for the regime and its measures. From June 1941 onward and even more so after the entry of the United States into the war, many Germans may have come to believe the slogans identifying the Jews as the ultimate enemy behind Stalin, Roosevelt, and Churchill, behind Bolshevism and plutocracy alike. Mainly, the vast majority continued to believe in Adolf Hitler and the regime. Even if his brand of anti-Jewish obsession was not shared by the majority of Germans, the faith in his leadership was such that his decisions were accepted with all their consequences.

As for the tens of thousands of killers, Germans and non-Germans alike, they were probably motivated by orders, by pack behavior, by constant and ever more ferocious anti-Jewish incitement, sometimes by prevalent and deep-seated anti-Semitic stereotypes, and probably more often than not by ordinary human sadism, the kind of sadism that incites to the worst cruelty against the weakest of the weak.

In summation, the killers were not essentially motivated by some kind of rabid eliminatory anti-Semitism that, according to Daniel Goldhagen's interpretation, was supposedly present in most of the German population. Rather, the population, the elites, the state agencies, and the Wehrmacht were suffused by a traditional religious and social anti-Semitism that, in and of itself, paralyzed any countervailing attitudes and proved to be a ready ground for the most extreme anti-Jewish steps. No less significant for the acceptance and often the active support of the regime's policies against the Jews was, as we mentioned, some measure of belief in official propaganda, nationalism, and "führer cult," on the one hand, along with material interests and opportunism, on the other.

But, in the absence of a powerful, endemic, anti-Jewish drive from within the population and therefore from within the Wehrmacht and the other state agencies, the murder campaign against the Jews could not have been systematically carried out and sustained for almost four years, in the face of constant organizational and bureaucratic problems and especially in the face of the growing constraints imposed by the war, had there not existed another driving force. This essential impetus came from the political leadership: from Hitler, the hard core of the party and its main terror agencies, where, as recent studies about the SD have shown, extreme anti-Semitism was prevalent.[24]

In Nazi Germany, murder on a large scale was easily implemented and rationalized by various groups. But—and allow me to repeat this decisive point—*initiating* the total extermination of millions of people and transporting them to killing sites from the farthest corners of the continent in the midst of an increasingly desperate general war demanded the fanatical drive of a pitiless ideological faith. This faith itself, Hitler's redemptive anti-Semitism, had its root in German history and in the Christian tradition. It also fed upon the potentially murderous instrumentalism inherent to modernity.

How unconscious the victims were of the oncoming events as the Final Solution started clearly appears from Victor Klemperer's diary entry of December 31, 1941: "Heads up for the painful last five minutes!"[25]

NOTES

1. For the text of Hitler's "Order of the day" of October 2, 1941, see Max Domarus, *Hitler. Reden und Proklamationen,* part 2, vol. 4 (Munich: Süddeutscher Verlag, 1965), pp. 1756–57. English translations of quotations from this source are mine.

2. Anson Rabinbach, *In the Shadow of Catastrophe: German Intellectuals between Apocalypse and Enlightenment* (Berkeley, Calif.: University of California Press, 1997), p.14.

3. Victor Klemperer, *I Shall Bear Witness* (New York: Random House, 1998).

4. Joseph Goebbels, *Tagebücher,* part 2, vol. 1, *July–September 1941,* edited by Elke Froehlich (Munich: K.G. Saur, 1996), p. 262. English translations of quotations from this source are mine.

5. Domarus, *Hitler,* pp. 1726–32.

6. Goebbels, *Tagebücher,* part 2, vol. 1, pp. 265–66.

7. French edition [Libres Propos], vol. 1, pp. 76–79. English translations of quotations from this source are mine.

8. Ibid., p. 87.

9. Ibid., p. 117.

10. Domarus, *Hitler,* pp. 1772–74.

11. Ibid., p. 1778.

12. Ralf Georg Reuth, *Goebbels* (New York: Harcourt Brace, 1993), p.299.

13. Memorandum of an Official of the Foreign Minister's Secretariat, November 30, 1941, *Documents on German Foreign Policy,* series D, vol.13 (Washington, D.C.: GPO, 1964), p.883.

14. Ibid., p. 1794.

15. Ibid., p. 1804.

16. Goebbels, *Tagebücher,* part 2, vol. 2, p. 498f.

17. Christian Gerlach, "Die Wannsee-Konferenz, das Schicksal der deutschen Juden und Hitlers politische Grundentscheidung, alle Juden Europas zu ermordern," *Krieg, Ernährung, Völkermord* (Hamburg: Hamburger Edition, 1998), p. 121. English translations of quotations from this source are mine.

18. Goebbels, *Tagebücher,* part 2, vol. 2, pp. 533–34.

19. Adolf Hitler, *Mein Kampf,* translated by Ralph Manheim (Boston: Houghton Mifflin, 1971), p. 206.

20. Domarus, *Hitler,* p. 1772.

21. For an analysis of Hitler's speech, see Saul Friedländer, *Nazi Germany and the Jews,* vol. 1, *The Years of Persecution 1933–1939* (New York: HarperCollins, 1997), pp. 142ff.

22. Ulrich Herbert, "Die deutsche Militärverwaltung in Paris und die Deportation der französischen Juden," in Christian Jansen et.al., *Von der Aufgabe der Freiheit* (Berlin: Akademic Verlag, 1995), p. 431. There were some exceptions. It seems that in Belgium the Wehrmacht command was slower in implementing the anti-Jewish measures; those were obviously implemented nonetheless.

23. Frank Bajohr, *Arisierung in Hamburg. die Verdraengung der Juedischen Unternehmen, 1933–1945* (Hamburg: Christians, 1997), pp. 328ff.

24. Michael Wildt, ed., *Die Judenpolitik des SD, 1935–1938: eine Dokumentation* (Munich: R. Oldenbourg, 1995), p.48.

25. Klemperer, *I Shall Bear Witness,* p. 436.

II.   P·E·R·P·E·T·R·A·T·O·R·S

Alvin Rosenfeld

Who Killed the Jews?
Reflections on a Riddle

AT FIRST GLANCE, THE QUESTION "WHO KILLED THE JEWS?" MAY SEEM
to be a strange one, but in fact some of the answers to this question
still elude us. To be sure, we know a great deal about the killers, and
yet we are still to fully absorb the extreme character of their crimes or
secure a clear place in memory for those who committed them. The
problem, as we shall see, has less to do with the facts as with the complex and sometimes contradictory manner of their presentation. It
also has to do with what the minds of most people are able and willing to take in. What is known and what is remembered, in short, are
not necessarily one and the same thing. To frame this problem in a
way that should be helpful, I begin with a poem:

> From Belsen a crate of gold teeth,
> from Dachau a mountain of shoes,
> from Auschwitz a skin lampshade.
> Who killed the Jews?
>
> Not I, cries the typist,
> not I, cries the engineer,
> not I, cries Adolf Eichmann,
> not I, cries Albert Speer.
>
> My friend Fritz Nova lost his father—
> a petty official had to choose.
> My friend Lou Abrahms lost his brother.
> Who killed the Jews?
>
> David Nova swallowed gas,
> Hyman Abrahms was beaten and starved.

• 51

Some men signed their papers,
and some stood guard,
and some herded them in,
and some dropped the pellets,
and some spread the ashes,
and some hosed the walls,

and some planted the wheat,
and some poured the steel,
and some cleared the rails,
and some raised the cattle.

Some smelled the smoke,
some just heard the news.
Were they Germans? Were they Nazis?
Were they human? Who killed the Jews?

The stars will remember the gold,
the sun will remember the shoes,
the moon will remember the skin.
But who killed the Jews?

William Heyen, the author of these lines, calls his poem "Riddle,"[1] for at the heart of it are the puzzling words, "Who killed the Jews?" This question is posed four times, and four times the answer is given, "Not I." All we know is that the Jews have been beaten, starved, and gassed and that "some men" are responsible for their brutalization and murder. Were these men "Germans?" "Nazis?" "Human?" The poem inquires into their identities in precisely these terms but provides no answers. Nor does it provide any answers to questions about the future memory of these killings apart from the fanciful one that memory will be stored in the heavens, among the stars, sun, and moon. Otherwise, in the absence of identifiable agents, we are left wondering: Who *were* the people who killed the Jews?

It may seem odd for such a question to be framed as a riddle, for surely by now, more than half a century after the defeat of Nazi Germany, we know who the killers were. Or do we? Most of those involved in the destruction of European Jewry left behind no written testimony to their crimes.[2] The historical literature on the perpetrators continues to grow, but the answers one discovers in this literature are often in conflict with one another and ultimately do not solve the riddle that Heyen poses. A review of more popular representations—

in novels, stories, poems, plays, television programs, films—yields an abundance of perpetrator images, but these, too, as we shall see, likewise prove unsatisfactory. To be sure, at the policy level, from Hitler on down, we know who the major perpetrators were. We also know that the lower level included the many thousands who did the work of registering and rounding up, confining and transporting, shooting and gassing. And yet, in spite of all we know, the killers resist coming into clear focus. There is something about these criminals and their crimes that remains inaccessible and creates a cognitive "unease," as Saul Friedländer has called it, which keeps the mind from being at rest.[3] Before exploring the nature of this unease, I find it necessary to open a wide parenthesis and acknowledge certain methodological assumptions that have guided this inquiry.

1. It is not primarily from historians that most people gain whatever knowledge they may acquire of the Third Reich and the Nazi crimes against the Jews but rather from novelists, filmmakers, playwrights, poets, television program writers and producers, popular newspapers and magazines, and the like.

2. Thus, the "history" of the Holocaust that is made available to most people most of the time is largely a product of popular culture and does not always derive from or necessarily resemble the history of the Jews under Nazism that professional historians strive to establish.

3. The public at large remains readily drawn by the specter of the Holocaust and is a receptive audience for stories and images of the Third Reich, yet one cannot assume that this popular fascination is equivalent to a serious interest in Jewish fate during the Nazi era. Images of mass suffering may awaken conscience, but they also have the power to perversely excite the imagination. A pornography of the Holocaust accompanies and may undercut a didactics of the Holocaust.

4. Far from being fixed, the image of the Holocaust is an ever-changing one. Within the evolving narrative of the Nazi era, the perpetrators obviously play a central role, but in both historiography and popular culture, representations of the perpetrators are varied, and explanations of who they were and why they did what they did elude anything like consensus. We have a fairly detailed and increasingly differentiated sense of the vic-

tims; a large literature has developed by and about the survivors; and, more and more, liberators, rescuers, and righteous gentiles are emerging as prominent figures within the changing typology of Holocaust narratives. With only few exceptions, however, the killers are weakly imagined types and generally live, if they remain alive to the imagination at all, as stereotypical figures. Thus, the seemingly simple question with which we began— "Who killed the Jews?"—remains a problematic one.

So much for the preliminaries. I turn now to some reflections on the place of the perpetrators in history writing and then offer a brief survey of the shapes the perpetrators have assumed in popular culture, where they have taken up what looks like permanent residence.

Raul Hilberg's *The Destruction of the European Jews* remains the most thoroughgoing study yet produced of the administrative apparatus and bureaucratic organization behind the Nazi crimes. Hilberg portrays the killers in exhaustive detail as technicians of a complex process of destruction. One comes to understand them as part of an extensive network of decision makers operating with efficiency and a kind of relentless logic toward the achievement of a deadly goal. The system is revealed through the disclosure of an endless chain of decrees, orders, agendas, letters, minutes, memorandums, invoices, inventories, schedules, tables, charts, and the like. These documents are copiously exhibited and carefully analyzed, and those who composed them and received them are named by name and rank, but in the main it was no part of Hilberg's purpose to show us the killers as individuals. The author says as much when he writes: "To grasp the full significance of what these men did, we have to understand that we are not dealing with individuals who had their own separate moral standards. The bureaucrats who were drawn into the destruction process were not different in their moral makeup from the rest of the population."[4] Thus, although one learns a great deal from Hilberg about the complex machinery of destruction, one does not come away from a reading of his book with a vivid sense of those who built and ran the machine. Rather, it is the machine itself that is the center of Hilberg's scrupulous attention and *it* that stands as the answer to questions about the identity of the killers: "Without regard to cost, the bureaucratic machine, operating with accelerating speed and ever-widening destructive effect, proceeded to annihilate the European Jews."[5]

To read *The Destruction of the European Jews* in this way is not to call into question Hilberg's immense achievement, for given the author's intentions, it is clear that his success is a formidable one. Nevertheless, if one seeks to move beyond his dominant trope of the killing machine and learn in more concrete detail who the killers actually were, one most likely will be frustrated. Given the task he set himself and the sources with which he worked, Hilberg chose to present the Nazi destruction of European Jewry within the relatively abstract framework of bureaucratic structures. Yet, as Judith Miller reminds us in her study of national memories of the Holocaust, "abstraction is memory's most ardent enemy."[6] Just as it is virtually impossible to imagine the individual victims within the by now canonized figure of "six million," so, too, is it hardly possible to see the faces of the killers if we dissolve them collectively into the categories of desktop murderers and industrialized killers.

In saying as much, I obviously do not want to deny the historical reality of those diffuse administrative and bureaucratic organizations that Hilberg has so meticulously described or to deny the reality of industrialized murder on a vast and impersonal scale. The issue is not one of the existence of these things, all of which are amply confirmed by the work of other historians, but of how their representation within the mainstream body of history writing presents us with a dilemma that is still to be resolved. Simply put, the dilemma is this: the Hilbergian analysis of the engineers of mass murder operating at a bureaucratic distance from the actual killings of the Jews is in conflict with the basic human desire to gain access to the hearts and minds of those who carried out the killings. One source of the cognitive unease that Friedländer points to, therefore, might be located precisely here, in the radical disjunction between the depersonalized nature of bureaucratically organized mass murder and the plain need to know, "one, by one, by one," who the murderers actually were.

In pursuit of the individual perpetrators, however, other problems arise. Is it possible to personalize the killers, for example, and not, at the same time, also hopelessly diminish the scope of the Holocaust or turn its enormity of pain and depravity into either banality or pornography? One of the ways in which those who murdered the Jews are likely to become real to us today is in public courtroom trials, where they tend to appear indistinguishable from other old men in neckties and jackets whom we pass on the street. These octogenarians discovered leading normal lives in Ohio suburbs, Canadian cities, French and South American towns and villages—is it possible that the unspeakable could have been done by men so unremarkable? The answer we know is "yes," yet the evidence before our eyes does not readily square with the images of atrocity that have passed down to us from the time of the Third Reich. No traces of murderous passion are detectable in the faces or voices of these suddenly exposed old men, either because such passions have long since dissipated or, as Hannah Arendt famously argued in writing about Adolf Eichmann, because they may never have been present in the first place. In the disjunction between the ferocious character of the remembered past and the ordinary appearance of some of those who were responsible for the ferocity, therefore, we might locate still another source of the "unease" that Saul Friedländer points to.[7]

The notion of the "ordinary" persists as a frequently invoked frame of reference for explaining the perpetrators, even if the identity of those who exemplify the "ordinary" remains mired in controversy. Read Christopher Browning, for instance, and it is apparent that those who did the killing were "ordinary men." Read Daniel Jonah Goldhagen, and the very same perpetrators appear as "ordinary Germans." These descriptive differences, far from signifying only minor semantic distinctions, point to a major historiographical debate about who the killers were and what motivated them. Browning sees them as human beings whose participation in mass murder might be explained by a range of situational factors as common as peer pressure and career ambition. Goldhagen, by contrast, offers an explanation that is almost anthropological in character and defines Nazi genocide in terms that are emphatically national and cultural. Between these two, there is obviously nothing resembling consensus.[8]

At its polar extremes, the debate between the intentionalists and the functionalists also renders remote anything like a common understanding of why and how the killings progressed as they did. And whatever else it may have been about, the notorious German *Historikerstreit* (historians' conflict) of recent years was similarly symptomatic of radical and unresolvable differences in historiographical analysis and explanation. Other historians have sought to identify the killers as products of a range of causative factors—some of them inherent in modernity itself, others attributable to the ideological and political underpinnings of "fascism," "totalitarianism," the "genocidal mentality," "eliminationist anti-Semitism," "redemptive anti-Semitism," a broad-gauged "ethnic cleansing," and so on.

Although frustrating for those who seek simple, monocausal explanations, this lack of consensus among historians has the positive effect of keeping open basic questions about the perpetrators, an openness that may indeed prevent the mind from being at ease but also guarantees it will remain active in its search for answers. The process is long and slow, nuanced and frequently contentious, but in the end (although no scholar ever truly reaches any such mythical place as "the end"), one may get close to the truth of how things really were. In the meanwhile, though, a fascination with the past, and particularly with *this* past, is ongoing, and the spaces left empty by the historians or filled in by them in ways that are so different and even contradictory will be eagerly occupied by art, which proceeds in other ways and appeals to other needs and desires.

Interestingly, Raul Hilberg himself has recently recognized the centrality of art—indeed, the inevitability of art—in the representation of the past. Here is how he puts the matter:

> To portray the Holocaust, Claude Lanzmann once said to me, one has to create a work of art. . . . The artist usurps the actuality, substituting a text for a reality that is fast fading. The words that are thus written take the place of the past; these words, rather than the events themselves, will be remembered.[9]

Once we make the shift away from documentary history to what "will be remembered," we enter the realm of art, which transforms reality according to its own imperatives and designs. Moreover, in a popular culture such as ours, it does so not just by written words but by visual and auditory images as well. These transformations do not necessarily depend upon the evidentiary base on which historians rest their accounts of the past but draw on other kinds of narrative conventions, some of which may be at odds with or even in defiance of the historical evidence. Be that as it may, when it comes to understanding what most people know of the crimes of the Holocaust and how they acquire such knowledge, the contribution of the arts, including the popular arts, is crucial.

Consider, for instance, the immense role that Steven Spielberg's film *Schindler's List* has played in projecting images of the perpetrators to tens of millions of people. The dominant figure of the killer in this film is that of Amon Goeth, the commander of the Plaszow labor camp, who murders Jews as easily as others swat flies. Far from being either an "ordinary man" or an "ordinary German," Goeth is clearly extraordinary in the brutal energy he displays as a psychopathic personality. Thus, while historians have argued that it is necessary to historicize understanding of Nazi Germany and move away from earlier categories of demonization, the demonic in fact retains a powerful appeal within popular culture. To cite only two examples among many, Spielberg's Goeth and the Mengele-like doctor of Rolf Hochhuth's play *The Deputy* fit no norm known to us other than the insanely sadistic or diabolical one. In both cases, we find imaginative projections of evil let loose in the world, mad and cunning killers who serve allegorical purposes more than they do historical ones. The type is repellent but also fascinating. To some, it may also carry the allure of the willful, transgressive criminal personality, an allure that the Nazi mystique solicits and strongly encourages. It is almost certainly men cast in this image of the evil killer and not "ordinary" men that a vast public believes were responsible for the mass murder of the Jews. For who else would have perpetrated such a crime if not cruel and crazy people like these? Or, to cite the craziest and most wickedly transgressive figure of them all, like Hitler himself?

The image of Hitler that prevails in the public domain is a complex one. The historian John Lukacs devoted a recent book to a comprehensive study of Hitler biographies only to conclude that we do not understand the leader of the Third Reich and cannot adequately explain him. For good reasons, Lukacs rejects the popular idea of the "mad" Hitler, but in its place he is not able to offer anything better than that he was "the greatest revolutionary of the twentieth century." Otherwise, as Lukacs sums up the matter, "We are not yet finished with Hitler. . . . [He] Was, Is and Remains a Problem."[10] Ron Rosenbaum, the author of *Explaining Hitler,* has given us a similar, if more popular, book and has reached analogous conclusions: Despite innumerable efforts by historians, biographers, filmmakers, psychologists, religious thinkers, and others, Hitler thus far remains elusive. As Rosenbaum puts it, in the search for the historical Hitler, "an enormous amount has been written but little has been *settled.*"[11]

And because so little has been settled, the Nazi mystique retains a hold on the popular imagination. An omnipresent figure in literature, film, television, popular magazines, science fiction, song, joke, and cartoon, Hitler remains before us in the most variegated shapes, not all of them repellent. As Gordon Craig has summed him up, "[Two] generations after his death in the bunker, Hitler was like the little man upon the stair in the old song. He wasn't there, but he wouldn't go away."[12]

In story after story, we have had the raging Hitler, the contrite Hitler, the artistic Hitler, the tender Hitler. There are fictions that bring him back to life as a woman; others that re-create him as a Jew. In the work of various comedians, he has been good for a joke. To the rockers he was the first rock star. To the pornographers, who like to re-create his private moments with Eva Braun (about which we know almost nothing), he is, as Nazism as a whole has become, a source of popular imagery for sadomasochistic sex.

To the public at large, Hitler remains a source of endless fascination. Such a figure, which, at one and the same time, seems to be able to satisfy our fantasies for power, madness, money, sex, murder, politics, pageantry, ambition, and art, obviously has appeal. It is not an appeal, however, that will help us better understand the Nazi persecution and slaughter of the Jews. On the contrary, the sustained fictionalization and popularization of Hitler and other Nazi perpetrators keeps alive a broad-based fascination with the Holocaust and, at the same time, keeps at a distance any truly serious efforts to understand the people who organized and carried out the killings.

Who, then, killed the Jews? "Not I, cries the typist, / not I, cries the engineer, / not I, cries Adolf Eichmann, / not I, cries Albert Speer." The denial that Heyen attributes to the perpetrators has been widespread. It has been eased somewhat but not truly overcome by the work of historians, much of which has focused on the technical and bureaucratic dimensions of the genocide, or on its political and ideological aspects, and not on its more human side. And because the human side of the catastrophe has been so understated, especially, as Omer Bartov has pointed out, in the work of German historians, who have "shown a complete inability to empathize with the victims, even while they [have] distance[d] themselves from the perpetrators,"[13] we are left with something like a faceless crime. The enormous volume of literature on Hitler seems to suggest that, if only we could locate him, it would be possible to pin at least the origins of the crime on the leader of the Third Reich, but he has become lost to the historians somewhere within the maze of contending theories about the nature and course of the killing machine that he set into motion and lost to the popularizers through the myriad recyclings of his image on stage, screen, picture book, record album, and pornography. Even if it were possible to retrieve him more successfully than has been the case to date, the Nazi genocide of the Jews, which can hardly be reduced to the doings of one man, will probably remain resistant to the normative categories of rational explanation, even as it retains its often perverse hold on the popular imagination.

"Der Tod ist ein Meister aus Deutschland" (Death is a master from Germany), another poet has told us, but we are still to identify the face or adequately explain the motives of this deadly Meister. Thus the question with which we began—"Who killed the Jews?"—remains before us, scandalously so, as more of a riddle than we might have supposed.

NOTES

1. The poem can be found in William Heyen, *The Swastika Poems* (New York: Vanguard, 1977), pp. 24–25.
2. See, in addition to the generally self-serving memoirs and autobiographical writings by Rudolf Hess and Albert Speer, the collection edited by Ernst Klee, Willi Dressen, and Volker Riess, *"The Good Old Days": The Holocaust as Seen by Its Perpetrators and Bystanders* (New York: Free Press, 1991); see also Gitta Serenyi, *Into That Darkness: An Examination of Conscience* (New York: McGraw-Hill, 1974).
3. Saul Friedländer, "The 'Final Solution': On the Unease in Historical Interpretation," in *Memory, History, and the Extermination of the Jews of Europe* (Bloomington: Indiana University Press, 1993), pp. 102–16.
4. Raul Hilberg, *The Destruction of the European Jews* (Chicago: Quadrangle, 1961), p. 649.
5. Ibid., p. 17.
6. Judith Miller, *One by One by One: Facing the Holocaust* (New York: Simon and Schuster, 1990), p. 287.
7. An important corrective to having the mass murder of the Jews appear commonplace was offered by Saul Bellow in his post-Holocaust novel *Mr. Sammler's Planet.* "The idea of making the century's great crime look dull is not banal," Artur Sammler remarks in a trenchant comment on Hannah Arendt's Eichmann thesis. "The banality was only camouflage. What better way to get the curse out of murder than to make it look ordinary, or boring, or trite . . . ? Do you think the Nazis didn't know what mur-

der is? Everybody knows what murder is. That is very old human knowledge." Saul Bellow, *Mr. Sammler's Planet* (New York: Viking, 1970), p. 18.

8. Christopher Browning, *Ordinary Men: Reserve Police Battalion 101 and the Final Solution in Poland* (New York: HarperCollins, 1992); and Daniel Jonah Goldhagen, *Hitler's Willing Executioners: Ordinary Germans and the Holocaust* (New York: Alfred A. Knopf, 1996). See also Christopher Browning, "Ordinary Germans or Ordinary Men: A Reply to the Critics," and Daniel Jonah Goldhagen, "Ordinary Men or Ordinary Germans?" in *The Holocaust and History: The Known, the Unknown, the Disputed, and the Reexamined,* ed. Michael Berenbaum and Abraham J. Peck (Bloomington: Indiana University Press, 1998), pp. 252–65 and 301–7.

9. Raul Hilberg, *The Politics of Memory: The Journey of a Holocaust Historian* (Chicago: Ivan R. Dee, 1996), p. 83.

10. John Lukacs, *The Hitler of History* (New York: Alfred A. Knopf, 1997), pp.258, 50, 51.

11. Ron Rosenbaum, *Explaining Hitler: The Search for the Origins of His Evil* (New York: Random House, 1998), p. xii.

12. Gordon Craig, *The Germans* (New York: G. P. Putnam's Sons, 1982), p. 2.

13. Omer Bartov, "'Seit die Juden weg sind . . .': Germany, History, and Representations of Absence," in *A User's Guide to German Cultural Studies,* ed. Scott Denham, Ireme Kacandes, and Jonathan Petropolous (Ann Arbor: University of Michigan Press, 1997), pp. 211, 221; see also, by the same author, a number of the articles collected in *Murder in Our Midst: The Holocaust, Industrial Killing, and Representation* (New York: Oxford University Press, 1996).

Peter Black

Officials of the Reich Central Office for Security

AS INTEREST IN THE HISTORY OF THE HOLOCAUST INTENSIFIES, THE ranks of participants and bystanders have widened. Responsibility for this still unique crime has evolved far beyond the early emphasis on the "Gestapo" as part of a larger SS "state within a state."[1] We now understand the essential role played by regional SS and police leaders and by the officials of other key SS main offices in Berlin: the Order Police Main Office, the SS Economic and Administrative Main Office, and the two race and settlement main offices: *the Reichskommissariat für die Festigung Deutschen Volkstums* (Reich Commissariat for Strengthening German Nationhood—RKFDV) and *Rasse- und Siedlungshauptamt* (Race and Settlement Main Office—RuSHA).[2] The essential participation of German civilian and military agencies—the German Foreign Office, the Reich Ministry of Transportation, the Reich civilian apparatus, and the German army—is now clear in general outline.[3] We now know much more about the complicity of the Axis powers in the Final Solution;[4] legal proceedings against Nazi collaborators in the United States have stressed the essential assistance of ethnic German and non-German auxiliaries in perpetrating genocide. Recent scholarly and popular attention has turned to the passivity, indifference, and even complicity not only of neutral powers such as Switzerland and Sweden but even of belligerents against Nazi Germany, particularly Great Britain and the United States.[5]

Yet, as the circle of indirect responsibility widens, we should not lose focus on the direct perpetrators, among whom the officials of the Reich Central Office for Security (*Reichssicherheitshauptamt*—RSHA) figure prominently. After all, the RSHA of SS-Obergruppenführer Reinhard Heydrich and Ernst Kaltenbrunner was responsible for conceiving, planning, and coordinating the implementation of the murder of the European Jews.

Shortly after Heydrich's death in June 1942, Himmler stressed the importance of the RSHA for the SS and the Nazi regime as a whole:

> Of the SS main offices, the Reich Main Office for Security alone has the possibility, through its predominantly political work, of having constant and direct contact with every phase of political development. I therefore order that all SS main offices direct all politically significant procedures to the Reich Main Office for Security for purposes of a uniform decision before these procedures are presented to me or directed to agencies outside the SS.[6]

The RSHA was created on September 27, 1939,[7] but its components had functioned together as a unit, if not always a harmonious one, at least since Heydrich's appointment as chief of the Security Police in June 1936. Heydrich ran the agency until his death. Until he settled on Kaltenbrunner as a successor, Himmler ran the RSHA himself.[8] Kaltenbrunner commanded the RSHA from January 1943 until 1945.

The RSHA drew its ideological zeal from the Security Service (*Sicherheitsdienst*—SD). The SD was established under Heydrich in 1931 as the intelligence service of the Nazi Party and in 1934 was designated the sole civilian intelligence agency in the Third Reich. Within the RSHA, SD officers who had made their careers in the Nazi movement ran five of seven departments, including personnel, administration, and the three intelligence-gathering departments. The commanders of the "mobile RSHA offices"—better known as the *Einsatzgruppen*—were SD officers.[9] During the 1930s, the SD developed a think tank for Jewish "matters." Commanded by Herbert Hagen and including among its staff Adolf Eichmann, this office II 112 suggested policy to Heydrich as he sought to assume a leading role in Reich policy development in "Jewish affairs."[10] The SD leaders perceived themselves as the intellectual elite and ideologically pure core of the "new community of harmony and strength" that the National Socialist movement would create.[11]

The RSHA developed its executive muscle from the Security Police, created in 1936 and 1937 out of the newly centralized political police (*Geheime Staatspolizei*—Gestapo) and Criminal Police (*Kriminalpolizei*—Kripo) forces. Originally pillars of the Security Police

Main Office, the Gestapo became Amt IV and the Kripo became
Amt V of the RSHA. The Gestapo and Kripo were run by professional policemen who had made successful careers in the Weimar police forces. So potentially independent and powerful was the RSHA
that Heydrich ordered its very existence to remain secret.[12]

With Himmler's support and guidance, Heydrich made the Security Police and SD key players in central policy direction regarding
the so-called Jewish question in the Third Reich. Security Police and
SD officials established a Central Office for Jewish Emigration in Vienna in 1938 and opened offices in Berlin and Prague in 1939 as a
one-stop agency for forcing Jewish emigration from Germany. In
1939, the *Einsatzgruppen* of the Security Police and the SD were
charged with the task of murdering Jewish and Polish opponents of
the German occupation in Poland and with orchestrating the concentration of the massive Jewish population of Poland into ghettos
near rail centers, from where they would someday be removed in accordance with a yet to be determined *Endziel* (final goal)[13]. At some
time prior to mid-January 1941, Heydrich was given the task of
developing an *Endlösungsprojekt* (Final Solution project) within
German-ruled Europe "on the basis of the extensive expertise in handling the Jews available in the agencies of the Chief of Security Police
and the SD."[14] Regardless of whether one believes that the "Final Solution project" meant the murder of all the European Jews, no one
can doubt that this Final Solution would be conceived, directed, and
at least initially implemented from the offices and under the guidance
of the Security Police and the SD.[15] Göring bestowed official confir-
mation of this responsibility upon Heydrich with his infamous Final
Solution decree of July 31, 1941.[16]

RSHA officials played a significant role in all phases of the implementation of the Final Solution. Though other units were involved, the *Einsatzgruppen* both coordinated and directed the murder of the Soviet Jews in conjunction with military commanders and
the Higher SS and Police Leaders (*Höhere SS- und Polizeiführer*—
HSSPF), Himmler's regional commanders of SS and police forces.
The Operation Reinhard deportations from the Polish ghettos were
carried out under the guidance of regional RSHA officials.[17] RSHA
Amt IV B 4 under SS-Obersturmbannführer Adolf Eichmann coordinated and supervised deportations from the rest of Europe; this office negotiated with police forces of the Axis nations, supervised the

deployment of indigenous forces in the occupied areas, and coordinated transit schedules with the Reichsbahn.[18] Each concentration camp, including Auschwitz, had a Gestapo office which monitored prisoners under protective detention. Though thousands were murdered in the camps without higher authorization, "official" murders were ordered by Himmler himself or the RSHA.[19]

The amalgamation of Security Police and SD developed from the ideas of Heydrich, Himmler, Werner Best, Walter Schellenberg, Arthur Nebe, and others related to the establishment of a *Staatsschutzkorps* (Corps for the Protection of the State). This ideological, if tactically flexible, police bureaucracy was expected, on the initiative of its leaders, to intervene proactively within the racial society to neutralize or eliminate racial and political enemies. Werner Best wrote in 1936 that even the term "political police" was too narrow for the National Socialist police function, which operated not according to "constrictive law or a formally defined leadership" but according to a "living idea" that the will of the *Volk* was "indivisible." Hence "each attempt to assert or even to adhere to another political ideal would be erased—without consideration for the subjective intent of its supporters—as a symptom of illness [*Krankheitserscheinung*] that endangers the healthy unity of the individual national organism [*Volksorganismus*]."[20] For Reinhard Heydrich, the Reich, as the political expression of the *Volk,* knew only *Volksfeinde,* and these were "opponents of the racial, völkischen and spiritual substance of our people." To ensure that these enemies, which included Jews, Marxists, internationalist Freemasons and "politicizing church officials," did not undermine the Nazi state and society from within, the Nazi state police must develop the ethos of a "corps-like community" whose members both understood the intensity of the danger and were permitted leeway by the structure of the National Socialist state to take the appropriate measures.[21] Kripo chief Arthur Nebe opined in August 1939 that crime was "a disease on the body of the *Volk*" that required "preventative measures" by a unified criminal police force consisting of "National Socialist persons" to uncover the "source of the infection."[22] As Walter Schellenberg put it in February 1939, the amalgamation of the SS, a party formation "equipped with its special laws of military discipline and ideological firmness," with the police would permit the creation of a "new *Staatsschutzkorps*" that would revise the image of the traditional police and "convey already a conceptually

completely differently developed pillar [of society] in the imagination of the individual *Volksgenosse.*[23] This obsession with future danger impelled the Sipo and SD to become a key engine driving the
implementation of the Final Solution.

Who were the men of the RSHA? Jens Banach has found that the
typical member of the Sipo-SD leadership core was born after 1900.
His father held a position either in the state or local bureaucracy or as
a white-collar employee in industry or commerce. He was likely to
have been part of the first or second family generation to make the
transition from the traditional *Mittelstand* of artisans, wholesalers,
and farmers to this new *Mittelstand* of bureaucrats and white-collar
employees. His formative years were spent in a dynamically optimistic, economically booming, yet defensively nationalistic German
empire that had pretensions of being a military, economic, and cultural world power.[24]

The Sipo-SD man made his transition to adulthood, however,
between 1914 and 1924. During these years, his father was absent or
preoccupied, often lost to World War I or economically undermined
in the catastrophic inflation that followed. The nation which he was
educated to revere as the present and future world power had collapsed suddenly and inexplicably; those explanations offered by authority figures pointed to foreign influence and treason by unworthy
people on the home front. Worse still, humiliating peace conditions
imposed foreign forms of government, the Weimar Republic and the
First Austrian Republic, to which at best he remained indifferent and
which seemed incapable of stabilizing the collapsing economy or
combating the new threat of Bolshevism without the help of free-
booter heroes determined to continue the good fight for its own sake.
Even during the prosperous 1920s, he was often unable to find or
hold a position that matched his ambitions. Nor was he able to latch
onto a sense of national-cultural mission to make the hard times seem
worthwhile.

The future Security Police and SD leader, now a university student or ex-university student, sought refuge in modernized versions
of the old dichotomy "them versus us" as reflected in elaborate theories of racial anti-Semitism, pseudo-Darwinistic theories that social
conflict had its sources in biological or genetic factors, and eugenic
ideas that better races and hence better cultures could be bred by
eliminating the physically and mentally disabled. Served up by intel-

lectuals consumed by national humiliation and fear of Bolshevism, such thoughts seemed modern, fashionable, and soothing as well as inspiring by this new-generation, middle-class, would-be professional. This man prided himself on his own *Härte* (toughness) and *Sachlichkeit* (objectivity)[25] reflected in a passionate yet reasoned commitment to the collective entity of his *Volk*, beyond which no value or law existed and for which he would fight and annihilate enemies. The struggle would be conducted without personal hatred, because it was rooted in the natural, scientific laws that prescribed order in a chaotic modern world.

Banach identified five prototypes of Sipo-SD men. The "older police officials" were common in the Kripo and Gestapo; they had served in the police during the Weimar period, though they had remained largely indifferent to the regime. Their ideological commitment to the National Socialist regime may have been suspect at times, but their enjoyment of the benefits that it offered law enforcement and their irreplaceable skills secured the continuity of the police apparatus and stabilized the regime. The "criminal commissar" was younger, born after 1900, and finished his training during the depression or under the Nazi regime. He rejected the old order, both Weimar and Kaiserreich, and was more ideologically in tune with National Socialism. The "SD-referent" worked in administrative positions, evaluating intelligence and managing finance, training, discipline, and personnel. He was young and ideologically committed and owed his career stability to the National Socialist regime and movement. The "jurist," likewise young and contemptuous of the old order, believed himself to be viewing the world coldly and objectively. His career was made by the rapidly expanding law-enforcement civil service under the Nazi regime. He aimed to fashion and serve a "new, racially pure, warlike, and tough Germany" that killed to survive without hatred but also without pity. Finally, the "SD intellectual" was an early adherent of the NSDAP, self-entrusted with developing a long-term vision of the future Reich and contemptuous of all bureaucracy and red tape that would restrict the realization of that vision.[26]

In two brilliantly conceived volumes, George Browder and Banach have dealt with the Security Police and the SD as a corporate group.[27] My more circumscribed purpose here is to look at the backgrounds of the very top leadership of the RSHA. These backgrounds appear to match those of what Browder has labeled "extraordinary men" who belonged to a privileged segment of society and whose obedience was based on respect and admiration rather than discipline and fear.[28] Their contribution to the most murderous policies of the Reich stemmed from a voluntary initiative that derived from an activist willingness to serve society and a consciousness of their own ability to do so. My admittedly unscientific sample includes Heydrich and Kaltenbrunner as well as office chiefs Werner Best, Bruno Streckenbach, Erich Ehrlinger, Hans Nockemann, Josef Spacil, Otto Ohlendorf, Heinz Jost, Walter Schellenberg, Franz Six, Paul Dittel, Heinrich Müller, Arthur Nebe, and Friedrich Panzinger.

Heydrich was born in Halle in 1904. His father was a composer and the director of a music conservatory; his maternal grandfather had founded a music conservatory in Dresden. As a child, Heydrich studied piano, cello, and composition. Though baptized a Protestant, Heydrich converted with his family to Catholicism. As a teen, he served as a courier in the Freikorps Maercker and the Freikorps Halle. His finished his *Abitur* (roughly the equivalent of an American high school diploma) at the Realgymnasium (*gymnasium* meaning secondary school) in Halle and escaped his family life in 1922 to join the navy. He had had some training in English, French, and Russian. He was serving as a signals officer when he was dishonorably discharged in April 1931. He joined the SS in July 1931 and the Nazi Party in August 1931. Heydrich was involved with the components of the RSHA from the beginning. He created a political intelligence service out of the SD and was Himmler's chief assistant in the 1933–1936 drive to take over and centralize the Security Police. His two main office SS commands, Security Police and SD, were fused into the RSHA in 1939. Heydrich was the chief of the RSHA until his death in June 1942, after he was mortally wounded by two Czech agents in Prague.[29]

Like Heydrich, Kaltenbrunner came from a highly educated, well-established, middle-class family. Born and baptized a Catholic in 1903 in Ried Im Innkreis in Upper Austria, Kaltenbrunner's great-grandfather had been a regionally renowned poet and a Hapsburg cultural bureaucrat. His grandfather and father had been small-town men but prominent lawyers who trained in Graz and practiced in the rural regions of Upper Austria. Kaltenbrunner himself spent the war years away from his parents attending the Realgymnasium in Linz.

After receiving his *Abitur* in 1921, Kaltenbrunner studied in Graz, was politically active in the student fraternity *deutschnationale Burschenschaft "Arminia,"* and earned a degree in jurisprudence in 1926. Though he found work as an attorney, he gave up his job in 1929 to join the *völkisch*-oriented Upper Austrian *Heimatschutz*. In October 1930, he shifted over to the Austrian Nazi Party; he joined the SS in July 1931. Rising up through the SS ranks in the underground Austrian Nazi movement, he fashioned with help from a small group of students in Vienna an intelligence service that provided Heydrich's SD with information on the political situation in Austria. After the *Anschluß*, Kaltenbrunner served as a Higher SS and Police Leader in Vienna until called to replace Heydrich in January 1943. He remained chief of the RSHA until the collapse of the Reich in May 1945. Kaltenbrunner was tried before the International Military Tribunal at Nuremberg as the representative of the SS and police. He was convicted, sentenced to death, and hanged in 1946.[30]

The personnel chiefs in the RSHA were SS-Brigadeführer Werner Best from 1939 until 1940, SS-Gruppenführer Bruno Streckenbach from 1941 until 1943, and SS-Oberführer Erich Ehrlinger from 1944 to 1945. Until 1940, Werner Best doubled as both personnel and administrative chief of the Security Police and SD. Born on July 10, 1903, in Darmstadt and baptized a Lutheran, Best was the son of a postal inspector who died of war wounds in the autumn of 1914. He attended gymnasium in his mother's hometown of Gonsenheim bei Mainz and received his *Abitur* in 1921. Best studied law at the university in Frankfurt, involved himself in right-wing student *Burschenschaft* politics and agitated against the French occupation of the Ruhr in 1923. He received his doctorate in law in 1927 from the University of Heidelberg and began serving his court clerkship in the Hessian administrative courts. Initially close to the German National Peoples' Party (*Deutschnationale Volkspartei*—DNVP), he joined the NSDAP in November 1930 and the SS in November 1931. After the Nazi takeover in 1933, Best was named state commissar for police matters in Hessen. Quarrels with the Hessian Party leadership, primarily over Best's efforts to bring talented, educated, but ideologically reliable people into the political police in preference over party stalwarts, led to his removal in September 1933. In September 1934, Heydrich called Best to Berlin to take over the administrative and training departments of the Berlin Gestapo. Between 1935 and 1939, Best was chief of Department I (administration and law) and Department III (counterespionage) of the Gestapo and played a key role in the development of the administration of the Security Police Main Office in 1936. Best ultimately quarreled with Heydrich over the issue of legal qualification for high-level Gestapo officials and was forced to resign his position in the RSHA in the winter of 1940.[31]

Streckenbach was born in 1902 in Hamburg and baptized a Lutheran. His father was a customs official in Hamburg, a first-generation bureaucrat after three generations of master handicraftmen. Streckenbach attended Realgymnasium, but his schooling was interrupted by military service in France from May through July 1918. He returned to school in the autumn of 1918 but never finished, joining the short-lived Freikorps Hermann in 1919 and then the Freikorps Bahrenfeld, which was incorporated into the Reichswehr (German army). At the end of 1919, he was mustered out of the army in accordance with the reductions mandated by peace treaty and became an apprentice in an import firm. He worked as a manager of an automobile rental business from 1924 until the depression, and he remained a member of various paramilitary organizations throughout the 1920s. As a member of the Freikorps Hamburg, he took part in the Kapp putsch; later he was a member of the *völkisch Norddeutschen Heimatbund* (the racist North German Homeland League) and the *Wehrwolf* until the latter drifted away from the extreme Right in 1928. In 1930 he joined the Nazi Party and the SA. He came to the SS in 1931. When the Nazis came to power in 1933, Streckenbach assumed a police position in Hamburg and came to the SD in December. He went to Poland as commander of Einsatzgruppe I in September 1939 and later served as commander of Security Police and SD (*Kommandeur der Sicherheitspolizei und des SD*—KdS) in Warsaw. In 1940, he returned to Berlin to run the reorganized personnel department of the RSHA. He acted as Himmler's deputy in the RSHA after Heydrich's death. In early 1943, after Kaltenbrunner's appointment became known, he transferred to the SS Cavalry Division at his own request.[32]

SS-Oberführer Erich Ehrlinger was born in 1910 in Giengen/ Brenz in Württemberg. The son of the local mayor, Ehrlinger joined the Nazi movement in April 1931. At the time, he had been studying law in Berlin and, similar to Kaltenbrunner, had been active as a liaison leader between German nationalist organizations at the universities. In 1933, Ehrlinger completed his first exams in jurisprudence after finishing his studies in Tübingen. He was serving in his first year as a *Gerichtsreferendar* (law student who has passed the first state examination) in Tübingen until the Storm Detachments (*Sturmabteilungen,* or "storm troopers") lured him into its Training Office in March 1934. Ehrlinger was working on his doctoral dissertation when he was brought into the SD Main Office as a staff officer in September 1935. He worked in the SD staff department and was deployed as a Security Police and SD official in the occupations of Austria and the Sudetenland. He was then deployed as an *Einsatzgruppe* officer in Poland and served as police advisor to the Quisling government in Norway. When the Germans invaded the Soviet Union, he commanded *Sonderkommando* 1b behind the front in the north-central Ukraine; after the civilian commissariat was created, he served as the commander of Security Police and SD (KdS) in Kiev. In September 1943, he was promoted to commander of Security Police and SD for all of the Reich Commissariat Ukraine (*Befehlshaber der Sicherheitspolizei und des SD*—BdS) and, after the German withdrawal from Kiev, continued in his function as BdS with seat in Minsk. In April 1944, he was appointed chief of the personnel office of the RSHA, in which capacity he served until the end of the war.[33]

SS-Standartenführer Dr. Hans Nockemann commanded Amt II, Administration and Law, after the departure of Werner Best. Born on November 16, 1903, and baptized a Lutheran in Aachen, Nockemann was the oldest child of a commercial agent; his grandfather had been a letter carrier. After receiving his diploma in 1922, he studied law in Bonn and Munich and earned his degree in 1929. During his university years he worked construction, apprenticed in a bank, and familiarized himself with his father's firm. Nockemann was politically active at an early age. He was arrested by the Belgian occupation authorities in Aachen during the passive resistance campaign of 1923 and, as a student in Bonn, joined the *Burschenschaft Alemannia.* He completed his initial jurisprudence exams in 1927 and worked as a clerk at the district court in Aachen and the court of appeals in Cologne. He earned his doctorate at Cologne in 1929 with a dissertation on the application of laws regulating the coal-mining industry. Appointed a *Gerichtsassessor* in October 1931, he worked at the administrative court in Aachen and as a prosecutor in Aachen and Cologne. In October 1931, Nockemann applied for membership in

the Nazi Party and served as legal advisor to the Nazi movement for
the Aachen region. He was accepted for membership in April 1932
and joined the SA in May. After the Nazis seized power, Nockemann
was appointed provisional chief of the state police office in Aachen.
Two years of training in various positions in local government were
followed by a permanent appointment as chief of the Gestapo in
Aachen in 1935. Nockemann then was appointed in late 1935 to
command the State Police Main Office in Koblenz. Nockemann
joined the SS in 1933 and the SD in 1935, surviving early criticism
for "not always demonstrating the good will to cooperate successfully
with others." He came to the RSHA in March 1941 to take over Amt
II. He was scheduled to command Einsatzgruppe A in June 1941,
when he was involved in a chargeable automobile accident in which
his wife was killed. An investigation on the count of vehicular
manslaughter was opened on Nockemann, who was replaced by
Stahlecker as prospective commander of Einsatzgruppe A and was in-
ducted as an SS-Untersturmführer of the Waffen SS in the Second SS
Division Das Reich on June 17, 1941.[34] He died in December 1941
of wounds received during the Soviet offensive before Moscow. The
impending proceedings, which had been stayed until the end of the
war and which did not prevent his promotion to SS-Oberführer in
November 1941, became moot.[35]

Josef Spacil, who took over Amt II of the RSHA in 1944, was
born in Munich on March 3, 1907, as the son of a businessman and
his professionally active wife. Baptized Catholic, Spacil attended
gymnasium in Munich between 1918 and 1921 and then trained at
a commercial school. He worked until 1931 as an accountant in the
Firm Hugo Stock, from which he was fired amid charges of embez-
zlement. Spacil found new employment in the SS, which he joined in
April 1931, joining the Nazi Party in August 1932. After serving in
the administrative office of the SS, he was transferred to the SS Training Camp at Dachau on September 9, 1936. He served as a chief administrative officer in various units, including the SS-Oberabschnitt
Donau in 1938, and the SS Death's Head Cavalry Standarte in
Poland in 1939–40. In 1941, Spacil joined the *Kommandostab* (command staff) of the Reichsführer-SS as it moved into the Soviet Union
in the summer of 1941. From the late summer of 1941 until the winter of 1944, he served as SS-*Wirtschafter* on the staff of Higher SS
and Police Leader Hans Prützmann, first in Riga and then in Kiev. In

April 1944, he took over Amt II of the RSHA, in which capacity he served until the Reich collapsed in May 1945.[36]

Chief of Amt III, SD-Inland was Otto Ohlendorf. Ohlendorf was born in 1907 in Hoheneggehen, Kreis Marienburg, the son of a prosperous farmer. Ohlendorf was Lutheran before leaving his church. He attended an academic gymnasium in Hildesheim between 1917 and 1928 and joined the Nazi Party and SA in 1925 as a teen. In 1927, he transferred to the SS. As a student of law and civics at Leipzig and Göttingen, he passed his initial jurisprudence exams in July 1931. After a year of study of the fascist movement in Italy, Ohlendorf returned to begin his training as a court assistant (*Referendar*) in Hildesheim. All the while he had been active in the National Socialist Student League. Ohlendorf had had little interest in law, however, and had attempted in 1933–36 with his former teacher, Jens Peter Jessen, to establish an Institute for World Economy in Kiel and then in Berlin. After the failure of both projects, Jessen was able to get Ohlendorf a job in the economic office of the SD in 1936. In September 1939, Ohlendorf became chief of Amt III in the RSHA and served in this position until the collapse of Germany in 1945. From May 1941 until July 1942, Ohlendorf served as commander of Einsatzgruppe D.[37]

Heinz Jost was born on July 9, 1904, and baptized a Catholic in Holzhausen. He was the oldest son of a pharmacist who suffered and eventually died from diabetes. He attended *gymnasium* in Bensheim an der Bergstrasse from 1914 until 1923. He studied law at Giessen and Munich and passed his *Referendar* exam in 1927. He completed his legal training in 1930 and hung out his shingle one year later in Lorsch/Hessen. A member of the conservative, nationalist, *Jungdeutschen Orden* (German Youth Order), Jost began working for the NSDAP without joining it. After graduating from the university, he became a member of the NSDAP in 1927 and the SA in 1929. He held several prominent local party positions in the early 1930s until his appointment as acting police director at Worms in March 1933. On January 10, 1934, he was confirmed as a police director in Giessen, where he became friendly with Werner Best. In July 1934, Best and Heydrich recruited Jost for the SD Main Office, and in January 1936, he became Heydrich's deputy as chief of counterespionage (III/1). When the RSHA was formed in 1939, Jost was appointed chief of Amt VI, SD-Ausland. In the spring of 1941, Heydrich assigned Jost as deputy commander of Einsatzgruppe A. In September 1942, he was shifted over to the Reich Ministry for Occupied Territories as a liaison to Army Group A, where Himmler found him in Nikolaev at Christmas 1943 with "nothing at all to do."[38]

Walter Schellenberg was born in 1910 in Saarbrücken and baptized a Catholic. His father owned a piano factory. Schellenberg later recalled the "horror of war" as a child in the winter of 1917 when his town was bombed by French planes and his family suffered through hunger, cold, and illness. After the war, his father was arrested by French occupation authorities for political reasons. Schellenberg received his *Abitur* in 1929 and studied law and political science at the university in Marburg, where he joined a *Burschenschaft*. He completed his *Referendar* exam in March 1933, at which time he joined the NSDAP and the SS. He served as a court clerk with the state prosecutor's office in Bonn and at the *Oberlandesgericht* (provincial high court of appeal) in Düsseldorf. In September 1935, he was called to Berlin to join the SD Main Office. He completed his law exams in 1936 and was recommended for promotion to officer status in the SS due to the fact that his "clear vision," "discretion," and "recognition of the 'big picture'" so impressed his superiors that they wanted him around as an adviser.[39] Schellenberg was moved over to the Gestapo in 1938, where he took over the counterespionage section (IV E of the RSHA). As Germany prepared to attack the Soviet Union in the spring of 1941, Schellenberg negotiated with the army's quartermaster general over the deployment of the *Einsatzgruppen* in combat zones. When Jost was assigned to Einsatzgruppe A, Heydrich appointed Schellenberg acting chief of RSHA Amt VI on July 2, 1941. On February 24, 1943, Schellenberg was confirmed as chief of Amt VI, in which capacity he served until the end of the war.[40]

SS-Standartenführer Franz Six, the chief of Amt VII of the RSHA, was born on August 12, 1909, in Mannheim and baptized a Lutheran. He was an exception in that his father worked at several trades, including furniture sales, upholstery, and interior decoration, although his paternal grandfather had been a theater musician. Due to financial difficulty, Six had to interrupt his secondary education for two years in 1927 to 1929. Nevertheless, he received his *Abitur* at the *Oberrealschule* (high school with emphasis on the sciences) in Mannheim in 1930. That autumn, he began his studies in Heidelberg in political science, history, political economy, and journalism.

One month before his high school graduation, Six joined the NSDAP, having been a member of the National Socialist Secondary School Pupils' League in Mannheim since the autumn of 1929. As a student, Six belonged to the SA and worked as a publicist on the pro-Nazi newspaper *Heidelberger Student*. When the Nazis came to power, Six received an assistantship in the Institute for the Study of Print Journalism at Heidelberg. After earning his doctorate in 1934, he obtained a professorship with party assistance at the University in Berlin. Six switched from the SA to the SS and joined the SD in 1935. From 1936, he supervised Zentralabteilung II/1 (Jews, Freemasons, and churches). As commander of Amt II (intelligence office) of the RSHA, Six participated in the key planning conferences for Security Police and SD operations in Poland. In 1941, his department received the new designation of intelligence on ideological enemies, Amt VII of the RSHA. Under his leadership, Amt VII sought to become a policy research center on the ideological enemies of the Third Reich. In June, Six was summoned to Berlin, where he took over the *Vorkommando Moskau* (Moscow forward command) of the Einsatzgruppe C, later B. After quarreling with both Heydrich and Nebe, he was transferred back to Amt VII in the late summer of 1941. He left the RSHA for good after Heydrich's death in the summer of 1942, joining Martin Luther's *Abteilung Deutschland* (Germany Department) in the German Foreign Office.[41]

Six was replaced in Amt VII by SS-Obersturmbannführer Paul Dittel. Dittel was born on January 14, 1907, in Mittweida/Saxony as the son of an elementary school teacher. Dittel was baptized a Lutheran. His paternal grandfather was a master locksmith. He attended the Reform-Real Gymnasium in Chemnitz, receiving his certificate of graduation in 1926. Between 1927 and 1931, he studied geography and history at the universities in Graz and then Leipzig. He spent a month in England in 1928 to solidify his English language skills and returned for several months in 1932, where he worked as a teacher and gathered material at the British Museum and the Geographical Society in London for his dissertation. Dittel joined the NSDAP in May 1933 and the SA in July and served as a trainer of new recruits in the 107th SS-Standarte in Leipzig while supplementing his income as a private tutor. He joined the SD in Leipzig in March 1935. Three months later, as he was securing his doctorate from the University of Leipzig, he transferred to the SD Main Office in Berlin. During the 1930s, he managed the SD archive in Zentralabteilung I/3 of the SD Main Office, developing an expertise in the organizations of the Freemasons. Deployed in Poland in 1939 primarily to seize archival material, Dittel replaced Six as chief of RSHA Amt VII in 1942, in which capacity he served until the end of the war.[42]

The chiefs of the Security Police offices in the RSHA were older men who had made their careers and achieved considerable personal success in the police independently of the Nazi movement and before the Nazis came to power. Both operated with a degree of personal and professional autonomy based on their considerable police skills, and both accommodated well to the regime, even if their ideological commitment to it was sometimes suspect. Chief of the Gestapo (Amt IV) from 1936 to 1945 was Heinrich Müller. Born on April 28, 1900, in Munich and baptized a Catholic, Müller was the son of a trained groundskeeper who had made a career as a medical orderly. Alone among his peers of lower-middle-class origin, Müller trained as an aircraft construction worker at the Bayerische Flugzeugwerke. After his apprenticeship was over, he volunteered for the air force and was highly decorated for his service as a pilot on the Western Front. Demobilized in June 1919, he landed a job with the Munich police directorate in December. While holding clerical jobs during the early 1920s, Müller managed to get his gymnasium diploma and entered regular police service. After passing the required technical examination in 1929, he became a *Polizeisekretär* (police secretary) and was deployed in section 6a of the Munich police directorate, which was responsible for dealing with left-wing opposition to the Weimar Republic.

Politically close to the conservative Bavarian People's Party, Müller was considered at best indifferent to the Nazi Party until 1933. A 1936 NSDAP evaluation condemned him as a man of "colossal ambition" and "pronounced status-seeking" who would have, "had it been his task, moved against the right and done all he could in this respect to earn the recognition of his 'system' superiors at the time." Müller was widely believed in party circles to have opposed the Nazi takeover of Bavaria in March 1933.[43] As a result of the party's concerns, Müller's entry into the SS was delayed until 1934, and he only joined the Nazi Party in 1939. Müller's experience in fighting German Communists and Soviet agents was deemed valuable by Heydrich and Himmler, who kept him on in Munich and then brought him to Berlin in early 1934 to take over subsection 1a of Department II of the Gestapo, which dealt with Communism, Marxism, and trade unions. After being named chief of the new Main Office Security Police in Berlin on June 26, 1936, Heydrich appointed Müller chief of Section II, the Gestapo, which was later incorporated into the RSHA as Amt IV. Whatever the nature of his internal ideological commitment to the regime, there is no question that Müller placed his considerable police and organizational skills at the disposal of the regime until the very end. He played a pivotal role in such key areas of Nazi policy as negotiating with the army on the issue of *Einsatzgruppen,* supervising the Eichmann deportation unit, which had found a home in the Gestapo, and incarcerating individuals in concentration camps and ordering their executions when requested by the camp staff. He remained outwardly loyal to the regime until the end.[44]

Arthur Nebe, the chief of the Kripo, had also made his career in Weimar Germany and indeed, in liberal, Social Democratic Berlin and Prussia. Born in the capital in 1894 and baptized a Lutheran, Nebe was the son of a gymnasium assistant principal. He earned a *Notabitur* (accelerated high school graduation in order to go to war) in August 1914 at the Leipzig gymnasium in Berlin and then served as a sapper in the 17th Pionierbatallion of the German army. Highly decorated, he remained in the Reichswehr as a battalion adjutant until March 1920, when, as he later claimed, he requested a discharge because he could not bear being monitored by "Social Democratic functionaries." His expertise in explosives secured him a position on the Berlin criminal police force in April 1920. Nebe's efforts to earn a doctorate in medicine and political economy failed, ostensibly due to financial difficulties. In 1923, he passed his examination and was appointed a *Kriminalkommissar* (criminal commissioner).

Nebe began his service in the Berlin Kripo with the homicide section. In 1926, he was appointed director of the narcotics bureau and became chief of the robbery section in 1931. Other than membership in German nationalist groups before 1923, little in his police career before 1931 foreshadowed his service to the National Socialist regime. He was a protégé of homicide detective Ernst Gennat, who, though lukewarm to the Weimar Republic, rejected the association of crime with heredity. In 1929, Nebe publicly acknowledged the support of the Jewish and fanatically pro-Republic Berlin vice president of police, Bernhard Weiß, for the Berlin narcotics section.[45] Nebe shared the frustrations of many detectives with the Weimar system, however: financial crisis and budget restrictions; blocked promotions (*Beförderungsstau*: Nebe was never promoted during the Weimar period); restrictions on police investigation imposed by inadequately trained personnel, outdated equipment, and constitutional protections of individual civil rights; the growth of petty crime and organized crime rings; and a media-driven sense that crime was flourishing in Weimar and that criminals were more exciting, attractive, and sympathetic than the poorly paid and equipped police officials who investigated them. He also shared the view of younger Kripo officials, influenced by eugenics ideas and reacting to the spread of organized crime, that a preventative strike against the "biological roots" of criminality was essential for the survival of society but impossible to conduct within the limits of the Weimar constitution. As chief of the narcotics bureau, Nebe had argued as early as 1929 that the "modern police [should] . . . operate in a preventative fashion, . . . if it wishes to be worthy of the designation as a friend of the population."[46]

Nebe secretly joined the NSDAP on July 1, 1931 (No. 574,307) and the SA in November 1931. In January 1932, he founded with two colleagues the *Fachschaft Kriminalpolizei* within the National Socialist Civil Servants Working Community (*Nationalsozialistische Beamten-Arbeitsgemeinschaft*—NSBAG). After the Nazis seized power, Nebe transferred to the new Secret State Police Office on April 1, 1933, and ran Department III, Movements, which monitored Marxist, anarchist, and conservative nationalist organizations and investigated acts of political sabotage within the armed forces, police, and paramilitary formations. Here he worked with Göring, Daluege, and Prussian Gestapo chief Rudolf Diels to staff the Secret State Police, maintaining a balance between professional police skills and ideological commitment to National Socialism. On January 1, 1935, Nebe was appointed chief of the Prussian State Criminal Police Office (*Landeskriminalpolizeiamt*—LKPA). When this agency was formally expanded to incorporate the entire criminal police force of the Reich within a Reich Criminal Police Office (*Reichskriminalpolizeiamt*—RKPA), Nebe remained its chief. With the formation of the RSHA in 1939, the RKPA became Amt V. As commander of the Kripo, Nebe was responsible for RSHA policies and operations against the Gypsy population of Germany and occupied Europe; officials of the Kripo's Criminal Police Forensics Institute (*Kriminaltechnisches Institut*—KTI) remained closely informed and involved in developing the means of mass murder, including the use of exhaust gas, and applying those means to the murder of the mentally disabled in 1939. The criminal police official Christian Wirth was perhaps the most important personnel link between the euthanasia program, which was managed by the Führer Chancery from 1939 to 1941, and the Operation Reinhard killing centers, run by the staff of the SS and Police Leader in Lublin.[47]

Nebe also served as commander of Einsatzgruppe B between June and November 1941. Like Müller, he was never fully ideologically committed to the National Socialist regime, however much he bought into its policies regarding an omnipotent police presence and campaigns against Gypsies, the disabled, and others who failed to meet the standard of middle-class conformity that the Nazis intended to impose on German society. Unlike Müller, he dabbled in contacts with conservative and military opponents of Hitler and was implicated in the July 20, 1944, conspiracy. Arrested in January 1945, Nebe was tried before the People's Court in March. He was convicted, sentenced to death, and executed.[48]

After Nebe's flight from Berlin in July 1944, his office was taken over by SS-Oberführer Friedrich Panzinger. Panzinger was born on February 1, 1903, in Munich and baptized a Catholic. Even before finishing high school, in 1919, Panzinger joined the Munich police. While serving in the Munich municipal police force, Panzinger finished his *Abitur* and studied law at the University of Munich, passing his final exams in 1934. He then served in the Bavarian political police until his transfer to the Berlin Gestapo in October 1937. In August 1940, he came into the RSHA to take over Gruppe IV A (Marxist movements). In September 1943, Panzinger was sent out into the field as BdS in Riga. Highly touted by both Müller and Kaltenbrunner, Panzinger was appointed to a three-man commission to investigate "lapses" committed by officials of the RSHA on July 6, 1944.[49] He played a key role in the RSHA during the July 20 putsch and the subsequent investigation. After Kaltenbrunner reluctantly decided that Nebe was indeed a suspect in the conspiracy, Panzinger was appointed to take over Amt V of the RSHA, in which capacity he served until the end of the war.[50]

What is so striking about the RSHA office chiefs is their youth and the level of their education. Only the professional policemen would reach the age of 45 in office; Müller in the last week of the Third Reich. Best, Kaltenbrunner, Ehrlinger, Nockemann, Six, and Dittel earned doctorates. The others, except for Heydrich, who joined the navy, and Streckenbach, who lacked the funds, attended university and completed degrees. With the exceptions of Müller and Six, all came from the solid middle-class families. There were none of George Browder's "shady characters" or even the "marginal set" among the RSHA chiefs; they all cherished self-images as "professional detectives" and "intellectual leaders."[51] Some, like Nebe, fashioned themselves as both. Nor should it surprise us much that highly educated or skilled middle-class men should have risen to the top of a central police and intelligence agency in Nazi Germany or in any other middle-class society where careers were open to talent, initiative, and education. As Gerhard Paul has found in his study of regional Gestapo chiefs, these men were by no means "desperados and 'human wrecks' who would not have advanced in normal law enforcement" but rather "children of the best society, often with liberal-humanistic academic training and distinguished with a doctorate in law."[52] Among the self-made men, like Müller and Nockemann, who were forced by financial and social circumstances to take jobs in order to finance their educations, we find qualities that we in a modern society otherwise tend to admire and reward, particularly in terms of initiative, hard work, and self-improvement in order to better develop one's own potential and better serve business or society.

This, then, was an elite of *Überzeugungstäter* (perpetrators from conviction) who knew what they were doing and did it out of conviction. What was unusual about their mixture of motivations was the lethal combination of power seeking, social ambition, and racist goals of the SS with the trauma of defeat, economic insecurity, and social crisis, and the conviction that economic and structural problems were traceable to biological-genetical sources and could and must be solved at a single blow once and for all.[53] This was an elite that could "do the dirty work" of murder, theft, and plunder as a "peripheral" assignment necessary to pursue the utopian future *völkische Gemeinschaft* (people's community), a transcendent mission that allowed them "that illusion of moral superiority or some rectitude."[54] Such moral "superiority" permitted Minsk Security Police and SD

commander Eduard Strauch the following outburst at civilian officials of the Reich Commissariat White Ruthenia:

> That we must carry out tasks that are sometimes difficult and un-
> pleasant is true, but it offends me whenever some people believe
> they must look down their noses at us. . . . Gentlemen! We can only
> practice this profession because we are convinced that someone
> must carry out the tasks. I can say with pride that my men, as evil as
> these tasks are, follow the straight and narrow path; they can look
> anyone in the eye and be fathers to their families at home. They are
> proud to serve their Führer out of conviction and loyalty.[55]

Today we emphasize education as a defense against a repeat of the
Holocaust. The backgrounds and careers of the RSHA office chiefs,
however, surely indicate that education, the achievement of a doctorate, even reinforced by initiative and hard work, is not in itself sufficient protection. Even education aimed at questioning authority
seems to be not enough; I can think of few generations in history that
questioned tradition and authority so profoundly and with such
lethal results as this generation of educated German men. No matter
how broad or deep an education might be, without the firm commitment to the value of human life—and I mean here each and every
human life, not some abstraction that can be adjusted to exclude—it
cannot prevent future mass murder. Sadly, without that commitment, education may only ensure the more thorough and efficient
murder of future victims under ever more imaginative and elaborate
justifications.

NOTES

The opinions expressed in this article are exclusively those of the author
and are not to be construed as official statements of the United States Holocaust Museum.

1. The popular notion of an all-powerful Gestapo undoubtedly
prompted the subtitle of the recent work of Gerhard Paul and Klaus-
Michael Mallmann, eds., *Die Gestapo: Mythos und Realität* (Darmstadt:
Wissenschaftliches Buchgemeinschaft, 1995). See also Robert Gellately,
The Gestapo in German Society: Enforcing Racial Policy, 1933–1945 (Ox-
ford: Oxford University Press, 1990); Eugen Kogon, *Der SS-Staat: Das Sys-
tem der deutschen Konzentrationslager* (Frankfurt: Gütersloh, 1946; reprint,
Bertelsmann Reinhard Mohn, 1974).

2. Christopher Browning, *Ordinary Men: Reserve Police Battalion 101 and the Final Solution in Poland* (New York: HarperCollins, 1991); Götz Aly and Susanne Heim, *Vordenker der Vernichtung: Auschwitz und die Pläne für eine neue europäische Ordnung,* 2d ed. (Frankfurt am Main: Fischer, 1994); Ruth Bettina Birn, *Die Höheren SS-und Polizeiführer: Himmlers Vertreter im Reich und in den besetzten Gebieten* (Düsseldorf: Droste, 1986); Yehuda Büchler, "Kommandostab Reichsführer-SS: Himmler's Personal Murder Brigades in 1941," *Holocaust and Genocide Studies* 1, no. 1 (1986): 11–26.

3. Christopher Browning, *The Final Solution and the German Foreign Office: A Study of Referat D III of Abteilung Deutschland, 1940–1943* (New York: Holmes and Meier, 1978); Hans Jürgen Döscher, *Das Auswärtige Amt im Dritten Reich: Diplomatie im Schatten der Endlösung* (Berlin: Siedler, 1987); Raul Hilberg, *Sonderzüge nach Auschwitz* (Frankfurt am Main: Dumjahn, 1981); Dieter Pohl, "Die Ermordung der Juden im Generalgouvernement," in *Nationalsozialistische Vernichtungspolitik, 1939–1945: Neue Forschungen und Kontroversen,* ed Ulrich Herbert (Frankfurt am Main: Fischer, 1998), pp. 98–121; Walter Manoschek, ed., *Die Wehrmacht im Rassenkrieg: Der Vernichtungskrieg Hinter der Front* (Vienna: Picus, 1996).

4. Randolph L. Braham, *The Politics of Genocide: The Holocaust in Hungary,* rev. ed. (New York: Rosenthal Institute for Holocaust Studies, 1994); Yeshayahu Jellinik, *The Parish Republic: Hlinka's Slovak People's Party, 1939–1945* (Boulder, Colo.: Columbia University Press, 1976); Susan Zuccotti, *The Holocaust, The French and the Jews* (New York: Basic Books, 1993).

5. Bernard Wasserstein, *Britain and the Jews of Europe* (New York: Oxford University Press, 1979); David S. Wyman, *The Abandonment of the Jews: America and the Holocaust, 1941–1945* (New York: New Press, 1998); William Slany et al., *United States and Allied Efforts to Recover and Restore Gold and Other Assets Stolen or Hidden During World War II* (Washington, D.C.: U.S. State Department, 1997); Jean-François Bergier et al., *Switzerland and the Gold Transactions in the Second World War* (Bern: Independent Commission of Experts, 1998); Richard Breitman, *Official Secrets: What the Nazis Planned, What the British and Americans Knew* (New York: Hill and Wang, 1998). For an exception, see Paul Levine, *From Indifference to Activism: Swedish Diplomats and the Holocaust, 1938–1944* (Uppsala: Uppsala University, 1996).

6. Circular of Himmler to SS Main Office Chiefs, June 25, 1942, Aktenmappe RSHA, Ordner 457, pp. 64–65, Bundesarchiv Berlin. English translation is the author's.

7. Decree of Himmler, "Die Zusammenfassung der zentralen Ämter der Sicherheitspolizei und des SD," September 27, 1939, Document L-

361, International Military Tribunal (IMT), *The Trial of the Major War Criminals* (Nuremberg, 1947), vol. 38, pp. 102–4.

8. Decree of Himmler, July 11, 1942, Bruno Streckenbach SS Officer File, RG-242, A3343, SSO-165B, National Archives and Records Administration (NARA); "Protokol über die Gruppenleiter- und Referentenbesprechung des Amt VI," June 10, 1942, File RSHA, R 58, Folder 1280, Bundesarchiv Berlin.

9. On the *Einsatzgruppen,* see Helmut Krausnick and Hans-Heinrich Wilhelm, *Die Truppe des Weltanschauungskrieges: Die Einsatzgruppen der Sicherheitspolizei und des SD, 1938–1942* (Stuttgart: Deutsche Verlags-Anstalt, 1981); Hans-Heinrich Wilhelm, *Die Einsatzgruppe A der Sicherheitspolizei und des SD, 1941/1942* (Frankfurt am Main: Peter Lang, 1996); Ronald Headland, *Messages of Murder: A Study of the Reports of the Einsatzgruppen of the Security Police and the Security Service, 1941–1943* (London: Associated University Presses, 1992); Peter Klein, ed., *Die Einsatzgruppen in der besetzten Sowjetunion, 1941/42: Die Tätigkeits- und Lageberichte des Chefs der Sicherheitspolizei und des SD* (Berlin: Edition Hentrich, 1997).

10. Michael Wildt, *Die Judenpolitik des SD 1935 bis 1938: Eine Dokumentation* (Munich: R. Oldenbourg, 1995), pp. 61–64.

11. George Clark Browder, *Hitler's Enforcers: The Gestapo and the SS Security Service in the Nazi Revolution* (New York: Oxford, 1996), p. 230.

12. Circular to all Inspectors of Security Police and SD and to RSHA office chiefs [signed Best], October 19, 1939, Akte RSHA, R 58, Folder 240, Bundesarchiv Berlin.

13. Circular Letter from the Chief of Security Police and SD [Heydrich] to the Chiefs of all Einsatzgruppen of the Security Police re: "Judenfrage im besetzten Gebiet," September 21, 1939, RG-242, Microcopy Group T-501, Roll 230, frames 18–23, NARA.

14. Memorandum of Dannecker [RSHA IV B 4] re: "Zentrales 'Judenamt' in Paris," January 21, 1941, reproduced in Serge Klarsfeld, *Vichy-Auschwitz: die Zusammenarbeit der deutschen und französischen Behörden bei der 'Endlösung der Judenfrage' in Frankreich* (Paris: Fayard, 1983–85), pp. 361–63. See the analysis by Richard Breitman, *The Architect of Genocide: Himmler and the Final Solution* (Hanover: University Press of New England, 1991), pp. 151–56.

15. As Dannecker and Eichmann made clear on separate occasions in Paris and Berlin in January and March 1941, see ibid. and file notation from the Reich Propaganda Ministry re: Evakuierung der Juden aus Berlin, March 21, 1941, RG-242, Records of the NSDAP, Microcopy T-81, Roll 676, frame 5485604, NARA.

16. Göring to Heydrich, July 31, 1941, Document 710–PS, IMT XVI, pp. 267–68.

17. For example, in the case of Lublin, Judgment of the Landgericht Wiesbaden in Proceedings against Lothar Hoffmann et al., March 1, 1973, File 8 Ks 1/70, Abteilung 468, Nr. 362, Hessischen Hauptstaatsarchiv.

18. Hans Safrian, *Die Eichmann-Männer* (Vienna: Europa Verlag, 1993), pp. 169–319.

19. Peter Black, *Ernst Kaltenbrunner: Ideological Soldier of the Third Reich* (Princeton, N.J.: Princeton University Press, 1984), pp. 143–44.

20. "Auszug aus den Ausführungen von Werner Best, *Deutsches Recht,* April 15, 1936, p. 125, "Die geheime Staatspolizei," File RSHA, R 58, folder 243, p. 120, Bundesarchiv Berlin. Emphasis in the original.

21. Reinhard Heydrich, "Die Bekämpfung der Staatsfeinde," *Deutsches Recht,* Heft 718, April 15, 1936, p. 121, ibid., pp. 123–25.

22. Arthur Nebe, "Der Aufbau der neuen deutschen Kriminalpolizei," in *Einweihung des Reichskriminalpolizeiamtes am 31. August 1939,* Berlin, o. J., pp. 1, 2, 4–5, 6; Arthur Nebe, "Aufbau der deutschen Kriminalpolizei," in *Kriminalistik* 12 (1938): 4.

23. Walter Schellenberg, "Reorganisation des Sicherheitsdienstes des Reichsführers-SS in Hinblick auf eine organisatorische und personelle Angleichung mit der Sicherheitspolizei," February 24, 1939, RG-242, T-175, Roll 239, frame 2728566, NARA.

24. Jens Banach, *Heydrichs Elite: Das Führerkorps der Sicherheitspolizei und des SD, 1936–1945* (Paderborn: Ferdinand Schöningh, 1998), pp. 35–86, 325–26.

25. Ulrich Herbert, *Best: Biographische Studien über Radikalismus, Weltanschauung und Vernunft, 1903–1989* (Berlin: J. H. W. Dietz, 1996), p. 528.

26. Banach, *Heydrichs Elite,* pp. 327–34.

27. Ibid.; Browder, *Hitler's Enforcers,* p. 230.

28. Browder, *Hitler's Enforcers,* pp. 170, 172.

29. Reinhard Heydrich SS Officer File, RG 242, A3343–SSO-55a, NARA. Until the 1990s, very little in the nature of scholarly work had been done on the RSHA chiefs or office chiefs. Even Heydrich, one of the most fascinating characters of the Third Reich, has not been the subject of a full-length, scholarly biography. See Joachim Fest's portrait in *The Face of the Third Reich: Portraits of the Nazi Leadership* (New York: Pantheon, 1970), pp. 98–110; Shlomo Aronson, *Reinhard Heydrich und die Frühgeschichte von Gestapo und SD* (Stuttgart: Deutsche Verlags-Anstalt, 1971); Charles W. Sydnor Jr., "Executive Instinct: Reinhard Heydrich and the Planning for the Final Solution," in *The Holocaust in History: The Known, the Unknown, the Disputed, and the Reexamined,* ed. Michael Berenbaum and Abraham J. Peck (Bloomington: University of Indiana Press, 1998), pp. 159–86; Syd-

nor, "Heydrich," in *Die SS-Elite,* ed. Ronald Smelser and Enrico Syring (Paderborn: Schöningh, 2000).

30. Ernst Kaltenbrunner SS Officer File, RG-242, A3343–SSO-150A, NARA. On Kaltenbrunner, see Black, *Ernst Kaltenbrunner,* 143–44; "Ernst Kaltenbrunner," in *Stufen zum Galgen: Lebenswege vor der Nürnberger Urteilen,* ed. Kurt Pätzold and Manfred Weißbecker (Leipzig: Militzke, 1996), pp. 119–49; and "Ernst Kaltenbrunner," in *Die SS-Elite,* ed. Ronald Smelser and Enrico Syring (Paderborn: Schöningh, 2000).

31. Werner Best SS Officer File, RG-242, A3343–SSO-064, NARA. See also Ulrich Herbert, *Best,* p. 528; Fritz Petrick, "Der liebenswürdige Dr. Best—Ein verhinderter Generalgouverneur," in *Die SS-Elite,* ed. Ronald Smelser and Enrico Syring (Paderborn: Schöningh, 2000); Sebastian Werner, "Werner Best: Der völkische Ideologe" in *Die Braune Elite II: 21 Weitere Biographische Skizzen,* ed. Ronald Smelser, Enrico Syring, and Rainer Zitelmann (Darmstadt: Wissenschaftliche Buchgemeinschaft, 1993), pp. 13–25. After leaving the RSHA, Best served in France and Denmark as the top civilian official in the German occupation administration. In 1948, he was tried, convicted, and sentenced to death by a Danish court. This sentence was eventually commuted; in 1951, Best was released and returned to Germany.

32. Bruno Streckenbach SS Officer File, RG-242, A3343–SSO-165B, NARA; Bruno Streckenbach RuSHA file, RG-242, A3343–RS-60073, NARA. See also Michael Wildt, "Der Hamburger Gestapochef Bruno Streckenbach: Eine nationalsozialistische Karriere," in *Hamburg in der NS-Zeit: Ergebnisse neuerer Forschungen,* ed. Frank Bajohr and Joachim Szodrzynski (Hamburg: Ergebnisse, 1995), pp. 93–124. Captured by Soviet authorities at the end of the war, Streckenbach was tried, convicted, and sentenced to twenty-five years hard labor. He was among the German military and police personnel released in 1955 in conjunction with the establishment of diplomatic relations between the Soviet Union and the Federal Republic of Germany.

33. Erich Ehrlinger SS Officer file, RG-242, A3343–SSO-177, NARA.

34. SS-Führungshauptamt to Ergänzungsamt der Waffen SS, June 14, 1941, Hans Nockemann SS Officer File, RG-242, A3343–SSO-352A, frame 470, NARA.

35. Hans Nockemann SS Officer File, RG-242, A3343–SSO-352A, frames 432–90, NARA; Hans Nockemann RuSHA file, RG-242, A3343–SSO-E03040, NARA.

36. Josef Spacil SS Officer File, RG-242, A3343–SSO-144B, esp. frames 294–95, 298, 309–12, 361–63, 382, 404, 408, NARA; Josef Spacil RuSHA file, RG-242, A3343–RS-F5389, frame 1094, NARA.

37. Otto Ohlendorf SS Officer File, RG-242, A3343–SSO-356A, NARA. See also Hanno Sowade, "Otto Ohlendorf: Non-Konformist, SS-Führer und Wirtschaftfunktionär," in *Die Braune Elite II: 21 Weitere Biographische Skizzen,* ed. Ronald Smelser, Enrico Syring, and Rainer Zitelmann (Darmstadt: Wissenschaftliche Buchgemeinschaft, 1993), pp. 188–200; David Kitterman, "Otto Ohlendorf—Nazism's Knight, Defender of the Holy Grail" in Smelser and Syring, *Die SS-Elite.* After the war, Ohlendorf was tried and convicted in the Einsatzgruppe Trial at Nuremberg. He was sentenced to death in 1948 and executed in 1951.

38. Hildebrandt to Kaltenbrunner, February 7, 1944, Heinz Jost SS Officer File, RG-242, A3343–SSO-141A, NARA. See also other correspondence in Jost's SS officer file. Like Ohlendorf, Jost was tried at the Einsatzgruppe Trial in Nuremberg and was convicted. Sentenced to life imprisonment, he was released in 1951.

39. Personal-Bericht, signed Albert, March 27, 1937, Walter Schellenberg SS Officer File, RG- 242, A3343–SSO-074B, NARA.

40. Walter Schellenberg SS Officer File RG-242, A3343–SSO-074B, NARA. Schellenberg was the only senior RSHA official to write memoirs, though he has not yet found a biographer. See Walter Schellenberg, *Aufzeichnungen: Die Memoiren des letzten Geheimdienstchefs unter Hitler* (Wiesbaden: 1979). See also George C. Browder, "Walter Schellenberg: A Cloak and Dagger Fantasy," in *Die SS-Elite,* ed. Ronald Smelser and Enrico Syring (Paderborn: Schöningh, 2000). Schellenberg was tried, convicted, and sentenced to six years' imprisonment at the Ministries Trial in Nuremberg. He was released due to ill health and died in 1952.

41. Franz Alfred Six SS Officer file, RG-242, A3343–SSO-139B, NARA. Franz Alfred Six RuSHA file, RG-242–A3343–RS-F5342, frames 2410–2418, NARA. See also Lutz Hachmeister, *Der Gegnerforscher: Die Karriere des SS-Führers Franz Alfred Six* (Munich: C. H. Beck, 1998). After the war, Six was convicted and sentenced to twenty years' imprisonment at the Ministries Trial in Nuremberg. He was released in 1952.

42. Paul Dittel SS Officer File, RG-242, A3343–SSO-155, esp. frames 205–27, 235–40, NARA; Paul Dittel RuSHA file, RG-242, A3343–RS-A5518, frames 2366–72, NARA.

43. Office for Officials of the NSDAP, Gau Munich-Upper Bavaria, "Politische Beurteilung des Kriminal-Oberinspekteurs Heinrich Müller," December 28, 1936, Heinrich Müller NSDAP File, Bundesarchiv Berlin.

44. Heinrich Müller SS Officer File, RG-242, A3343–SS0–331A, NARA. See also Andreas Seeger, *"Gestapo-Müller". Die Karriere eines Schreibtischtäters* (Berlin: Metropol, 1996); "Vom bayerischen 'Systembeamten' zum Chef der Gestapo: Zur Person und Tätigkeit Heinrich Müllers (1900–1945)," in *Die Gestapo: Mythos und Realität,* ed. Gerhard

Paul and Klaus-Michael Mallmann (Darmstadt: Wissenschaftliches Buchgemeinschaft, 1995), pp. 255–67; and "Heinrich Müller—Der Gestapo-Chef," in *Die SS-Elite*, ed. Ronald Smelser and Enrico Syring (Paderborn: Schöningh, 2000). Though his body was never found and his whereabouts after the war have been the source of much speculation, Müller is believed to have been killed attempting to escape Berlin or to have committed suicide in Berlin on April 29, 1945.

45. Arthur Nebe, "Kriminalpolizei und Rauschgifte," *Kriminalistische Monatshelfe*, no. 3 (1929), p. 61.

46. Ibid., pp. 61, 83, 85.

47. Henry Friedlander, *The Origins of the Nazi Genocide* (Chapel Hill: University of North Carolina Press, 1997), p. 298; Yitzak Arad, *Belzec, Sobibor, Treblinka: The Operation Reinhard Death Camps* (Bloomington: University of Indiana Press, 1987), pp. 24–28.

48. Arthur Nebe SS Officer File, RG-242, A3343–SSO-345A, NARA. See also the impressionistic and sympathetic Hans-Bernd Gisevius, *Wo ist Nebe? Erinnerungen an Hitlers Reichskriminaldirektor* (Zurich: Droste, 1966); and Peter R. Black, "Arthur Nebe: Nationalsozialist im Zwielicht," in *Die SS-Elite*, ed. Ronald Smelser and Enrico Syring (Paderborn: Schöningh, 2000).

49. See memorandum of Bender [SS-Richter beim RFSS] to Hauptamt SS Gericht, July 6, 1944, Friedrich Panzinger SS Officer File, RG-242, Roll A3343–SSO-364A, NARA.

50. Friedrich Panzinger SS Officer File, RG-242, Roll A3343–SSO-364A, NARA. Panzinger was captured by Soviet troops and incarcerated in the Soviet Union until 1955. After returning to Germany, he collapsed and died in 1959, shortly after his arrest by West German police.

51. Browder, *Hitler's Enforcers*, p. 242.

52. Gerhard Paul, "Ganz normale Akademiker," in *Die Gestapo: Mythos und Realität*, ed. Gerhard Paul and Klaus-Michael Mallmann (Darmstadt: Wissenschaftliches Buchgemeinschaft, 1995), pp. 236–54, quote on p. 238.

53. Banach, *Heydrichs Elite*, p. 332.

54. Browder, *Hitler's Enforcers*, p. 174.

55. Speech of Strauch, April 10, 1943 in "Protocol of the Conference of Gebietskommissare, Main Department leaders and Department leaders of the General Commissar in Minsk from April 8 to April 10, 1943," July 16, 1943, R 93/20, pp. 137–46, Bundesarchiv Berlin.

Henry Friedlander

The Administrators in the Concentration Camps

THE SS OFFICERS WHO ADMINISTERED THE CONCENTRATION CAMPS could be called "managers," the term I used to describe the men who administered the T4 killing centers, although the term in common usage has been *Schreibtischtäter* (writing desk perpetrators). I prefer the former term, because the latter implies a distance from the killings, which applies only to bureaucrats in the interior, finance, or foreign ministries. The T4 managers and the managers of the concentration camps, however, were hands-on types of administrators who did not hesitate to visit the killing fields.

In my opinion, the Nazi German perpetrators form three relatively distinct groups, who do, however, overlap at the margins. One group is composed of the policy makers who initiated the killings, usually described as the chief perpetrators (*Haupttäter*), including Hitler, Göring, Himmler, Heydrich, Kaltenbrunner, and their peers. Most of them have been analyzed in individual biographies, and we know a great deal about their ideological commitments, institutional concerns, and personal ambitions.[1] Another group is composed of the rank-and-file killers, both men and women, who were essential for the implementation of both terror and genocide in the killing centers and killing fields. We know they were selected almost at random and were not always members of the SS and sometimes not even of the Nazi Party. Although ideology undoubtedly played some role, most historians agree that other factors must explain their behavior; acceptance of authority, peer pressure, personal advancement, avoidance of frontline duty, or situational pressures are usually cited as primary reasons.[2]

The managers, members of the third group, formed an essential link between the other two groups of perpetrators, but their history and their motives have received relatively less attention.[3] They differ from the chief perpetrators in that they did not have the status, power, or flexibility to initiate, stop, or significantly alter killing operations. But they implemented the killing orders, and they had a great deal of leeway within the parameters set by their superiors. Some historians committed to the functionalist interpretation of the Nazi period have even argued that as a group they not only influenced but also compelled policy decisions.[4] I do not agree. The evidence indicates that while they carried out their orders with alacrity, initiative, and thoroughness, they were usually very careful to protect their backs by getting explicit orders orally or in writing and by not exceeding them.[5]

Whether a person belonged to the group of managers, and not to that of the policy makers, often depended not on his rank but on his personality and the setting in which he operated. A good example is Richard Glücks, the inspector of the concentration camps during World War II. His patron and predecessor, Theodor Eicke, created and shaped the camp system and must thus be counted as a policy maker; Oswald Pohl, his boss after the WVHA absorbed the camps in 1942, was one of Himmler's close advisers who influenced policy during the war.[6]

Glücks does not fit the role of leader and initiator; he was in many ways the perfect example of a manager. Born in the Rhineland in 1889 as the son of a businessman, he attended the city gymnasium in Düsseldorf until 1907 and thereafter worked for his family's insurance company in various cities. He served his one-year voluntary military service with the artillery; thereafter, he attended business college in Leipzig and later traveled in England and Argentina to obtain needed language skills. He served as first lieutenant with the artillery during World War I, earned iron crosses of the first and second class, moved with his unit into a Free Corps in 1919, and thereafter into the postwar Reichswehr (German army). He served there in various staff jobs, including as liaison officer with the Allied Control Commission, until downsizing led to his separation in 1931. As a serving officer, he had abstained from political participation and did not join the Nazi Party until 1930. In November 1932 he entered the SS.[7]

Glücks's professional experience during the sixteen years preceding his separation from the Reichswehr had been limited to military service, and his prospects during the depression could not have been bright. The SS provided an obvious opportunity to practice his profession. He advanced rapidly. He had entered the SS as a private, was soon appointed adjutant of his local SS battalion in Essen, moved to serve as personnel officer for the SS division in Düsseldorf, and thus advanced in less than a year to the rank of technical sergeant. Soon he replaced the division's staff officer and in November 1933 was promoted to second lieutenant.[8] In his letter recommending Glücks for promotion, his commanding officer, Gruppenführer Fritz Weitzel, later Higher SS and Police Leader (HSSPF) in Norway, described him as a "dependable and conscientious" officer who "possesses the aptitude and ability" of a staff officer.[9] Within two years he advanced to the rank of lieutenant colonel.[10]

In April 1936, Glücks transferred to the SS Death Head units to serve as chief of staff for Theodor Eicke, the inspector of the concentration camps. Like Weitzel, Eicke considered Glücks perfect for the job. In his 1936 evaluation, Eicke described Glücks as an "expert, an energetic collaborator with a pronounced sense of responsibility"; one year later, after he had been promoted to colonel, Eicke wrote that "Glücks is an example of what a staff officer ought to be."[11] Indeed, Glücks's "bureaucratic nature" made him a perfect complement for the temperamental Eicke.[12] After Eicke left to assume command of the Death Head Division he had created for the Waffen SS, Glücks succeeded him as inspector but without Eicke's additional title of commander of the Death Head units; Glücks's job was that of an administrator and not that of a military commander.[13] He did not remain independent for long; in March 1942, the inspectorate was incorporated into the WVHA as Office D, and Glücks served, in fact if not in name, as Pohl's staff officer.[14] As such, he advanced during the war to the rank of major general and as late as January 1945 was awarded the German cross in silver.[15] Glücks remained at his post until the end but escaped retribution by dying in May 1945.[16]

Glücks's résumé reveals that career considerations were his primary motivation. He was, of course, a man of the Right; he fought in the Free Corps, was a member of the Stahlhelm, and joined the Nazi Party in 1930. But he joined the SS to continue his military career. We do not know how he met Eicke and thus entered the concentration camp system.[17] Still, he served there as conscientiously as he had served in the Reichswehr and the General SS. There is no evidence that he was a particularly rabid Nazi, although he undoubtedly agreed with the ideological tenets of the movement, including its leadership principle, its antidemocratic and antiparliamentarian posture, its racist and anti-Semitic outlook, and its devotion to the *völkisch* community. But there is no evidence that he personally enjoyed or participated in brutalities. Still, he was not just an armchair perpetrator; he inspected all the concentration camps, including Auschwitz, and was privy to all killing operations.

Glücks did not differ substantially from the T4 managers I have described and analyzed elsewhere.[18] In addition to their ideological commitment, those managers were motivated by career and personal considerations: promotions, allowances, exemption from service at the front, and ultimately personal power and influence. These motivations applied also to the men who, under the direction of the T4 managers, commanded the T4 killing centers on German soil and later the extermination camps of Operation Reinhard in the East. Of course, there were individual differences; some were more brutal, corrupt, or ambitious than others. Elsewhere, I have described these lower-level managers as "supervisors."[19] The concentration camp commandants who operated below Glücks were comparable "junior managers"; few advanced above the rank of lieutenant colonel. Although they had risen within the camp system, they did not differ substantially from the T4 supervisors who had not had previous camp experiences before they were assigned to killing centers. Of course, there were differences. In the concentration camps, the line dividing managers from junior managers was relatively narrow, and men moved easily from one group to the other; several men served as commandant and also at the inspectorate. Further, the job of concentration camp commandant required more administrative and command experience than the job directing a killing center. While the killing center's only job was the mass murder of human beings, the concentration camp commandant had in addition to administer a large complex, command troops, and direct a labor force.

For this discussion—to see whether my conclusions about the T4 supervisors can apply also to their peers in the concentration camps—I have selected twenty-five camp junior managers, SS officers who had served for a relatively long time in the concentration camps under Eicke and Glücks and who advanced to the position of commandant. The twenty-five were a diverse group; still, they had much in common. Some were managers like Glücks, but most had absorbed the activist approach preached by Eicke. A preliminary analysis of this group might give us hints about the motivations of the junior managers of Nazi terror and mass murder.[20]

First, some generalizations. These junior managers were young men. The youngest—Richard Baer—was born in 1911 and was therefore only twenty-two the year Hitler came to power and thirty-three at the time he was appointed commandant of Auschwitz I in 1944. Several were not much older: Johannes Hassebroek, born in 1910, was thirty-four when he assumed command of Gross-Rosen; Heinrich Schwarz, born in 1908, was appointed commandant of Auschwitz III at thirty-five. The oldest was Hermann Baranowski, the commandant of Sachsenhausen; he was born in 1884 but died in 1940. Hermann Pister, the commandant of Buchenwald, was only one year younger. But these two were exceptions; the next three in age were ten years younger.

These men did not have a great deal of formal education. Only one, Günther Tamaschke, had taken the *Abitur,* the examination upon leaving the gymnasium that made university admittance possible. They came from working or lower-middle-class backgrounds and entered blue- or white-collar jobs. They were bakers, electricians, mechanics, carpenters, farmers, clerks, and salesmen. Because of their age, only a few had served in the war and a few more in the postwar Free Corps. However, five men had become professional soldiers in the postwar Reichswehr (Adam Grünewald, Friedrich Hartjenstein, Anton Kaindl, Arthur Liebehenschel, and Franz Xaver Ziereis) and one in the police (Hans Loritz). Only one, Martin Weiss, had mastered a profession—electrical engineering—by attending a technical school. Most were unemployed or underemployed in 1933; active service in the SS provided a job as well as upward mobility.

They did, of course, have ideological commitment. All joined the Nazi Party and the SA or SS prior to January 1933 (Hartjenstein, Kaindl, and Ziereis joined later but only because service in the military prevented them from joining earlier). But most joined after 1929, only a few during the 1920s. The records, however, indicate that they were not early activists; Rudolf Hess, who fought with the Free Corps in the Baltic and served in prison for a Feme murder, was an exception.[21]

Almost all of these men rose through the ranks and thus served for many years on the staff, in the guard units, as adjutants, and as camp leaders (*Schutzhaftlagerführer*) before they were appointed commandant. In this way they absorbed the Eicke lessons of "hardness" against the "internal enemy." They were rewarded for maintaining draconian order; the managers overlooked their failings, even their incompetence, as long as the camps produced the expected results: guard discipline, inmate compliance, work quotas, and, later, mass murder. But similar to the T4 killing centers, the total power granted to the SS in the camps led to brutality, cruelty, depravity, licentiousness, and corruption. The senior managers, however, only intervened if such behavior interfered with the smooth operation of the terror system or became too noticeable.

Some of the men who served as commandant were disciplined. Walter Chmielewski was born in 1903 and worked as a wood-carver but found himself unemployed in 1930. He joined the SS in 1932 and thus found employment as an auxiliary policeman in March 1933. He joined the staff of the office of the Reichsführer SS in November and worked there as a cashier until June 1935. He was then transferred to the staff of the Columbiahaus concentration camp in Berlin and one year later to Sachsenhausen, where he was promoted to second lieutenant. In 1940, he was promoted to captain and assigned as camp leader to the Mauthausen subsidiary Gusen. In January 1943, the inspectorate appointed him commandant of the Herzogenbusch (Vught) camp in Holland. But he did not manage well and was removed in October 1943. The reasons are not clear, but they probably concerned the need to keep conditions secret from the Dutch population. The SS and Police Court of Berlin sentenced him to fifteen years, and he first served pretrial detention in Sachsenhausen and thereafter his sentence in the SS and police penal camp at Dachau.[22]

We know a little more about his successor at Vught. Adam Grünewald was born in 1902 and trained as a baker. He served in the Free Corps and thereafter in the Reichswehr until 1931. That year he joined the Nazi Party and the SA but transferred to the SS in 1934, probably to obtain a job with the guard unit at the Lichtenburg concentration camp. He had been a lieutenant colonel in the SA and therefore entered the SS as a captain and was promoted to major in 1941. He served as camp leader in Dachau from 1938 to 1939, thereafter with the Waffen SS Death Head Division until 1942, when he was posted to Sachsenhausen as camp leader. Grünewald was commandant at Vught until early 1944. He was then removed and placed on trial. Under his authority and in his presence, eighty-seven women inmates were crowded into two small cells and left there overnight. As a result, ten women ended up dead and twenty seriously injured. Grünewald was not disciplined because of his brutality but because the events became known to the Dutch public. As he had been warned about public relations, his actions were considered a dereliction of duty. The SS and police court sentenced him to three years and six months. The Reichsführer changed the sentence: Grünewald was reduced to private and transferred to the Waffen SS; in 1945, he was killed in action in Hungary.[23]

The cases of Chmielewski and Grünewald show that the vitae of SS officers seldom revealed the true realities of the concentration camp system. Promotions and assignments of increasing responsibility were accompanied by positive evaluations that concealed the true facts; alongside the vaunted *Führerprinzip* there operated an SS peer review system that protected the incompetent, the vicious, and the corrupt. Of course, not all evaluations were positive. In April 1937, for example, an evaluation of Arthur Rödl, then camp leader in Sachsenburg, advised that this "loyal and honest National Socialist" should not be continued in a responsible position in the camps, because he was incompetent and a functional illiterate.[24] But this evaluation did not prevent Rödl's 1941 appointment as commandant of Gross-Rosen.

There obviously had to be competent men or the camp system would have ceased to function. Martin Weiss and Rudolf Hess were two such SS officers; both finished their careers as managers at the WVHA. Weiss had joined the SS in 1932 and was one of the most educated SS camp officers. He was responsible for engineering problems at Dachau in the 1930s before his appointment as commandant of Neuengamme in 1940, then of Dachau in 1942, and finally of Lublin in 1943 to clean up the mess created there by his predecessors.[25] Hess started his career at Dachau in 1933 as a noncommissioned officer who was promoted to second lieutenant in 1936 in part because he had known both Heinrich Himmler and Martin Bormann.[26] But he was also competent and as commandant of Auschwitz later created there the largest concentration camp and killing center. Obviously, the mass murder practiced in Birkenau and the random murder practiced in the Stammlager and at Monowitz did not detract from his image as an honest and hard-working commandant.

Himmler and his managers took notice of the massive corruption in the camp system only when internecine warfare or public disclosures forced them to do so. Colonel Günther Tamaschke, the only commandant with the *Abitur,* had served as camp leader in Dachau, staff officer at the inspectorate, and commandant of Lichtenburg before he was dismissed from the SS Death Head units in 1939 because of economic corruption; in 1942 the Reichsführer excluded him from the SS altogether, because he had used his office to acquire an Aryanized Jewish business.[27]

Corruption inside the camps was taken more seriously if it disrupted the smooth functioning of the camps and the morale of the troops. This happened in Buchenwald and Lublin. Both Karl Koch, commandant of Buchenwald and Lublin, and Hermann Florstedt, camp leader of Buchenwald and commandant of Lublin, were executed for corruption shortly before the end of the war.[28] Koch symbolized the brutality and corruption of the camp system. Born in 1897 as the son of a government clerk, he served in the war, was captured, and spent 1918 to 1919 in Britain as a POW. After the war he worked at a bank, ending up as senior clerk. Having joined the Nazi Party and the SS in 1931, Second Lieutenant Koch headed SS Special Commando "Saxony" in 1933 and the Sachsenburg concentration camp in 1934; from there he moved to command the guards at Esterwegen until 1935. He served as camp leader in Lichtenburg, adjutant in Dachau, and acting commandant at the Columbiahaus and was appointed commandant first at Esterwegen and then Sachsenhausen. In 1937, he was promoted to colonel and appointed commandant of the newly established Buchenwald camp; that year he also married Ilse Köhler. After the departure of Eicke, who had protected Koch, an investigation of corruption in Buchenwald launched by Prince Waldeck-Pyrmont, HSSPF in Weimar, led in November 1941 to Koch's transfer to Lublin. A mass escape of Soviet POWs from the Lublin camp in July 1942 led not only to Koch's removal as commandant but also to an inquiry that not only revealed corruption and mismanagement in Lublin but was also broadened to include conditions at Buchenwald. Koch was arrested in 1943 and, together with other Buchenwald officers as well as his wife, placed on trial before an SS and police court. He was convicted and eventually executed.[29]

The case of Arthur Liebehenschel illustrates better than any other the irrational nature of the SS ethos and the camp system. Born in Posen in 1901, Liebehenschel served in the Free Corps in 1919 and in the Reichswehr until 1931; he joined the Nazi Party and the SS in 1932. In 1937, Major Liebehenschel entered the camp system as staff member in Lichtenburg. Thereafter, he served on the staff of the Death Head units until 1940 and as chief of staff for Glücks at the WVHA until 1943. In November 1943, Lieutenant Colonel Liebehenschel was appointed to succeed Hess as commandant of Auschwitz, where he improved conditions for the prisoners. His career appeared to flourish, but, suddenly, in May 1944, he was transferred to Lublin, where he remained as commandant until he joined the staff of the HSSPF in Trieste in August.[30]

Liebehenschel's removal from Auschwitz had nothing to do with his competence or his honesty. At the WVHA, he had started an affair with Anneliese Hüttemann, who worked as a secretary for the inspectorate. He divorced his wife, established a joint household with Hüttemann in Auschwitz, and applied for permission to marry. During a routine investigation, the inspectorate discovered that in 1935 Hüttemann had briefly been placed in protective custody because she had slept with a Jew. Considering the setting—Auschwitz—there then developed a bizarre scenario. Oswald Pohl refused permission for the marriage, transferred Liebehenschel to Lublin, and sent his adjutant, Richard Baer, to Auschwitz to replace Liebehenschel and to report on developments. Baer consoled Liebehenschel and insulted Hüttemann. Liebehenschel accepted the transfer but refused to part from his lover; Hüttemann took her case to Himmler. In the end, the Reichsführer permitted the marriage because Hüttemann was with child; in 1948, Liebehenschel was executed in Poland.[31]

The information about the men who served as commandant, as well as all other senior SS officers in the camps, is still extremely fragmentary, and we need to know much more before we can be certain about their motivations. Still, some preliminary conclusions are possible: Those who served in the camp system were committed to Nazi ideology and the SS ethos, but most entered and remained in the system because it opened a career providing the status, power, and comfort neither education nor talent could have obtained for them elsewhere.

NOTES

1. For a recent biography of one of these chief perpetrators, see Ulrich Herbert, *Best: Biographische Studien über Radikalismus, Weltanschauung und Vernunft, 1903–1989* (Bonn, 1996).
2. For recent analyses, see, for example, Christopher R. Browning, *Ordinary Men: Reserve Police Battalion 101 and the Final Solution in Poland* (New York, 1991); Dick de Mildt, *In the Name of the People: Perpetrators of Genocide in the Reflection of their Post-War Prosecution in West Germany: The "Euthanasia and Aktion Reinhard" Trial Cases* (The Hague, 1996); and Henry Friedlander, *The Origins of Nazi Genocide: From Euthanasia to the Final Solution* (Chapel Hill, 1995), pp. 232–45.
3. For one recent study of this group of perpetrators, see Hans Safrian, *Die Eichmann-Männer* (Vienna, 1993). See also Friedlander, *Origins of Nazi Genocide,* chap. 10.
4. Recently, this position has been forcefully argued by Götz Aly, *"Endlösung": Völkerverschiebung und der Mord an den europäischen Juden* (Frankfurt, 1995).
5. See Friedlander, *Origins of Nazi Genocide,* pp. 67–68, 284–85.
6. On Eicke, see Berlin Document Center (BDC), dossier Theodor Eicke; Charles W. Sydnor, *Soldiers of Destruction: The SS Death's Head Division, 1933–1945* (Princeton, 1977), chap. 1; and Henry Friedlander, "Die Entwicklung des NS-Konzentrationslagersystems," *Revue d'Allemagne* 27 (1995): 151–64. On Pohl, see BDC, dossier Oswald Pohl; and *Trials of War Criminals before the Nuremberg Military Tribunals under Control Council Law No. 10,* 15 vols. (Washington, 1950–52), vol. 5. The acronym WVHA stood for SS Wirtschaftsverwaltungshauptamt (SS Central Office for Economy and Administration).
7. BDC, dossier Richard Glücks: SS-Karteikarte; handwritten Lebenslauf [curriculum vitae], 21 August 1933; SS-Stammrollenauszug; Personalnachweis with Dienstlaufbahn [documentation of service] and typed vita. See also Johannes Tuchel, *Konzentrationslager: Organisationsgeschichte und Funktion der "Inspektion der Konzentrationslager," 1934–1938,* Schriften des Bundesarchivs, no. 39 (Boppard on the Rhine, 1991), pp. 232–34.
8. BDC, dossier Richard Glücks: Dienstlaufbahn; Gruppenführer Fritz Weitzel to Reichsführer SS, 28 July, 22 August, and 13 September 1933; Vorschlagsprotokoll des Führerkorps der SS Gruppe West, 19. Sep-

tember 1933. Glücks's noncommissioned SS rank was Obertruppführer, because, prior to the Röhm affair a year later, the SS still used SA ranks; the equivalent later SS rank would have been Hauptscharführer. For the same reason, his first commissioned rank was Sturmführer, later known as Untersturmführer.

9. BDC, dossier Richard Glücks: Weitzel to Reichsführer SS, 13 September 1933.

10. BDC, dossier Richard Glücks: Dienstlaufbahn.

11. BDC, dossier Richard Glücks: Personal-Bericht on Richard Glücks by Theodor Eicke, 8 August 1936 and 3 August 1937. English translation is the author's.

12. Klaus Drobisch and Günther Wieland, *System der NS-Konzentrationslager, 1933–1939* (Berlin, 1993), p. 256.

13. Sydnor, *Soldiers of Destruction,* p. 133 n. 22.

14. See, for example, Rudolf Hess, *Commandant of Auschwitz: The Autobiography of Rudolf Hoess,* trans. Constantine FitzGibbon (New York, 1961), pp. 232–35.

15. BDC, dossier Glücks: Dienstlaufbahn; Fernschreiben [telex], 27 January 1945.

16. He was admitted with heart problems into the naval hospital at Flenburg-Mürwik. Rudolf Hess described him as "half-dead" at that time: *Kommandant in Auschwitz: Autobiographische Aufzeichnungen des Rudolf Höss,* ed. Martin Broszat (Munich, 1963), p. 148. Other reports indicate that he committed suicide at the hospital. Johannes Tuchel, *Die Inspektion der Konzentrationslager, 1938–1945: Das System des Terrors,* Schriftenreihe der Stiftung Brandenburgische Gedenkstätten, No. 1 (Berlin, 1994), p. 58.

17. Tuchel, *Inspektion der Konzentrationslager,* p. 233.

18. Friedlander, *Origins of Nazi Genocide,* pp. 41–42, 68–69, 190–98.

19. Ibid., pp. 202–8.

20. The twenty-five, selected because their BDC files are in my possession, are the following: Hans Aumeier, Richard Baer, Hermann Baranowski, Karl Walter Chmielewski, Hermann Florstedt, Adam Grünewald, Friedrich Hartjenstein, Johannes Hassebroek, Rudolf Franz Hess, Anton Kaindl, Karl Otto Koch, Max Koegel, Josef Kramer, Arthur Liebehenschel, Hans Loritz, Max Pauly, Hermann Pister, Arthur Rödl, Albert Sauer, Heinrich Schwarz, Fritz Suhren, Günther Tamaschke, Martin Weiss, Franz Xaver Ziereis, and Egon Zill. My analysis is based on information contained in their BDC dossiers; some of these have been published in Henry Friedlander and Sybil Milton, eds., *Berlin Document Center,* vol. 11, parts 1–2 of *Archives of the Holocaust* (New York, 1992).

21. On Hess, see also *Kommandant in Auschwitz,* pp. 34–39.

22. LG Ansbach, Urteil 11 April 1961, Ks 1ab/61, in *Justiz und NS-Verbrechen,* vol. 10, no. 505, pp. 153–55.

23. BDC, dossier Adam Grünewald: SS- und Polizeigericht den Haag, Urteil 6 March 1944, St. L.I 20/44.

24. Friedlander and Milton, *Berlin Document Center,* 2: 222–23.

25. See also Johannes Tuchel, "Die Kommandanten des Konzentrationslagers Dachau," *Dachauer Hefte* 10 (1994): 86–88.

26. BDC, dossier Rudolf Höss: Hans Loritz, Kommandant Dachau, to Theodor Eicke, Inspekteur der Konzentrationslager, 24 June 1936.

27. Friedlander and Milton, *Berlin Document Center,* 2: 276: Heinrich Himmler to Günther Tamaschke, 5 January 1942.

28. Staatsanwaltschaft Köln, Anklageschrift Hermann Hackmann [Majdanek case], 130 (24) Js 200/62 (Z), 15 November 1974, p. 110.

29. See BDC, dossier Karl Otto Koch, for the documents concerning Koch's career and downfall. See also Eugen Kogon, *Der SS Staat: Das System der deutschen Konzentrationslager* (Munich, 1974), pp. 323–26.

30. See Hermann Langbein, *Menschen in Auschwitz* (Frankfurt, 1980), pp. 357–60.

31. For the Liebehenschel-Hüttemann affair, see BDC, dossier Arthur Liebehenschel; Friedlander and Milton, *Berlin Document Center,* 2: 55–75.

Michael Allen

Technocrats of Extermination
Engineers, Modern Bureaucracy, and Complicity

IN DECEMBER 1943, WERNER JOTHANN, THE CHIEF OF ENGINEERS AT Auschwitz, took the time to write what was, by bureaucratic standards, a heated letter to a subcontractor, the HUTA AG. HUTA had fallen delinquent in the payment of its own subcontractor, Müller of Hamburg. Although Jothann had no direct dealings with Müller, he went out of his way to warn HUTA: "This firm was completely destroyed by enemy bombing at the end of July, 1943 but has now once again reached full production capacity through emergency measures. It is therefore a duty that goes without saying to handle the settlement of such a firm's accounts as a first priority."[1]

One wonders what in the nature of this business could have inspired Jothann to appeal to some "duty that goes without saying [*selbstverstaendlich,* literally 'self-understood']." The whole business involved only the housings for pipes, hardly a pressing need. Dry matters of accounts payable were usually handled in standardized letters, and for this reason, if no other, Jothann's moralizing would have stood out to HUTA. The very insignificance of the correspondence makes it noteworthy for other reasons, however. It was highly abnormal to intervene in the affairs of sub-subcontractors. One of the advantages of bureaucratic institutions was supposed to be that one did not ever have to, let alone go out of one's way to do so. Jothann drafted this letter instead of doing what was easier and far more typical, namely, ignore Müller and stick to Auschwitz's own pressing business. Nevertheless, Jothann took the time to indulge a flourish for moralization.

Even in such a trivial business, a sense of "duty" or moral propriety, for whatever reason, still mattered to him. This in itself would hardly be worth pointing out if so many did not persist in identify-

ing bureaucracy, technocracy, or "instrumental reason" as a fundamental cause of the Holocaust (all of which seem to have placed precious few constraints upon Jothann's actions). Zygmunt Bauman, for
instance, writes that a "meticulous functional division of labor" led to
the "substitution of technical for a moral responsibility," which facilitated the Holocaust.[2] One could make too much of Jothann's letter,
but if Jothann could appeal to "duty that goes without saying" over
pipe housings, how much more implausible are the historical judgments of Bauman and others when it comes to the Holocaust itself,
in which the Nazis' most cherished racial fantasies were at stake?

The following essay is a small attempt to seek out a more accurate
understanding of how men and women behave in modern organizations, because these were the organizations which perpetrated the
Nazi genocide. This is all the more necessary in the wake of *Hitler's
Willing Executioners* precisely because Daniel Goldhagen has provided a powerful ideological interpretation of perpetrators' motives
in modern institutions. Although Goldhagen is rightly criticized for
proffering a simple answer to complex questions, existing scholarship
has hardly been innocent in this respect, proposing for instance that
the popularity of the Nazi Party can be explained *only* with reference to
"material self interest" (William Brustein) or that the concentration
camps can be explained *only* as an expression of absolute power in
which ideological explanations are "superstition" (Wolfgang Sofsky).[3]
Such accounts would have us believe not only that victims came like
sheep to the slaughter but that their butchers did so as well.[4]

Entire symposia and even TV talk shows have convened to dis-
credit Goldhagen before an educated public, yet no similar reaction
has accompanied the publication of books like Brustein's *The Logic of
Evil* or Sofky's *The Order of Terror*. This is not to say that prominent
reviewers have failed to criticize these and countless other books written in the same spirit, but unlike *Hitler's Willing Executioners,* they do
not, as a rule, become part of what I would call an "anti-canon," a text
that becomes acceptable to discuss among scholars only in derision.[5]
This contrast would seem to suggest that we are much more comfortable with causal explanations couched in social structures than
agency and genuine motivation, something that misrepresents modern organization as much as it does Nazi perpetrators.[6] István Deák is
scarcely atypical in criticizing Goldhagen because "it is wrong to
eliminate social function as a source of study."[7] Rarer are calls for ac-

curate answers to Goldhagen's *right* questions, namely: What commitments endowed complex social structures with their dynamism?
How does ideology function in organizational settings?[8]

A useful framework might be to consider how and why bureaucrats like Jothann appealed to shared principles, an ethos, in order to
mobilize the structures in which they worked. Recently, Karin Orth
has addressed this very theme with poignant results. She has pursued
the biographies of almost three hundred concentration camp personnel, from the pettiest lieutenants to the highest-ranking *Kommandanten.* Of relevance here, she notes the repetitive comments like
"healthy human understanding" or "old national socialist" in SS personnel evaluations (the latter, ironically, often applied to very young
men). These are the same vapid appeals to "self-understood" consensus that Jothann deployed above over pipe housings. Instead of dis-
missing them, Orth notes that these "speak of an orientation of the
(historical) subject on principles that were felt to be 'normal' and 'un-
questionable' within a social community, that could be reproduced
without any reflection whatsoever. Recourse to theoretical maxims or
norms anchored outside the group, by contrast, seemed as unnecessary as they were highly suspect."[9]

As the constant repetition of clichés uncovered by Orth suggests,
moral decisions based upon ideology remain imbedded in quotidian
bureaucratic operations. They lie at the root of collective identity and
consensus, which in turn play an important function in bureaucratic
structure that we can understand best by considering the nature of
modern management in general. The techniques of modern management were and are intended to render local, individual experiences
and material artifacts fungible, that is, amenable to collation, interchangeability, and abstract transfer. Thus otherwise banal statistics depend upon agency—the maintenance, input, trust, and cooperation
of people—namely, the new masses of midlevel managers, engineers,
and white-collar workers who appeared at the end of the nineteenth
century and were coming to dominate the twentieth. Siegfried Kracauer called them "the model of the future."[10] The SS put them to
work on the tasks of genocide.

At the juncture of personal as well as collective trust among managers, professional ethos played an indispensable role. It lent credibility to the entire process by which information was pared down to the
bare essentials. Consensus created trust, a powerful time-saver, and it

saved the most time precisely when it did not have to be put into words, constantly reiterated, and read in lengthy tedium. The sparse mention of explicit ideological doctrines in bureaucratic memos cannot, therefore, be considered evidence of their absence; as frustrating as this is to historical research, the absence of any articulated motivation is all too often evidence of an unreflective consensus.

By selecting a discrete work community of engineers like Jothann within the SS Business Administration Head Office (SS-Wirtschafts-verwaltungshauptamt, or WVHA), this essay seeks to reinvest "structural" analysis with an understanding of agency that aids our historical understanding of both. I have selected engineers precisely because no other group could be more pertinent to the argument at hand. This profession was supposedly the most prone to the "technocratic" mentality, which, as Albert Speer and others have argued, kept them far too preoccupied with the minutiae of daily work to concern themselves with overarching ideological or moral considerations.

ENGINEERING THE NEW ORDER

The most competent branch of the WVHA was its civil engineering corps, the Office Group C-Construction, and the most decisive event in its formation was the arrival of Dr. Engineer Hans Kammler in mid-1941. Many of the men he subsequently recruited shared a relatively homogeneous career profile. They came from civil service, especially from those innovative branches that owed their existence to the National Socialist regime, such as the Luftwaffe and the Organisation Todt (OT); the SS was itself one such branch.

The technical nature of the Office Group C-Construction obviously required a relatively homogeneous professional background: all but two officers were trained engineers or architects. Most (twenty-eight of thirty-eight) had enjoyed advanced technical training, either at Germany's polytechnic universities (*Technische Hochschulen*, seventeen officers) or higher technical colleges (*Höhere Technische Lehranstalten*, eleven officers). Four additional officers had attended polytechnic universities without graduating. Almost all had progressed beyond primary school.[11] The relative homogeneity of educational experiences in itself constituted a powerful source of common career identity, which did not come without its own ideological color. Technical universities of the 1910s and 1920s consciously strove to instill specific ideals of social reform. While this topic is beyond the scope of this article, the "social structure" of polytechnic education had sought to mold engineers to seek out work that served German "culture" long before the Nazi period. Werner Durth, Karl-Heinz Ludwig, and others have shown that polytechnic schools taught German students to draw a direct causal link between industrial growth and social progress, between the steady promotion of technical innovation and the betterment of humankind.[12] This powerful message associated technical expertise with a mission. This was especially true of disciplines like architecture and structural engineering (*Hochbau*), which had traditionally shared a closer integration with the humanities in the engineering curriculum than others.[13]

Civil engineering education was roughly split along three different subspecialties: *Tiefbau* (below-grade civil engineering including hydraulics), *Hochbau* (above-grade, especially structural engineering), and *Architektur* (architecture, which I will count in common with civil engineering here, because it often involved the same practices as *Hochbau*). *Hochbauer* in above-grade work were known to have more "cultural" background than *Tiefbauer* or hydraulics engineers; architects more than building engineers. In the SS, architects and *Hochbauer* predominated. The historical prestige attached to their professional training had shifted only recently, and as Eckhard Bolenz has shown, civil engineers made arguments for higher status in terms of "the arts" (*Kunst*) and "culture" (*Kultur*—a much more loaded term than the literal English), in other words, in terms of the humanities. *Hochbau* began to include more artistic and aesthetic training in the late nineteenth century so that its graduates could compete with architects for civil service positions.

Similarly, both *Hochbauer* and architects sought to claim legitimacy as part of the so-called "free professions" like lawyers and doctors, who had earned degrees at Germany's famous humanistic universities and more often than not outranked engineers in the hierarchies of state service. To compete with established elites, ambitious civil engineers tried to distance themselves from the empirical science-based curricula required of other technological specialists. Within civil engineering, this meant diminished prestige for *Tiefbau*. Before the advent of scientific management and new materials like steel-reinforced concrete, *Tiefbau* had actually surpassed architectural training or structural engineering in sophistication, one example being the rigorous study of hydraulics. Far from counting this a deficit, however, *Hochbauer* and architects pointed to their own grounding in the humanities in order to make the point that they, not narrow specialists, were more qualified to represent the public interest. They were more than mere technicians; they were equipped to engineer the public good.[14] More than others, these technical men were taught to make the reform of society their business. Their very professional ethos included a predilection for ideological concerns; they counted themselves more sophisticated purveyors of ideology than other technical professionals.

The content of the ideals that would animate them in the 1920s and 1930s were not inconsequential. Viewed abstractly, the drive to teach engineers to serve society is perhaps laudable, but the moral crux lies in *what kind of society* lay at the center of engineers' vision of a better world. As difficult as it is to believe now, many young, intelligent, idealistic construction engineers and architects looked to National Socialism to fulfill their visions of "culture" and "the arts." Increasingly in the late 1920s, the extreme Right succeeded in mobilizing the activism of elite engineering students. By the early 1930s, the student bodies of the technical universities were overwhelmingly National Socialist.[15] At the Polytechnic University of Munich, for example, the Nazis carried fifteen of thirty seats in the student council in November 1932. A further ten seats were carried by other radical Right representatives. These were the last elections for student-body representatives before Hitler's seizure of power. The voter turnout reached 90 percent. Liberals or socialists carried not a single seat. Nine years earlier, Polytechnic students had held rallies just days after the Beer Hall Putsch of November 1923, and fully 70 percent of those present had spoken out in favor of Hitler and demanded leniency.[16]

Of course, in the lower echelons of the SS engineering corps, many officers were construction foremen, skilled workers, or non-engineering specialists such as clerks. Yet among top officers, "cultural" or humanistic technical education predominated. Out of a total of twenty-six officers above the rank of captain (*Hauptsturm-führer*)—those who planned and implemented the blueprints for genocide rather than merely filling them out—half were *Hochbauer* or architects; only one was a *Tiefbauer*. The remaining twelve came from eclectic backgrounds: five had risen from careers as *Bauführer* (foremen), one from status as a skilled worker, and six from either other engineering backgrounds (mechanical or electrical engineering) or financial administration (*Kaufmänner*). In terms of specific roles within the organization, the importance of "cultural" training was even more exaggerated. *Hochbauer* and architects monopolized nearly all top positions. Thus the structure of these SS engineers' education and, subsequently, the structure of their organization encouraged them to take ideology more, not less, seriously. We have more, not less, reason to consider their technical training as complementary to National Socialist convictions.

In these top officers' collective biographies, the importance of the humanities becomes even clearer. In one instance, an SS officer listed his professional training in *Kunstbauten*, or artistic buildings; another had studied at the Bauhaus. Both of them worked for the SS's central construction directorate at Auschwitz building the gas chambers. Another SS engineer had trained in the atelier of Paul Ludwig Troost, one of the architecture professors who taught Albert Speer to consider himself an "artist" and who built the National Museum in Munich. Another had also worked in the SS's Main Bureau for Culture excavating Germanic ruins in an effort to provide evidence for Heinrich Himmler's racial theories.[17] The chief of SS engineers, Hans Kammler, also took care to encourage a sense of cultural mission within his organization: The SS had a double task, both to preserve past tradition and to propel the German "race" to new "great construction programs of a cultural and social kind."[18]

Kammler's entry into the SS corps of engineers further clarified its specific ethos and ideology. He and those he recruited entered the WVHA at a time when SS construction was expanding radically throughout the Reich and the occupied territories of the Soviet Union and Poland. A specific mission drove this expansion, what the Reichsführer SS and Chief of German Police Heinrich Himmler would label the "New Order." The SS aimed to settle German citizens in racially pure communities throughout the conquered East in order to insure the demographic and cultural hegemony of the Third Reich over its newly won territories. As newly appointed Reichskommissar for the Strengthening of Germandom (*Reichskommissar für die Festigung deutschen Volkstums*—RKF), Himmler received the mandate both to plan and to implement these policies of domination in late 1939.[19] Up to 1941, the SS had maintained regional Building Directorates at concentration camps, but these were decentralized, dissolute, and limited to scattered projects. The SS now recruited Kammler to rectify the poor organization of the past and ready an SS construction corps for future expansion.

Investigation of Kammler's past reveals a strong identification with the Nazi movement in general and settlement projects in particular. He published a book in 1934 whose dry title suggests nothing more than pragmatic methods of organization: *Basics of Cost Accounting and Organization of Building Enterprise for Housing and Settlement Construction.* Indeed, the book delivered the technical information promised, including the methods of time-motion studies and outlines of the structure of modern bureaucratic corporations. But ideological statements accompany these practical methods of building-site management. "We are convinced," states the introduction, "that a unification of cost accounting and price calculation has as its prerequisite a complete transformation of employers and employees from the liberal-capitalistic to the National Socialist economic order."[20] A section titled "The Meaning of the Building Sector for Housing and Settlement Construction" continues:

> [Under liberal capitalism] houses and settlements were seen as a commodity. . . The production and maintenance of this commodity became a good business . . . Man and the soil did not stand at the center of these measures but rather materialism, bureaucratic technicalities, legalities, and the sales-man's point of view. The measures of National Socialism are now dedicated to the firm connection of the man to the soil through hearth and home as the basic foundation of the people (*Volk*) and the state. The German man's hereditary health and the hereditary health given by the German soil therefore stand at the focal point of the German Reich's program of renewal.[21]

No censorship in the building trades required such statements, and there is no reason to suspect that Kammler was in any way disingenuous. The SS Race and Settlement Head Office, which Kammler served as a consultant at this early time before the RKF, sought to build these values into the physical structure of housing developments.

Ideological variations bear much more extensive treatment than allowed here, but even in the foregoing short quotation, the glorification of state power, anticapitalism, racial supremacy, and agrarian romanticism readily come to the fore. As a collectivity, the SS wished to institutionalize them all in subbureaus and departments. On the other hand, once embedded in organizational hierarchies, no one tenet needed inspire all SS men; likewise, no one individual needed identify with each and every principle. Above all, ideology cannot be reduced to functional variables that mechanically determined organizational outputs, and Robert Gellately has warned against such oversimplification.[22] But the WVHA functioned best when it succeeded in evoking the active identification of its officers—for whatever reason—with elements of its social mission, and one reason that the New Order could mobilize collective identity so effectively was because the SS's fantasies of the East were so capacious that they subsumed almost every darling Nazi cause. Once officers identified with the institution and their fellows, if only with fragments of this grand mission, their specialized skills could be mobilized in unison for the whole. And of no lesser importance to the preservation of collective identity, no one was alienated.

As he built up his engineering bureau, Kammler sought to shepherd an esprit de corps. He seems to have approached the institutionalization of dedication in the very structure of his organization as part of his job. He began with structural changes, to be sure. He organized regional Building Inspections with divisions and subdivisions, nested Central Construction Directorates and Construction Directorates. Control was centralized and administered from Kammler's bureau in Berlin, whence this branching organization extended over the whole of central Europe. They included SS machine parks, building-supply stockpiles, and concentration camps as labor depots.[23] The nature of technical management on this geographical scale necessarily demanded that Kammler place his trust in other engineers at building sites beyond his direct control, and the far-flung organization placed a premium on the fungibility of experience. It had to, for all of Kammler's officers could not know each other personally. Kammler therefore used his own institutional position to reinforce collective identity.

All SS personnel sheets included a category for the estimation of *Weltanschauung,* or ideology. Typically, this slot was filled with perfunctory statements like "old National Socialist," whose importance should not be exaggerated. Nevertheless, in some cases, Kammler took the evaluation of dedication seriously and even barred some from advancement on ideological grounds. Regarding one officer he wrote, "For the chief of his office he is not suited." As one reason, he gave the lack of "ideological equipment."[24] In other cases, Kammler emphasized the dedication of those he did promote, often praising technical and ideological capacity in the same sentences. "He is especially enthusiastic about his work, he understands in an outstanding way how to use the possibilities at hand," Kammler once wrote of an officer he wished to promote, and then added, "He possesses the old *Staffel* Spirit."[25] By "*Staffel* Spirit" Kammler meant the *Schutzstaffel,* the SS. He was referring to the ethos which, as the chief of Office Group C, he actively sought to create and uphold. Precisely because such issues mattered, Kammler and engineers like him would have rejected the label of "technocrat" applied to them after the war ahistorically. The argument that the stale structure of their organizations enervated human agency would have likewise seemed bizarre to them, for he attempted to cast these structures of human interaction in order to promote initiative and mobilize the whole in collective endeavor.

Kammler's first directive of 1941 showed his keen sensitivity to matters of personal motivation among subordinates: "All members must know . . . that all depends upon the work of each individual, totally irrespective of where he is positioned and which task he has to fulfill."[26] Here, Kammler stressed the importance of each officer's identification with his task and underscored the fact that bureaucratic duties are double-edged: They demand submission to large, impersonal institutions but also bestow the power to direct and exploit the enhanced capacity of collective work that no single individual could ever achieve. A memorandum from one Central Building Authority clearly showed acute awareness of this double edge: "The Office Group Chief C [Kammler] has ordered that the leader of each service position and department in the coming time will be totally responsible for the work under their supervision and will be made accountable."[27] The SS civil engineers were the big fish in their ponds of regional authority, and they were conscious of their command, as the following examples demonstrate at the Central Building Directorate of Auschwitz.

EXEMPLARY BIOGRAPHIES: HEINRICH COURTE, MAXIMILLIAN KIEFER, AND KARL BISCHOFF

First, however, the question remains: Did Kammler's corps respond to his call? Currently I have collected data on thirty-eight officers who comprised the elite leadership of the SS Office Group C-Construction, no less than two-thirds of Kammler's Building Inspections' elite.[28] Their biographies yield evidence that they dedicated themselves to the purposes that Kammler defined for them. The "pragmatic" technical competence of these officers undoubtedly enabled their success; however, the existence of collective identity strongly suggests that they conceived of their tasks in terms of a collective identity: this in turn, I argue, facilitated their cooperation in an impersonal hierarchy.[29]

Active engagement can be proven for nearly half of the thirty-eight officers, eighteen in all, by which I mean those who made conscious statements or decisions of ideological sympathy. This number may plausibly be extended to twenty-six if one counts an additional eight officers who joined the Nazi Party before January 1933 (but who have left no statements of engagement), that is, before membership became fashionable and professionally advantageous.

Of course, such qualitative evidence must be carefully weighted. Some officers engaged their creativity to promote National Socialism while others only sympathized or participated without taking a leading role. Among those who were participants but not activists, evidence also yields a differentiated conglomerate of issues with which they identified. Therefore let us start with these weaker cases.

Take, for example, the thirty-two-year-old former Organisation Todt engineer, Heinrich Courte. Courte was like many new officers of the total war era: Kammler did not recruit him directly to the Office Group C-Construction; rather, the Office Group C snapped him up out of the mass of men who enlisted in the Waffen SS in 1942.[30] Various indicators suggest that he found himself at home among ideologically driven men like Kammler. First, at the Polytechnic University of Aachen, during what was probably the beginning of his political consciousness, he joined the Student Platoon of the SA and then switched after a few months to the SS, in which he took time out from studies to participate in special training for military construction. Second, after receiving his diploma in engineering, Courte went to work for the Organisation Todt. Part of the "social structure" of the German engineering profession included a traditional association of the full mobilization of the nation's technical capacity with social progress (a sentiment by no means unique to engineers in Germany). It is therefore probably safe to assume that Courte believed Nazi construction projects and the full employment of civil engineers they helped create to be a positive contribution to German society. Third and last, another hint of ideological sympathy for the Nazi movement is contained in his curriculum vitae, in which he took pains to explain his father's suicide as the result of the "general disintegration" of the Weimar Republic.[31]

Taken together, however, Courte's biography remains ambiguous. As a student, he may have joined the SA to "fit in." Thomas Zeller, and Franz Seidler have pointed out that Organisation Todt engineers discussed the very form of bridges, the vistas offered by parkways, the architecture of rest stops, and plantings on medians as symbols of a Nazi renaissance.[32] Thus the "structure" of these organizations almost inevitably included exposure to such ideals, literally in the blueprints; nevertheless, even if Courte would have had to be extremely ignorant to miss the meanings attributed to his work in the Nazi media or among colleagues, the historian must still admit to such possibilities: perhaps Courte was oblivious. In addition, even his condemnation of the Weimar Republic may have been disingenuous, for SS racial theories linked the German "will" and racial supremacy to bloodlines. Suicide in the family could be viewed as a sign of poor genetic or spiritual mettle. Courte had an interest in explaining away his father's death in a way that would appeal to his superiors. Further, even if he held a wholehearted, genuine disgust for the Weimar democracy—a disgust widespread among technical men in the 1920s and 1930s—this would prove only a certain affinity for Nazism but not necessarily active belief.[33] In light of available evidence, one can only wager the conclusion that men like Courte interpreted aspects of their lives in ideological terms, and, judging from their service, they also willingly participated in Kammler's organization.

For one quarter of the officers of the Office Group C, however, historical evidence reveals proven activists. These men did more than just participate in the Nazi movement. Either by building organizations or by promulgating ideology, they consciously sought to propel the movement forward. Several participated in agrarian settlement clubs; others promoted overtly National Socialist organizations; others sat in jail for their political beliefs; and some suffered injuries in political street fights.

Maximillian Kiefer is a prime example. He was a *Hochbauer* trained at the Polytechnic University of Munich. He never joined the party and only joined the SS after 1935, yet his sacrifices of time on behalf of Nazi organizations betray an energetic man who held National Socialism foremost in his mind. He served as an instructor at an SS officer school at Arrolsen and set aside spare time to plan housing developments for SS officers even as he worked full time for the Luftwaffe. In the Luftwaffe, he was also involved in idealistic, "agrarian" settlement planning.[34] If the historian were to forget that part of Kiefer's job was to oversee forced labor brigades in which tens of thousands of prisoners were worked to death, his dedication might even seem humorous. During wartime, he volunteered to submit his wife (at forty-three years of age) to medical examinations so that the married couple might increase Germany's birthrate: "Our common will for progeny remains now as before unshakably strong," he announced to the SS's Race- and Settlement Main Office.[35] Kiefer and men like him assured the Office Group C a dedicated cadre of leaders. If these were technocrats, they were messianic technocrats, and National Socialist settlement policies as well as other programs were their crusades.[36]

For twelve officers there is no hard evidence of ideological engagement. They may have been dedicated participants (although not activists) or they may have been mere fellow travelers. The success of the Office Group C still depended no less upon their cooperation. More precisely, it depended upon the *absence* of any counteracting dissent. It is therefore significant that *no evidence* reveals any resistance to the leadership and organizational structures initiated by Kammler. Since, as Kammler well knew, formal bureaucratic directives alone could provide only slender ties within his organization, at the very least it is safe to say that the vast majority of officers in the Office Group C had nothing against radical SS ideology. Precisely because large bureaucratic structures are so susceptible to relatively small-scale disruption, perhaps nothing was more powerful than the lack of contravening dissent in Kammler's organization, dissent that officers could have otherwise found opportunity enough to express in petty administrative obstruction. The actions of even those officers who expressed little ideological engagement still spoke of their dynamic initiative in an organization that demanded the interchangeability of daily experience in collective action.

Here a brief example might be made of the Central Building Directorate of Auschwitz. As is hardly atypical in any large, impersonal bureaucracy, Kammler's subordinates broke and bent the rules. But they consistently did so to reinforce their organization. Preceding Werner Jothann (met with at the beginning of this essay), the Central Building Director of Auschwitz was Karl Bischoff. He defied the orders of his regional Building Inspector in order to deal directly with the Ministry of Armaments and War Production. He did so, however, to speed up the construction of Auschwitz and secure key raw materials.[37] It is important to remember that he could have chosen to act otherwise. Had he merely "followed orders" as his institutional niche formally prescribed, Bischoff could have easily chosen to let schedules fall by the wayside and might have even pointed out his fidelity to formal instructions by way of deflecting blame from his own office. In other bureaucratic niches of the WVHA occupied by individuals who did not readily identify with the SS, this is exactly what happened. For example, the chief engineer at an SS-owned factory near Auschwitz refused to deliver shipments to Bischoff's construction corps and based this obstruction on petty state and municipal regulations that prohibited such transactions—regulations over which the SS routinely ran roughshod.[38] By contrast, Bischoff ignored a steady stream of complaints from the municipality of Auschwitz in order to push ahead with the construction of the concentration camp.[39]

Bischoff himself belongs among the "participants" like Courte, not the "activists." While he had worked for the Luftwaffe, he had also served the German Workers Front as a cell leader. Ronald Smelser has noted the general ideological commitment of those who usually served in such positions.[40] Thus the structure of this organization would lead us to suspect Bischoff's commitment, but nevertheless no evidence speaks of his activism. At Auschwitz, on the other hand, he clearly did not go out of his way in the cause of Nazi fundamentalism. When queried by the local party leader (*Ortsgruppenleiter*) of the NSDAP and the *Kommandant* staff of Auschwitz whether his subcontractors were "free from foreign and Jewish capital" and if "the owners of the firms and their wives are of Aryan descent and Reich-German," Bischoff blandly replied that he did not know and the local party leader should seek such information elsewhere.[41] The engineer was not exercised by such issues, yet when this same engineer requested that the Gestapo arrest some civilian workers for shirking, he added that they were "for the most part lazy Poles" (the German is somewhat stronger: *polnische Bummelanten;* an American construction manager might use "jerk offs"). Likewise Jothann, who appealed to lofty "duty" over pipes and housings earlier, referred to foreign workers as worthless loafers who shirked "in order to live in their homeland of donothingness or alms and handouts."[42] Letters requesting Gestapo intervention to punish shirking workers were ordinarily very standardized. They were used widely not only by the SS but also by its civilian subcontractors. The most usual practice was merely to copy the same paragraph over and over while filling in new names. Those petitions to the Gestapo quoted previously differed, however; Bischoff and his subordinates added unbidden slurs to existing stock phrases, a sort of racist flourish upon otherwise fungible information.

This unusual deployment of racial stereotypes cuts to the quick of theoretical issues surrounding human agency in bureaucratic structure. Earlier, Bischoff had lifted not a finger to "prove" the Aryan character of his subcontractors. Regarding workers, on the other hand, he and Jothann were ready and willing to add extra slurs to routine Gestapo requests. Why? Wolfgang Seibel has recently advanced one answer. He stresses the ways in which bureaucratic context structures agency. Even when those structures represent established pathways of action, they are inert without the activation energy provided by initiative, motivation, and interest. On the other hand, little is likely to happen even when consensus exists that "something must be done" if institutionalized pathways are lacking, at least without organizational innovation. Yet when institutions and intentions reinforce each other—even competing institutions or otherwise contradictory intentions—the consequences are usually swift and decisive.[43]

When the regional party leader appealed to Bischoff to uphold the racial hierarchy of National Socialism among his contractors, the engineer found himself called upon to take initiative that lay far beyond the bounds of his normal activity. In the Central Building Directorate he already had plenty to do and no time to chase down what must have seemed extraneous gossip. Prying into the private lives of other businessmen was police work, work for which he and his staff had neither training nor resources. But this hardly meant that an ethos of racial supremacy did not matter to him as soon as "business" made it relevant, and there seems to have been a consensus in his office that poor performance among prisoners or civilian workers was due to their nature as Poles, Jews, Czechs or whatever "racial" category could be made to fit. Neither Bischoff nor Jothann hesitated to mobilize bureaucratic organization by appealing to this consensus. They seem to have added the racial slurs in their arrest requests to get more prompt action or harder punishment; at the very least, the added sentences would have differentiated their requests from otherwise standardized formulations.

Some may ask whether Bischoff or Jothann really believed in such stereotypes or whether they merely used them cynically to "fit in." The point seems moot. They worked within a radicalized institution (the SS) within an already radical political movement (National Socialism) that associated efficiency with racial supremacy and inefficiency with "ballast existences" and "unnecessary eaters." Engineers under Kammler gave vent to their contempt for "typically Polish" misrule in matters of technical and organizational proficiency in the East.[44] Likewise in the slang of engineers at Flossenbürg, inferior building stones were referred to as "Jews."[45] If the appeals of Bischoff and Jothann could and did spur the Gestapo to a more prompt response, this could have only served as "evidence" to confirm their belief in racial tautologies. There is no necessary dividing line between the pragmatic operation of institutional structure and fanaticism in such a case.

The ethos of the SS corps of engineers facilitated appeals for collective action between men who would have otherwise had to consider each other strangers. By appealing to common values, even out of a sense of propriety, they continually reinforced that ethos and confirmed themselves as like-minded men. These officers had internalized Nazi racial supremacy to some degree (and likely to a much greater degree—they were, after all, engineering genocide). Perhaps Bischoff was not a man to demonstrate in the streets on behalf of Nazi ideals; on the other hand, everything suggests that he had nothing against the most radical Nazi policies, and some evidence suggests he identified with them passively.

To return to the preoccupation with a sinister, disembodied "instrumental reason" with which this essay began, it is interesting to remember that many once placed great hopes for salvation in messianic technocracy. Franz Neumann expected German engineers to undermine Hitler's rule precisely because of their unique training:

> [The engineer] will later constitute . . . the most serious break in the regime. The engineer exercises the most rational vocation and he knows what beneficent powers the productive machinery can wield. Every day sees how this machinery becomes an instrument of destruction rather than of welfare.[46]

This was merely an earlier, optimistic version of current "postmodern" preoccupations with rationality. Both share a belief that technical or scientific knowledge can compel individuals to act independently of human passion or ideology; that "reason" is somehow divorced from such preoccupations. Neumann had faith that engineers would prove the most intransigent opponents of dehumanizing ideology; theorists like Bauman or Sofsky merely identify disembodied rationality as a dehumanizing force itself.[47] The human nature of professional engineering is denied in either case. But it should be no surprise that these supposedly most "rational" of professionals, the SS engineers, took culture, values, and racial supremacy seriously—even in the micromanagement of Gestapo arrests.

As in any other professions, engineers learn the rigorous techniques and methods appropriate to specialized tasks in large, bureaucratic institutions. Yet that same training also instills common principles—including expectations of social reform, even missions of national grandeur. Acculturation within institutions only reinforces this; moreover, it serves a purpose. It lends cohesion within impersonal organizations that can potentially mobilize the talents of many to accomplish what none can do alone. But only bonds of trust, a common ethos, collective identity—whatever we might call it—can animate the structures of bureaucratic hierarchy; its content inevitably shapes agency and structure simultaneously. Thus, while, István Deák is clearly right—it may well be wrong to ignore social function—we would be equally in error to discount the social function of ideals and the perpetrators' culture of consensus when considering the Holocaust.

NOTES

I am indebted to Therkel Straede, Paul Jaskot, Ronald Smelser, and Matthew Payne for their comments on this essay.

1. Jothann to HUTA AG, undated copy, from 16 or 17 December 1943, and see also Firma Müller to ZBL Auschwitz, 11 December 1943, United States Holocaust Memorial Museum, Microfilm Collection, RG-11.001M.03: Roll 29 (502:1:154). Hereafter cited by record group: roll. In parentheses are the original call numbers of the documents from the secret KGB archive of Moscow where the documents were filmed. English translations throughout this chapter are mine unless noted otheriwse.

2. Zygmunt Bauman, *Modernity and the Holocaust* (Ithaca, N.Y.: Cornell University Press, 1989), 98.

3. William Brustein, *The Logic of Evil: The Social Origins of the Nazi Party, 1925–1933* (New Haven, Conn.: Yale University Press, 1996); and Wolfgang Sofsky, *Die Ordnung des Terrors. Das Konzentrationslager* (Frankfurt am Main: S. Fischer Verlag, 1993), esp. 32–33.

4. Daniel Goldhagen, *Hitler's Willing Executioners: Ordinary Germans and the Holocaust* (New York: Alfred A. Knopf, 1996). Although Goldhagen's critics are right to point out the book's methodological and substantive flaws, there can be little doubt that Goldhagen has had such wide acclaim because he addressed the role of ideology, which many historians have neglected. An example is the tradition of Alltagsgeschichte, in which motives for action in the Third Reich are overwhelmingly ascribed to petty material interest. The most widely used text in English is likely Ian Kershaw, *Popular Opinion and Political Dissent in the Third Reich: Bavaria 1933–1945* (Oxford: Clarendon Press, 1983). Kershaw's contrast between Bavarian complaisance toward the transport of Jews as opposed to their strident opposition to euthanasia deftly shows that people's belief in what was right and wrong set limits on Nazi programs (p. 372). Nevertheless, the majority of Kershaw's emphasis falls upon the banal self-interests of "ordinary Germans," the ebb and flow of their disgruntlement, and their overwhelming indifference. The most profound conclusions of Alltagsgeschichte seem to be those that *are not there.* Having set out to investigate popular resistance and opposition, it has found almost none. Its positive assertions are more tenuous.

5. Some might object that these books have never become international best-sellers and therefore have not warranted the critical energy leveled on Goldhagen. Sofky's *Order of Terror* has been speedily translated into English by Princeton University Press, and his essay appears as the concluding commentary to *Die nationalsozialistischen Konzentrationslager,* ed.

Ulrich Herbert, Christoph Diekmann, and Karin Orth (Göttingen: Wallstein Verlag, 1998), 1141–70. This would seem to suggest that appeal to an anonymous, agentless "order of absolute power which conceals within itself the dynamic that springs all bounds of violence" (p. 1144) holds considerable appeal.

6. See Michael Thad Allen, "The Banality of Evil Reconsidered: SS Mid-Level Managers of Extermination through Work," *Central European History* 30 (1997): 253–94.

7. István Deák, "Holocaust Views: The Goldhagen Controversy in Retrospect," *Central European History* 30 (1997): 306.

8. Christopher Browning's attempt to isolate moments of individual decision is a notable exception: *Ordinary Men: Reserve Police Battalion 101 and the Final Solution in Poland* (New York : Asher Books, 1992).

9. Karin Orth, *Die Konzentrationslager SS: Sozialstrukturelle Analysen und biographische Studien* (Göttingen: Wallstein, 2000), 301.

10. Siegfried Kracauer, *Die Angestellten* (1929; reprint, Frankfurt am Main: Suhrkamp, 1971), 7; Hans Speier, *German White-Collar Workers and the Rise of Hitler* (New Haven, Conn.: Yale University Press, 1986); Michael Prinz, *Vom Mittelstand zum Volksgenossen. Die Entwicklung des sozialen Status der Angestellten von der Weimarer Republik bis zum Ende der NS-Zeit* (Munich: R. Oldenbourg Verlag, 1986). On the nature of modern management in general, see also James Beniger, *The Control Revolution: Technological and Economic Origins of the Information Society* (Cambridge: Harvard University Press, 1986); Olivier Zunz, *Making America Corporate 1870–1920* (Chicago: University of Chicago Press, 1990); and Alfred Chandler, *Scale and Scope: The Dynamics of Industrial Capitalism* (Cambridge: Harvard University Press, 1990), which takes a comparative perspective. Regarding the German case, see Jürgen Kocka, *Die Angestellten in der deutschen Geschichte 1850–1980* (Göttingen: Vandenhoeck and Ruprecht, 1981).

11. These biographies are collected from trial affidavits, testimony, and contemporary personnel files deposited in the Berlin Document Center, hereafter cited as BDC. I hope I will be allowed to include architects with Bauingenieure as one category of technical career. Especially in the Amtsgruppe C, architects functioned predominantly as project managers, not designers. The competition and coexistence of civil engineers and architects in the 1930s was especially common, even though the attempts of architects to argue for their distinction as a separate profession had never been more vocal. See Eckhard Bolenz, "Baubeamte, Baugewerksmeister, freiberufliche Architekten—Technische Berufe im Bauwesen Preußen/ Deutschland, 1799–1931" (Ph.D. diss., University of Bielefeld, 1988), 33–39, 62–69, 116–25, 280. This is reflected in Kammler's own scholarly

work, including his dissertation at the TH-Hannover, which he dedicated to managerial techniques for building sites and not to aesthetic principles of form.

12. Werner Durth, *Deutsche Architekten. Biographische Verflechtungen 1900–1970* (Braunschweig: Friedr. Vieweg und Sohn, 1986): 23–40, 65–86. Karl-Heinz Ludwig and Wolfgang König, *Technik, Ingenieure und Gesellschaft: Geschichte des Vereins Deutscher Ingenieure 1856–1981* (Düsseldorf: VDI-Verlag, 1981).

13. Karl-Heinz Ludwig, *Technik und Ingenieure im Dritten Reich* (Düsseldorf: Droste Verlag, 1974), 44–53; for Technische Hochschulen in the Nazi period, 105–8. See also Werner Durth, *Deutsche Architekten. Biographische Verflechtungen 1900–1970* (Braunschweig: Friedr. Vieweg und Sohn, 1986), esp. 17, for the importance of settlement projects among Bauingenieure and Architekten; regarding the education of a generation, 41–65. Though it deals less directly with engineering education, see also Gerd Hortleder, *Das Gesellschaftsbild des Ingenieurs: Zum politischen Verhalten der Technischen Intelligenz in Deutschland* (Frankfurt am Main: Suhrkamp, 1970): 73–74, 103–8. The best book on the institutions of engineering professionalization that I have found is Kees Gispen, *New Profession, Old Order: Engineers and German Society, 1815–1914* (Cambridge: Cambridge University Press, 1989).

14. Bolenz, "Baubeamte, Baugewerksmeister," esp. 116–25.

15. Karl-Heinz Ludwig, *Technik und Ingenieure im Dritten Reich* (Düsseldorf: Droste Verlag, 1974): 20–35, 105–9.

16. Ulrich Wengenroth, "Zwischen Aufruhr und Diktatur Die Technische Hochschule 1918–1945," in Wengenroth, ed., *Die Technische Universität München Annährungen an ihre Geschichte* (Munich: Faktum, 1993): 215–23.

17. These were Karl Eggeling, Fritz Ertl, Thilo Shneider, and Hans Schleif, respectively.

18. Heinrich Himmler reply to Oswald Pohl and Hans Kammler, 31 January 1942, BAK NS19: 2065.

19. The RKF is treated extensively in Robert Koehl, *RKFDV: German Resettlement and Population Policy 1939–45, A History of the Reich Commission for the Strengthening of Germandom* (Cambridge: Harvard University Press, 1957); Götz Aly and Susanne Heim, *Vordenker der Vernichtung. Auschwitz und die deutschen Pläne für eine neue europäische Ordnung* (Frankfurt am Main: Fischer, 1993); and Rolf-Dieter Müller, *Hitlers Ostkrieg und die deutsche Siedlungspolitik. Die Zusammenarbeit von Wehrmacht, Wirtschaft und SS* (Frankfurt am Main: Fischer, 1991).

20. This was coauthored by Dr.-Ing. Edgar Hotz and Dr.-Ing. Hans Kammler, *Grundlagen der Kostenrechnung und Organisation eines Baube-*

triebs für den Wohnungs- und Siedlungsbau in Stadt und Land (Berlin: Verlagsgesellschaft R. Müller, 1934), vii.

21. Ibid, 1.

22. Robert Gellately, "'A Monstrous Uneasiness': Citizen Participation and Persecution of the Jews in Nazi Germany," in *Lessons and Legacies: The Meaning of the Holocaust in a Changing World,* ed. Peter Hayes (Evanston, Ill.: Northwestern University Press, 1991), 180.

23. This organization was directly connected to the policies of genocide both through the construction of "stationary crematoria, incineration stations, and execution installations of various kinds" at Auschwitz-Birkenau by early 1942 and through practices of extermination through work. See Kammler, "Bericht des Amtes II: Bauten über die Arbeiten im Jahre 1941," end of December 1941, received by ZBL Auschwitz 1 August 1942. In United States Holocaust Memorial Museum, Microfilm RG-11.001M.03:19 (502–1–13).

24. Kammler, evaluation of Franz Eirenschmalz, 17 November 1944, BDC SS Personal Akten Franz Eirenschmalz.

25. Kammler evaluation, 26 April 1944, BDC SS Personal Akte Robert Riedl.

26. Ibid.

27. ZBL Auschwitz to All BL, 2 August 1944, "Geschäftsbetrieb bei den ZBL mit den angegliederten Bauleitungen und Abteilungen," RG-11.001M.03: 24 (502–1–84).

28. The structure and personnel needs of Amtsgruppe C are given in Kammler, "Bericht des Amtes" and Kammler, 23 December 1942, "Jahresbericht der Amtsgruppe C für das Jahr 1942," RG- 11.001M.03: 18 (502–1–2). Total elite officer corps was projected as seventy-eight top-ranking officers. This was a wishful estimate, as many officers occupied dual positions in Kammler's hierarchy; furthermore, due to the general shortage of skilled personnel in the Third Reich, not all Kammler's personnel slots could be filled.

29. Gunther Mai, "Die Oekonomie der Zeit. Unternehmerische Rationalisierungstrategien und industrielle Arbetisbeziehungen," *Geschichte und Gesellschaft* 23 (1997): 311–27, notes the importance of "corporate culture" in both formal managerial curricula as well as current scholarship by historians of business and organization. Corporations "care" about such issues precisely because they recognize their importance in daily function. It is past time that we stop considering corporate or modern bureaucratic organizations in the Nazi period to have been any different, as if matters of "corporate culture" did not concern German managers from 1933 to 1945.

30. BDC Personal Akte Heinrich Courte.

31. BDC RuSHA Akte Heinrich Courte.

32. Thomas Zeller, "Landschaften des Verkehrs Autobahnen im Nationalsozialismus und Hochgeschwindigkeitsstrecken für die Bahn in der Bundesrepublik," *Technikgeschichte* 64 (1997): 323–40; Ulrich Hartung, "Bauästhetik im Nationalsozialismus und die Frage der Denkmalwürdigkeit," in *Raktionäre Modernität und Völkermord Probleme des Umgangs mit der NS-Zeit in Austellungen und Gedenkstätten,* ed. Bernd Fankenbach and Franz-Josef Jelich (Essen: Klartext-Verlag, 1994): 71–84; Franz Seidler, *Fritz Todt Baumeister des Dritten Reiches* (Frankfurt am Main: Verlag Ullstein, 1988).

33. Gerd Hortleder, *Das Gesellschaftsbild des Ingenieurs,* 111.

34. Kiefer to SS Personal Hauptamt, 27 August 1935; Zeugnis from Reichsminister der Luftfahrt, 8 February 1942, BDC SS Personal Akten Max Kiefer. For settlement planning in the Luftwaffe, whose racial tenor was hardly less strident than the SS's, see Rolf-Dieter Müller, *Hitlers Ostkrieg,* 125 (Dokumentenanhang).

35. Kiefer to Amtsgruppe A des WVHA, 13 January 1944, BDC Personal Akte Max Kiefer.

36. I thank Matthew Payne for suggesting this phrase. He has studied similar enthusiasm among Soviet engineers.

37. Regarding Bischoff's altercation with his immediate superior, Gustav Rall, see the correspondence Bischoff to Kammler, Rall to Bischoff, and Kammler to Rall, July–September 1942, RG-11.001M.03: 23 (502–1–82).

39. See Michael Thad Allen, "The Puzzle of Nazi Modernism: Modern Technology and Ideological Consensus in an SS Factory at Auschwitz," *Technology and Culture* 37, no 4 (1996): pp. 550–57.

39. On the ongoing feud between the municipality of Auschwitz and the SS building authority at the concentration camp, see Polenz, 3 December 1942, "Besprechung am 3.12.42 in Kattowitz," RG-11.001M.03: 23 (502–1–78); Amtskommissar Butz der Stadt Auschwitz to ZBL Auschwitz, 7 July 1942, RG-11.001M.03: 23 (502–1–72); and same to ZBL Auschwitz, 13 July 1942, with Bischoff's reply, 13 July 1942, RG-11.001M.03: 23 (502–1–76).

40. BDC Personalakte Karl Bischoff. He was Zellenleiter from 1936 to 1938 in Munich. Ronald Smelser, *Robert Ley, Hitler's Labor Front Leader* (New York: Berg, 1988), 155, and on DAF ideology of organization, 98–179 in general.

41. Ortsgruppenleiter der NSDAP bei Kommandantur Auschwitz to Bischoff, 24 April 1942 and reply of 29 April 1942, USHMM RG-11.001M.03: 25 (502:1:99).

42. First quote: Karl Bischoff to HUTA AG, 18 March 1943, "Verhaengung von Strafen ueber Zivilarbeiter," RG-11.001M.03:22 (502:1:58).

Second quote: Werner Jothann to Gestapo Auschwitz, 2 August 1944, "Wiederbeibringung von 2 auslaendischen Arbeitern," USHMM RG-11.001M.03: 22 (502:1:70).

43. Wolfgang Seibel, "Staatsstruktur und Massenmord. Was kann eine historisch-vergleichende Institutionenanalyse zur Erforschung des Holocaust beitragen?" *Geschichte und Gesellschaft* 24(1998): 539–69.

44. Hotz and Kammler, *Grundlagen der Kostenrechnung,* 1; Kammler, "Zur Bewertung von Geländeerschliessungen," 37. See the anonymous report, 22 May 43, "Besprechung mit dem Amtsgruppenchef C. Besuch am 21.5.43," United States Holocaust Memorial Museum, Microfilm RG-11.001M.03:20 (502–1–25).

45. Amt II to Neubauleitung Flossenbürg, 10 August 1940, BAK NS4/59. This slur was apparently common in the building trades. Joachim Wolschke-Bulmahn, "Biodynamischer Gartenbau, Landschaftsarchitektur und Nationalsozialismus," *Das Gartenamt* 10 (1994): 640.

46. Franz Neumann, *Behemoth: The Structure and Politics of National Socialism 1933–1944* (New York: Harper and Row, 944), 472.

47. For recent laments on the "authoritarian" nature of rationality, science, and technological knowledge (in which the Holocaust is often a central trope), see the following essays in Andrew Ross, ed., *Science Wars* (Durham: Duke University Press, 1996): Hillary Rose, "My Enemy's Enemy Is—Only Perhaps—My Friend," 89, 98; Sarah Franklin, "Making Transparencies: Seeing through the Science Wars," 156; and esp. Richard Lewontin, "A la recherche du temps perdu: A Review Essay," 299. Compare Michael Thad Allen, "Modernity, the Holocaust, and Machines without History," in *Technologies of Power,* ed. Gabrielle Hecht and Michael Thad Allen (Cambridge: MIT Press, 2001).

Hannes Heer

How Amorality Became Normality
The Wehrmacht and the Holocaust

BACKED BY OVERWHELMING EVIDENCE, HISTORICAL RESEARCH HAS
proved that the Wehrmacht participated in and shared responsibility
for the Nazi genocide. It has not yet been able to answer the question
of how millions of "completely normal German men" could become
perpetrators, helpers, and witnesses. No history of Wehrmacht mentality has yet been written, be it of the high command or the generals,
the officer corps or the troops. What we have are the first, and certainly
quite remarkable, endeavors. For example, in his book *Die Wehrmacht
im NS Staat* (*The Wehrmacht in the Nazi State*), Manfred Messerschmidt has demonstrated how from 1933 onward, the military leadership systematically shaped the Wehrmacht as an institution into the
"second column" of the Nazi system, forming it into a compliant tool
of its extermination policy. Taking a view from the bottom end, based
on three divisions stationed on the eastern front, Omer Bartov has examined the reality of this extermination policy in penetrating detail.[1]
By analyzing the calculated interplay of military situation and propaganda, his study manages to overcome the static focus restricted
to ideological issues proposed by Messerschmidt and his school. There
remain, however, several points for objection. By ascribing the war after 1942 to the condition of an overall "de-modernization," he over-
looks the numerous wars that took place within the one eastern war.
By attributing the "barbarization" of the troops to their desperate situation, he fails to mention the deliberately planned and implemented
erosion of morality during their advance, and while he ascribes the
"distortion of reality" to indoctrination, he underestimates the soldiers' own capacity for moral assessment rooted in the prewar period
and the prevailing military situation.

I therefore propose an approach that is oriented toward three categories:

1. Disposition taken as the entirety of the formative influences and interpretational patterns previously internalized by the soldiers.
2. Situation viewed as the sum of the various determinants resulting from military phase, operational area, issued orders, and function.
3. Legitimization defined as the interpretation of events based on personal experience (and in most cases backed up by propaganda), which, contrary to all logic, persistently made the war appear just and necessary.

It is my contention that during the first phase of the war, when the army was on the advance and scoring victories, the political and military leadership succeeded inculcating amorality as a normal condition. This basic mind-set, in which the individual soldier was immersed like a protective shield, was reinforced in the course of the war by being supplemented with further attitudes (such as those analyzed by Omer Bartov).

To quote from the diary of Private Werner Bergholz:

The war with Russia. 31/6/41. When . . . we passed through Rovno all the shops were raided and everybody took whatever he could lay his hands on. . . . 2/7. At night two of our sentries were shot. A hundred men were put up against the wall for this. It must have been Jews.

And the diary of Senior Private Richter:

1/7/1941. We shot 60 prisoners at headquarters. . . . 7/7. Matula and I rummaged around a bit in our quarter. We acquired some booty: 25 eggs and a sack of sugar. . . . 19/7. Uto captured a guerrilla in the woods and hanged him.

From the diary of Captain Reich:

2/7/1941. Jews shot. 3/7. We leave. 22 Russian soldiers, some of them wounded, shot in a peasant farmyard. Fruitful valley. Windmills. . . . 6/7. Rest at a Ukrainian cottage. Air attack . . . 7/7. Bombers. 9/7. Commissar executed by machinegun squad. 10/7. Departure north by train. . . . 13/7. German airman killed; 50 Jews shot.[2]

Take the following entry by Private Heinz Bellig:

25/7. Gave "coup de grace" to wounded Russians in the roadside ditch, prisoners are not to be taken. 2/8. Partisans have destroyed the railway line; all inhabitants were lined up against the wall, their fate is certain.[3]

The diary of Sergeant Friedrich Fiedler states:

7/8/1941. We march from Shitomir to Korostichev and lie down there in the school where 72 shot Jews lie buried in the garden . . . 17/8. Semionovka: There seem to be no Jews here or only a few . . . 22/9. The sugar factory in Grigorovka serves as a prisoner camp. At night about 900 Russian deserters arrived, guarded by 1 sergeant and 6 men, who were driven across the Dnieper by starvation . . . About 35 pol[itical] commissars and functionaries are sorted out from the prisoners and physically liquidated . . . 17/10. In Mirogrod: in the evening we get commissary vodka which *Kamerad* Habich has brought with him, and he tells the following story he experienced on his return from Lubny. With the headline "modem resettlement" . . . 1,600 Jewish men, women and children are divided into groups of sixty and, guards using clubs, are herded into a sand pit. Clothes, furs and jewelry are collected in sacks, and with backs bared the Jews are made to lie down in rows, two SS men shoot each one in the head with a machine gun. The next victims have to lie on top of the corpses and are physically exterminated in the same way. When the first shots are fired everyone starts screaming in fear and tries to get away, but the guards' clubs are faster and no one escapes. By the afternoon at around 3 o'clock the entire Jewish population of Lubny has been resettled in heaven. For my comrades this heroic act "calls for a drink," merry songs are struck up. *Kamerad J.* pitches in with the freedom song "The Jews are traveling along and away, traveling over the Red Sea, the waves crash down, the world is left in peace," and I quietly go to bed, teased by some for my sloppy sentimentality.[4]

SHOCK AND RENORMALIZATION

If, as Clausewitz claims, war is "an act of violence" which persists "ruthlessly and without regard to loss of blood" until the aim of "forcing the enemy to fulfill our will" has been achieved,[5] then the transition from civil life into this aggregate condition represents for all participants a reversal of the hitherto prevailing system of values and codes of behavior, which surely must cause at least a temporary loss of orientation, confusion, and fear. So what then would be the reaction of soldiers on entering a war which, as indeed was the case in the "war of *Weltanschauung*" and the "war of extermination" between 1941 and 1944, not only revoked the rules of civil society but repudiated even the hitherto accepted codex of war?

Thus the tale told by the letters written by the majority of soldiers who invaded the Soviet Union in summer 1941 is one of shock. There is talk of experience having turned them "into a different person," of a process of "inner change" having occurred, of being forced to "completely readjust" and also of having to "throw overboard several principles held in the past."[6] A minority of the men experienced this "adjustment" as a harrowing process of "split consciousness," which ended either in their resigned withdrawal into a world of subjective privacy—"One loses interest in anything that extends beyond one's own little self"—or in a defiant emigration into "the silent nobility of solitude"; or alternately, as in the case of Sergeant Fiedler, this process leads to an indulgence in the luxury of "sloppy sentimentality."[7] But most soldiers managed to adapt effortlessly to the shock: they became "hard," "indifferent," and "heartless," as the previously quoted diary entries by the soldiers Bergholz, Richter, Reich, and Belling demonstrate.[8] One letter from the front describes this "adjustment" and the "inner change" in the following terms: "It's like growing a shell around you that's almost impenetrable. But what happens inside this shell? You become part of a mass, a component of a relentless whole which sucks you up and squeezes you into a mold. You become gross and insensible. You cease to be yourself."[9] What this sentence describes is fraught with consequences. If someone ceases to be himself, he severs his own history and relinquishes his moral principles; he ceases to see with his own eyes and is no longer capable of absorbing fresh experiences into his own identity. "I have forgotten myself" is how someone else describes this process in another letter.[10] And a third soldier, writing home to his wife, says, "One has to be ruthless and unmerciful. Don't you have the impression that it's not me but a different person who is speaking to you?"[11] The results of such self-denial are manipulability and a dependence upon the collective and its standpoints. These were provided in the form of basic orders and daily propaganda.

Hitler had planned the war against the Soviet Union, long in advance, as a campaign beyond the norms of international law. In order to camouflage this scenario, the enemy itself was accused of breaking international law; Stalin was alleged to have made preparations for an attack which the German Reich had just managed to forestall, and, due to its national character and political mentality, the Soviet military leadership had put itself beyond all military conventions. Since "in the fight against Bolshevism . . . it is unlikely that the enemy's behavior will follow the principles of humanity or international law," the German command, so the argument ran, had no choice but to react with the same methods so as "to avoid being put at a disadvantage."[12] Repeatedly invoking the stereotypically bigoted foe image of "perfidiousness, hatred, cruelty," the primary orders drawn up prior to the invasion accordingly instructed that the political commissars be immediately "eliminated," that Soviet prisoners of war be treated as "criminals," that the civilian population generally be regarded as "partisan suspects," and, therefore, that the instructions for and execution of coercive measures be put under the direct responsibility of the combat troops and not of the cumbersome military courts.[13]

Both assertions—that this was a "defensive war" and that the enemy was "brutish"—were adopted by the troops and assimilated into their own argumentation. The fact that neither Hitler's basic desire for peace nor his proclaimed reluctance at having to wage war on two fronts was seriously doubted was the outcome of his skillful political maneuvers in the prewar years, which represented him as "chancellor of peace" assailed by a world of enemies.[14] In the eyes of the ordinary soldier, still further proof that the Russians had been preparing an invasion was provided by the enemy's military conduct, in other words, by its determined and brutal resistance. "Although I have always been fairly skeptical and critical about pronouncements made by the government, I must now unreservedly state the truth about statements concerning the combat zone. While on our side you wouldn't find a single wire barrier, antitank obstacle or minor field fortification, you saw masses of them on Russian territory."[15] Or: "The German people has a gigantic obligation toward our führer, because if these brutes, who are our enemies, had got to Germany this would have produced the greatest slaughter the world had ever witnessed."[16]

In *Mein Kampf,* Hitler had analyzed the crucial role played by English atrocity propaganda in deciding the outcome of the First

World War. By demonizing the Germans in advance as "Huns," it allowed English soldiers to view anything done by the Germans as proof of the notorious "brutality of the barbarian foe."[17] Correspondingly, the Supreme Command (OKW/OKH) inundated the German army with a veritable flood of pamphlets describing the "brutish enemy" and the "Russian [subhuman] *Untermensch*." This too was accepted by the soldiers because it evidently coincided with their own experience of an alien and threatening world. "The conditions here are antediluvian. Our propaganda certainly didn't overdo it, maybe even understated things."[18] Or: "The crudeness repeatedly shown by the Russian can only be explained by their indoctrination. These are people who would need a long and thorough education to ever become human beings."[19] Or: "Prisoners often come toward us, alone or in crowds, apathetic, bestial and tattered but often perfidious too."[20] Or: "Recently things have been totally crazy. You are not fighting against men, but against animals. . . . All the prisoners I encounter are killed, there's no two ways about it. This has been our motto in the infantry for some time now."[21]

These quotations are evidence of a recovery from the shock and of an acceptance of the crime. For most men, this renormalization offered relief, since it enabled them to attune to the demands of war without being plagued by worry and self-reproach.

THE IMPLANTATION OF THE HOLOCAUST INTO THE WAR: THE
MILITARIZATION OF THE "JEWISH QUESTION"

We have not yet spoken about the Jews and their fate at the hands of the Wehrmacht. In his brilliant study *The Germans and the Final Solution*, David Bankier has shown how, from 1941 onward, at a time when the deportation trains were being filled and dispatched to the extermination camps, the majority of Germans in the *Heimat* (at home) escaped into a mental warp of not-seeing and not-wanting-to-see.[22] Such evasion was denied to soldiers on the eastern front. They drove Jews into ghettos, cordoned off the mass graves where Jews were shot by the SD and the police, and executed hundreds of thousands of them of their own volition. What made possible this transition from anti-Semitic resentment to actual violence against Jews, from hating to murdering the Jews?

It began with the definition of the enemy written into the "Guidelines for the Conduct of the Army in Russia" issued on May 19, 1941, which instructed each soldier that, besides "Bolshevist agitators, guerrillas, saboteurs," "the Jews" are also be viewed and treated as the enemy.[23] After the Wehrmacht crossed the border on June 22, the Jews were held responsible for every act of sabotage and for every enemy action. When it came to the retaliatory shooting of hostages, the troops were under orders to execute Jews if the culprits could not be found.[24] As "agents of the Bolshevist system," they were also given the blame for murders of ethnic Germans and political detainees, particularly in the Ukraine and in the Baltic region, which were committed by the retreating NKVD (Soviet secret service). An extract from an army chaplain's letter from the front to his wife: "It wasn't long before they got their comeuppance. The Jews who were the wire-pullers behind the whole thing were killed where they were found. Of course, as usual the worst ones were not caught, they all escaped to safety in Russia. Whatever remained was sometimes just done away with using a shovel. . . . Putting someone up against a wall, everyone could agree on that, but not just killing in a disorderly way."[25]

It was only a small step from the "Jew as a wire-puller" to the "Jew as partisan." This job was undertaken by the divisional situation reports, which became the instrument for a systematic campaign. The following passages have been selected from reports during the first weeks and months: "It is clear that everywhere where Jews live, 'mopping up the area' runs into difficulties because the Jews support the creation of partisan groups and disruption of the area by scattered Russian soldiers. Due to this finding, the evacuation of all male Jews from all villages north of Bialoviza has been ordered, effective immediately."[26] Or: "In all these measures it is finally most important to remove the influence of the Jews. . . . These elements must be disposed of with the most radical means, because . . . they are exactly those who maintain connections to the Red Army and the resistance groups." In the margin, the regiment commander had noted, "The solution to the Jewish question must take more radical forms."[27] Or: "The Jewish population is Bolshevik and capable of any attitude hostile to Germany. In terms of how they are treated, there need be no guidelines." And: "In case after case, it is clear these are the sole support the partisans find in order to survive both now and through the winter. Their annihilation is therefore to be carried out in whatever manner."[28] By autumn 1941, the prevailing watchword all along the front was: "The Jews are without exception identical with the concept of partisan."[29]

The stigmatization of the Jew as a partisan and the wire-puller of resistance signaled the transfiguration of the Jews as political opponents into the declared military enemy. Officially, Himmler's *Einsatzgruppen* were responsible for political enemies, but the military opponent in fact fell in the domain of the Wehrmacht. This had consequences that went far beyond the brotherhood in arms shared by the SD and the army; this ever changing and extended notion of the enemy called for a new definition of the soldier's duties. In his notorious order of October 10, 1941 (which Hitler instructed be distributed all along the eastern front, leading to a series of similar orders from Field Marshals Manstein and Hoth), the commander of the Sixth Army, General Field Marshal von Reichenau, phrased this new status in terse language: "The soldier in the East is not only a fighter by the rules of war, but also the carrier of an inexorable *völkisch* idea and the avenger of all bestialities inflicted on the Germans or related races."[30] It was no longer merely about the "Jewish question" or "the Jews." Each individual Jew in the occupied territories was identified as the enemy and had to be eradicated. It was first Hitler in his annual speech to his old comrades (*alte Kampfgefährten*) in Munich on November 8 and then, one week later, Goebbels who gave final shape to this position. In an article published through his mouthpiece, the magazine *Das Reich,* on November 16, 1941, and which was discussed along the entire eastern front, Goebbels used illustrations from the realm of pathology to describe the danger represented by each individual, however amiable-seeming, Jew, and in the style of a hygienic prevention campaign, he announced their impending eradication. The article, which bore the headline, "It's the Jew's Fault," concluded with ten key points. They stated: "The Jews are our ruin. They plotted and then brought about this war. . . . This plan must be thwarted." And then: "Every German soldier who falls in this war must be answered for by the Jews. They have him on their conscience and so they will also be made to pay for it."[31] This was tantamount to enjoining each soldier to identify the murder of Jews with military duty. The timing of this radicalization was anything but accidental. The beacon which was lit in the gorge of Babi Yar on September 29 and 30, 1941, marked the first wave of ghetto massacres. At the same time, the Wehrmacht started its Operation Taifun, an assault on

Moscow, as the final attempt to mount a decisive *Blitzsieg* in the hope
of winning the war.

An argument still prevalent among German historians is that the
orders issued by Reichenau and the other generals were pure propaganda, that no one actually believed them.[32] Nonetheless, these orders were carried out: whether out of racist delusion or because it was
believed that this was the only means of achieving victory; whether in
revenge for dead comrades or in anger that, contrary to all promises,
fighting was still going on in Russia and no end of the war was in
sight. Stephen Fritz's book *Frontsoldaten: The German Soldier in
World War II* provides a wealth of evidence for such motives.[33]

Things didn't stop at the stigmatization of the Jews as militarily
threatening "partisans." When the murder operations in the ghettos
got underway (in most cases assisted by the Wehrmacht), these massacres were justified with the argument that the ghetto Jews were
"*unnütze Esser*," worthless mouths to feed. Hence they would only
place a burden on the already overstretched supplies of the troops.
The selections carried out at the ghetto gates were based on the logic
of "fit for work, not fit for work." Jews who were determined to be
not able to work placed strain on the German war campaign, so they
were consigned to the bullets or the gas vans. The recollections of a
former Wehrmacht soldier reveal that the blurring of moral categories
had been successful and military operations could no longer be distinguished from genocidal actions: "Even those incidents which in
fact clearly indicated the genocidal nature of this 'war' were interpreted by me (and probably by most soldiers at the front) as part of the
general, if not 'normal' process of war, and as military operations."[34]

This confusion which, within a short time, caused most soldiers
to lose all sense of moral orientation, was not only a result of the war
situation and individual or collective interpretation. It had already
started in the prewar period and belonged to most soldiers' basic
frame of mind. Let me describe it in a brief digression with one example—violence and the willingness to violence—that might explain what I define as "disposition."

The core of Hitler's program—as can be read in *Mein Kampf*—
was focused on war. Given that the laws of nature dictated the course
of history according to the right of the strongest and eternal selection
of the best, war then offered the "highest expression of life" for any
race and the nation's only chance of survival. Due to a historical an-

tagonism, the enemy had long been identified: the Jews, as the "cancerous ulcer" of history, and Bolshevism, as the most extreme embodiment of this evil. The only conceivable aim of some future call to arms would be the annihilation of these "universal contaminators" and the forcible annexation of lebensraum in the East. For the purposes of such a war, any strictures anchored in international agreements or prevailing moral consensus would no longer be binding. The future war, so Hitler argued, is a "just war," so consequently it would be permissible to wage it with all means, even "the most inhumane."[35]

National Socialism used the period between 1933 and 1939 to entrench war as an overriding social project. German society physically experienced this process as a gigantic mobilization aimed at establishing the military spirit as an essential virtue, thus creating a shift from civilian society to military community. This was brought about by reversing various important advances that had been made toward a modem civic culture. Their own mortal fear had made it easier for citizens to accept the state's monopoly of violence and to relinquish the ideals of heroic resistance in favor of the middle-class "spirit of cowardice." Instead of this, National Socialism preached "the end of all fear and the return to bravery and death."[36] This risk was rewarded with the promise of total power over all enemies of National Socialism. As an explosive means of forging collective identity, violence played an important role in the period, which saw the constitution of nation-states in Europe, and had thereafter been regimented within rituals and symbols into a "culture of violence."[37]

It was now removed from these shackles and established as an intoxicating "cult of violence."[38] This cult was founded on the ruins of pity and empathy. The curricula practiced in the *Napola* (national political education schools) and the educational targets of the quasi-medieval *Ordensburgen* (SS order castles), the war games drilled by the *Hitlerjugend* (Hitler Youth), and the endurance training performed in the elite SS *Junkerschulen* (cadet schools) all reveal the face of this new category of barbarian warrior. There was no opposition to be feared from any socially accepted sense of justice when National Socialism finally denied the authority of law that was founded in natural law or religious tradition and in the place of this authority interpreted laws or rights as direct (and thus permanently changing) concepts derived from the concepts of "movement" and "racial community." This destruction of human rights coupled with the conscious awareness of these rights corresponded to the substitution of the "culture of guilt"—based on personal responsibility—with the "culture of shame," which was bound by collective values and watched over by the collective. These observations are not the result of thorough research but indicate where such research could begin.

THE MORALIZATION OF CRIME

We were . . . indeed . . . for a time the masters of the world and everything was done our way . . . we always had right of way, we always had priority . . . everything had to make way for us, and if a town was in the way, a building was in the way, or a forest, then these things had to get out of our way too.[39]

This self-glorifying image of a German Wehrmacht hurtling forward, evoked by a veteran soldier who was still enrapt with fascination years after the war, collapsed in December 1941 on the outskirts of Moscow. In the following weeks, the mightiest military power the world had ever seen appeared simply to dissolve in a series of crumbling fronts, mass-retreating armies, and panic-stricken commanders. The best soldiers in the world, who in a three-pronged attack, battles of encirclement, and victory had managed to conquer half of Europe, were now forced to erect entrenchments, take evasive action, dig in, and flee. Soldiers' letters paint a plain picture of the situation. But even in the chaos of the retreat there emerged a new myth. To have survived against such pitiless natural conditions and against an enemy that ruthlessly sacrificed masses of its own men revealed qualities of "sacrifice" and "quiet heroism."[40] What this suggested in outline—the transformation of the victoriously advancing invader into an imperturbable and enduring defender—was rounded off into a finished and conclusive picture by the Nazi leaders. On January 30, 1942, Hitler presented a first balance of the previous weeks in a speech in the Berlin *Sportpalast:* "Any weakling can handle victories. But only the mighty can endure the blows of fortune! Providence will give the ultimate and highest prize only to those who are capable of dealing with the blows of fortune."[41] And Goebbels outspokenly characterized the winter crisis as a "great test of character." Just as the soldier on the eastern front had shown a "heart of bronze" and "true

virility," the whole nation had also undergone a "great transformation"; instead of "bringing [the war] to an end as soon as possible" and
at whatever cost, everyone "wants it to be continued until full victory
is secured."[42]

Sentences such as these, long before Stalingrad, point to a new
type of hero. The soldier on the eastern front now displayed a new
character trait hitherto unknown in the intoxication and arrogance of
blitzkrieg warfare: the silent and reliable performance of duty. "At
first we acted out of conviction, later we acted out of duty": this
wartime caesura was described thus by two former soldiers, completely independently of one another, in a film interview in 1995.[43]
The notion of duty, which consciously evoked the frontline fighter
myth of the First World War, aroused in contemporaries a whole
range of connotations that stretched back to a time long before National Socialism and had the power to mobilize greater loyalty than
party political programs and propaganda could muster. One veteran
Wehrmacht soldier characterized it with the idea of "soldierliness"
(*das soldatische*) and described his fascination thus:

> Well, for me, being a soldierly person means encountering another
> man with a clean and decent attitude, it means representing view-
> points which conform to universal moral laws. But soldierliness also
> means showing . . . courage . . . not in the sense that you are brave
> if you kill your enemy before he kills you, but as a strong inner con-
> viction toward problems, you encounter in private and personal
> life. . . . I was . . . more inclined to say, alright, it's not to your taste
> what they are expecting of you, . . . but if from the point of view of
> the state and our philosophy this is required, well for God's sake,
> you'll have to do your duty, you must summon up the necessary un-
> derstanding to say that this just has to be done. Fulfilling your duty
> is very close to the spirit of sacrifice. . . . There were things where
> you simply accepted that you have to participate, because the whole
> thing, the collective purpose, just requires you to do it.[44]

A moral codex and the collective purpose, performance of one's
duty and the readiness to make sacrifices, this constituted the cate-
chism German soldiers carried in their kit bags from 1942 onward.
Again and again, this is referred to by the "decent" men, those who
showed insight and expressed remorse after the war. We have Klaus
von Bismarck (the former president of the Federal Republic of Germany's Goethe Institute and in wartime a regimental aide), who be-

neath the snow next to the runway discovers the piled-up corpses of executed prisoners of war. When the general field marshal responds to his outraged report with a gesture of disapproval, he is forced to decide whether he should accept the crime or tender his resignation. He took, as he sees it, a third course: "I couldn't just abandon my regiment; to desert my men would have meant assuming guilt. So I decided . . . to try and keep my entrusted regiment's conscience as blameless as possible."[45] Peter Bamm, a captain in the medical corps in the southern sector of the eastern front, behaved similarly. In his postwar bestseller called *The Invisible Flag,* he reports how, when confronted with the monstrous crimes against Ukrainian Jews, for example, he and his comrades opted against resistance in favor of the daily self-sacrificing performance of duty in the hospital: "By helping those in suffering, countless acts of heroism have been carried out. Thousands have given their lives in doing this."[46] These justifications were all honorable. The men who chose to look after their regiment, fulfill their duty as doctors, follow the military oath, or safeguard the people and the fatherland also seemed to be choosing moral principles. The fatal mistake, though, was that these principles were derivative, secondary virtues. As Hannah Arendt pointed out, "because they had lost all sense of a higher moral values," their decency was morally worthless.[47]

But even the most infamous murderers, who admitted nothing and witnessed nothing, pleaded that they had only been doing their duty. In the evidence he gave in the Jerusalem trial, Eichmann said "he was doing his duty . . . he didn't just obey orders, he also abided by the law." In other words, his behavior followed the categorical imperative outlined in Kant's "idea of duty."[48] That might sound cynical, but he did it in all honesty; besides, he was also backed by a certain philosophical tradition. Kant's attempt to stress the unconditionality of the ethical dictate by formulating the categorical imperative lured him toward empty formalism. Instead of representing the awareness of a particular moral issue or principle, conscience for him represented "that consciousness which bears duty unto itself." Hegel's attempt to fill this gap by embracing family, society, and state in his definition of "true conscience" was countermanded by Nietzsche. He severed the link between conscience and universal and natural laws, redefining it in terms of its correspondence to life with all life's creative and destructive energies. Nietzsche postulated a notion of the human subject who is "'fortified by wars and victories, for whom conquest, adventure, danger, pain have even become a need.' Man thus conceived is 'beyond good and evil' in moral terms."[49]

This is the person we encounter in millions under National Socialism, be it in the extermination camps, beside the dug-out mass graves behind the front, in the prisoner-of-war camps, in the "partisan operations," or on death marches. These were men with a "trans-moral conscience," as Paul Tillich termed it. In their minds, misdeeds figure as good deeds, and criminal behavior becomes the enactment of the moral code.[50] This is possible only under certain conditions: by conquering one's "weaker self " in favor of demands externally dictated "by the state or philosophy *[Weltanschauung]*" or by setting aside the wishes formed in one's "private and personal life" in favor of "the greater entity," in other words, of the Wehrmacht, Germany, or simply the führer.

The former soldiers Bismarck and Bamm described how they were faced with the temptation to put up resistance against barbarity, to call a halt or to disobey it. Instead they chose duty. Hannah Arendt's dictum that in the Third Reich "evil [had] lost the attribute which makes it recognizable for most people—it no longer appeared to them as a temptation" relates to this choice. People were only brought into temptation by goodness, by moral probity. "But," so she continues, "they had, God knows, learned to control their inclinations and to resist temptation."[51] Which is why, in the belief they were acting morally, the soldiers of the German Wehrmacht murdered so well and in such numbers, and why, even up to the present, they neither wish nor are able to remember any crime.

NOTES

1. Manfred Messerschmidt, *Die Wehrmacht im NSStaat. Zeit der Indoktrination* (Hamburg, 1969); Omer Bartov, *The Eastern Front, 1941–1945, German Troops and the Barbarisation of Warfare* (Houndmills, 1985).

2. Bergholz, Richter, and Reich diary entries quoted from *True to Type: A Selection of Letters and Diaries of German Soldiers and Civilians, Collected on the Soviet-German Front* (London, 1945), pp. 11, 19, 22, 23.

3. From the collection of the author. English translations throughout the chapter are mine unless noted otherwise.

4. Ibid.

5. Carl von Clausewitz, *Vom Kriege* (Berlin, 1915), pp. 3ff.

6. Joachim Dollwet, *Menschen im Krieg, Bejahung und Widerstand? Eindrucke und Auszüge aus der Sammlung von Feldpostbriefen des Zweiten Weltkrieges im Landeshauptarchiv Koblenz,* in *Jahrbuch für westdeutsche Landesgeschichte,* vol. 13 (Koblenz, 1987), p. 299 (letter of 29 July 1941).

7. Lothar Steinbach, *Ein Volk, ein Reich, ein Glaube? Ehemalige Nationalsozialisten und Zeitzeugen berichten über ihr Leben im Dritten Reich* (Berlin, 1983), pp. 204–205; Edwin Grützer's notes, in Rolf-Dieter Müller, ed., *Die deutsche Wirtschaftspolitik in den besetzten sowjetischen Gebieten 1941–1943. Der Abschlussbericht des Wirtschaftsstabes Ost und Aufzeichnungen eines Angehörigen des Wirtschaftskommandos Kiew* (Boppard am Rhein, 1991), p. 615 (entry of 13 November 1941); Siegbert Stehmann, *Die Bitternis verschweigen wir. Feldpostbriefe 1940–1945* (Hanover, 1992), p. 219 (letter of 29 July 1942), p. 154 (letter of 26 December 1941).

8. Dollwet, *Menschen im Krieg,* p. 299 (letter of 26 June 1941) and p. 299 (letter of 19 July 1941).

9. Birke Mersmann, *"Was bleibt vom Heldentum?" Weiterleben nach dem Krieg* (Berlin, 1995), p. 34 (father's letter in spring 1942).

10. Stehmann, *Bitternis,* 152 (letter of 27 December 1941).

11. Letter of 28 June 1941 in Karl Fuchs, *Sieg Heil! War Letters of Tank Gunner Karl Fuchs, 1937–1941,* ed. and trans. Horst Fuchs Richardson (Hamden, Conn., 1987), p. 116.

12. "Richtlinien für die Behandlung politischer Kommissare" ("Guidelines for the Treatment of Political Commissars"; 6 June 1941), cited in Gerd R. Ueberschär and Wolfram Wette, *Der Deutsche Überfall auf die Sowjetunion, "Unternehmen Barbarossa" 1941* (Frankfurt am Main, 1991), p. 259.

13. Ibid., p. 260; *Anordnungen über die Behandlung sowjetischer Kriegsgefangener in allen Kriegsgefangenenlagern* (Instructions for the treatment of Soviet POWs in all POW camps; 8 September 1941), cited in Gerd R. Ueberschär and Wolfram Wette, *Der Deutsche Überfall auf die Sowjetunion, "Unternehmen Barbarossa" 1941* (Frankfurt am Main, 1991), p. 297; *Erlass über die Ausübung der Kriegsgerichtsbarkeit im Gebiet "Barbarossa" und über besondere Massnahmen der Truppe* (Law concerning the practice of military law in the "Barbarossa" area and about special army operations; 13 May 1941), cited in Gerd R. Ueberschär and Wolfram Wette, *Der Deutsche Überfall auf die Sowjetunion, "Unternehmen Barbarossa" 1941* (Frankfurt am Main, 1991), p. 252.

14. Wolfram Wette, *Ideologien, Propaganda und Innenpolitik als Voraussetzung der Kriegspolitik des Dritten Reiches,* in *Das Deutsche Reich im Zweiten Weltkrieg,* vol. 1 (Stuttgart, 1979), p. 128ff.

15. Dollwet, *Menschen im Krieg,* p. 298 (letter of 26 June 1941).

16. Ortwin Buchbender and Reinhold Sterz, eds., *Das andere Gesicht des Krieges. Deutsche Feldpostbriefe 1939–1945* (Munich, 1983), p. 74 (10 July 1941).

17. Adolf Hitler, *Mein Kampf* (Munich, 1941), p. 199.

18. Buchbender and Sterz, *Gesicht*, p. 79 (letter of 22 August 1941).

19. Ibid., p. 76 (letter of 1 August 1941).

20. Ibid., p. 84 (letter of 15 October 1941).

21. Rolf Demeter, letter to Ursula Bischof of 28 July 1941, Staatsarchiv Bremen, 7, lOGG383.

22. David Bankier, *Die öffentliche Meinung im HitlerStaat. Die "Endlösung" und die Deutschen. Eine Berichtigung* (Berlin, 1995), pp. 177ff.

23. "Richtlinien für das Verhalten der Truppe in Russland," cited in Gerd R. Ueberschär and Wolfram Wette, *Der Deutsche Überfall auf die Sowjetunion, "Unternehmen Barbarossa" 1941* (Frankfurt am Main, 1991), p. 258.

24. OKH (GenStdH/H Wes.Abt. Abw.) Az.Abw., III. Nr. 2111/41 of 12 July 1941, BAMA RH 27–7/156; AOK 17, Gruppe Ic/AO Br. B. Nr. 2784/41 of 30 July 1941, BAMA, Alliierte Prozesse 9 NOKW 1693; similarly, the command given by AOK 6 on 19 July 1941, 62.ID KTB Ic/Eintragung (entry) of 21 July 1941, BAMA RH 2662/40; Berück Süd Abt.,VII/Nr. 103/41 of 16 August 1941, BAMA RH 22/6; AOK 2 Ic/AO Nr. 1388/41 of 17 July 1941 BAMA RH 202/1090.

25. Steinbach, *Ein Volk*, p. 221.

26. 221. Sich. Div., KTB Nr. 2, Eintrag (entry), 17 August 1941, BAMA, RH 262210, p. 87.

27. Inf. Rgt. 350, U. Batt, An das Regiment, 18 August 1941, BAMA, RH 262212l, pp. 294ff.

28. Der Kommandant in Weissruthenien (Belorussia) des Wehrmachtbefehlshabers Ostland/Abt. Ia, Lagebericht (field report), 10 September 1941, BSA Minsk, 65111, p. 25; Der Kommandant in Weissruthenien/ Abt. Ia, Befehl (order) NT. 24 of 24 November 1941, BSA Minsk 3781698, p. 32; Der Kommandant in Weissruthenien/Abt. Ia (Tagesbefehl), 16 October 1941, BSA Minsk 3781698, pp. 12–13.

29. Cited in Hannes Heer, "Killing Fields," in *Vernichtungskrieg. Verbrechen der Wehnnacht 1941 bis 1944,* ed. Hannes Heer and Klaus Naumann (Hamburg, 1995), p. 67.

30. Armeebefehl des Oberbefehlshabers der 6. Armee, Generalfeldmarschall von Reichenau, dated 10 October 1941, cited in Gerd R. Ueberschär and Wolfram Wette, *Der Deutsche Überfall auf die Sowjetunion, "Unternehmen Barbarossa" 1941* (Frankfurt am Main, 1991), p. 285.

31. Joseph Goebbels, "Die Juden sind schuld," in *Das eherne Herz. Reden und Aufsätze aus den Jahren 1941–1942* (Munich, 1943), pp. 85ff.

32. Jörg Friedrich, *Das Gesetz des Krieges. Das deutsche Heer in Ruß-land 1941 bis 1945. Der Prozess gegen das Oberkommando der Wehrmacht* (Munich, 1993), pp. 424ff.

33. Stephen Fritz, *Frontsoldaten. Der erzählte Krieg* (Berlin, 1998).

34. Martin Schröter, *Held oder Mörder. Bilanz eines Soldaten Adolf Hitlers* (Wuppertal, 1991), p. 76.

35. H. A. Jacobsen, *Krieg in Weltanschauung und Praxis des National-sozialismus 1919–1945,* in *Beiträge zur Zeitgeschichte. Festschrift für Ludwig Jedlicka zum 60. Geburtstag,* ed. R. Neck and A. Wandruszka (St. Pölten, 1978), pp. 238ff.

36. Bernd Guggenberger, "Der erste der letzten Kriege? Nachdenken zum Golfkrieg," in *Universitas* 6 (1991): 559; Ernst Jünger, "Über den Schmerz" (1934), in *Sämtliche Werke (Complete Works),* vol. 7 (Stuttgart, 1970).

37. R. Kössler and T. Schiel, "Nationalstaaten und Grundlagen eth-nischer Identität," in *Nationalstaat und Ethnizität,* ed. R. Kössler and T. Schiel (Frankfurt am Main, 1994), pp. 17ff.

38. T. Scheffler, "Ethnizität und Gewalt im Vorderen und Mittleren Orient," in *Ethnizität und Gewalt,* ed. T. Scheffler (Hamburg, 1991), p. 21.

39. Mersmann, *"Was bleibt vom Heldentum?"* p. 250.

40. Buchbender and Sterz, *Gesicht,* p. 90 (letter of 7 December 1941), p. 94 (letter of 25 February 1942).

41. Max Domarus, *Hitler. Reden und Proklamationen 1932–1945,* vol. 2 (Würzburg, 1993), p. 1826, p.1831.

42. Goebbels, "Wanderung der Seelen" and "Neue Perspektiven," in *Das eherne Herz. Reden und Aufsätze aus den Jahren 1941–1942* (Munich, 1943), pp. 191–92, 252.

43. *Jenseits des Krieges,* a film by Ruth Beckmann.

44. Steinbach, *Ein Volk,* 31–32.

45. K. von Bismark, 5 March 1995.

46. Peter Bamm, *Die unsichtbare Flagge* (Munich, 1989), p. 76.

47. Hannah Arendt, *Eichmann in Jerusalem* (Munich, 1964), p. 277.

48. Ibid., pp. 173f.

49. Paul Tillich, "Das transmoralische Gewissen," in *Glaube und Handeln. Grundprobleme evangelischer Ethik,* ed. Heinz Horst Schrey (Bre-men, 1956), p. 284.

50. Ibid.

51. Arendt, *Eichmann in Jerusalem,* p. 189.

Peter Hayes

The Degussa AG and the Holocaust

UNTIL ITS NAME BEGAN TO SURFACE REPEATEDLY IN THE MEDIA OF late, the Degussa AG of Frankfurt am Main was a relatively little-known German chemical company, even at home. Always in the shadow of either IG Farben or its successors (Bayer, BASF, Hoechst), it attracted public attention only intermittently during its rise to the status of Germany's tenth largest chemicals firm in 1927, on average its fifth or sixth largest following World War II.[1] Thanks in part to its historically low profile, even the American occupation authorities in the late 1940s took a benign view of the enterprise, largely exempting it from their trust-busting efforts and overlooking the ways in which it had capitalized on Nazi economics and, in particular, the persecution of the Jews. Specifically, during the Nazi era, Degussa had: (1) greatly expanded its commercial position through the takeover of formerly Jewish-owned property, including ten companies, substantial stockholdings in three other firms, ten parcels of real estate, and at least one patent; (2) smelted, refined, and sometimes resold the majority of the gold and silver pillaged by the Reich from Jews between 1939 and 1944; (3) "leased" over 3,000 forced laborers (about 40 percent of them Jews) from the SS and put them to work in at least four factories; and (4) controlled the distribution of the Zyklon B gas that was used to murder over one million people at Auschwitz and Majdanek.

In recent years, the rediscovery of Degussa's role in processing plundered precious metals, along with a generational change in the firm's leadership, have produced an increasing corporate willingness to reexamine the firm's past. Following the examples of Volkswagen, the Deutsche Bank, and the Allianz insurance firm, Degussa in 1997 began seeking a professional historian to review its own and other relevant records and write the firm's history in the Nazi era, then approached me. Several months of negotiation yielded a contract obligating the enterprise to provide me all of the rather extensive documentation in its possession, but giving the firm no control, not even a right of review, over what I write. This essay is a first, of necessity abbreviated, report on what the sources reveal about Degussa's involvement in the dispossession and persecution of the European Jews. Two emergent conclusions seem particularly well founded and, in different respects, troubling: (1) Degussa's behavior appears to have been typical of that of most large German firms, in that the enterprise played almost no direct role in causing the policies that produced so much misery but exhibited little reluctance about benefiting from and, in the process, facilitating them; and (2) the "profits" made on this participation were so incommensurate with the degree of suffering related to it that assessing what obligations, if any, Degussa still bears toward the victims is not so simple a matter as billing the company for the present value of its erstwhile gains.

Understanding why and how Degussa came to play so frequent a part in events related to the Holocaust requires a brief review of the firm's development prior to 1933. The German Gold and Silver Separation Society, Inc. (Aktiengesellschaft Deutsche Gold- und Silber-Scheideanstalt vormals Roessler) was incorporated in January 1873 in order to carry out the consolidation of the German coinage following national unification. Over the next forty years, building upon their father's technical experience as head of the former Frankfurt mint, the five Roessler brothers who headed the new firm and its foreign branches gradually expanded their smelting and refining operations to embrace the liquefied application of precious metals to ceramics and porcelain. This entailed increasing involvement with sodium and potassium compounds, including cyanides, which provided the eventual link to Zyklon B. Meanwhile, thanks to the experimental genius of Otto Liebknecht, the son and brother of the famed Social Democrats Wilhelm and Karl and Degussa's most creative chemist until he left the firm in 1925, this specialization led to a substance called Perborat. It became the essential active ingredient in the Henkel company's phenomenally successful detergent, Persil.[2] As a result, despite the loss of all of its foreign operations at the end of World War I, Degussa entered the Weimar era as a rather narrowly focused but potentially quite profitable firm, and this combination set the agenda for subsequent development.

In 1919, reflecting the founding family's declining interest and influence in the firm, Degussa elected Ernst Busemann, the prewar leader of the firm's Belgian metals-processing subsidiary, to the managing board, and he emerged as primus inter pares long before being named chairman formally in 1930. Busemann set out not only to reinvigorate the parent enterprise, which in his opinion had "slept through" the First World War while competitors expanded mightily, but also to diversify it in order to reduce its financial dependence on Henkel's orders. In the process, he and his successors wanted to develop a position strong enough to establish a durable modus vivendi with the German organic chemicals producers, especially those that fused to form the giant IG Farben concern in 1925. Much more a salesman than a scientist, Busemann thought the best route to this objective lay not through expensive research but through mergers and acquisitions, since "one could always buy good production processes" for less than the cost of inventing and developing them.[3] The onset of the depression only reinforced his dedication to this strategy. Depreciating newly acquired plant seemed to offer the only way both to sustain earnings during a time of economic downturn and to insure his enterprise against a possible devaluation of the Reichsmark. As a result, in the early 1930s, Busemann applied the steady flow of cash from Henkel to a buying spree that included the complete absorption of a longtime subsidiary, the HIAG wood carbonization firm and its scattered plants, and a venture into the manufacture of carbon black, an additive for rubber tires. More important for the purposes of this essay, Busemann's diversification drive predisposed Degussa to seize more readily than most other large German firms on the opportunities presented by Nazi pressure on Jewish enterprises after 1933.

Given the close fit that emerged in the early years of the Third Reich between the Nazi policies of "Aryanization" and autarky and Ernst Busemann's corporate strategy, it is worth emphasizing that the enterprise's leaders do not appear to have anticipated the match. None of the nine full members of the managing board were Nazis prior to Hitler's accession, and only three of them ever subsequently became Nazi Party members. Two department heads later elevated to the board, Hermann Federlin and Helmut Achterath, already had enlisted in the party during the previous summer but apparently found it prudent to keep their political loyalty secret from the firm's leaders until after the Nazi takeover.[4] A third up-and-comer in the company was also a convinced Hitlerite, however, and he was much more vocal. Hans Menzel had joined the movement in Stuttgart in 1922, received membership number 1830, and risen during the 1920s to be district party treasurer in Frankfurt. Though not yet even a deputy member of the managing board, his status as the grandson of Degussa's founder and the nephew of its supervisory board chairman had given him ample chance to advertise for Nazism among the firm's leaders.[5] Most of them appear to have supported the German People's Party in the 1920s, then fallen prey to the prevailing political disorientation of the German bourgeoisie in the crisis years. Their sense of detachment from politics was mirrored by the subsequent conduct of Busemann. He toyed with having the entire board enroll in the Nationalsozialistische Deutsche Arbeiter Partei (NSDAP) in the spring of 1933, then drew back; at his death in 1939, he had still not taken the plunge. Only one of his colleagues tried to go ahead anyway, but he was probably the most important one: Hermann Schlosser, the commanding and convivial son of a Protestant pastor and Busemann's eventual successor as head of the firm. Schlosser apparently applied to join the party for both pragmatic and ideological reasons. Above all, the Nazis' emphasis on the people's community and the end of class warfare appealed to the romanticized ideology of *Frontkämpfer* (front-fighter) solidarity that he had imbibed during World War I and would continue to extol throughout his life. Although purists in the Frankfurt party apparatus managed to block his admission on a technicality until 1939, his application marked the first of his many successful steps toward cultivating good relations with the Gauleitung (NSDAP administration).[6]

Nazis, in short, were well placed in Degussa in 1933 but not predominant, and something similar might be said regarding the prevalence of anti-Semitism. To be sure, while fending off attacks by the Nazi *Westdeutscher Beobachter* during 1933, Degussa claimed not only to have no practicing Jews among its 1,850 workers and employees as the Third Reich began but also never to have hired any.[7] If so, that policy implies a substantial degree of exclusion on the part of a company headquartered in a city where the Jewish population came to almost 5 percent of the whole in 1933. Converts, however, had and did occupy significant posts, notably Dr. Theodor Pohl and Dr. Ernst Eichwald, both of whom remained with the firm until the pogrom of

1938. On that occasion, Eichwald and his wife were ousted from their home by the SA and then hidden by friends in the company until they escaped to England in March 1939; Pohl remained in Germany and survived the war by virtue of his marriage to a non-Jew.[8] Six members of the supervisory board were also Jews by Nazi definitions in 1933. While the firm's management was not above informing them that their presence was creating difficulties, it allowed them to determine the pace of their departures or to serve out their terms over the next four years.[9] In the surviving documents, I have found but two examples of the way in which Hitler's triumph made crude remarks about Jews more "salonfähig" (socially acceptable) within the corporation than previously, one a furious reference by a board member to two businessmen who outnegotiated him over a piece of property as "diese Rassejuden" (these Jews), the other a letter from Hans Menzel to the Nazi Gauwirtschaftsberater in Frankfurt in August 1933, denouncing the leaders of a rival firm as "unverschämte Juden" (impudent Jews).[10]

In general, however, the firm's behavior with regard to the so-called Jewish question in the 1930s conformed to the ambivalence that the chairman of its supervisory board, Fritz Roessler, set down on paper between 1933 and his death in 1937. On the one hand, convinced "that their influence grew to a frightening degree after 1918 and became a cultural danger," Roessler had no objections "to pushing the Jews back strongly, to limiting or even prohibiting access to certain professions." On the other hand, he found it "impossible to approve of the ruthless destruction of the livelihoods of thousands of Jewish and half-Jewish fellow citizens, many of whom had done great service to Germany and its science and culture." Unable to believe in even the existence of pure races, not to mention their supposed essences, destinies, missions, and relative worths, he dismissed talk of Aryan supremacy as "absolutely without scientific basis" and ridiculed as "a fixation" the Nazi image of "a horrible conspiracy of international Jewry with Marxism." By the time his life was drawing to a close, he regretted having let his prejudices neutralize his senses of justice and reason during the initial years of the Third Reich, and he admitted, at least with regard to his old fraternity's agreement to purge its non-Aryan members, "the correctness of all those who were against all concessions from the beginning and would rather have disbanded than offend their fundamental principles."[11]

The fact, in other words, that Degussa became one of the more vigorous corporate Aryanizers in Germany during the 1930s did not reflect obvious political or racist zeal on the part of the firm's upper echelons but rather the confluence of an ongoing corporate strategy with new, politically created opportunities. Convenience, as well as an absence of *Zivilcourage* and the presence of Roessler's patrician sort of irresolution on the "Jewish question," assured that the prevailing spirit among Degussa's leaders regarding economic "Aryanization" became that which Ernst Busemann articulated in July 1937 but practiced from the beginning of Nazi rule: "It is pointless to swim against the stream."[12] But the enterprise neither tried to roil the waters further nor attempted to breach the dikes Jewish businessmen threw up around their companies—at least for a time. Prior to January 1938, while the anti-Semitic current in the corporate sphere was being driven by extralegal party intimidation and harassment, Degussa played a generally reactive and "decent" role, usually making acquisitions after being approached by the threatened sellers, who often were long-standing business partners, and paying commercially fair prices that were arrived at by normal business processes of evaluation. Although the five corporate takeovers and two acquisitions of large blocks of stock that occurred during this period took place under varying degrees of implicit or explicit duress, there is no evidence that Degussa helped exert or profiteered from it. But after a flood of official decrees in early 1938 turned the stream of dispossession into a torrent that threatened to sweep away some of Degussa's own interests, the firm stopped throwing lifelines. Its remaining annexations proceeded in almost heartlessly self- interested fashion.

There is not space here to review each of Degussa's "Aryanizations" in detail.[13] But a few remarks about the most revealing and representative cases will convey the gradual deterioration of the firm's conduct toward Jewish partners during the ten-year history of its expansion at their expense. Prototypical of Degussa's behavior in the years prior to 1938 were its first two, and by far its largest, takeovers, those of the Chemische-Pharmazeutische Werke Bad Homburg AG in September 1933 and of the Degea AG (formerly and later again known as the Auergesellschaft) in two stages between September 1933 and July 1934.[14] In both cases, the Jewish owners—Arthur Abelmann and Alfred Koppel, respectively—were driven to sell out by the prospect of Nazi-controlled customers—the national health insurance system and the Defense Ministry, respectively—ceasing to purchase their products unless the companies changed hands. In both cases, failed efforts to camouflage the proprietors' continuing leadership induced them to offer majorities of their stock to Degussa, which supplied intermediate products to each company. In both cases, the written record indicates a good-faith effort on Degussa's part to keep these men on as managers or junior partners and then agreement on generous financial terms for their departures when these proved inescapable. Abelmann was not just paid the full audited value of his firm, including an allowance for forgone future earnings—a total of almost 1.9 million Reichsmarks, or eight times the face value of the stock purchased, two-thirds of it in Swiss francs. He was also extended a long-term salary and pension contract as the firm's sales representative in western and southern Europe, which guaranteed him and his family another 427,000 Swiss francs through 1948. Koppel got Degussa to pay the full market value of his shares as of the fall of 1933, a rate of just over 130 percent and a sum of 9.3 million marks.

Unexceptionable as these arrangements were in commercial terms, the sales were hardly voluntary, and each transaction had an ugly side. Out of deference to the power of IG Farben, Degussa cut it in on the acquisition of Homburg and then acquiesced in its insistence that Arthur Abelmann had to go. Literally heartbroken at not being able to remain in his homeland and pursue his life's work, he died in Switzerland within eighteen months of selling out. Though Koppel got the prevailing market price for his stock, it had not yet recovered to the level of his firm's intrinsic value, with the result that Degussa obtained assets worth some fourteen million marks for the expenditure of just over nine million. Moreover, the firm's improving fortunes between the first and second stages of the takeover seemed to Koppel to warrant renegotiation of the purchase rate for the remaining stock, but Degussa rejected that idea, arguing that the improvement might prove fleeting, a contract was a contract, and Koppel had set the terms during the preceding autumn. An arbitrator largely concurred. At least the sellers in both cases not only got fair returns on their accomplishments but also the chance to take most of those returns with them into exile, thanks in part to Degussa's lobbying with the German authorities.

In short, Degussa's behavior in these takeovers was "correct" and somewhat considerate, and the same adjectives apply to its subsequent "Aryanizations" between 1934 and early 1938: the acquisition of the Neptunhaus in Frankfurt in February 1934 for the asking price, which netted the owners more than three times what they had paid for the property a decade earlier; the purchase of Richard Merton's 435,000 Reichsmarks worth of shares in the Metallgesellschaft at the market rate of 85 percent in September 1934; the takeover from a long-bankrupt holding company of the Carbidfabrik Wyhlen for 1.5 million marks in March 1936; the 36 percent participation in a consortium that bought out most of the Hirsch family's vinegar and preserves operations for 454,000 marks in May 1936; the annexation of the L.C. Marquart scrap metal reclamation firm for 187.5 percent of par in August 1936; and the obtaining of Hydrocarbon KG, a small maker of carbon black from acetylene, for twice its net worth in the spring of 1938.[15] Only the takeover in March and November 1935 of adjoining plots of real estate in Frankfurt—which, together with the Neptunhaus, Degussa's corporate headquarters still bestride—deviates somewhat from this pattern. In this case, the firm worked hand in glove with the creditors, to whom the bankrupt Jewish owner had ceased paying taxes and mortgage interest in 1931, in order to buy up the land in return for settling the debts. Only at the last minute, as Degussa was about to acquire the larger part of the site for less than half what the owner had paid prior to World War I, did the enterprise extend 1,800 Reichsmarks to the destitute remaining family members in Frankfurt so that they would stop trying to obstruct the sale in court.[16]

When the individuals subjected to "Aryanization" were personally known to Degussa's leaders, they were on occasion even generous, as indicated by the case of the Meyer family.[17] Three of its members still held 12 percent of the stock in a Degussa subsidiary, the Chemische Fabrik Grünau AG, and seats on its supervisory and managing boards in 1937, having repeatedly been protected from party pressure during the preceding years. A new crisis erupted in July of that year, however, thanks to a Nazi whispering campaign against Grünau's products and the application of the German Labor Front organization in the plant for designation as a *Nationalsozialistischer Musterbetrieb* (National Socialist model plant). It was the request of Grünau's business manager for instructions on how to handle the resulting situation which precipitated Busemann's remark about the pointlessness of swimming against the stream. But the rest of Busemann's response is also worth quoting as testimony to his respect for the people involved and sense of obligation to them:

> Your message troubled me greatly because I know the Meyer gentlemen as capable, completely fair businessmen. They have stood by Degussa and me and shown us loyalty since even before the new political conditions began. . . . now comes the moment when I must negotiate with them over a further considerable reduction in their influence. These negotiations will be all the more difficult for me because two equal partners will not be present, but rather there will be, for the most varied reasons, nothing that can be done about my decision. . . . Our effort must be, for the sake of the firm as well as the Meyer family, to retain Theo and Viktor Meyer for our plant. . . . I hope that the gentlemen trust you and me enough to arrange matters as best as possible. I will try hard to justify the faith in me that they have shown for years.[18]

When the Meyer brothers finally were driven from Grünau's managing board and their father from its supervisory one in January 1938, Degussa exchanged their stock for shares in IG Farben on such advantageous terms that the Nazi regime later challenged the settlement.

With the inauguration of the regime's official drive to force the pace of economic "Aryanization" in the early months of 1938, the tone and nature of Degussa's takeovers changed strikingly. No longer were dismissals of personnel the consequences of political pressures applied to particular plants; no longer were acquisitions the results of private negotiations undertaken when the sellers found remaining in Germany intolerable but conducted between parties with at least formally equal legal rights. Henceforth ousters and takeovers occurred in compliance with an ever expanding web of governmental regulations, designed at first to force Jews out of ownership or leadership positions and then to dictate the terms on which firms and shares changed hands.[19] In early 1938, therefore, the remaining Jewish employees at subsidiaries such as Marquart and the Auergesellschaft were abruptly dismissed.[20] As for Jews' property rights, Degussa's first experience with the new ground rules reveals how quickly corrupting they proved. At issue was the presence at the time of the Anschluss of members of the Margulies family as managers and owners of 26 percent of the stock in the Österreichische Chemische Werke GmbH (ÖCW), a firm dominated by Degussa, though it divided the re-

maining shares equally with IG Farben as a "silent partner."[21] Faced
with the circumstances that the number of Jewish executives in the
firm and the proportion of Jewish-owned capital both narrowly exceeded the permissible limits established by Nazi decrees in early
1938, Degussa feared that ÖCW might be declared a "non-Aryan"
enterprise. Moreover, the Margulies family's similar holding of 26
percent in Leukon AG, a Degussa–IG Farben marketing firm in
Switzerland, made that firm seem similarly endangered. As a result,
Degussa swiftly purged the Jewish personnel of ÖCW and began ex-
ploiting the sellers' desperation to get themselves and some fraction
of their wealth out of the country by offering to pay only far less than
the market or intrinsic worth for the shares. After one of the family
members broke ranks with the others and came to terms in September 1938, thus removing any basis for a "non-Aryan" classification,
Degussa not only merely waited for the Reich to confiscate the remaining stock in their hands and then bought it at auction for about
three-quarters of its nominal value but also encouraged the Reichsbank to seize the family's shares in Leukon. Only after the latter ma-
neuver barely miscarried did Degussa enter into negotiations with
the Margulieses, who had found refuge in Switzerland, to purchase
that stock on reasonably fair terms.

The Margulies Aryanization case was the first in which Degussa
actually worked to obtain what can only be called legally stolen property, but it was neither the last nor the crudest. The acquisition of
Kulzer & Co. of Frankfurt constituted a "compulsory Aryanization"
in an even more extreme sense, in that the Gauleiter of Hessen adjudicated the sale, and the three Jews among the four owners played
almost no role in the negotiations whatsoever. Because the firm man-
ufactured high-quality dental prosthetics and related materials, in
part for export and on the basis of rationed precious metals that were
denied to Jewish firms by the decrees of early 1938, its swift
"Aryanization" was a matter of some importance to the local and national economy and of some rivalry among the metals-refining firms
that saw a chance to expand their businesses vertically. All of this
helps explain both Degussa's interest and the Gauleitung's intervention.[22] By February 1939, the regime and the competing parties had
worked out a solution that divided Kulzer evenly between Degussa
and the Heraeus platinum firm and provided for the remaining Gentile owner to stay on as business manager and retain a substantial

share of revenues via license fees. Two of the Jewish partners got a sum in Reichsmarks equal to about two-thirds the commercial value of their shares, most of which was subsequently confiscated, and the third, who had emigrated to the United States, was paid with rights to an American patent and profits from an American firm that had belonged to Kulzer. While Degussa appears to have had little to do with the unfairness of the price, which was fixed by the regime's agents, the firm's leaders must have been far more preoccupied with their good fortune than with the injustice in which they were participating. Within a year, the new Paladon GmbH had delivered a profit to Degussa that exceeded its share of the takeover costs. Equally blinding was the price at which the Reich allowed Degussa to acquire in late 1939 some 700,000 shares in the Metallgesellschaft that Richard Merton had been forced to give over to the Prussian State Bank as he was expelled from Germany. At 115 percent of the face value per share, instead of the 160 percent at which the stock was trading, Degussa was enabled to "save" over 300,000 Reichsmarks on the purchase.[23]

The Margulies, Kulzer, and Merton cases carried Degussa's leaders across a moral line. That their behavior thereafter became even more actively exploitative is made clear by the takeover of the Aurora Nasch & Co. precious metals refinery of Brünn (Brno), which was representative of Degussa's four "Aryanizations" in the so-called Protectorate of Bohemia-Moravia.[24] The installation itself was, from Degussa's point of view, so run-down as to be virtually worthless. Aurora, however, had inventories of precious metals valued at about 100,000 Reichsmarks in May 1939, and it was entitled to annual allotments of gold, platinum, and other metals from the National Bank in Prague, which continued throughout the German occupation. Therefore, Degussa quickly entered into arrangements with Erwin Scheinost, the ethnic German in Brünn who had been assigned temporary management of the Aurora firm, calling for him either to arrange its sale to Degussa or to buy it himself temporarily and then resell it to the German firm; in either event, he would then take up a new job in Frankfurt. But the scheme ran into three problems straightaway: While two of the Jewish owners, Sidonie Nasch and Samuel Frankfurter, were willing to go along, they also wanted a higher price than Degussa hoped to pay; the lawyer for the third partner, Bruno Elsner, who had fled abroad, took a dilatory approach to all proposals; and the local NSDAP expressed its opposition to both the "concern building" entailed in Degussa's expansion and the loss of German blood in the region that would result from the departure of Scheinost and his family. By August 1939, following a lobbying effort by Hans Menzel with the Gauleiter and his regional economic advisor, Degussa had removed the first and third obstacles and seemed poised to make the takeover indirectly, through its wholly owned subsidiary in Vienna, Louis Roessler & Co. But Elsner had chosen well—his lawyer was savvy and politically well connected enough to delay matters for almost another year.

At this point, seven years after embarking on the course of "Aryanization," Degussa completed its descent from taking advantage of Nazi pressure on Jews to instructing the Gestapo on how to exert it. Walter Roessler, the now exasperated head of the Vienna branch, called at the Gestapo office in Brünn to explain that Elsner was, in fact, a Polish citizen of a town that Germany had annexed and hence was now subject to German laws, including the one that permitted the seizure of property belonging to German subjects who had fled to enemy territory. In short, "his citizenship must be revoked and his property confiscated," as Roessler proudly reported to Frankfurt on April 5, 1940.[25] Though all sorts of legal and bureaucratic stumbling blocks postponed the final takeover until 1943, Degussa ended up pocketing Aurora's metals inventories and quota allotment essentially for free, while the Reich raked off the firm's recent earnings in the forms of the purchase price and an "equalization payment" to the Reichsprotektor.

Although the takeovers in the protectorate constituted the only "Aryanizations" of firms that Degussa carried out in occupied Europe, they did not mark the end of the corporation's involvement in earning money from the despoiling of the Jews.[26] Indeed, even as the Aurora imbroglio was just beginning, Degussa already was in hot pursuit of a second sort of business opportunity presented by the Nazi regime's stepped-up campaign of robbery in the aftermath of Kristallnacht. At stake were virtually all the gold, silver, and platinum possessions of Jews in Greater Germany, which the Nazi government resolved in November 1938 to confiscate. In a series of decrees to that end between then and February 1939, the regime first authorized the use of such objects to pay the "fine" levied on the Jewish population following the pogrom, then forbade any other disposal of them, and finally ordered their surrender to the state-run pawnshops.

From the outset, it was plain that this *Judenmetallaktion* (Jewish metals action) was a cruelly confiscatory operation, despite the veneer created by a formal system of compensation. The payments to the erstwhile owners amounted to only 90 percent of the international wholesale price of the estimated fine-metal content of the jewelry, tableware, and religious and decorative objects handed in (i.e., sometimes to as little as 20 Reichsmarks per kilogram of silver and 1–1.6 marks per gram of gold) and made no allowance for antiquity or workmanship.[27] Usually deposited directly and in stages to blocked Reichsmark accounts that the nominal owners could barely access, the resulting sums were first "skimmed" by Nazi-appointed "trustees" for the accounts and then confiscated by the regime when the Jews emigrated or were deported. Meanwhile, the pawnshops withheld the remaining 10 percent of the international wholesale price as a handling fee when they either resold the objects and remitted any resulting profit to the Reich Finance Ministry or lumped them into lots that were collected by the refining and smelting firms. These paid the pawnshops the lowest standard Berlin price for the fine metal that resulted (33–35 marks per kilogram of fine silver and 2.8–3.4 marks per fine gram of gold), processed and purified the metals, and sooner or later either sent the equivalent weight in bars on to the Reichsbank at a small markup (2 marks per kilo of fine silver, 15.9 pfennigs per gram of fine gold) or directed the metals at the regime's behest to other firms at the highest standard Berlin price, from which the refiners could deduct a higher commission (3 marks per kilo of silver and 30–36 pfennigs per gram of gold) before transferring the net proceeds to the Reichsbank. The regime thus bought gold and silver at extortionist prices and sold at normal ones, made sure that it eventually would also reclaim even its initial outlays, and meanwhile rewarded the intermediaries who administered the process, in this case including Degussa, with small percentages of the loot.

Limited as the potential returns on this process were, Degussa volunteered its assistance eagerly. In part, this resulted from the fact that the influx of metals posed a potential threat to the administrative position the firm had secured since 1935 as the executor of the national rationing system for precious metals developed pursuant to

Hjalmar Schacht's New Plan. More important, however, was the depressed state of Degussa's metals business. Because of the weakness of the German trade balance, the virtual nonconvertibility of the Reichsmark, and the hoarding of gold by the Reichsbank, Degussa's refineries were limping along at well below capacity by 1938. Their intake of silver had fallen from 493 metric tons in the business year 1935–36 to 391.6 in 1937–38, that of gold from 17 metric tons to 10.4.[28] The value of the firm's inventories of precious metals had dropped as a result by more than 3 million marks (over 25 percent) since September 1934.[29] Given this trend and the reality that, in the Nazi system of bureaucratic rather than market competition, usefulness to the authorities was the only way to maintain or gain access to key supplies, it is not surprising that Degussa leaped at the new source of business that the "metals action" represented. In the spring of 1939, the firm quickly worked out distribution quotas with the industries that most needed the metals, offered the Reich a 5 to 8 percent discount on the usual smelting rates, negotiated with the Reichsbank the pricing scheme outlined earlier, and lobbied that institution intensively for a disproportionate share of the stolen silver with the argument that Degussa could process it far more cheaply than could its smaller competitors.[30] Any other course would have jeopardized the firm's ability to maintain its market share and control. As a result, at the price of concessions to the smaller smelters regarding their shares of what the firm's documents explicitly labeled *Judensilber* (Jewish silver), Degussa acquired the rights to most of the income on processing the precious metals being plundered (80–90 percent of the gold, 50 percent of the platinum, and 40 percent of the silver collected in Germany, plus an unspecified portion of that gathered in the so-called Ostmark for L. Roessler & Co.).[31] Over the next year and a half, Degussa also managed to secure a system of supplementary payments to compensate for lost interest on the capital the firm tied up in the metals during the long intervals that developed between paying the pawnshops and disposing of the refined product.[32]

If the firm's determination to get a piece of the action is thus clearly established, the question of how much Degussa made by this process of governmentally sanctioned plundering is harder to answer definitively. The proceeds are not listed separately in the firm's accounts, and the relevant offices went to great lengths in February 1945 to destroy pertinent records.[33] But the quantities involved can be reconstructed from surviving documents. These reveal that by 1941, all the German precious-metals processors had turned the goods provided by the pawnshops into about 135,202 kilograms of fine silver (i.e., almost 149 U.S. tons), most of which went to industrial consumers, such as IG Farben's film-making factories, and some 1,300 kilograms of fine gold (i.e., about 1.5 U.S. tons), the equivalent of virtually all of which went to the Reichsbank.[34] Degussa refined over half of the first 52,700 kilograms of fine silver that had resulted by the end of 1939 (two-thirds, when one includes the total for L. Roessler) and more than one-third of the next approximately 78,400 (just under half, when L. Roessler's output is added) smelted through February 1941, for a total of 70,746 kilograms.[35] A report to the German Commissioner for Price-Setting in August 1941, by which time nearly complete returns were in, notes that altogether 72,321 kilograms of silver (roughly 54 percent of all that collected from Jews) and 1,113 kilograms of gold (86 percent) had "passed through" Degussa's facilities in consequence of the *Judenmetallaktion*.[36] On the basis of the refining and transfer fees outlined earlier, it appears, therefore, that Degussa probably earned at least 217,000 Reichsmarks on silver taken from the Jews of Germany and Austria, along with some 18,000 marks on the gold; the firm's total proceeds, then, came to the equivalent of US $940,000 in today's currency.[37] Despite the preferential fees offered the Reich, which Degussa soon regretted and sought to change without success, the sums were virtually pure profit, involving limited additional costs at the underutilized smelters.

Building on this experience, Degussa became the predominant precious-metals processor for the Reich in the far more extensive pillaging of Jews throughout Europe that attended the ghettoization, expropriation, deportation, and finally annihilation of most of them during the period 1940 to 1945. Once more, the chief beneficiary of this robbery was the German Treasury, but Degussa's share of the loot appears to have risen by virtue of the disappearance of the special rebate on the smelting charges. To date, the laborious efforts to tabulate the total value of the metals seized from Jews by the Nazi regime or to piece together the entries in Degussa's smelting books have not been completed, so an estimate of the firm's proceeds from this thievery must be speculative and rough. It is clear, however, from those books that Degussa processed at least 1,015 kilograms, probably

1,374 kilograms, and perhaps as much as 1,962 kilograms of fine gold from the forty-four infamous deliveries of metal plundered from Jews that were both delivered to the Reichsbank by SS-man Bruno Melmer and subsequently refined (thirty-two further deliveries never reached the smelters and were captured in raw form by the U.S. Army in 1945). These quantities would have yielded smelting fees of 17,471 Reichsmarks, 23,655 Reichsmarks, and 33,746 Reichsmarks, respectively, according to the fee structure of 17.2 Reichsmarks per kilo laid down in the Smelting Convention of 1938, which probably was applied.[38] If one proceeds from the likely assumption, however, that Degussa actually processed 80 to 90 percent of all the gold that the Swiss Commission of Experts has estimated was stolen from Jews by German agencies, including the Wehrmacht and the Haupt-treuhandstelle Ost in Poland, and then refined into internationally recognized form—in other words, 80 to 90 percent of all the formerly Jewish-owned gold that became truly usable by Germany—then the volume that emanated from Degussa's refineries may have been between 7,200 and 8,200 kilograms, which would have yielded the firm some 141,000 Reichsmarks, at most, or US $ 574,000 in today's currency.[39] Far more lucrative would have been the silver business, owing to the larger quantities seized and the possibility of commercial resale, although more of this material may have remained in the countries of origin. But only fragmentary statistics have yet emerged regarding Degussa's intake of "Jewish silver" from outside of Germany and Austria. If one assumes, for the present, a ratio of silver-to-gold earnings of over 12:1, as in the Greater German case of 1939 to 1941, my best guess at the moment is that the firm may have received a maximum of 2 million Reichsmarks (US $8 million in today's currency) on the process of plundering Jewish-owned gold and silver, from beginning to end.

This is a substantial sum of money, and reaping it was important enough to make Degussa elbow a subsidiary aside and to pay no mind to the provenance of the metals.[40] Of that, some officials in the metals division of the firm were surely aware, since their offices in the Französische Strasse in Berlin received deliveries directly from some sources, such as the Lodz ghetto administration, and remitted the postcommission proceeds to accounts in their names at the Reichsbank.[41] With regard to the articles received via the Reichsbank from the Gestapo or the SS, including metals extracted from the mouths of corpses, illusions about the origins were possible for a time, since the shipments arrived in compressed form that rendered the components no longer immediately recognizable, and reprocessing dental gold was, in any case, a common activity in the smelting business. But, on some occasions, as a former assistant in Degussa's Reinickendorf smelter in Berlin has recalled, deliveries came in a condition that made drawing conclusions hard to avoid.[42] Whether this became a matter for discussion further up the corporate line is not provable from the extant documents, but it seems probable that the principal officers in the metals division knew something of the illegitimate origin of the material coming to them, given their feverish efforts to destroy records in 1945. Establishing their knowledge conclusively seems, however—from a historian's point of view if perhaps not a lawyer's—almost beside the point. There is simply no reason to believe that the firm's leaders would have rejected the shipments even if they had been fully informed.

In all probability, Degussa took part in the plundering of the Jews not just or primarily to obtain immediate profits but rather for the sake of prospective ones and in order to avoid the penalties that noncooperation might have entailed. Knowledge of the gruesome process by which these metals were obtained would not have altered the calculations that motivated the firm's behavior. Degussa had nothing to gain in 1939 from refusing to carry out a task the state was bound to request of the predominant firm in the industry, but something to lose, namely its quasi-monopolistic market position, if the regime had to look elsewhere. The firm meanwhile could hope for future consideration regarding the pricing of its services and access to other metals supplies that might become available. Indeed, after the victories in the West in 1940, such calculations paid off. During the winter of 1941, Degussa took in and processed almost three times as much fine gold taken from Belgian supplies alone, for example, than it produced from the looting of the German and Austrian Jews altogether; in the single month of February 1941, the firm reprocessed fine silver from France and Belgium that came to 127 percent of the total yielded by the *Judenmetallaktion*.[43] In this period, sharing the general German illusion of impending victory, the leaders of Degussa's metals division began to entertain visions of taking leadership in the European silver business from London after the war, and that made them all the more eager to prove useful to the Reichsbank.[44] These larger stakes help account for the fact that no one in Degussa's leadership so much as questioned what the firm was becoming engaged in.

Conversely, the relative unimportance of the plunder from Jews to the firm's overall business in precious metals facilitated the absence of reflection as time passed. Even if Degussa indeed took in as much as two million Reichsmarks on thefts from Jews in the seven calendar years 1939 through 1945, that figure amounts to only 14 percent of the firm's receipts for metals processing in the single business year 1941–42 and to only 1.2 percent of the receipts of the metals division in the three business years between September 1941 and September 1944 alone (174.5 million Reichsmarks).[45] Another way of contextualizing the firm's behavior is to note that the metals plundered from Jews that passed in and out of Degussa's refineries from 1939 through 1941 came to only 5 percent of the total fine-gold flow in kilograms, to only 10.5 percent of the intake and 6.3 percent of the output of fine silver during that period. Projecting from these data and those of the Swiss Commission, as I have previously, the maximum possible share of Jewish-origin precious metals in the firm's total outflows by weight from 1939 to 1945 currently appears to have been less than one-fifth of the 42,444 kilograms of fine gold produced in this period and perhaps one-quarter of the 2,192,789 kilograms of silver.[46]

But there is something else to say about Degussa's initial eagerness to take part in the metals business, something that reflects the atmosphere not only in the country in the period 1939 to 1941, but also within the concern itself. These two years mark the apogee of the firm's ties to the regime, indeed, of its identification with the Third Reich. Ernst Busemann's death and the ascent of Hermann Schlosser in October 1939 was accompanied by the election of Carl Lüer, a convinced Nazi of long standing, as head of the supervisory board; by the election to that body of Wilhelm Avieny, who was later to become the local Nazi Gau Economic Advisor; and by the achievement of a controlling interest in the firm's stock by the Henkel company, which, in turn, had come under the control of Werner Lüps, a protégé of Hermann Göring. Shortly thereafter, Hans Menzel finally got, with the support of the Gauleiter of Hessen-Nassau, the seat on the managing board he had long desired. Five of the six other men elected to that body with him in 1941 were also all Nazi Party members. This was not a period in which second thoughts about Germany's ends or means were common within Degussa.

The real growth sector of Degussa's business under the Nazis, however, and especially after 1939, was not in precious metals, proceeds from which held relatively constant from 1937–38 to 1941–42 while their contribution to the concern's income fell from 43 percent to 32 percent, but in the division of the firm that formerly been rooted in wood carbonization and distillation.[47] This loose set of operations grew ever more important to Degussa, increasing its share of total income from 25.5 percent to over 35 percent in the same period and drawing the corporation into a more personal form of complicity in the persecution of the Jews, their exploitation as forced labor. That practice began in June 1939 at the Aryanized Hydrocarbon carbon black factory at Blankenburg in the Harz. Unable to keep German workers from leaving for jobs offering far better working conditions, the plant management decided to take advantage of the new regulations by which the Nazi regime, having stripped most German Jews of their livelihoods, began assigning them to labor battalions.[48] The executives applied for and received a handful of compulsory laborers, who were paid at officially prescribed and discriminatory wage rates and, as Degussa's Nazi foreman (*Betriebsobmann*) Adolf Hilpert noted with some satisfaction, kept apart from the rest of the workforce, given "the most unpleasant work," and supervised by "reliable Aryan work comrades."[49] Initially numbering perhaps a dozen sometimes elderly men, this Jewish work group swelled to about twenty-five people before being gradually reduced at the turn of 1942–43, then "dissolved completely" in February 1943 and replaced by Polish workers.[50] By then, the use of Jewish labor was broadening into a massive system involving no payments at all to tens of thousands of workers drawn from ghettos and concentration camps.

The biggest employers of inmate labor among Degussa's operations became the factories of the Auergesellschaft at Oranienburg and Guben, but few of the inmates involved were Jews. During the final six to ten months of the war, in conjunction with a massive program to produce gas masks for the German civilian population and under considerable pressure from Walter Schieber, the official in the Speer Ministry responsible for both this initiative and the application of camp inmates to armaments production, these plants came to have about 2,000 prisoner workers between them, most of them Eastern European women transported from Ravensbrück. Virtually all records concerning them, however, appear to have been destroyed just before or after Soviet troops arrived in 1945, either by the enormous American air raids that leveled the plants or by the actions of German or Russian officials. About all that can be said with anything approaching certainty is that Auer paid the camp four Reichsmarks per laborer per day, minus a charge for the inadequate rations; that the women probably worked twelve hours per day at least six days per week; and that at least thirty of them died on the site and some 247 in the air raids.[51]

Slightly to much better documented is the history of Jewish forced labor at the only two Degussa installations that appear to have had recourse to such workers. Both were, as was more typical than not of the early phases of the slave labor program, construction projects at locations in central and eastern Germany that had been selected, in part, for their distance from British air bases. At Fürstenberg on the Oder (now Eisenhüttenstadt), Degussa sought to build a giant *Konzernwerk* that would replace and consolidate its scattered, often cramped chemicals manufacturing installations after the war. At Gleiwitz in Upper Silesia, the corporation was to play the main role in constructing and operating a carbon black factory owned by the Deutsche Gasrußwerke GmbH, in which Degussa owned half the stock. Interestingly, in the planning documents regarding both factories, the question of where the workforces were to come from receives relatively little attention compared to issues of financing, topography and transport, and raw materials supply. Only in the spring of 1941, as the time for ground breaking approached at each location, did it become apparent to the planners that the assurances local authorities had proffered in this regard had no chance of being fulfilled.[52] Disappointment, delay, and desperation thus provided the springboards for the readiness with which Degussa's managers on the sites accepted suggestions from the respective local labor allocation offices in January 1942 that Jews be added to the workforces. In March and April, the first such construction workers began to arrive, 200 men from the Lodz ghetto at Fürstenberg and 200 men from Auschwitz at Gleiwitz.[53]

At both plants, the procedures governing the Jewish laborers were extensions of those earlier developed with regard to the "leasing" of workers by German firms from prisoner-of-war camps. The firms built and paid for the stripped-down barracks that government regulations ordained for forced laborers and for the food and lodging of the so-called *Werksschutz* of guards but otherwise subcontracted the German Labor Front to provide nourishment, bedding, heat, and the like. The fee per worker appears to have been roughly 3–3.5 Reichsmarks per day, of which 1.50 went to the Labor Front for these expenses, another 20–30 pfennigs was withdrawn for taxes, and all or virtually all of the remainder was paid to the provider of the laborers, that is, to ghetto or concentration camp administrations.[54] In short, the Jewish compulsory workers were cheaper than free laborers would have been, costing roughly one-quarter to one-third of what Degussa was paying its German laborers on average at western locations such as Rheinfelden and Knapsack per eight-hour day, one-third to one-half of the prevailing hourly rates for Germans in Brandenburg and Silesia and for POWs, and one-half to two-thirds of what recruited or conscripted Eastern European civilians would have received. But the Jews were not free. Fürstenberg projected the guard costs alone at 44,000 marks per year. At Gleiwitz, the bill for "Jewish wages" in 1943 totaled more than 584,000 Reichsmarks.[55] Degussa eagerly accepted forced laborers because they seemed, both initially and increasingly, to be the only ones that could be had (their percentages of the total workforces peaked at perhaps 40 percent at Fürstenberg and 76 percent at Gleiwitz), not because they represented an immediate "windfall." Indeed, in both cases, Degussa embraced the use of Jewish inmate labor only after its applications for *Ostarbeiter* (workers from Eastern Europe) and Russian POWs had been completely or substantially rejected. Not to use these workers meant, it appeared, not completing the plants on schedule or at all, and this the firm and its leaders simply refused to contemplate.

In this context, the day-to-day treatment of the Jewish laborers appears to have depended in part on the willingness of each plant management to concern itself with their welfare, and this correlated strongly with their replaceability. Where the tasks they performed required no experience and fresh workers could be relied upon to arrive periodically, Degussa's managers and those of the subcontractors on the building sites needed to expend no time and energy on the condition of their Jews. Indeed, they succumbed frequently to the temptations to resort to mindless brutality and to extend the workday in order to extract a few extra pfennigs' worth of labor out of the 3–3.5 Reichsmarks fee. But, where skills mattered and no new contingents could be predicted, the corporation had to behave differently. In short, if the firm thought it had little choice about whether to "lease" human beings, whom it paid for but did not pay, and even though every aspect of their lives from the number of calories to be provided them per day to the amount of wood to be expended in the construction of their barracks was subject to elaborate government regulations, the record of Degussa's conduct toward these people suggests that it showed some leeway regarding how it treated them.

This conclusion results from two variations regarding the fates of Jewish laborers suggested by the surviving records. First, the on-site mortality rates of male construction workers may have diverged considerably between Fürstenberg and Gleiwitz. The former site did not enjoy priority status as a war plant and hence never could get its workforce up to the targeted level of 500 laborers and was, in fact, never finished. With every worker therefore precious and Jews a minority among the foreigners on the site, Degussa's managers expressed their dissatisfaction in mid-1943 with the *Deutsche Arbeitsfront*'s ("German Labor Front," DAF) provisioning of the workers by threatening to turn the job over to the Organisation Todt and won improvements.[56] There is no sign in the surviving records of "selections" having taken place, despite the weak condition in which many of the laborers arrived, or of any deaths among the workers prior to the indeterminate date of their withdrawal from the factory. At Gleiwitz, on the other hand, where the projected output of carbon black (*Ruß*) was desperately needed for the tires on which the Wehrmacht ran, the supply of male Jews to the site became steady enough for their number to swell from 200 in 1942 to about 400 in May 1943 to some 500 in December 1944 and for the installation to begin production in April 1943 and become fully operational during the fall of 1944. Meanwhile, some 90 percent of the initial contingent died there or was sent back to the camp system within a year, and another 100 were selected out in November 1943.[57] When concerns about the Labor Front's underfeeding of workers emerged, the result was that the SS assumed direct control of the workers' barracks in May 1944, conducted another "selection," and began running the site like an outpost of Auschwitz, while Degussa accepted direct responsibility for provisioning the workforce. So pleased were Degussa's local

managers with the resulting situation that they expressed the desire
to replace the remaining free French, Italian, and Bulgarian laborers
with inmates![58]

Second, the mortality rates for workers at Gleiwitz diverged
strongly between women and men. Virtually none of the females,
who worked indoors in eight-hour shifts supervising important machinery and packing the final product, died between 1942 and the
evacuation of the plant in late January 1945; the only two documented deaths were by suicide. Attrition among the men, however,
who performed interchangeable tasks outdoors on the building site,
was as murderous as just described, producing the deaths or "transfers" of some 300 people during the same period. This is not to say
that the females were treated well; survivors recall being constantly
cold, hungry, and plagued by skin sores resulting from vitamin defi-
ciency, hence by the constant threat of infection owing to the omnipresent soot and the absence of medicines.[59] Nonetheless, something more than relatively advantageous working assignments seems
necessary to account for such widely divergent fates. It appears that
Degussa's managers at Gleiwitz recognized the difference between ex-
pendable workers, the treatment of whom it was pleased to delegate
to either the DAF or SS, and nonexpendable ones. Willing to turn a
blind eye to malnutrition, illness, and murder on the construction
site, the plant's leaders would not permit the wasting away and
culling out of the more valuable female workers.[60]

Of course, in the long run, Degussa expected to profit from the
brutality in which it partook, in that the plants were being built to
yield appreciable returns eventually. But the enterprise neither earned
nor "saved" large sums on the exploitation of the inmate laborers.
Fürstenberg, on which Degussa had spent 23.6 million marks by January 1945, never produced anything more than a small quantity of
formaldehyde in 1944.[61] Gleiwitz's construction costs aggregated to
10.5 million marks and its total expenditures to over 21 million as of
the end of 1944, by which time its total sales to date had come to 2.3
million Reichsmarks in 1943 and, at most, twice as much in 1944.
The plant did not begin to produce at a profit over its unit costs until May 1944, which means it "made" money in the simplest sense for
some nine months, showing an operating profit for the year of 1.2
million marks. All things considered, Gleiwitz was still 3 million
marks in the red when it was overrun by the Soviet army.[62] Still, that

it came into operation at all was due, as the management's report for May 1943 explicitly noted, to the fact that it "succeeded . . . in obtaining female Jewish workers."[63]

Calculating what the company's "true" labor costs might have been, that is, what it would have paid regular, free laborers, had they been available, is extremely difficult, since the length of their workdays would have been shorter, in all likelihood, and their base wages would have varied considerably by length of employment, gender, skill levels, and marital and parental status, as required by law. A very rough way of proceeding is to say that if the sum of the monthly numbers of Jews working on the site in 1943 comes to 6,333 and their "wages" to 584,159 Reichsmarks, then the wage bill for the sum of roughly 1,500 Jewish laborers there in 1942 would have been 146,000 marks and that for the 7,880 Jewish workers reported for all the months of 1944 would have been 730,199 marks, for a total of just under 1.5 million Reichsmarks paid for Jewish labor by the Gleiwitz plant. Assuming that the wage bill for native German laborers would have averaged out to a figure about three times this high, we may conclude that the Gleiwitz factory "gained" on the order of 3 million marks from the use of "slave" labor, which is to say by some US $12 million in today's currency. If one makes the same sort of calculation for the average of 1,500 exclusively female Ravensbrück inmates who labored at Oranienburg for the Auergesellschaft for ten months in 1944–45, the "gain" comes to US $3.6 million. While these are unhistorical calculations, since Gleiwitz would never have been built and the Auergesellschaft's production would not have been expanded under normal conditions in the labor market, the arithmetic does convey some sense of the extent of what Degussa would have implicitly pocketed by virtue of the slave labor system, if Germany had won the Second World War—about $16 million.

Perhaps the most dramatic aspect of Degussa's connection to the Holocaust concerns the production of Zyklon B, the vaporizing form of hydrogen cyanide used to asphyxiate at least one million people at Auschwitz and Majdanek.[64] With regard to this, the principal revelation to emerge from Degussa's archives is probably that the product was a Degussa operation, rather than an IG Farben one, contrary to what observers have thought ever since the trial of that giant concern's directors before an American Military Tribunal in Nuremberg in 1947–48. Degesch, the firm that at the end of World War I assumed

the patents for the fumigant Cyklon, which had been developed for
use in barracks and U-boats by chemists working for the German
War Ministry, was owned in the 1920s exclusively by Degussa. During this period, it bought up a process devised by Walter Heerdt to
capture the poison in cottonlike pellets until they were exposed to air
and then brought out the resulting product as Zyklon B. To head off
competition in the pesticides field, however, Degussa had to cede
shares in Degesch to IG Farben and the Theo Goldschmidt corporation in 1930–31, thereby reducing its own holding to 42.5 percent of
the stock. But Degesch's chief executives were always Degussa men:
Hermann Schlosser until he became head of Degussa in 1939, and
then Gerhard Peters, who remained officially a Degussa employee.[65]
The firm's offices were located in Degussa's headquarters buildings in
Frankfurt; its books were kept by a Degussa department, which cir-
culated monthly summary statements to two of Degussa's board
members, Hermann Schlosser, the chairman, and Ernst Bernau, the
chief financial officer.[66]

Equally closely linked to Degussa were the two German sales
agencies for Zyklon, Heli (Heerdt-Lingler) and Testa (Tesch &
Stabenow). They divided the German civilian market more or less
along the Elbe River, while Testa was the exclusive purveyor to the
German military and the SS. Degesch owned a majority in both firms
until June 1942 but then sold its holding in Testa when its attempt
to oust Bruno Tesch as head of the firm was blocked by his Nazi Party
connections.[67] Degussa did not own the company that actually man-
ufactured most of the Zyklon B, the Dessauer-Werke, but it long had
controlled 13.35 percent of the shares in the firm that produced
about one-third of the product, the Chemische Werke Kolin in Bohemia. Hermann Schlosser became the effective head of that company from 1942 on, and Degussa probably intended to absorb or liq-
uidate it completely if Germany won the war.[68] In short, Degesch and
its sales representatives belonged to Degussa's sphere, not IG Farben's.
That firm's executives, in fact, took little interest in the company, beyond blocking any attempts for it to expand from vaporizing into
sprayed pesticides.[69]

Not only a Degussa operation, Degesch was largely dependent on
Zyklon B. It produced one-half to two-thirds of the firm's sales in the
years 1940 through 1944 and consistently two-thirds or so of its profits. Both rose to unprecedented heights at the middle of the war,

largely on the strength of enormous military demand, which Testa cultivated by, among other things, offering training courses to the Wehrmacht and the SS on applying the substance.[70] As a result, Degussa earned almost 100,000 Reichsmarks in dividends from Degesch in the years 1941 through 1943, after which orders dropped off again, and the firm lost money.[71]

But did the Degussa's leaders know that Zyklon B was being used after September 1941 not only to kill lice but also to kill human beings whom the Nazi regime regarded as such? The central problem in providing a conclusive answer is the gap between general, circumstantial indications and the specific record. It is very unlikely that Peters ran Degesch without close consultation with Schlosser. The latter man intervened personally in the crisis with the party that led to Heerdt's removal at Heli in 1941; he was deeply concerned with Kolin's prospects.[72] And, it is clear that Peters knew that the SS was using Zyklon B to eliminate "inferior" people, including but probably not limited to criminals and the mentally deficient. Obersturmführer Kurt Gerstein told him so sometime during 1943, and not even the German appeals court that finally let Peters off on a technicality in 1955 believed that he was unaware of Zyklon B's application and had done anything to prevent it.[73] But did he actually tell Degussa's leaders? They said no, and so did he, as one would expect in view of the facts that Hans Scherf, a Degussa Vorstand member, served as one of Peters's lawyers after the war and Degussa offered to pay up to 150,000 Deutschmarks as bail money in order to keep Peters out of jail during the appeals of his initial conviction.[74] In short, one cannot prove that Degussa's leaders knew about the use of Zyklon B in the gas chambers. However, even after discounting secondhand postwar claims that such things were overheard being discussed—and Auschwitz referred to by name—in Degesch's offices in Frankfurt, it seems unlikely that Peters failed to take counsel from Schlosser on so grave a matter as the product's application to human beings.[75]

One thing is sure: If Peters did not tell Degussa's chief executives, they could not have figured out the use to which Zyklon was being put from the sales figures. Total shipments to Auschwitz came to approximately 23,000 kilograms in the years 1942 through 1944, for which the price was just under 105,000 Reichsmarks, or about $42,000 at the time.[76] In contrast, total Zyklon B sales amounted to over 3.6 million marks in 1942 to 1943. The only reason to take any notice of the SS's orders was that the ones Kurt Gerstein placed were never paid for, hence his name appears rather conspicuously on the lists of bills outstanding that circulated in the final months of Nazi rule.[77] Nor does Degussa's intense interest in increasing Zyklon B production necessarily provide grounds for suspicion; German military demand was completely explicable and sufficient to make serving it a matter of great concern to Degussa.

Interestingly, had Degussa known what Zyklon B was being used for and wanted to prevent it, the firm would have had, in theory, an easier time doing what Kurt Gerstein hoped to provoke by telling Peters of the product's murderous application—that is, ceasing deliveries to the SS—than it would have had balking at the regime over the smelting of stolen metals. Whereas Degussa could not hide behind any alternative usage of its refineries, Degesch could have claimed that the military demand had exhausted the supply of Zyklon B, since competing uses for cyanide, notably in making Plexiglas for airplane cockpits, were constantly undercutting the flow of raw materials. In practice, however, stanching the flow of the fumigant to Auschwitz would have been impossible thanks to Bruno Tesch, the head of the Testa sales agency, who would have been loathe to let his sales to the SS go, since they made up a far larger portion of Testa's income than of Degesch's. He would quickly have seen through the situation and denounced Degesch, hence Degussa, to his friends in the SS, who had revealed to him what the product was being used for at Auschwitz. In fact, he and his chief aide, Karl Weinbacher, were sufficiently untroubled and indiscreet about their knowledge that they could be made to pay for it with their lives by a British military court in 1947.[78]

How much did Degussa make on selling the Zyklon B that killed people? If one calculates by the dividends Degesch paid to Degussa that can be tied to sales of the product to Auschwitz, the amount is tiny, perhaps 4,000 Reichsmarks from 1941 through 1944 ($16,000 today); if one assesses Degussa for its share of all proceeds on Zyklon B sold to Auschwitz, the total is still surprisingly low, roughly $168,000 today. The as yet undocumented quantities ordered by Majdanek are unlikely to raise this figure appreciably, given the relatively small size of that camp.

The duty of a historian is generally to discover what happened, then to show why it did so, often by showing how. That is the chief purpose of this essay and of the book that covers in greater detail the

matters discussed here, along with other aspects of Degussa's history
in the Nazi period. The mainsprings of Degussa's behavior, in every
one of the instances discussed here, seem to have been similar: each
form of persecution ("Aryanization," confiscation, forced labor, and
murder) presented the firm's executives with opportunities or imperatives that the firm had every commercial or political reason to accept
or accede to and only moral reasons to reject. Involvement in each dimension of the Holocaust appeared irresistible, not least because each
was legally sanctioned and encouraged, and each entailed a series of
small extensions of previous practices rather than abrupt descents
into viciousness (recall the slippery slopes from purchasing Jewish
property to encouraging the state to seize and sell it, from employing
POWs and unwilling foreigners at reduced pay to accepting Jewish
inmates of camps or ghettos at none). Moreover, the nonexercise of
any of the new business prospects promised to have adverse commercial consequences, and the worst results of what the firm was
doing were obscured from view by various means (e.g., gentlemanly
negotiations in the pre-1938 Aryanization cases; specious compensation under the system of metals seizures; delegation of the feeding of
inmate laborers to the DAF) until an apparent point of no return had
been crossed, after which looking reality in the face was so emotionally or professionally threatening as to be impossible. Caught up increasingly during the 1930s in the Nazi regime's siege mentality, then
in the extremity of a war, wishing to do their perceived national duty
and not wishing to risk the consequences of seeming not to do so, the
leaders of Degussa became part of a system of exploitation and death.

But the highly charged discussion that surrounds the class-action
suits recently launched against German corporations, including Degussa, in American courts means that readers will be interested in
some attempt to state the implications of the historical record for the
scale of the firm's liability in claims for restitution for its actions in
connection with the Holocaust. The easiest matter to deal with conclusively is "Aryanization," since nearly all of the twenty-five transactions to which Degussa was party were the subjects of either postwar
restitution proceedings or confiscation by successor governments to
Nazi Germany (Austria, Czechoslovakia, and the German Democratic Republic). As a result of settlements, in and out of court, Degussa
paid approximately two million Deutschmarks and other forms of
compensation and/or returned the properties still in its hands to the

former owners or their heirs.[79] By 1962, only four of the firms acquired from Jewish owners remained to produce for the postwar Degussa: Wyhlen, which had not been obtained, strictly speaking, via "Aryanization," hence was not contested after 1945; and Homburg, Marquart, and Kulzer, for each of which the heirs had sought and received indemnification. While the lost Eastern European properties all had given off profits during the war that Degussa still may be legitimately asked to relinquish, these come to rather little in contemporary values, certainly no more than $400,000 and probably less. If one adds to this the sums calculated earlier—$8 million (metals), $15.6 million ("unpaid" wages), and $168,000 (Degesch)—and estimates that the final figure for "unpaid" wages will rise as we learn more about Fürstenberg and Guben to a number in the range of $19 million—then the total quantifiable liability of Degussa for its participation in the persecution of the European Jews will amount to roughly $28 million in current U.S. currency. That sum, of course, should be augmented to allow for the pain and suffering inflicted by virtue of the processes of dispossession, imprisonment, malnutrition, and brutality in which Degussa enlisted. Even so, the final total is not likely to seem commensurate with the enormous human damage to which Degussa lent a hand.

Neither does or will the $28 million traceable to the Holocaust suffice to justify assertions that Degussa's postwar prosperity rests on the persecution of the Jews. If the company's headquarters still literally do so, its financial and commercial strength do not. The gains involved were, frankly speaking, too small, and the proceeds were largely eaten up by bombing and defeat (especially in the instances of the use of inmate labor). While "Aryanization" did have lasting benefits, in the form of the productive components that remained to Degussa after the war, ironically, it constitutes the only form of complicity in persecution concerning which the legal and restitution issues long have been judicially settled. It is a worthy objective to seek to recover what was stolen and squeezed from helpless people and a virtuous goal to seek compensation for the cruelties to which they were subjected. These efforts must be pursued on principle and for the sake of precedent, even though circumstances have prevented their fulfillment for so long that few of the victims will be able to collect what they are owed. But it is far less warranted to lay claim to large portions of Degussa's current assets on the basis of fantastic claims regarding earlier profits. One aspect of the Holocaust, one more of the many reasons for all the descendants of the perpetrators, victims, and bystanders to remember its horrors, is that, as it devastated the lives of so many, it enriched, in the end, very few.

NOTES

All documents cited are in the Degussa-Hüls AG archive unless preceded by one of these initials: BAL (Bundesarchiv Lichterfelde), LAB (Landesarchiv Berlin), HHSA (Hessisches Hauptstaatsarchiv, Wiesbaden), NR-WHSA (Nordrhein-Westfälisches Hauptstaatsarchiv), or RA (Archiv der Mahn- und Gedenkstätte Ravensbrück, Fürstenberg/Brandenburg). All English translations are mine unless noted otherwise.

1. Hannes Siegrist, "Deutsche Großunternehmen vom späten 19. Jahrhundert bis zur Weimarer Republik," *Geschichte und Gesellschaft* 6 (1980): 93. See also Martin Fiedler, "Die 100 größten Unternehmen in Deutschland—nach der Zahl ihrer Beschäftigten—1907, 1938, 1973 und 1995," and "Die 100 größten Unternehmen von 1938 Bein Nachtrag," *Zeitschrift für Unternehmensgeschichte* 44 (1999): 32–66 and 235–42.

2. On the formative years of Degussa, see Mechthild Wolf, *Im Zeichen von Sonne und Mond* (Frankfurt am Main: Degussa AG, 1993), pp. 13–123; and Birgit Bertsch-Frank, "Eine etwas ungewöhnliche Karriere. Otto Liebknecht," in *Immer eine Idee besser: Forscher und Erfinder der Degussa*, ed. Mechthild Wolf (Frankfurt a.M.: Degussa AG, 1998), pp. 54–75.

3. Biographische Unterlagen Dr. Koloman Roká, memo by G. Pichler, 9 February 1968, reporting the contents of a conversation with Hermann Schlosser.

4. BAL, NSDAP Mitglieder Kartei, Federlin's membership card, dated 1 August 1932; on Achterath, HHSA, Abt. 483, Akte 10989, Gaupersonalamt, 13 June 1942; on the secretiveness, Biographische Unterlagen Fritz Roessler, *Zur Geschichte der Scheideanstalt* [1937], Abschrift, p. 137.

5. BAL, NSDAP Mitglieder Kartei, Menzel's membership card, dated 15 April 1925, the date of his readmission after the "refounding" of the NSDAP, and Biographische Unterlagen Hans Menzel, Lebenslauf, 4 February 1932; on his proselytizing among the firm's leaders, Biographische Unterlagen Fritz Roessler, *Zur Geschichte*, p. 137, and "Nationalsozialismus, Dez. 1933," p. 1.

6. On Busemann's abandoned plan, Biographische Unterlagen Fritz Roessler, *Zur Geschichte*, Abschrift, pp. 137–38; BAL, Schlosser's party membership file, shows that he enlisted as of 1 May 1933, but that a long wrangle ensued because of his failure to resign promptly from the Free-

masons. In October 1934, a Party Court finally rejected his candidacy. Only in December 1939, by special dispensation of Hitler himself, was Schlosser taken into the party.

7. DL 11.5./21, Bekanntmachung an alle Zweigniederlassungen und Verkaufsstellen, 31 March 1933.

8. Biographische Unterlagen Hermann Leyerzapf, including the records of his expulsion from the NSDAP in 1936 for refusing to terminate his open friendship with "the Jew Eichwald"; Sch 1/4, Eichwald to Leyerzapf, 28 August 1947. Re Pohl, Biographische Unterlagen Ernst Baerwind, Tagebuch, entry for 28 June 1945; Biographische Unterlagen Theodor Pohl, Vereinbarung between him and Degussa, 1 April 1946.

9. See especially Biographische Unterlagen Fritz Roessler, *Zur Geschichte*, Abschrift, p. 98. The minutes of Degussa's supervisory board meetings record that Paul Hammerschlag died on 24 June 1933, shortly after the Nazi takeover, and that the departures of the others occurred as follows: Georg Schwarz on 17 October 1933, Max von der Porten on 9 January 1934, Freiherr von Goldschmidt-Rothschild on 6 November 1934, Alfred Merton on 6 December 1935, and Ludwig Deutsch on 8 January 1937. Richard Merton's term as the replacement for his brother ended when he followed him into exile in 1938. Indicative of the firm's willingness to encourage but not force resignations are Busemann to Roessler, 18 July 1933, and Roessler to Goldschmidt-Rothschild, 28 December 1933.

10. IW 1.2/3, Besprechung mit den Herrn Gebrüder Lorch in Gegenwart von Herrn Baer, 19 February 1934; DL 11.5./21, Menzel's Expose in Sachen Degussa gegen Dr. L.C. Marquardt AG, 23 August 1933, enclosed with Menzel, as Stadtrat and Kreisschatzmeister, to Gauwirtschaftsberater Eckhardt, 25 August 1933.

11. See Peter Hayes, "Fritz Roessler and Nazism: The Observations of a German Industrialist, 1930–37," *Central European History* 20 (1987): esp. 73–74.

12. IW 22.5/4–5, Chem. Fabr. Grünau, Busemann to Herzog, 30 July 1937.

13. Interested readers will find a nearly complete account of Degussa's takeovers in Peter Hayes, "Die Arisierungen der Degussa AG: Geschichte und Bilanz," in *"Arisierung" im Nationalsozialismus*, Jahrbuch 2000 des Fritz Bauer Instituts, ed. Irmtrud Wojak and Peter Hayes (Frankfurt am Main: Campus, 2000), pp. 85–123; and a comprehensive one in Peter Hayes, *From Cooperation to Complicity: Degussa in the Third Reich* (New York: Cambridge University Press, 2001), chap. 2.

14. The principal documentary sources in Degussa's archive regarding the takeover of Homburg are in the following files: DL 3.Busemann/4, IW 46.4/1 and IW 46.5/3; also relevant is material in the Bayer-Archiv, Lev-

erkusen, Sig. 6/14. On Auer, the main relevant headings at Degussa are DL 3.Busemann/4 and IW 24.2/1, 24.4/1 and 24.4/4–7.

15. The pertinent documentary collections at Degussa are: on the Neptunhaus, IW 1.2/3 and UV 4/44; on Merton's shares, RFI 4.3/1; on Wyhlen, IW 38.4/1, DL 3.Baerwind/17, and DL 3.Busemann/5; on the Hirsch holdings, IW 41.4/1; on Marquart, IW 21.2/1; and on Hydrocarbon, DL 3.Baerwind/21 and PCA 2/13. It should be added, however, in this connection that Ignaz Hirsch was being subjected at the time of that sale to constant police harassment; he later perished in the Lodz ghetto. See Nordrhein-Westfälisches Hauptstaatsarchiv, RW 58–11288, Gestapo-Akte Ignaz Hirsch, especially Stichwortartige Darstellung des politischen Lebenslaufes, 31 May 1941, telegram from the Bayerische politische Polizei to the Staatspolizeistelle Düsseldorf, 14 April 1936, and Gestapoleitstelle Düsseldorf to Vorsteher des Finanzamtes in Eisenach, 16 October 1942.

16. IW 1.2/3 and UV 4/44 contain the documentation of this case.

17. See IW 22.5/4–5 for the documents concerning this case.

18. IW 22.5/4–5, Busemann to Herzog, 30 July 1937.

19. On the transformation of the situation in early 1938, see Peter Hayes, "Big Business and 'Aryanization' in Germany, 1933–1939," *Jahrbuch für Antisemitismusforschung* 3 (1994): 265–67, 269–70.

20. IW 24.5/2, Reichsanzeiger, 15 February 1938, and Notiz für Herrn Dr. Busemann by Federlin, 7 April 1938.

21. AW 5.2/1 and AW 5.2/3 are the relevant file headings.

22. Most of the documentation is to be found in D2/18, DL 11.5/48, and GBE 1/119–20.

23. DL 11.5/41, UV 1/46, and DL 3.Scherf/1.

24. On the Aurora case, see GEH 6/11, DL 3.Baerwind/42, and AW 2.4/1. Degussa also acquired the Fröhlich, Ing. Jermár & Co. of Prague, a glazing firm (see DL 2/1 and GKF 2/5), and, via the Auergesellschaft subsidiary, two further installations in Prague (see IW 24.9/12 and 24.5/5).

25. DL 3.Baerwind/42, Bericht über Besuche in Brünn und Prag in Angelegenheit der Arisierung der Firma Aurora, 5 April 1940.

26. In 1944, Degussa's branch in Vienna also acquired a patent for gold-plating dental products; AW 2.6/1.

27. LAB, Rep. 39, Restitution Court decision 3W2683/62, 20 February 1963; testimony of Hartmann, former director of the Pfandleihanstalt Frankfurt, 10 January 1955, in case ORG/A/3317.

28. GEH 5/5, Degussa to Hermann Göring, Betr.: Verlängerung der Scheidgut-Konvention, 1 December 1939.

29. RFI 4.8/5, Körperschaftsteuer Berichte, 30 September 1934 and 30 September 1938, Anlagen 2b.

30. GEH 6./11, memos by R. Hirtes, 9 and 15 June 1939.

31. GEH 4/1, Judensilber, 30 June 1939, signed by Dr. Eitel, lays out the quotas allotted to the silver refiners.

32. LAB, Rep. 039–01, Nr. 325, Bl. 20–23, Degussa to the Kammergericht, Berlin-Charlottenburg, 7 July 1960; DL 11.5/51, protocol of conversation between Hans Schneider, Degussa, and Joost of the Reichsbank, 8 November 1939.

33. See DL 3. H. Schlosser/1, Deppe to Hirtes, 8.ii.45.

34. Ralf Banken, "Der Edelmetallsektor und die Verwertung konfiszierten jüdischen Vermögens im 'Dritten Reich,'" *Jahrbuch für Wirtschaftsgeschichte* 39 (1999): 152. Banken's figures, based on the reports of the Reichsstelle für Edelmetalle, appear conclusive regarding gold. Contemporary reports from the refiners regarding the fine silver obtained from the pawnshops' intake are neither consistent nor entirely reconcilable, however; cf. GEH 3.Schnieder/1, Degussa to the Reichskommissar für die Preisbildung, 27 August 1941, and DL 11.5/51, Leihhaus-Silber. Stand vom 25. Februar 1941, signed by Becker. Readers should be aware that the actual total may have been between 131 and 139 metric tons.

35. DL 11.5/51, Degussa to the Reich Economics Ministry, with enclosed tabulations for each refinery as of 31 December 1939, 16 February 1940; DL 11.5/42, Notiz. Betr.: Silber-Zuteilung, signed by Benz, 19 October 1940, and Bestände an Judensilber, 25 February 1941. That Degussa's de facto share exceeded its quota allotment probably resulted from the inability or unwillingness of the smaller firms to comply with the requirement that they pick up the silver from the principal points of collection.

36. See GEH 5/5, Degussa to the Reichskommissar für die Preisbildung, 27 August 1941. Cf. Banken, "Edelmetallsektor," *Jahrbuch für Wirtschaftsgeschichte* 39 (1999): 152, 155, which gives 33,000 kg of fine silver and 1133 kg of fine gold as the totals produced by Degussa. The latter figure, based on a meticulous review of the entry books of Degussa's refineries, may be an advance on the information provided by the contemporaneous documents; the former assuredly is not.

37. In converting the currencies and estimating present values, I have divided the number of Reichsmarks by 2.5 (according to the official exchange rate of the Nazi era), then followed the generally accepted practice of the Bergier and Eizenstat commissions and multiplied the resulting number of dollars by 10.

38. Ralf Banken, "Melmer Gold" (paper presented at Humboldt University, Berlin, June 1999).

39. See Independent Commission of Experts, Switzerland—Second World War [Bergier Commission], "Switzerland and Gold Transactions in the Second World War; Interim Report," May 1998, Table I, p. 39. In ad-

dition, Degussa earned small distribution fees on the 28 kg of this gold that was allocated to it and modest charges for reformatting the portions of plundered gold that the Deutsche and Dresdner banks were permitted to sell abroad, mostly through Turkey. See Jonathan Steinberg, *Die Deutsche Bank und ihre Goldtransaktionen während des Zweiten Weltkrieges* (Munich: Beck Verlag, 1999); and Johannes Bähr, *Der Goldhandel der Dresdner Bank im Zweiten Weltkrieg* (Dresden: Gustav Kiepenheuer Verlag, 1999).

40. See GEH 4/1, the correspondence between Schneider of Degussa and Eitel and Warlimont of the Norddeutsche Affinerie, May-August 1939; and GEH 6/11, Hirtes' Notiz Betr.: Verständigung Degussa/Affinerie, 9 November 1942.

41. See the documents from 1943 to 1944 in *Dokumenty i Materialy, Tom III, Getto Lodzkie* (Warsaw: 1946), pp. 156–57, 163.

42. See Biographische Unterlagen Erna Spiewack, p. 128, where she remarks that, on occasion, "To the smelter also came gold teeth in crates, which, as one later knew, probably were from concentration camps. At the time, such suppositions were not expressed."

43. See the documents in GEH 6/10 and 6/20 prepared for the Belgian Military Mission in Frankfurt in 1946 to 1947, and GEH 6/11, French tally of 6 February 1941.

44. GEH 6/11, Notiz, signed by Hirtes, 31 July 1941.

45. BET 10/1, Bilanzbericht an den Aufsichtsrat über das Geschäftsjahr 1943/44, 24 Mai 1945; and D 2/3, Wertmässige Absatzzifern der wichtigsten Produkten-Gruppen der Degussa im Geschäftsjahr 1937/38, 1941/42, 1946/47.

46. These are the totals that Dr. Ralf Banken has arrived at by adding all the entries in the In- and Outflow Books of the Degussa refineries (Banken, "Melmer Gold").

47. Degussa's proceeds from the precious metals division came to 55.6mRM in 1937/38 and 55.1mRM in 1941/42; D2/3, Wertmässige Absatzziffern der wichtigsten Produkten-Gruppen, and D 2/6, the pie graph of this table.

48. Wolf Gruner, *Der Geschlossene Arbeitseinsatz deutscher Juden* (Berlin: Metropol Verlag, 1997), esp. pp. 55–106.

49. PCA 2/15, Akten-Notiz Betr. Besuch der Hydrocarbon Gesellschaft für Chemische Produkte GmbH, 1 July 1939.

50. The numbers and small turnover in this workforce must be deduced from the data in the monthly reports of the Blankenburg plant in PCA 2/18.

51. Concerning the pressure from Schieber, see IW 24.6/1 and Bernhard Lorentz, "Heinrich Dräger und das Drägerwerk: Industrieelite und

Wirtschaftspolitik 1928–1945" (Ph.D. diss., Humboldt-Universität zu Berlin, 1999), pp. 318–38. Degussa's documentation concerning the compulsory labor force at these plants is extremely sparse, amounting, as of this writing, to a single reference to "1700 female inmates" at Oranienburg in DL 3. H. Schlosser/1, Quasebart to Schlosser, 17 February 1945. Earlier reports on this site and Guben refer to *Ostarbeiter* and prisoners of war among the workforce but not specifically to inmate laborers; see IW 24.9/11, assorted Gefolgschaftsberichte. The records at Ravensbrück establish, however, that the first transports from there to the Auer-Werke Oranienburg occurred in the summer of 1944 (e.g., RA IV, Nr. 11a, Sign. 22, Liste der 5. Überstellung, 20 July 1944) and that the number of women provided quickly reached 900 to 1,200 (RA Bd. 22, Bericht 211, Affidavit by Fritz Suhren, Commandant at Ravensbrück from 1942 to 1945, 17 June 1946). On the wages and deaths, RA Bd. 11, Berichte 67a, 538, and 610. The arrival of such workers at Guben may be inferred from the authorization to construct two new barracks conveyed in IW 24.5/5, exchange of letters between Quasebart and Schlosser, 11 and 16 September 1944.

52. See, especially, TA 2/72, Bericht über die Reise der Herren Obering. Brobeil und Gg. Metz, February 1941, and Betr. Fürstenberg, 11 March 1941, by Retze.

53. On Fürstenberg, see TA 2/73, Schmidt to Degussa, 20 February 1942, and Schmidt to Hemmer, 14 April 1942, as well as TA 2/75, Niederschrift über die "F"-Besprechung am 21. April 1942. With regard to Gleiwitz, see PCA 2/4, Besprechung über Material- und Arbeitsfragen in Gleiwitz am 27 January 1942, by Pross, which notes that "the use of Jews was suggested and accepted in principle by the construction management," and Ziegler's memo of 21 April 1942.

54. See TA 2/78, Schulz, Aktennotiz, 23 February 1942.

55. See TA2/75, Niederschrift über die "F"-Besprechung am 31.3.42, 1 April 1942, for the estimate; and PCA 2/2, Zwischenbilanz vom 31.12.1943, Gewinn- und Verlustrechnung, for the expenditures for *Judenlöhne* (Jewish wages).

56. On this matter, which was fought out at length in the summer of 1943, the key document is TA 2/79, Dencke's Aktennotiz. Betr. Fürstenberg—Lagerverwaltung DAF, 21 September 1943.

57. Of the first 200 Jews sent to Gleiwitz in April 1942, 130 were "exchanged" for fresh personnel in April 1943; PCA 2/1, Monatsbericht Nr. 24, 12 April 1943. According to the unpublished memoir of Coen Rood, a survivor of the labor battalion at the plant, only 10–15 members of the initial contingent remained behind to train the new arrivals, which suggests that some 60 men had died during the year. That is consistent with the rec-

ollections of Martin Sojka, another survivor, with whom I spoke in Frankfurt on 22 October 1998. PCA 2/2, Betriebsbericht Nr. 7, 9 December 1943, comments that in November, 100 Jews were "given up" because of a shortage of guard personnel. This has the look of a "selection," and it was recalled as such by Wolff (Willy) Luksenberrg, who was there, when I spoke with him in Bethesda, Maryland, on 14 August 1998.

58. PCA 2/2, notes to the Zwischenbilanz of 31 May 1944, and Betriebsbericht Nr. 13, 5 June 1944, signed by Pross, where the actual wording is, "Wir streben an, die Ausländer nach und nach ganz durch jüdische Häftlinge zu ersetzen."

59. Manya Friedman and Helen Luksenberrg, conversation with author, Bethesda, Maryland, 14 August 1998.

60. The total number of deaths can be only approximately established. I am estimating that at least as many construction workers died on average per month at the Gleiwitz site after April 1943 as before, which produces a minimum figure of 175, even if one does not include those "exchanged" and "given up" during 1943. Given the worsening conditions in the Lager as the war went on, and the more brutal discipline after the SS took the barracks over in 1944, this is a very conservative calculation.

61. TA 2/86, Genehmigte Investitionen, Anlage Fürstenberg/O., 21 January 1945.

62. PCA 2/1, Endabrechnung der Bauarbeiten, Stichtag 31. Dezember 1944, 26 July 1945; PRO 1/12, Schlussabrechnung DGW Gleiwitz, 8 October 1945; PCA 2/2, Gegenüberstellung von Gestehungskosten und Erlösen [for 1943]; PCA 2/2, Bisherige Betriebsergebnisse des Werkes Gleiwitz, 14 August 1944; and, for the profit and deficit figures, BET 9/5, Bericht über die Prüfung der Bilanz nebst Gewinn- und Verlustrechnung per 31. Dezember 1944, 5 November 1945.

63. PCA 2/2, Betriebsbericht Nr. 1, 5 June 1943, p. 6.

64. See, for the most up-to-date account of this subject, Hervé Joly, "L'implication de l'industrie chimique allemande dans la Shoah: le cas du Zyklon B," *Revue d'histoire moderne et contemporaine* 47 (2000): 368–400.

65. The most informative Degussa files regarding Degesch are to be found under the headings IW 57.2/1 and IW 57.5/1. SCH 1/44, Bernau and Scherf to Peters, 28 November 1946, confirms that "you have been, not a Degesch, but a Degussa employee."

66. Jürgen Kalthoff and Martin Werner, *Die Händler des Zyklon B* (Hamburg: VSA-Verlag, 1998), p. 80.

67. Ibid., pp. 114–17; IW 57.14/3.

68. Concerning Dessau, the most important documents are in IW 32.2/1 and 32.15/1; regarding Kolin, the main files are AW 33.2/1, 33.5/1,

33.6/1, and 33.15/1, and in DL 3. H. Schlosser/14, especially Westphal's report of 9 March 1942 and Feldman's memo of 30 January 1945.

69. This was one of Peters's principal objectives from 1943 on, largely because of Degesch's heavy dependence on sales of Zyklon B; see especially IW 57.2/1, Notiz für Herrn Schlosser, signed by Peters, 7 August 1944.

70. See Kalthoff and Werner, *Händler des Zyklon B,* pp. 107–09, 152–57.

71. BET 9/43, Gewinn- und Verlustrechnung, Heerdt & Lingler; Anlagen zum Geschäftsbericht der Degesch für 1943; and Beantwortung der Fragen in der Anweisung der amer. Militärregierung für Deutschland betr. Dekartellisierung, Anlage zu 6a; BET 10/7, Aufteilung des Brutto-Erlöses 1930–44. That Degesch was acutely conscious that its business rested on Zyklon B is clear from DL 3. H. Schlosser/1, Peters to Schlosser, 26 May 1944, and Stoecker to Schlosser, 28 August 1944.

72. On the Heerdt crisis, IW 57.14/2 provides an extensive record; the numerous documents concerning Kolin in DL 3. H. Schlosser/14, show how interested Schlosser remained in that firm.

73. Biographische Unterlagen Dr. Gerhard Peters, especially the Third Judgment of the Schwurgericht Frankfurt, 27 May 1955.

74. Clariant Werksarchiv Gersthofen, Ordner 125, Hans Scherf to Theo Goldschmidt, 4 July 1950. I am grateful to Dr. Stephan Lindner for bringing this document to my attention.

75. For an example of such a claim, BR 01/12, Notiz für Spruchkammerverfahren Dr. Peters, by Zirkelbach, 17 June 1947.

76. SCH 1/44, Scherf to Oberstaatsanwalt beim Landgericht Frankfurt, 1 March 1948, says that a check of Testa's order books revealed that its shipments to Auschwitz came to 19,653.5 kilograms in 1942 to 1943, and that Degesch independently sent the camp another 3,400 kilograms in 1943 to 1944. These figures were buttressed by testimony and additional documents submitted to the various court proceedings against Peters that culminated in the decision of 1955. Not included in these totals are the shipments to Kurt Gerstein at the SS offices in Oranienburg, which came to 3,790 kilograms between June 1943 and 31 May 1944, according to BRO 1/12, a copy of the account book page for Gerstein's Konto-Nr. G 36 at Degesch.

77. Bericht über die Prüfung des Jahresabschlusses vom 31. Dezember 1943, 10 August 1944, p. 12; BET 9/43, Geschäftsbericht fuer 1943, Anlage; BET 10/7, Gewinn- und Verlustrechnung für 1944; and DL 11.5/60, Degesch to Bachmann, 12 July and 12 August 1946, which reports that the bill of 17,101.70 RM for all 3,790 kilograms delivered to Gerstein remained unpaid.

78. See Peter Hayes, *Industry and Ideology: IG Farben in the Nazi Era* (New York: Cambridge University Press, 1987), p. 363.

79. For a detailed treatment of the individual settlements and specific references to the sources, see Hayes, "Arisierungen der Degussa AG," in *"Arisierung"im Nationalsozialismus,* Jahrbuch 2000 des Fritz Bauer Instituts, ed. Irmtrud Wojak and Peter Hayes (Frankfurt am Main: Campus, 2000), pp. 108–13.

Sybil Milton

The Case against Switzerland

THE RECENT SPOTLIGHT ON ECONOMIC ASPECTS OF THE SECOND World War and the Holocaust has caused new interest in the Nazi machinery of dispossession and despoliation. This preoccupation is reflected in a growing quantity of governmental and corporate histories in France, Germany, Great Britain, Sweden, Switzerland, the United States, and elsewhere.[1] The focus of these investigations has spread from accounting for the "dormant or unclaimed Nazi-era bank accounts" of Holocaust victims in Switzerland to research about various types of stolen property and valuables, including but not limited to gold, real estate, insurance, securities, jewelry, looted art, and forced labor.

Gold symbolizes the German appropriation of all types of looted victim assets; dental gold and wedding rings also represent the murder of human beings. The intrinsic link between looting and genocide had been clear since April 7, 1945, when U.S. Army officers entered the Kaiseroda salt mines near Merkers, discovering bags of gold and silver bars and coins as well as dental fillings, wedding rings, jewelry, and precious stones. This cache also included some of Melmer's "shipments" to the Reichsbank, the partial records of the Reichsbank, and thousands of works of art.[2] General Dwight David Eisenhower visited this mine several days later, before inspecting the liberated concentration camps at Ohrdruf and Buchenwald. Already in 1945, it was clear that economic and physical liquidation were closely linked aspects of one crime.

Since German looted gold had to be transformed into foreign currency to purchase raw materials indispensable to the arms industry and conduct of the war, it was essential to find a place to exchange resmelted gold. Switzerland served in this capacity because of its political neutrality, its established role as an international financial center, and the convertibility of the Swiss franc. Moreover, Switzerland's geographical proximity to the German Reich enabled both countries to complete business with minimum risk, largely unnoticed by the public.

Let me digress for a moment to say something about how historians have viewed Switzerland's relationship with Nazi Germany. Although there is an extensive literature about many aspects of Switzerland during World War II, the fact that gold transferred by Nazi Germany to Switzerland included persecutee-origin gold had been peripheral for most scholars until the May 1997 Eizenstat report, the London gold conference, and the Independent Commission of Experts interim "gold" report.[3] Switzerland served as a major conduit for German looted gold and other assets plundered by the Germans.

In Amos Elon's words in the *New York Times,* Switzerland was "surely not the Auschwitz of the Alps," but it had "its own politics of memory . . . shrouded by powerful national myths. This landlocked country in the heart of Europe had always seen itself as a special case."[4]

THE GERMAN BACKGROUND

The systematic theft, confiscation, plunder, and exploitation of state and private property from the countries Nazi Germany occupied during World War II is relatively well known. At the International Military Tribunal in Nuremberg, crimes involving property were muted in comparison to other Nazi German atrocities. However, in ten of the twelve subsequent American Military Tribunal trials at Nuremberg, property crimes and rapacious Nazi policies became a major component of each indictment. In the Jurists', the Flick, and the Ministries cases, Nazi property confiscations were central to the specification of charges. Aryanization as well as the seizure of property from political opponents, Freemasons, and churches before 1939 were also considered crimes against humanity. The defendants in the I. G. Farben and Krupp trials faced the charge that their participation in the Four Year Plan constituted intent to wage aggressive war. German occupation policies that robbed civilian populations and exploited foreign civilians and concentration camp prisoners as slave labor provided the justification for additional war crimes charges. However, the complexity of property crimes and their short statutes of limitations meant that postwar trials between the mid-1950s and

1990s largely ignored crimes against property. Claims for misappropriated property reemerged in the mid-1990s with the end of the cold war, including individual and class-action Jewish survivor claims for confiscated and nationalized properties, for dormant bank accounts, for forced labor, for looted art, and for "looted victim gold."

After 1933, the cumulative escalation of the economic restrictions designed to isolate Jews, as well as Gypsies, the disabled, and political and religious opponents in Nazi Germany initially included boycott, exclusionary legislation, expulsions from professional organizations, and employment discrimination. The combination of terror, propaganda, and legislation was so effective that two-thirds of all Jewish-owned or -operated businesses in Germany (ca. 100,000 in all) had been sold or liquidated "voluntarily" by 1938. Jewish owners, desperate to emigrate or to sell a failing business, often accepted selling prices that were up to 70 percent below actual value. After the incorporation of Austria in March 1938, the pauperization of Jews and the expropriation of Jewish-owned property and capital proceeded even more rapidly in Austria than it had in Germany. Immediately after the November 1938 pogrom, Aryanization entered its second stage: the mandatory transfer of all Jewish enterprises to non-Jewish ownership. Every remaining Jewish business was assigned an Aryan trustee to oversee its immediate compulsory sale. The trustee's fee for this required service was often only slightly less than the sale price and was paid by the former Jewish owner. A further percentage of sale profits funded Hermann Göring's Office of the Four Year Plan, launched in September 1936.

The Four Year Plan rapidly prepared the German economy for war. The massive funds needed to initiate large-scale armaments production were in part raised through the confiscation of property and valuables. German Jews wishing to emigrate were compelled to forfeit much of their property. Part of these assets went directly to the Reich government in the form of a special "flight tax" (*Reichsfluchtsteuer*), while the rest was deposited as liquid assets into special nontransferable bank accounts whose access was severely restricted. The assets of those Jews who remained in Germany were likewise placed in blocked accounts; their owners were allowed to withdraw only a fixed monthly sum, the bare minimum needed for meeting expenses. Moreover, after the November 1938 pogrom, German Jews were required to pay one billion Reichsmarks as a penalty; the state also confiscated all insurance payments that should have been paid to Jewish property owners. The latter were held responsible for all property repairs for damage they had incurred during the looting and vandalism of the November pogrom.[5]

As early as February 1939, compulsory levies required Jews to surrender tangible property, such as precious metals, diamonds, pearls, securities, and stock or bond certificates. These were often resold for the Reich Ministry of Economics and Four Year Plan in the United States after laundering the stolen property via Swiss middlemen.[6] Later levies in 1941 included the confiscation of cars, cameras, radios, telephones, and optical and electrical equipment. Ultimately, all property involuntarily left behind at deportation was either sold by state auctioneers, with the revenue going to state coffers, or taken over by Aryan neighbors and subsequent tenants. The victims and their heirs were seldom compensated for all of these losses after the war.

Jews were not the only victims of this property confiscation and employment restriction in the German Reich and occupied Europe. Any group or organization considered detrimental was discouraged, disbanded, expropriated, and destroyed. Thus, already on July 14, 1933, the Law for the Confiscation of Subversive and Enemy Property was initially used for the seizure of assets (property and possessions) of proscribed and denaturalized political opponents, thereby impoverishing them. The automatic loss of citizenship, including property rights, made many socialists and Communists unwelcome as transients or residents in countries of exile where they sought temporary sanctuary. This law was also applied inside Nazi Germany to Jews (until the 11th decree of November 1941), to Gypsies (until the 12th decree of 1942), and to Jehovah's Witnesses after 1935. These measures against racial and political outsiders in Nazi Germany and incorporated Austria impacted the flow and timing of emigration for political and racial "enemies," and, in turn, their accelerating destitution decreased prospects for flight and survival outside the Nazi empire. The interlocking series of prohibitions and confiscations created a pattern of lost jobs, lost incomes, lost properties, and ultimately, lost physical existence. Thus, the processes of economic and physical liquidation were closely linked aspects of one crime: mass murder and genocide.

By late 1941, systematic deportations from Germany to the East had begun. When notified by German authorities of their impending "resettlement to the East," a euphemism for forced deportation, Jews and other victims received specific instructions. The SS and police made it clear to all deportees that failure to adhere to these instructions would mean immediate prosecution or death. These rigid and precise orders included instructions to pack about 100 pounds of their possessions to take with them. For the deportees, these instructions created an illusion of survival to the very end and enabled relatively small numbers of SS to control the large numbers of deportees arriving in the camps. The steps prior to deportation included the following:

1. All deportees were required to complete a property inventory form, detailing what they were forced to leave behind. This property was then confiscated by local authorities and the inventory forms were countersigned by the deportee. The involuntarily abandoned property was sealed by the police. House keys were to be marked and delivered to the police and all drawer keys were to be placed in their locks with all desk and closet locks left open.

2. All rent and debts were to be paid by the deportee prior to deportation and all utilities (gas, water, electricity) were to be shut off.

3. All securities, currency, bank books, and other valuables were to be surrendered to the police before departing for the assembly center or train station for deportation. Cameras, bicycles, and typewriters, were to be surrendered to the local police prior to departure.

5. Deportees could pack and take along a suitcase of a fixed weight containing prescribed articles of clothing and maintenance (blankets and kitchen utensils). They could also carry a knapsack with bedding and linen and a briefcase or satchel with food for the trip. The baggage was to be marked on the outside with the name and evacuation number of the deportee.

6. All deportees were searched bodily at assembly centers and the contents of their luggage was searched by Gestapo and local police before the train departed. This enabled local police to confiscate concealed valuables such as currency, jewelry, precious metals, or precious stones.

On arrival at the ramp in the East, all arriving prisoners were told to leave their larger pieces of luggage. In reality, the luggage they had so painstakingly packed was taken on arrival at Auschwitz to a series of special warehouses known collectively as "Canada." Canada was the term for the Birkenau warehouses where the belongings of the newly arrived victims were sorted and stored by the SS. In Poland, the name and country Canada symbolized a place of great riches, and as such, it is still used as an idiom for wealth in contemporary Poland. At Canada, prisoner labor would open and sort the contents for reutilization in the German war economy. This included clothing, personal possessions like hairbrushes and toothbrushes, and eventually also by-products of the killing process such as dental gold and human hair (used as fleece linings in military jackets).[7]

In February 1943, Oswald Pohl, head of the SS Central Office for Economy and Administration and responsible for all SS economic activities in the concentration camps, reported that exactly 781 train cars had left Auschwitz for Germany. Of these, 245 freight cars were filled with clothing and one with human hair. Gold fillings retrieved from the corpses and from human ashes were smelted down and sent by special courier as ingots to the Reichsbank for further processing. By October 1942, Himmler had been informed that the SS had enough dental gold (more than 50 kilograms) from dead inmates of concentration camps to handle all SS dental needs for at least five years; future gold deliveries of this type were to be processed via the Reichsbank.[8] On January 11, 1943, SS Lieutenant Colonel Arthur Liebehenschel, Chief of Office D-I, of the SS Central Office for Economy and Administration (*Wirtschaftsverwaltungshauptamt,* or WVHA), notified all subsidiary concentration camps that they should not forward gold teeth every month but should send only larger amounts once a year.[9] Some of the SS-looted victim gold from the Operation Reinhard camps (Auschwitz and Majdanek) had been conveyed to the Reichsbank by SS Captain Bruno Melmer. (The Reichsbank list of the 46th shipment of so-called Melmer dental gold to the Prussian State Mint [24 November 1944] was used by the U.S. prosecution at the Ministries Trial in Nuremberg.)[10]

At the beginning of 1943, the Allies first warned neutral nations against purchasing gold from Germany, but at first this warning had no immediate tangible consequences. The Allied declaration about gold purchases on February 22, 1944, also later warned neutral nations about accepting looted gold.

SWITZERLAND AND THE DISPOSAL OF SS-LOOTED VICTIM GOLD

Current research gives us an approximation of the magnitude of the gold transactions between Germany and Switzerland. Seventy-nine percent of all Reichsbank gold shipments abroad were delivered to Switzerland. The Swiss National Bank accounted for 87 percent and Swiss commercial banks for 13 percent of such transactions. The U.S. State Department estimated that out of a total sum of about $398 million worth of gold purchased by Switzerland from Germany during the war, a minimum of $185 million and a maximum of $289 million included looted gold. There were three types of looted gold: (1) gold obtained from confiscation and looting from individuals in Germany and occupied territories after 1938; (2) gold from murdered victims of Nazi German extermination policies ("victim gold"); and (3) gold from currency reserves belonging to the central banks of occupied countries, which Germany transferred to Berlin. This third category was statistically the most important for German gold transactions in Switzerland.

Let me again digress for a moment. Since January 1997, I have personally been involved in two official historical reports about looted assets. First, as senior historian of the U.S. Holocaust Memorial Museum Research Institute, I was part of the interagency team that investigated "the disposition of SS-looted victim gold" for the first Eizenstat report,[11] and later in 1997, as vice president of the Independent Commission of Experts: Switzerland—Second World War (ICE), I was involved in the interim report *Switzerland and Gold Transactions in World War II*.[12] These two reports are complementary, revealing our growing knowledge about the scale of the centralized German liquidation and plunder of the property and assets of European Jews, Gypsies, political opponents, and conquered civilian populations.

The May 1997 Eizenstat report demonstrated conclusively that "victim-origin gold was incorporated into Germany's monetary reserves" and subsequently included in gold transactions with Switzerland and other neutral states. It will probably never be possible to determine definitively the total value of gold that the Reichsbank received from the SS. The total value of gold in this partial surviving record of Melmer shipments to Switzerland amounted to at least $2.9 million.

The ICE report issued in 1998 concluded that during the first two years of the war, the Reichsbank's gold transactions were primarily with commercial banks in Switzerland. After 1942, gold shipments from the German Reichsbank went mainly to the Swiss National Bank (SNB). The SNB had made no effort to distinguish between legally obtained and looted gold supplied by the Reichsbank. These transactions cannot be fully reconstructed today based on fragmentary available sources. The report concluded, "Viewed from today's perspective, the SNB's claims that it acted in good faith and that Swiss neutrality obliged it to accept the gold offered by Nazi Germany are clearly not justified. . . . Swiss neutrality in no way obliged the country to accept stolen gold. . . . As to the theory put forward by the SNB that the gold purchased from the Reichsbank helped dissuade Germany from invading Switzerland, it must be pointed out that Hitler's policies . . . were not guided by rational or pragmatic reactions to measures of economic deterrence. . . . Profit was not the main reason for the SNB's accepting delivery of gold from Germany. This motive did, however, play a role in the sale to third parties of gold the SNB had purchased."[13] During the war, the SNB earned 18.4 million francs on trade in gold that it had acquired from the German Reichsbank and subsequently resold. This represents about 20 percent of all gross returns of SNB business during the same period. Germany's last gold shipment to the SNB took place on April 13, 1945. In 1946, the United States knew about gold transactions between the Reichsbank, the SNB, and Swiss commercial banks. The Washington agreement of May 25, 1946, specified that Switzerland was required to pay an indemnity of 250 million francs as settlement for its gold transactions. In return, the United States and its allies declared on behalf of fifteen countries that they would relinquish all claims against the Swiss government and SNB for gold purchased by Switzerland from Germany during the war.

The fascination with humongous figures makes it clear that current research is still defined by governments focusing on central banks, although the discussion by survivors and their heirs about heirless and dormant Nazi-era assets and accounts (*nachrichtloses Vermögen*) has placed mass murder center stage, because lack of contact with Swiss bank accounts was not about missing assets but about missing customers and thus a by-product of Nazi genocide. From 1945 to 1997, our emphasis has changed from the needs of governments for the reconstruction of Europe to the moral and material claims for restitution to elderly Jewish survivors of the Holocaust.[14]

In late 1996, the Swiss Federal Council commissioned two historians, Peter Hug and Marc Perrenoud, to study compensation agreements between Switzerland and Eastern Europe (especially Poland and Hungary) after the war. Essentially, the unclaimed heirless assets of Jewish victims of Polish or Hungarian nationality were used to compensate Swiss citizens for assets nationalized under these Communist governments.[15] Let us be clear about what is happening here: not only were accounts which previously had been announced as either nonexistent or not locatable, and which had been withheld from heirs because of inadequate documentation, identified, but legal title and contents were transferred to Swiss citizens whose claims against Hungary or Poland might hinder future profitable Swiss trade with those countries.

I should point out in passing that scant attention has so far been paid to the financial aspects of Switzerland's refugee policies, although this is related to the question of dormant assets. Until 1938, Switzerland nominally maintained its traditional policy of asylum for refugees, admitting 10,000 to 12,000 refugees between 1933 and 1938. Refugee policies were initially decentralized and vested with the cantons rather than with federal authorities, although refugee policy was increasingly centralized after 1938. Refugees were usually not allowed to work and were generally under police surveillance. Moreover, they had no access to their finances during their stay in Switzerland, although mandatory security deposits were required before certificates of residence could be issued. Permits valid for three to six months' temporary residence for refugees in transit were the norm, and renewals were allowed. It was mandatory to deposit "collateral" (*Kaution*) for "tolerance permits" (*Toleranzbewilligung*), usually 5,000 Swiss francs per person, for temporary residence permits. This bond or collateral was to be repaid when a refugee left Switzerland. Tolerance permits issued for more than two years needed approval by Swiss federal authorities.

In March 1940, the Swiss Federal Council ordered the construction of labor and internment camps for all refugees, and on March 18,

1941, they decreed that refugees with assets were subject to a "solidarity tax" (*Solidaritätsabgabe*) to assist indigent fellow refugees. These measures meant that refugees were liable for their own expenses and subsistence after 1941. Their money and personal valuables were seized after 1940 when refugees were interned in labor camps and homes, and this money was involuntarily placed under the trusteeship administration (*Treuhandstelle*) of the Federal Justice and Police Department in Bern. Jewelry and precious stones taken from interned refugees could be sold and converted to cash (Swiss franks) at the request of the federal police under an agreement between the police and the Schweizerischer Volksbank on May 18, 1943.

Usually when refugees left Switzerland, the deposited funds reverted to them minus bank charges and fees. Sometimes, personal valuables confiscated at the refugee's arrival disappeared in the internment camps and the value of such objects was repaid, if at all, at arbitrarily low figures. Although the administration of refugee property ended in March 1947, many accounts were continued on police instructions.[16]

In 1955, the Volksbank transferred about 20,000 Swiss francs to the federal treasury; it had liquidated 107 accounts and still retained an additional 37 accounts. In April 1963, the police, as required under the Federal Registration Decree for dormant assets of December 1962, reported 50 refugee accounts valued at 18,524 Swiss francs. The Swiss office (*Meldestelle*) responsible for the reporting of dormant assets refused to accept jurisdiction over this money, since these sums did not fit within the definitions of the 1962 decree. In 1967, the Federal Justice and Police Department placed this money in an interest-bearing account in the Federal Ministry of Finance. The account was subsequently terminated, and 42,820 Swiss francs were transferred to the Swiss Central Office for Refugee Assistance.[17] It is thus probable that dormant refugee accounts and assets have not been fully restituted to the original depositors or their heirs.

The national mythology of Switzerland's "special position" can be characterized by the buzzwords "neutrality/independence" and "national redoubt/resistance." The deconstruction of these myths in a growing critical literature about Swiss refugee policies and anti-Semitism has resulted in the reinterpretation of Switzerland as Germany's "silent partner."[18] This belated debate as the twentieth century draws to a close is parallel to the German historians debate of the

1980s. Since Switzerland was neutral in the First World War, there was no historical debate about war guilt in 1914 (like the Fritz Fischer controversy in Germany), no discussion about the continuities from Bismarck to Hitler, the "uniqueness" of Nazi genocide, the role of the Wehrmacht, or the Goldhagen debate. Instead, a painful and often frenzied reevaluation of Swiss historical taboos and self-deceptions, usually under pressure from abroad, is essentially putting the past belatedly on trial in the press, on television, in films, and in historical publications.[19] Obviously a more nuanced and comprehensive reevaluation of Switzerland's relationship to Nazi Germany is being addressed by historians both in and outside Switzerland.

I would like to close with a quotation from Max Frisch's book *Reminiszenz* (1974) that reveals the insular nature of 1930s Switzerland and, conversely, Swiss accommodation to German anti-Semitism: "In 1936, when I wanted to marry a Jewish student from Berlin, I went to Zürich city hall to get the necessary papers (birth certificate, citizenship certificate, etc.) and also received, without asking, an official Aryan identity form with the stamp of my home town. . . . I tore up this document immediately. Switzerland was not then occupied by Hitler; it was then what it still is today—independent, neutral, free."[20] A growing understanding of the consequences of neutrality and independence is part of the examination of the case of Switzerland during World War II.

NOTES

1. U.S. Department of State, *U.S. and Allied Efforts to Recover and Restore Gold and Other Assets Stolen or Hidden by Germany during World War II: A Preliminary Study,* coordinated by Stuart E. Eizenstat and edited by William Z. Slany (Washington, D.C.: Department of State Publication 10468, May 1997), hereafter cited as *1st Eizenstat Report;* U.S. Department of State, *U.S. and Allied Wartime and Postwar Relations and Negotiations with Argentina, Portugal, Spain, Sweden, and Turkey on Looted Gold and German External Assets and U.S. Concerns about the Fate of the Wartime Ustasha Treasury* (Washington, D.C.: Department of State, June 1998), hereafter cited as *2nd Eizenstat Report;* Independent Commission of Experts Switzerland—World War II, ed., *Switzerland and Gold Transactions in the Second World War* (Bern: EDMZ, 1998), hereafter cited as ICE, *Switzerland and Gold;* Historians in Library and Records Department of the For-

eign and Commonwealth Office, ed., *Nazi Gold: Information from the British Archives* (London: Foreign and Commonwealth Office, September 1996); 2d rev. ed. (Jan. 1997); Historians in Library and Records Department of the Foreign and Commonwealth Office, ed., *Nazi Gold: Information from the British Archives: Part II* (London: Foreign and Commonwealth Office, May 1997); Historians in Library and Records Department of the Foreign and Commonwealth Office, ed. *British Policy towards Enemy Property during and after the Second World War* (London: Foreign and Commonwealth Office, April 1998); Foreign and Commonwealth Office, *Nazi Gold: The London Conference* (London: HMSO, 1998); Historical Commission for the History of the Deutsche Bank, *The Deutsche Bank and Its Gold Transactions during the Second World War*, edited by Jonathan Steinberg (Munich: C. H. Beck, 1999); and Johannes Bähr, *Der Goldhandel der Dresdner Bank im Zweiten Weltkrieg* (Leipzig: Gustav Kiepenheuer Verlag and Hanna Arendt Institut, 1999).

Interim reports have also been published by commissions in Sweden (Commission on Jewish Assets in Sweden at the Time of the Second World War, ed., *The Nazi Gold and the Swedish Riksbank* [Stockholm, July 1998], interim report ca. 150 pages, also online at www.ud.se), Norway (Ministry of Justice and Police, White Paper No. 82 to the Storting, *Historical and Moral Settlement for the Treatment in Norway of the Economic Liquidation of the Jewish Minority during World War II* [June 1998]), France (Report Mattéoli Commission: Premier Ministre, *Mission d'étude sur la spoliation des Juifs en France* [December 1997]), Belgium (Commission d'Étude sur le sort des biens des membres de la communauté Juive de Belgique spoliés ou délaissés pendant la guerre 1940–1945, *Réport intérimaire* [1998]), Spain, Portugal, and Argentina (Commission of Inquiry into Activities of Nazism in Argentina [CEANA], *Second Progress Report* [July 1998]). See also Bundesarchiv (Berlin) and the German Bundesbank, ed., *Der Verblieb der Unterlagen der Deutschen Reichsbank: Ein Rechercheberict*, Document No. R 4—2850/18 (Berlin, August 1988).

2. Greg Bradsher, "Nazi Gold: The Merkers Mine Treasure," *Prologue* 31, no. 1 (spring 1999): 6–21.

3. The exception was the Swiss journalist, Werner Rings, *Raubgold aus Deutschland: Die "Golddrehscheibe" Schweiz im Zweiten Weltkrieg* (Zurich: Chronos, 1996), who explains Swiss laundering of looted and victim gold as motivated by profiteering and expediency. See also Arthur L. Smith, *Hitler's Gold: The Story of Nazi War Loot* (Oxford: Berg, 1989).

4. Amos Elon, "Switzerland's Lasting Demon," *New York Times Magazine,* 12 April 1998, 40.

5. Gerald D. Feldman, "Confiscation of Insurance Assets: Special Is-

sues," in U.S. Department of State and U.S. Holocaust Memorial Museum, *Washington Conference on Holocaust-Era Assets,* edited by J. D. Bindenagel (Washington, D.C.: U.S. Government Printing Office, 1999), 599–604.

6. National Archives, College Park, Md. (hereafter NARA II): RG 260, Box 58, OMGUS- Finance Division, correspondence between the import-export jewelry dealer Ernst Färber in Berlin and the Reich Ministry of Economics about the sale of Jewish jewels and diamonds via Switzerland in the United States, May 1939–October 1940.

7. See Andrzej Strelecki, "Der Raub des Besitzes der Opfer des KL Auschwitz" and "Die Verwertung der Leichen der Opfer des Lagers," *Hefte von Auschwitz* 21 (1997); manuscript of German translation courtesy of Auschwitz-Birkenau Memorial Museum.

8. NARA II, RG 238, Box 44, Entry 174: Nuremberg Doc. NO-2305, letter from Hans Frank, then governor-general of occupied Poland, to Himmler, 8 October 1942.

9. Bundesarchiv Koblenz, NS 3/426, reproduced in Henry Friedlander and Sybil Milton, eds., *Archives of the Holocaust,* vol. 20, *Bundesarchiv of the Federal Republic of Germany, Koblenz & Freiburg* (New York: Garland, 1993), 480 (Doc. 179).

10. NARA II, RG 238, Doc. NI(D) 15534; published in the *Trial of War Criminals before the Nuremberg Military Tribunals under Control Council Law No. 10* [Green Series], 14 vols. (Washington, D.C.: U.S. Government Printing Office, 1950–52), 13: 370.

11. *1st Eizenstat Report.*

12. ICE, *Switzerland and Gold;* and Elizabeth B. White, "The Disposition of SS-Looted Victim Gold during and after World War II," *American University International Law Review* 14:1, pp. 213–24; manuscript courtesy of Dr. E. B. White, Chief Historian, Office of Special Investigations, U.S. Department of Justice, October 1998.

13. ICE, *Switzerland and Gold,* 191–93.

14. Swiss Federal Archives, ed., *Fluchtgelder, Raubgut und nachrichtenlose Vermögen: Wissensstand und Forschungsperspektiven,* Bundesarchiv Dossier 6 (Bern: EDMZ, 1997).

15. Peter Hug and Marc Perrenoud, *In der Schweiz liegende Vermögenswerte von Nazi-Opfern und Entschädigungsabkommen mit Oststaaten,* Bundesarchiv Dossier 4 (Bern: EDMZ, 1997).

16. Guido Koller, "Die Finanzierung der schweizerischen Flüchtlingspolitik im Zweiten Weltkrieg: Fakten, Zahlen und Hintergründe," (Bern: Schweizerisches Bundesarchiv, 1997; photocopy).

17. Uriel Gast, *Von der Kontrolle zur Abwehr: Die eidgenössische Fremdenpolizei im Spannungsfeld von Politik und Wirtschaft, 1915–1933* (Zurich: Chronos, 1996); and Jacques Picard, "Die Schweiz und die Ver-

mögen verschwundener Nazi-Opfer," *Die Schweiz und die Flüchtlinge: Zeitschrift des Schweizerischen Bundesarchivs, Studien und Quellen* 22 (1996): 271–324.

18. Guido Koller, "Entscheidungen über Leben und Tod: Die behördliche Praxis in der schweizerischen Flüchtlingspolitik während des Zweiten Weltkrieges," *Zeitschrift des Schweizerischen Bundesarchivs* 22 (1996): 17–106 [special issue "Die Schweiz und die Flüchtlinge 1933–1945"]; Jacques Picard, *Die Schweiz und die Juden 1933–1945* (Zurich: Chronos, 1997); and Jakob Tanner, "'Réduit national'und Aussenwirtschaft: Wechselwirkungen zwischen militärischer Dissuasion und ökonomischer Kooperation mit den Achsenmächten," in *Raubgold—Réduit—Flüchtlinge: Zur Geschichte der Schweiz im Zweiten Weltkrieg,* edited by Philipp Sarasin and Regina Wecker (Zurich: Chronos, 1998), 81–103.

19. See the anthology, Georg Kreis and Bertrand Müller, ed., *Die Schweiz und der Zweite Weltkrieg* (Basel: Schwabe, 1997).

20. Swiss Federal Archives, ed., *Fluchtgelder, Raubgut und nachrichtenlose Vermögen,* 63 n. 14.

Gitta Sereny

Questioning the Perpetrators

QUESTIONING PERPETRATORS, LET ME SAY IT RIGHT AWAY, IS DIFFICULT, demanding, and immensely costly, to yourself and to others. Which is, of course, one reason why so few people have done it, or indeed are doing it now in Bosnia, in South American and African countries, where it urgently needs to be done.

But let me try to tell you what doing this work involves, for—contrary to what many people may think—it isn't "interviewing" people. I call myself a journalist because of many other things I do, but this isn't really journalism. What it requires first of all, is the acquisition of knowledge: it is entirely irresponsible to touch, even marginally, upon this kind of historical, or social, journalism without a background of real knowledge in history, law, and psychology. That, of course, you can gain by education and experience. But there is need for more fundamental decisions which, once made, will almost inevitably profoundly affect the way you lead your life. For you must first of all be prepared to commit unlimited time. What motivates you cannot be just an ambition, or even a desire, but a need inside yourself to know, to understand. You need to be capable of opening your mind to even the worst, the most unbearable things human beings can do, and manage the consequences, both in yourself and to a degree the other—the person who thus confides in you—your subject, I will call them.

I have of course by now worked like this with many people, and all of them, with their story and their feelings, good or bad, are in my books. But what I will do today, rather than generalize, is to tell you about a few of these people, quoting what seems to be essential to help you see how it is done and what it can—and at times cannot and perhaps should not—produce.

In doing this, I need of course to use my own books, so let me apologize in advance to those of you to whom some words or descriptions will be familiar. At the risk of preempting myself, or doubts that you may want to express at the end, let me first confront two questions I am frequently asked.

They have arisen again in England with the publication of my newest book, *Cries Unheard*,[1] which is not in fact about perpetrators in the Third Reich but about an eleven-year-old girl who killed two little boys thirty years ago, an act familiar to you after what happened in Oregon and Arkansas in the spring of 1997. Mary Bell—that was her name, now changed—was tried in 1968 in an adult British court and sentenced to life imprisonment. In 1996, then thirty-nine years old, she spent eight months talking with me in an attempt—as she put it—to find out how she became such a child. The reason I mention her here is because, as you will see in *Cries Unheard*, although there is a world of difference in the backgrounds, there is little difference in technique between questioning someone who had a harrowing childhood and finally killed, and a former Nazi who murdered or acquiesced to murder.

Some people find it hard to accept some of the things these people find themselves discovering and divulging to me. And the questions put to me, which of course are implied doubts or criticisms, are always the same: Are you not getting too close to the subject to remain capable of objectivity and judgment? And the other, closely related: Are you not afraid they lie to you, and are you aware—and tell them so—when they do?

Let me tackle the first one. It is not possible to do this sort of . . . not interrogating, but questioning, which is really a dialogue . . . without establishing a relationship of some sort. Of course the nature of that relationship varies, depending on the subject, but it can't be fake or faked: it has to be true, and you need to be capable of demonstrating and sustaining this truth.

My—particularly difficult—relationship with Mary Bell, the woman who killed as a child, was really that of an adult . . . an adult woman at that . . . talking with a child. She needed to be the child she had never been allowed to be, and when she felt sure I understood and could accept this, she felt able to respond.

My relationship with Albert Speer—as those of you who have read my book about him may have noticed—was really quite . . .

stern, but on the other hand it was two civilized people working together: It demonstrated clearly my enormous intellectual interest in him and acknowledged not only his formidable intellect but also my awareness of his battle to remake himself into a different, a moral, man. Sensing this awareness—or if you like, this faith—in me was what allowed *him* to respond to me, to divulge what he had not been able to divulge before.

My relationship with Franz Stangl, commandant of Treblinka, was totally different and totally one-sided: I learned everything or nearly everything about him, but he knew nothing about me; it would have been outrageous to allow the monstrous man he had become—and as I would find, had remained—even that amount of familiarity. And for him who—as he showed to me—knew quite despairingly what he was, this was right. Anything else would have been impossibly confusing; this was the relationship to which he could respond.

But whatever the relationship one creates, what is always essential, and only possible to achieve with experience and discipline, is to retain distance—spiritual, emotional independence from the subject, a kind of neutrality. Intellectual involvement is right; sympathy and compassion are natural and not to be suppressed, as otherwise you risk your own humanity. Empathy, however, is dangerous and needs to be . . . not suppressed, but withdrawn back to the limits which you have set . . . the distance which you must always maintain.

As for lies—if one undertakes this work, one has to know and accept that there will be lies: some unimportant, to try you out, but mostly about matters the subject has long lied about to him- or herself, because the truth cannot be faced, cannot be lived with.

The ability to both recognize the lies and deal with them is again a matter of knowledge and experience: preknowledge about the subject's circumstances and experience in listening to tones of voice and observing what—I assure you—is unfakeable body language. After that it becomes a matter of judgment whether one forces the lies out or leaves them fallow where perhaps, to save the subject's sanity, they need to be.

To illustrate this, let me briefly tell you about a man called Hans Munch who was an SS doctor in Auschwitz. I wrote a profile of him in 1982 for the *Times* in London; he is also in my book on Albert Speer. But the reason why it is entirely relevant to speak about him here, now, is because the German Magazine *Der Spiegel* recently rediscovered him, and it appears that *60 Minutes* will have him on television here, very soon. Here is my talk with Munch, who was then 71; now he is 87 and, as I can clearly see from what he says to *Spiegel* and how he will, of course, be encouraged to speak on *60 Minutes,* he is on the way to an inability to distinguish between what was good or less good in him—a fact which the reporter, out for a story on the memories of perpetrators, is not aware of or deliberately ignores. "Bad" makes better reading and indeed better viewing than "good."

When I talked to Munch in 1982, he and his wife were living, as they did before the war, in a small, peaceful Bavarian village. The windows of his living room looked out over ski lifts and practice runs, but the feeling within that comfortable house was anything but peaceful. There was a deep rift between this bearded, elderly man and his wife and between him and his three grown children.

But here, remarkably, the difficulty was not as it has been with many other German families, because of the husband's crimes under the Nazis and his later denial or silence about them, but, on the contrary, because of his comparative courage during those times and his need ever since to question publicly the limits of that courage.

Although excused from military service early in the war and assigned to take over two older doctors' practices, by late 1942 Munch felt embarrassed to be safe when others were serving in the forces. One day in Munich he bumped into a former classmate who was in the Waffen SS. "He told me he could get something for me pretty quickly in his outfit, in one of my specialties, pathology," he said.

Within weeks, after a brief basic SS training course, he was posted to Rajsko, a medical institute which was part of Auschwitz, where research was done into mass immunization methods against infectious diseases. Apart from one other SS pathologist, the whole staff in the installation he now headed—seventy-one men and a few women—were Auschwitz prisoners. Many of them had been eminent scientists in Poland and France, and 90 percent of them, he was soon told, were Jews.

"He treated us as human beings," one survivor said on German TV later. "He shook hands with us on arrival, and addressed us as Herr Doktor or Herr Professor—it was unheard of."

Munch does not deny that he experimented on prisoners at Auschwitz's infamous Block 10 and was aware too of the other experiments that were being carried out there by the abominable

Dr. Mengele. He soon found out too, of course, about the gassings at nearby Birkenau and knew that his own patients, however long he extended his treatments, inevitably ended up there when he had finished with them.

He had refused to attend selections or to watch gassings, he told me, but he had seen victims being pushed into the gas chambers and, on one occasion, passing by, he had heard their death moans. "A sound like no other," he said. "Very soft."

All the SS officers, particularly the doctors, talked endlessly about the Final Solution, with intellectual curiosity but emotional indifference. "That's what happened to one," he said. Still, many of them, while acknowledging the "necessity" (his word) of removing the Jews from Western European society, deplored the gassings and would have preferred resettlement in remote areas, he said.

I asked if he himself acknowledged such a "necessity."

"I knew you would ask that," he said sadly. "I would like to say 'no,' but I don't think I can. I have no excuse. I was there, and did take part. I cannot—I don't have the right now—to answer your question with 'no.'"

Eventually he was forced to take a stand. It was decided that since, with the arrival in 1944 of the Hungarian Jews, all the SS doctors were overworked, the two Rajsko research physicians had been sufficiently coddled and would now have to take part in the selections. "I took the night train to Berlin that very evening," said Munch, "and I told my department chief that doing that was against all my ethical principles and that I refused." The chief agreed, and he never had to do selections.

At the end of the war, forty Auschwitz doctors were arrested by the Russians and handed over to the Poles. The trial in Krakow, Poland, ended on December 22, 1947, with twenty-three of the accused sentenced to death, six to life imprisonment, and ten to prison for between three and fifteen years. Munch alone was acquitted. Nineteen former prisoners had testified in his favor.

Since then, now more than fifty years, he has not ceased to question himself and to lay himself open to questions from others, even though his wife has begged him to stop. "I can't stand it any more," she said to me. "It is torture for me. And the children—he owes something to us too."

"I know she feels like that," Munch said. "But how can I stop? To stop talking about it is the same as to stop thinking about it. But I have to think about it; I have to understand. How could I stand it? How could I, as a human being, bear to stay?"

In an eerie echo of Speer, who had just died, he added, "I cannot understand myself, and somehow I must find the answer before the end."

You can see clearly, can't you, as I did, that Munch at Auschwitz was a flawed man. But as Primo Levi said, was anyone not flawed in these infernos? And if a man so exceptional rose, even partly, beyond his flaws, is it not this, for our own sakes as much as his, we should allow him to be remembered by? That is why I regret the tone of the *Spiegel* piece and deplore any further public exposure of this man, for it abuses the fact that most human beings who have gone through traumas in their lives in old age recall the worst they have lived, not the best they have done. For it is "bad" that pursues the spirit, not "good" that then alleviates it.

When I began to speak with Franz Stangl, who built Sobibor and then became commandant of Treblinka, it was very shortly after his conviction and his sentence to life imprisonment. The case was on appeal, however, because West German law decreed that a man could only be found guilty of murder if he himself was proven to be a murderer.

The fact is that Stangl did not himself murder anyone; as one of his SS men, Sergeant Suchomel, said to me, "Why should he have? He had lots of others to do that for him." Stangl no doubt thought—mistakenly of course—that what I would write could help his appeal. It was essential to disabuse him of this idea from the start.

When I met him in Düsseldorf prison, Stangl gave the disquieting impression of an imposing and dominant personality, in full control of himself. After we had been left alone, he immediately began in gratingly familiar terms to rebut various accusations made during his trial: he had done nothing wrong; there had always been others above him; he had never done anything but obey orders; he had never hurt a single human being. What had happened was a tragedy of war and—sadly—there were tragedies of war everywhere. "Look at Katyn," he said, "look at Dresden, Hiroshima and now Vietnam."

I listened to him all morning, almost without interrupting. Shortly before breaking off for lunch, I told him that having listened to him for two and a half hours, I thought I had better explain what

I really wanted. I said that I knew all the things he had said that morning; all of them had been said by any number of people. To argue the
right or wrong of any of it was pointless. What I had come for was
something different: I wanted him to really talk to me; to tell me
about himself as a child, a boy, a youth, a man; to tell me about his
father, his mother, his friends, his wife and his children; to tell me not
what he did or did not do, but what he loved and what he hated, and
what he felt about the things in his life which had eventually brought
him to where he was sitting now.

If he didn't want to do this, but preferred to go on in the vein of
that morning's recital, then I would stay to the end of the afternoon,
go back to England, write a little something and that would be the
end of it. But if, after thinking about it, he decided to help me delve
deeper into the past—his past, because things had happened to and
inside him which had hardly happened to anyone else, ever—then
perhaps we could find some truth together, some new truth which
would contribute to the understanding of things that had never yet
been understood. I told him too that he had to know from the start
that I abhorred everything the Nazis had stood for and done but that
I would promise him to write down exactly what he said, whatever it
might be.

What one is doing, I suppose, is making the truth tempting to
people. This isn't a trick, but the fact is that most people, good or bad,
need to talk about themselves, and the more troublesome, the worse
their lives have been, the more puzzled, even mystified they are, the
greater, more often than not, is their need to understand and be understood.

There was, of course, an enormous difference between what I
sought in Stangl and those who worked and even those who lived
with him, and what I looked for in Speer. With Stangl, who without
any doubt, became a monster, I wanted to know what he *felt*. With
Speer I needed to know what he *knew*.

I met him and his wife, Margarete, when I was to do a profile of
him for the London *Sunday Times*. Over dinner the first evening, I
told him at once about the ambivalence of my feelings toward him—
it is essential to state your own position from the start: no lies or pre-
tense on your side. I said that I was surprised by the similarity of the
questions he was invariably asked and did not like his almost monot-
onously uniform answers. I warned him that I would attempt to

break through this pattern and the glibness I detected in him. He shrugged and said everybody came with that intention. All of them wanted to trap him into admitting the same thing—his knowledge of the murder of the Jews. "You will too," he added with weary resignation.

Conversations such as I intended having with him needed to be structured, and though difficult with a man such as this, the control had to be mine. His denial of knowledge of the murder of the Jews was, of course, central, but to my mind it needed to be left in abeyance, in a way refusing him the relief of denial until everything else hade been said.

There were two essential things I wanted to focus on: (1) Hitler and his personality, about which he knew more than anyone else, and the origin of the evil in him; and (2) Speer's realization of it and participation in it.

Hitler's genius in part was to corrupt others, but the evidence I have collected suggests that with extraordinary skill he deliberately protected those closest to him—who from 1934 on included Speer—from any awareness that could have disturbed them or the harmony of their relationships with him. But corruption is insidious. Speer, in the course of his growing relationship with Hitler, inevitably became—though for a long time unwittingly—a part of it.

Speer, I was already convinced, had never killed, stolen, personally benefited from the misery of others, or betrayed a friend. And yet, what I felt neither the Nuremberg Trial nor his own books had really told us was how a man of such quality could become not immoral, not amoral, but somehow infinitely worse—morally extinguished.

Eventually he had gained knowledge of the abominations and recognized that they originated with Hitler. What then kept this man in place? What had prevented him, whose possibilities for escape were unlimited, from taking himself and his family out of it?

The reasons for this and for his later denial of knowledge, I felt sure, needed to be uncovered slowly by exploring, with his help, all of his life. So on that early spring evening in his patrician Heidelberg family home, I told him that I needed to learn about all the things he hadn't written or talked about: his childhood, his parents, "this house where you lived as a boy," I said.

"I hate it," he interrupted, with surprising vehemence. "I hate being here."

His wife winced. "But Albert," she said helplessly, "my friends . . . the children . . ." And to me, "He doesn't mean it."

He did. He hated this house of his childhood misery. But showing his feelings had been a momentary slip quickly corrected. He could see, he said lightly, that I intended to tax his endurance. If it got too near the knuckle—he smiled, "then Don here will come to my aid." My husband, Don Honeyman, a tall, blond Iowan who had been a *Vogue* photographer for years, was to photograph him for the *Sunday Times* profile. Speer had quickly formed an easy relationship with him. Don, I explained, would be going back to London after taking the photographs he needed in Heidelberg.

"Oh, what a pity," he said. "I was counting on him to protect me." This flippancy and Speer's very real charm were integral parts of his whole persona and, I would discover later, always had been. I knew well that if anything of value was to come out of our conversations, I would have to get him to divest himself of the glibness which he had cultivated over a dozen years of continuous publicity, behind which I believed there could be another—perhaps a worse, possibly a better—man.

For all those whom one questions, in my experience, the root of it all is unfailingly to be found in their childhoods. I have never yet done this work with anyone who did not long to speak of his childhood and in whom those memories did not begin the process of truth. Stangl feared his father, a crude and cruel man.

"I was scared to death of him," he said. "I remember one day—I was about four or five and I'd just been given new slippers. It was a cold winter morning. The people next door to us were moving. The moving-van had come—a horse-drawn carriage then, of course. The driver had gone into the house to help get the furniture and there was this wonderful carriage and no one about.

"I ran out through the snow, new slippers and all. The snow came halfway up my legs but I didn't care. I climbed up and I sat in the driver's seat, high above the ground. Everything as far as I could see was quiet and white and still. Only far in the distance was a black spot moving in the whiteness of the new snow. I watched it but I didn't recognize what it was until suddenly I realized it was my father coming home. I got down as fast as I could and raced back through the deep snow into the kitchen and hid behind my mother. But he got there almost as fast as I. 'Where is the boy?' he asked, and I had to come out. He put me over his knee and leathered me. He had cut his finger some days before and wore a bandage. He thrashed me so hard, his cut opened and blood poured out. I heard my mother scream, 'Stop it, you are splashing blood all over the clean walls.'"

Would he have become what he became if he had not been a beaten child who forever after needed to prove himself worthy of— as it happens, his wife's—love? I doubt it. Let me read you, quite out of sequence, my most unbearable moment with Stangl—*the* moment in fact when I nearly gave up on him; when I not just felt but *knew* that what he was was harming me and therefore was of danger to my family, my children.

It was when we were about two-thirds through our conversations; I had asked him whether he had ever had any contact with the so-called work-Jews, the men and women who were selected on arrival to stay alive, for a while, to take part in the operation of the camp.

"Yes," he said, "I did have contact with the work-Jews, quite friendly relations. You know, you asked me a while ago whether there was anything I enjoyed. Beyond my specific assignment, that's what I enjoyed: human relations. I always tried to give as many jobs as possible to Vienna Jews. After all, I was Austrian. . .

"Blau was the one I talked to most, he and his wife. No, I don't know what his profession had been; business, I think. I'd made him the cook in the lower camp. He knew I'd help whenever I could.

"There was one day when he knocked at the door of my office about mid-morning and stood to attention and asked permission to speak to me. He looked very worried. I said, 'Of course, Blau, come on in. What's worrying you?' He said it was his eighty-year-old father; he'd arrived on that morning's transport. Was there anything I could do? I said, 'Really Blau, you must understand, it's impossible. A man of eighty. . .'

He said quickly that yes, he understood, of course. But could he ask for permission to take his father to the Lazarett (the fake hospital where people were shot rather than gassed). And could he take his father first to the kitchen and give him a meal. I said, 'You go and do what you think best, Blau. Officially I don't know anything, but unofficially you can tell the Kapo I said it was all right.'

In the afternoon, when I came back to my office, he was waiting for me. He had tears in his eyes. He stood to attention and said, 'Herr

Hauptsturmfuehrer, I want to thank you. I gave my father a meal.
And I've just taken him to the Lazarett—it's all over. Thank you very
much.' I said, 'Well, Blau, there's no need to thank me, but of course
if you want to thank me, you may.'"

"What happened to Blau and his wife?"

"I don't know."

Of course he knew, but it was the answer he gave me, each time I
asked about any individual victim. This story and the way it was told
represented to me the starkest example of a corrupted personality I
had ever encountered and came very near to making me stop these
conversations. I broke off early that lunchtime and went to sit for
nearly two hours in a pub across the street, wrestling with the most
intense malaise I'd ever felt at thought of listening further to these disclosures.

I think the reason I did finally return to the little room in the
prison was because I came to realize—perhaps as a result of the intensity of my own reaction—that for a man whose view was so distorted
that he could tell that story in that way, the relatively simple terms
"guilt" or "innocence," "good" or "bad" no longer applied; what was
important was that he had found in himself the need—or the
strength—to speak. Even as I acknowledged my own apprehension at
continuing with these talks, I also knew for certain, at that moment,
that if I did, he would end by telling me the truth—some truth.

This is what you must be willing to confront, willing to accept if
you want to do this work: that if you are asking a human being to lay
bare the worst they felt, the worst they were, then you owe them at
least your presence, as promised.

Would Speer have needed so much and looked so hard for a hero
if his mother had not disliked him and his father—whom he thought
of as a hero—had not had such contempt for him? I doubt it. Again
preempting the sequence of events, let me give you one small proof
of the feelings of Speer's parents. We are looking at the deep winter of
1942 and Hitler's looming defeat in Stalingrad. In the middle of it,
Speer wrote in *Inside the Third Reich,*

> I had panic-stricken calls from my parents: my brother Ernst, serv-
> ing in an advance observation unit, is caught at Stalingrad. They
> have alarming letters from him: he has the Sixth Army disease,
> jaundice, and is lying in a primitive field hospital with fever,
> swollen legs and kidney pains. There is little food and a minimum

of drinking water. . . . The "hospital" is in a horse-stable, only partly roofed and without walls; no heating, the wind and snow blow in; the men die of hunger and exhaustion.

"My mother, who never showed her emotion," he told me later, "sobbed into the telephone. 'You can't do this to him,' she said, as if I was doing it, and then my father, sounding like a broken man, added, 'It is impossible that you, you of all people, can't do something to get him out.'"

His written account continued,

I had last seen my brother the previous summer when he was home on leave. He came to see me at the office but I had people waiting, an official lunch, meetings scheduled. Even so, going against Hitler's rules which prohibited people holding high rank in government from extending privileges to their relatives, I promised that I would get him out of Russia at the end of this campaign and get him into a construction battalion in the West for the remainder of the war.

Later he told me the rest of the story. "Sitting beside me in my office, phones ringing, people running in and out, he saw I was pressed for time," Speer said. "'Ah well, thanks,' he said, and automatically came to attention, to my embarrassment. 'Goodbye then,' he said, and he was gone before I could even stand up. After a moment I did rush out trying to catch him. I was going to walk out on the luncheon and take him out. But he was gone. I hadn't even shaken his hand."

Annemarie Kempf, Speer's extraordinary private secretary (whose account of her life is almost as important as Speer's) told me the end of this story, when Speer's mother phoned him in Berlin the day they received the dreaded telegram that Ernst was missing. Annemarie put the call through and—she never forgave herself for it—stayed on the line and listened. "You—" Speer's mother screamed into the telephone. "It should have been *you* who died."

Speer described to me his first experience of hearing Hitler speak; the speech was for students, teachers, professors. Speer, by then doing postgraduate work in architecture in Berlin and working as first assistant to his professor, Tessenow, was dragged to the speech by Tessenow's students.

He expected to see Hitler in uniform and to hear him speak loudly and wildly; instead, he saw a thinnish man wearing a dark blue suit who spoke quietly—"like a professor, you know," Speer said. "Hitler was like a chameleon, he changed 'colour'—i.e., personality, expression, behaviour, above all his manner of speaking—depending on the group he was with, the place, the time of day . . . but it was almost always calculated. That was part of his genius, but also part of his need."

When the speech and the enthusiasm of the five thousand intellectuals present was over, late at night, Speer drove his small car out of the city and went to walk in the woods. The meeting, and the lonely walk, changed Speer's attitude to Hitler and helped to change his life.

"Above all else," he said quietly to me, "—and it was obviously the greatest mistake of my life—I felt he was a human being; I mean by that, I felt he cared: not only about Germany, which in his own terrible way of course he did, but that he cared about people. If you like, though it would never have occurred to me to put it like that, that he cared about me . . . I mean . . ." he corrected himself, "about us, the young, individually. I am still convinced now that this was his greatest gift: to convey, not in words but by a kind of mass—and individual—hypnosis, that he cared about each of us; even, if you forgive the term, that he loved us. I didn't expect to feel that, you see; I abhor, yes abhor vulgarity and loudness, and that is what I had associated with him before that night.

"So you see, I made a double mistake in judgment, one before that night—for he was certainly not vulgar—and one afterwards, for certainly he could not love, at least in the accepted sense of the word. But it took me years—a kind of lifetime—to realise that. That night, of course, what he said appealed to me. Believe me, in the context of the world then—the enormous growth of communism, and of its danger to Germany—it made sense."

Over the next years, Speer did architectural odd jobs for the party, but it was only in 1934 that his career took off. It began with an inspection by Hitler of renovations of the chancellor's residence, accompanied as usual by the building supervisor and Speer, who was assistant to the chief architect.

"But you know," Speer told me, "I had the feeling he didn't even see me; he never looked at me. During the many inspections he made of our progress, although he asked many questions—some of which were up to me to answer—he never addressed me directly. I came to feel that was just his way; I accepted it as, well, normal. Why should the great man talk to me? It was enough for me just to be there."

And then one day, at the end of the usual noon visit, Hitler, who had never seemed to notice him, suddenly turned to him as he was leaving and said, "Come along to lunch."

"Can you imagine this?" said Speer. "Here I was, young, unknown and totally unimportant, and this great man for whose attention—just for one glance—our whole world competed, said to me, 'Come and have lunch.' I thought I'd faint. Just that morning, climbing about on the site, I'd got some plaster on my suit and Hitler noticed me looking doubtfully at my dirty sleeve. 'Don't worry about that,' he said, 'We'll fix it upstairs.' And upstairs he took me into his private quarters and told his valet to get his dark blue jacket. And before I knew it there I was, walking back into the drawing-room behind Hitler, wearing his own jacket.

"The party elite were assembled for lunch—soon afterwards I would discover that he always had large groups for lunch—and Goebbels's eyes popped. He immediately noticed what I hadn't seen, Hitler's golden party badge, the only one of its kind. 'What are you doing?' he said sharply. 'What are you wearing there?'

"'He is wearing my jacket,' Hitler said, and pointed at the seat next to him. 'Sit down here,' he said.

"Can you conceive what I felt?" Speer said again. "Here I was, twenty-eight years old, totally insignificant in my own eyes, sitting next to him at lunch, wearing his clothes and elected—at least that day—as virtually his sole conversational partner. I was dizzy with excitement."

I hope you understand that I am not trying, either in my book or here with you, to make you feel sympathy for Speer. As much as by his love, indeed his worship of Hitler, he was, no doubt at all, very soon driven by wild ambition which, in the course of only a few years, made him—who had been born with such gifts, with such a moral mind and spirit—impervious to morality. I saw as one of my main tasks with him to find out how he had felt about the fourteen million East European slave laborers who were brought to Germany on his orders, a huge number of whom had died of starvation and maltreatment.

And I found that except for one experience, he felt no guilt whatever about them. I don't think he felt that they were *Untermenschen,* as Hitler referred to them: that is the point. He felt nothing about them.

Except about Dora, the terrible underground factory near Weimar, where prisoners from the Buchenwald concentration camp, political prisoners more than Jews, built the Nazis' rockets. Thirty thousand of them died there.

The creation of this underground camp was a direct result of a meeting at the Rastenburg Headquarters between Hitler, Speer, and Himmler on August 22, 1943. Himmler guaranteed complete secrecy about the rocket production if the work were entirely produced by concentration camp prisoners, all of whose contact with the outside world would be eliminated. He offered to provide all the necessary technicians from among the prisoners. All industry would have to provide would be the management and the engineers. The factories would be built in the caves of the deep Harz Mountains, where they would be safe from Allied bombs and prying eyes. The workers would be drawn from the nearby Buchenwald concentration camp and would be under the authority of the SS.

The Peenemunde scientific team under its head, Colonel Walter Dornberger, and its most famous scientist, Wernher von Braun (both of whom would live peacefully and productively in America after the war) would be responsible for the technical side; Speer's ministry would bear the financial responsibility for the project, and the SS construction section would be in charge of building.

On August 23, 1943, the day after this initial meeting, the first one hundred prisoners from Buchenwald were brought to the site, and construction was started that very morning. But it was three months before Speer's Ministry doctor told him he must go there— *without* warning the SS that he was coming.

"It was a cold day in December when I went," Speer told me. "I was completely unprepared; it was the worst place I have ever seen. Even now when I think about it, I feel ill." The prisoners, he said, lived in the caves with the rockets; it was freezing cold, humid.

Jean Michel, a French slave laborer, described it in his book *Dora:*

The missile slaves . . . from France, Belgium, Holland, Italy, Czechoslovakia, Hungary, Yugoslavia, Russia, Poland and Germany . . . toiled eighteen hours a day . . . for many weeks without tools, just with their bare hands . . . ammonia dust burnt their lungs . . . they slept in the tunnels in hollowed-out cavities.

"I was outraged," Speer told me. "I demanded to see the sanitary provisions."

Michel described them:

No heat, no ventilation, not the smallest pail to wash in: death touched us with the cold, the sensation of choking, the filth that impregnated us. . . . The latrines were barrels cut in half with planks laid across. They stood at each exit from the rows of sleeping cubicles."

One of the SS guards' favorite jokes, he wrote, was to watch the slaves sit on the plank, laugh, and push them into the barrel.

"We all had dysentery. They laughed and laughed when we tried to get up and out of the shit."

"I walked past these men and tried to meet their eyes," said Speer, despair in his voice. They wouldn't look at me; they ripped off their prisoners' caps and stood at attention until we passed. I demanded to be shown their midday meal—it was an inedible mess." After the inspection was over, he found out that thousands had already died. "I saw dead men . . . they couldn't hide the truth," he said. "And those who were still alive were skeletons." He had never been so horrified in his life. "I ordered the immediate building of a barracks camp outside, and then and there signed the papers for the necessary materials."

Michel in *Dora:*

It was not until March 1944 that the barracks were completed. At Dora, the work was as terrible as ever, but we could at least leave the tunnel for the six hours of rest allowed.

"There, yes," said Speer, "I was appalled." What about the other camps, the other slaves, I asked. He shook his head. "I never saw them—wherever I went, I was a VIP."

It was a strange thing, this matter of "knowledge" in Nazi Germany. Here is what happened in 1944 to fourteen-year-old Martin Bormann, Bormann's eldest son and Hitler's godson. He was, of course, a passionate young Nazi, immensely proud of his "strict but just" father and of his führer. Significantly enough, his family and Hitler's circle called young Martin "Kronzi," the Crown Prince. But late in the war, in a small house near Berchtesgaden, he had an experience that would plant the seeds in him for what was eventually to become a very different life.

That day in 1944 he was at home on the Berghof, on holiday from his elite boarding school. In the mornings he was busy, as usual during holidays, running errands for his father and Hitler, carrying films, photographs, and maps to and fro. One afternoon, however, Himmler's mistress, Hedwig Potthast, whom he had installed with their two children in a villa nearby, invited Martin's mother to bring him and his younger sister Elke for tea. "She gave us chocolate and cake; it was nice."

Later, Frau Potthast said she would show them something interesting, a special collection Himmler kept in what had become his special lair. She led the way up to the attic.

"When she opened the door and we flocked in, we didn't understand what the objects in that room were—until she explained, quite scientifically you know," Martin said, his voice now toneless. "It was tables and chairs made of parts of human bodies. There was a chair . . . the seat was a human pelvis, the legs human legs, on human feet. And then she picked up a copy of *Mein Kampf* from a pile of them—all I could think of was that my father had told me not to bother to read it as it had been outdated by events. [Speer had told me that Hitler had said exactly the same thing to him.] She showed us the cover—made of human skin, she said—and explained that the Dachau prisoners who produced it used the Ruckenhaut, the skin of the back, to make it."

He said they fled, his mother pushing them ahead of her down the stairs. "Eike was terribly upset," he said, "and I was too."

Not much more than a year later, when it was all over, Martin, now a penniless fifteen-year-old refugee on a mountain farm in Austria who didn't know where his family was and whether his mother and siblings or father were alive, saw photographs in a Salzburg paper of the horrors that had been discovered in the concentration camps. "People said that the photographs had to be fakes, but I knew that it was all true," he said, his face red with stress. "After what I had seen in that attic, I had no doubts at all, ever . . ."

"The swine," said someone who was present as he told the story.

"To call those people swine," said Martin Bormann's son, "is an insult to swine."

Speer would of course never have known about anything like that. In fact, however difficult it is to believe, most of Hitler's young aides, his secretaries, and all the intimate Hitler circle knew nothing of the increasingly horrific plans for the civilian population in the East and for the Jews of Europe.

I have asked a number of these people what they would have done if they had known of Hitler's plans for the murder of Poland's and Russia's cultural elite and of the Jews. It is a measure of their honesty that none of them simply said they would have departed in horror. I think several of them spoke the truth when they said they would have felt horrified. But I believe that all of them would have tried to put it out of their minds, not because any of them were monsters but because they were totally convinced that Hitler wasn't and that therefore whatever they might have heard couldn't have been quite as bad as it sounded—not "if the führer knew."

Not everyone agrees with me. I am convinced that Speer—though certainly aware of the so-called resettlement of German Jews in the East and doubtless aware too, on a different level, of the infamous *Kommissar Befehl,* Hitler's order to the army in the East to kill Soviet kommissars—knew nothing of the planned genocide of the Jews.

At least he did not know the complete truth until the Gauleiter meeting on October 6, 1943, in Posen. The morning of that day was devoted to a speech by Speer, who chided the Gauleiters for their lack of discipline and personal greed and threatened them with dire consequences if they didn't concentrate their entire efforts toward the pursuit of the war.

That afternoon, after three other short addresses, Himmler delivered what is generally known as the worst speech ever delivered. Though many of you will know it, I will quote a little of it:

> I want to speak now, in this most restricted circle, about a matter which you, my party comrades, have long accepted as a matter of course, but which for me had been the heaviest burden of my life—the matter of the Jews. . . . The brief sentence, "The Jews must be exterminated," is easy to pronounce, but the demands on those who have to put it into practice are the hardest and the most difficult in the world.
>
> I ask that you only listen but never speak of what I am saying to you here today. We, you see, were faced with the question, "What about the women and children?" And I decided, here too,

to find an unequivocal solution. For I did not think I was justified
in exterminating—meaning kill or order to have killed—the men,
but to leave their children to grow up to take revenge on our sons
and grandchildren. The hard decision had to be taken to have this
people disappear from the face of the earth. For the organisation
which had to carry out this order, it was the most difficult one we
were given . . .

(Incidentally, in an almost identical speech to the generals, four
months later, he emphasized even more that he was obeying an order.)

I think I can say that it has been carried out without damaging the
minds or spirits of our men and our leaders. The danger was great
and ever present. For the difference between the two possibilities . . . to become cruel and heartless and no longer respect human
life, or to become soft and succumb to weakness and nervous break-
downs . . . is appallingly narrow.
  I considered it my duty to speak to you, who are the highest
dignitaries of the party . . . for once quite openly about this question . . . to tell you how it was.
  And with this I want to finish about the matter of the Jews. You
are now informed, and you will keep the knowledge to yourselves.
Later perhaps we can consider whether the German people should
be told about this. But I think it is better that we—we together—
carry for our people the responsibility . . . responsibility for an
achievement, not just an idea . . . and then take the secret with us
to our graves . . .

Even in this dreadful speech, as in the others he delivered before and
afterward on this subject, Himmler carefully avoided describing the
method of these murders—the words "gas chamber" never appeared—and the probability remains that all those who heard him,
most of whom already knew about the shootings in Russia, thought
that this continued to be the way the Jews were killed. The existence
of the gas chambers, in which half these millions died, and which the
so-called revisionists have so busily denied ever since, was apparently
unmentionable even for Himmler, Hitler's master of death.
  Speer has always claimed, to me too, that he wasn't there that afternoon; he and a friend had left before lunch to drive to Hitler's headquarters. It may be true; a number of people said it was, and actually,
of the many people I spoke with who were there, I found no one who
had actually seen Speer that afternoon. But this is finally immaterial.

Whether he was there or not, Speer had three good friends among the Gauleiters, and all of them following Himmler's terrible speech proceeded on an overnight train to Hitler's headquarters, where Speer—so he claimed—had arrived late the previous evening and spent the night. I consider it impossible—and of course told Speer so—that, spending all that next day until 3 a.m. the next morning with Hitler and with men who had been at Posen, he would not have been told about this speech. He was, as I describe in the book, very hurt that I felt this.

But in fact the disillusionment of those last months of 1943 made him ill. He very nearly died after Posen and Dora. It certainly was, up to a point, an emotional parting of the ways with Hitler, even though he remained loyal to him until the end, even while working against him from March 1945 on, by stopping as many of Hitler's "scorched earth" orders as he could, thereby without doubt saving Germany's economic life.

You may say—and many people feel like this—does this make him any better, any more forgivable? In a review of *The Secret Diaries* Speer once brought out to show me, the historian Lucy Davidowicz had written, "what his 'Diaries' do not mention are any sleepless nights . . . or dreams about Auschwitz."

"But that is exactly what *does* give me sleepless nights," he said, sounding very weary; this was the last day of our original three weeks together.

"I think I know what you knew about the Jews," I said. "But could you yourself not go a little further?"

"I can say," he said slowly, "that I sensed (*dass ich ahnte*) . . . that dreadful things were happening with the Jews. . ."

"But if you sensed," I said, "then you knew." He opened his hands in a gesture of despair. "You cannot sense or suspect in a void. You knew."

He did know, and suffered atrociously under the knowledge which, except on two occasions toward the end of life—one of them to me when I said this—he could not confront, he could not admit.

Is he forgivable? Are any of them forgivable? I have never felt that it was up to me, or anyone else, to "forgive." What I can recognize, however, and acknowledge, is the humanity, the morality in men who cannot forgive themselves. Munch was one of them; so were a number of men and women I worked with—listened to—for the Speer

book: above all, of course, Speer himself. And their inability to forgive themselves may not redeem them, but it helps the rest of us who
were alive at the time and did too little.

NOTES

1. Gitta Sereny, *Cries Unheard: Why Children Kill: The Story of Mary Bell* (New York: Metropolitan Books, 1999).

III.   T·H·E   C·O·U·R·T·S

Michael R. Marrus

History and the Holocaust in the Courtroom

FOR MANY YEARS SCHOLARS AND OTHERS HAVE WORRIED ABOUT HOW
the Holocaust should be represented. "We are dealing with an event
which tests our traditional conceptual and representational categories,
an 'event at the limits,'" says Saul Friedländer, in a work dedicated to
exploring the problem.[1] Those who seek to bear witness or record,
he observes, face constant pitfalls—distortions, banalizations, half-
truths, and even worse. This essay examines some of these pitfalls in
one particular mode of discourse, Holocaust-related trials, for the
most part trials of Nazis and others accused, exclusively or among
other crimes, of the wartime murder of European Jews. While re-
specting the impulses behind such trials, or rather most of these trials, I concentrate on what has sometimes gone wrong with trials as
a way of representing the wartime destruction of European Jewry. Of
course, trial transcripts, material submitted in evidence, and pretrial
interrogations have all been useful for historians of the Holocaust, including myself. But it seems to me that people have often expected trials to contribute more than source material for historical understanding: Trials were supposed themselves to teach history lessons, often
painful lessons, otherwise ignored. I think this is often a mistake. Trials have been far less effective vehicles than many people think for registering a historical account of the Nazis' assault on European Jewry.

A glance at particular claims on behalf of historical representation
for many of these trials puts this critical assessment into context. The
case against the major Nazi war criminals at Nuremberg, American
chief prosecutor Robert Jackson told U. S. president Harry Truman,
had to be "factually authentic and constitute a well-documented history of what we are convinced was a grand, concerted pattern to in-
cite and commit the aggressions and barbarities which have shocked

the world." What Nazism perpetrated had to be recorded "with clarity and precision," Jackson continued. If not, "we cannot blame the future if in days of peace it finds incredible the accusatory generalities uttered during the war."² The British chief prosecutor, Sir Hartley Shawcross, spoke similarly to the Nuremberg court, stating that "this Tribunal will provide a contemporary touchstone and an authoritative and impartial record to which future historians may turn for truth and future politicians for warning."³ Jackson and Shawcross would certainly have agreed with a much more junior prosecutor, Robert M. Kempner, for whom Nuremberg and its subsequent proceedings were "the greatest history seminar ever held in the history of the world."⁴

Israeli prime minister David Ben-Gurion, whom Hannah Arendt called "the invisible stage manager" of the trial of Adolf Eichmann in Jerusalem in 1961, declared unabashedly that trial's didactic purpose: "We want to establish before the nations of the world how millions of people, because they happened to be Jews, and one million babies, because they happened to be Jewish babies, were murdered by the Nazis."⁵ "The [Eichmann] trial is not necessary for this defendant, whose name we need not soil our mouths by pronouncing it too often," said the Communist Knesset member Moshe Sneh. "This trial is necessary because we need to remind the world of what happened during World War II, something many would like to consign to oblivion."⁶ Far from diminishing with time, the goal of "reminding the world" has become more insistent with the passage of time, at least in the minds of some. "Reminding" by means of the courtroom has also been seen as an answer to Holocaust denial. This is the view of Irwin Cotler, a law professor at McGill University. "Every time we bring a suspected Nazi war criminal to justice, we repudiate by the legal process the Holocaust Denial movement," he contends. "Conversely, every time we abstain, for whatever reason, and do not bring suspected Nazi war criminals to justice, it allows the inference to be drawn that if there were no criminals, it's because there were no crimes."⁷

My own view is that trials cannot and should not be expected to do the job of historians to teach history. Trials do not in themselves represent the past, or at least do not so without pitfalls that regularly arise. Interestingly in view of Ben-Gurion's remarks noted earlier, this was the opinion of Judge Haim Landau and the Jerusalem District Court, which originally heard the Eichmann case. The District Court refused "to be enticed into provinces which are outside its sphere," it said in its judgment. "The judicial process has ways of its own, laid down by law, and these do not change, whatever the subject of the trial may be. . . . The court does not have at its disposal the tools required for the investigation of general questions. . . . Accordingly, its ability to describe general events is inevitably limited. As for questions of principle which are outside the realm of law, no one has made us judges of them, and therefore no greater weight is to be attached to our opinion on them than to that of any person devoting study and thought to these questions."[8] This was a wise response, I want to suggest in this short essay.

The trials to which I refer differ widely by virtue of their legal and political contexts and hence their intended historical focus. It is well to recall just how divergent these points of departure have been in the past and for what different purposes the history raised by them is presented. Indeed, the very diversity of courtroom encounters with the Holocaust suggests a qualification to the expectations of many that these processes promote historical understanding. As we shall see, some may; others may not. I want to turn now to these contexts. Looking at the jurisdictions in which trials of Nazi war criminals having to do with the Holocaust have occurred, I identify six kinds of trials and hence six very general ways of contending with the historical material.

The highest instance is of course international, and here we have only one trial, of twenty-two major German war criminals, commonly known as the Nuremberg Trial, before the International Military Tribunal (IMT) with judges from the United States, Britain, France, and the Soviet Union. This yearlong trial, which began in November 1945, was intended by the four prosecuting powers to present a grand summing-up of Nazi criminality. According to the American secretary of war Henry L. Stimson, one of its principal architects, the trial was to "afford the most effective way of making a record of the Nazi system of terrorism and of the effort of the Allies to terminate the system and prevent its recurrence."[9]

While not at the very center of attention, the murder of European Jews figured importantly in this trial, particularly in two of the four counts against the accused—war crimes and crimes against humanity. Shocking evidence on the process of mass murder, much of it freshly publicized, stunned the court and the many spectators who attended the proceedings. Most important, the trial gave a sense of the great scale of the Nazis' slaughter of European Jews and of the connections with other criminal policies such as the euthanasia program and the devastation of Eastern Europe. This, together with the tabling of vast quantities of evidence about high-level Nazi decision making about the killings, may well have been the most important contribution of the trial to the historical study of the Holocaust. Nuremberg's interpretation of that event, however, was heavily conditioned by the prosecution's trial plan, a legal strategy in which the murder of European Jewry played a distinctly secondary role.

For various reasons, the four powers that organized the Nuremberg Trial came to accept the American view, which placed crimes against the peace, and the conspiracy to commit such crimes, at the very center of attention—"the supreme international crime," declared the judges, "differing only from other war crimes in that it contains within itself the accumulated evil of the whole."[10] In consequence, as one scholar sums it up, Nuremberg understood the Holocaust "essentially as the horrific consequence of a war of aggression."[11] More particularly, the origins of the Holocaust were seen to lie in the *conspiracy* to launch the war, a conspiracy held to be a core element of Nazism. From this, as Christopher Browning has noted, came the dominant interpretation of the first wave of Holocaust historians, what he calls the "Nuremberg view"—the Holocaust as the product of "criminal minds, infected with racism and antisemitism, carrying out criminal policies through criminal organizations."[12] War, however, was the heart of their criminality; everything else the Nazis did, including their anti-Jewish campaign, tended to be seen in instrumental terms—as a means to hold the Nazi movement together, eliminate enemies, consolidate power, mobilize support, or carry out robbery or intimidation.

The Holocaust flitted through a second category of proceedings, trials held by the victors, part of the Allied war crimes policy defined in the latter part of the war. Soviet trials in Krasnodar and Kharkov occurred in 1943 and were widely publicized in the West. Trials of lower-echelon war criminals by military tribunals of the major occupying powers began soon after the collapse of the Third Reich. With the Nuremberg trials under way, the four victorious Allies agreed to try more important criminals in their respective zones of occupation, charging them with crimes originally defined in the preparation of the IMT. Agreeing on a uniform basis for the prosecution of such crimes in Control Council Law No. 10, the Allies promised to cooperate for this purpose. For the next few years, these "zonal" trials proceeded under British, French, American, and Russian auspices, continuing until 1949.

Generally speaking, these trials dealt only intermittently with the murder of European Jews. Understandably, given the domestic preoccupations of the victor nations, they focused on crimes committed against Allied military and civilian personnel. In the American zone, the largest proceeding, and the one that probably attracted most publicity, was the trial of seventy-four SS soldiers who had massacred American GIs in the Belgian village of Malmedy during the Battle of the Bulge in 1944. However, the twelve "subsequent proceedings" held under American auspices did raise important themes of Holocaust history. These included the legal foundation for the persecution of Jews in Germany, Aryanization, the concentration camps, the *Einsatzgruppen,* slave labor, the so-called medical crimes, and links between heavy industry and the Auschwitz camp complex. The Russian trials are the least well known, but here the relevant point seems to be a remarkable lack of interest in punishing Germans for the wartime ordeal of the Soviet people. To be sure, with the onset of the cold war, Western powers did not help matters, showing reluctance to cooperate with the Russians and even refusing the extradition of Soviet citizens accused of collaborating with the Germans. Certainly, the Soviets were ill disposed to address the special victimization of Jews usually referred to in the Kharkov and Krasnodar trials as "peaceful Soviet citizens."[13] East and West, there was little attention to the singularity of Nazi Jewish policy. As Raul Hilberg notes, "the high point of Allied sentiment for massive punitive measures was reached in the spring of 1945 with the widespread publication of detailed accounts of wartime German atrocities."[14] Thereafter, interest rapidly flagged.

A third group of trials, by the successor regimes in formerly occupied countries, had been contemplated by Allied war crimes policy. In Moscow, in November 1943, representatives of the United States, Britain, and the Soviet Union agreed that war criminals who were not of the first rank would be "sent back to the countries in which their abominable deeds were done in order that they may be judged and punished according to the laws of these liberated countries and of the Governments which will be erected therein."[15] And so they were. Trials were conducted across Europe, and many of these raised having to do with Jews. Most important for the latter in the postwar period were the trials held in Poland, where some 5,500 criminals were brought to justice. Particularly relevant to the Holocaust were the trials of Rudolf Hoess, commandant of Auschwitz; Arthur Greiser, the Gauleiter of the Warthegau; Jürgen Stroop, the SS and police leader in charge of the suppression of the Warsaw ghetto uprising; and Hans Biebow, the German administrator in charge of the Lodz ghetto. But there were dozens of others, held in virtually every occupied country. And these did not deal only with Germans. From the start, perhaps the most passionately pursued charges were against local collaborators, many of whom were accused of the wartime persecution and murder of Jews. The widely followed trials of collaborationist leaders—notably those of Pétain and Laval in France, Quisling in Norway, Tiso in Czechoslovakia, Bárdossy in Hungary, and Antonescu in Romania—included substantial material on the fate of European Jews.

"Successor justice is both retrospective and prospective," Otto Kirchheimer observed. "In laying bare the roots of iniquity in the previous regime's conduct, it simultaneously seizes the opportunity to convert the trial into a cornerstone of the new order."[16] To varying degrees, but virtually everywhere in the immediate postwar era, successor trials were conducted against a background of turmoil and dislocation, in which powerful forces sought to legitimize themselves through patriotic consolidation. Most commonly, this meant accenting the collective national victimization at the hands of the Germans, rather than the singling out of Jews. In a word, Jewish issues were submerged. This was most obvious in those parts of Europe that were coming under Communist control. "People's tribunals" in those countries pursued their task in what were often civil war conditions in the liberation period; in many places, the punishment of the crimes of the occupation broadened into a savage assault upon "fascists" or "reactionaries"—those who were seen as enemies of the new regimes.

Beneath the surface, there were desperate power struggles: nationalists, many of them anti-Semites, battled Communists and others who sought to impose the Soviet system. In Western Europe as well, Jewish issues were deemphasized. There, since wartime complicity in the persecution of Jews had been widespread, and since local bureaucracies and police had done much to assist the Germans, established interests militated against a judicial reckoning and the continuing divisions that would entail. And even where Holocaust-related evidence was presented, as in the 1954 trial of Karl Albrecht Oberg, the SS commander in France from 1942 to 1944, and his adjutant Helmut Knochen, the public missed the symbolic importance of the event. National priorities lay elsewhere.[17]

Most important of the successor trials from the standpoint of evidence generated for future historians were those organized by the two German regimes, continuing into the Federal Republic of Germany and the German Democratic Republic. For obvious reasons, these were the trials that made the deepest inroads into the masses of perpetrators and those that continued the longest, extending far beyond the mid-1950s, when trials in the other successor states had virtually come to an end. As a leading German authority, Adalbert Rückerl, observes, West German trials proceeded through various stages, defined first by the rules of the Allied occupation and then by the German criminal code.[18] A national investigative agency, the Zentralstelle der Landesjustizverwaltungen, established in Ludwigsburg in 1958, launched hundreds of inquiries and led to important prosecutions in the Federal Republic. Some of these trials became famous and contributed importantly to a public understanding of the Holocaust. Most important, these proceedings raised questions about lower-echelon perpetrators, shifting the attention from major decision makers to the legions of ordinary Germans who were involved in one way or another.

German courts, however, often focused far less on the elucidation of the historical past than on technical issues. Crucial to these prosecutions was applicability of specific provisions of the German criminal code to specific atrocities, to questions of time limits for prosecution, and to the precise motives for the commission of murders in wartime matters involving sometimes fine distinctions that were nevertheless crucial in determining whether individuals could be charged or found guilty according to German law.[19] Quite often these legal questions may have thrown historians off the historical trail. Some *Einsatzgruppe* and *Einsatzkommando* leaders, for example, testified generously about orders to kill all Jews ostensibly issued before the attack on the Soviet Union on June 22, 1941, seemingly giving force to overall German culpability; in all likelihood, such evidence was shaped much more by the dynamics of the legal process, notably the effort to prove binding orders upon individual defendants, than by the quest for historical accuracy.[20] Raul Hilberg's conclusion is that while the evidence collected in investigations was useful for historians, the achievement in juridical terms was singularly unimpressive. Entire classes of offenses fell away from judicial consideration as the statute of limitations came into force. Many perpetrators reentered public life after a short period of disgrace or imprisonment. Countless numbers escaped justice altogether.[21]

Successor trials continue on to our own time, their periodic if infrequent irruption into public consciousness usually signaling some egregious failure in the past of the judicial or political process. In France, where governments for many years were remarkably unenergetic in pursuing French collaborators for wartime acts against the Jews, but where crimes against humanity were declared imprescriptable in 1964, there have been several affairs and much legal effort underscoring the failure to bring former Vichy officials to justice after the war for crimes associated with the Holocaust. The recently initiated trial in Bordeaux of the former Vichy official Maurice Papon is only the most recent of these. In 1985, the French Supreme Court of Appeal (Cour de Cassation) redefined "crimes against humanity," providing the basis for a successful prosecution in 1987 of Klaus Barbie, the former Gestapo chief of Lyons. To date, only one French citizen, Paul Touvier in 1994, has been convicted of such crimes. Typically, much of Touvier's life involved encounters with the law in which, needless to say, there was little satisfactory historical reflection on his crimes against French Jews and others: sentenced to death in absentia in March 1947, effectively amnestied in 1967, pardoned in 1971, charged with crimes against humanity in 1981, arrested in 1989, released in 1991, cleared in 1992 but reconvicted that year, and finally convicted again in 1994. In another case in the summer of 1996, an Italian military court presided over a trial of the former SS captain Erich Priebke, then eighty-three, charged with shootings of 335 Italian civilians, including 35 Jews, in the Ardeatine Caves outside Rome in 1944. The court found Priebke guilty of the crime but also ruled that because he did not display premeditation or special cruelty, punishment was ruled out under a thirty-year statute of limitation.

A fourth set of trials, Holocaust-related trials of Jews by other Jews, is unquestionably the least well known because these proceedings were conducted within a very restricted Jewish fold—except in a few cases, which I shall mention in a moment. A handful, of which we know practically nothing, were underground proceedings organized by members of the Jewish resistance, hearing charges brought against alleged Jewish collaborators. In early 1943, the eighty-year-old Alfred Nossig faced such a secret trial in Warsaw; apparently the members of the court were divided in their opinions, and it was only when they reassembled after a month that they found Nossig guilty. He was shot on February 22, 1943.[22] Following liberation, the thirst of many Jewish survivors for justice prompted them to organize "courts of honor," often in displaced-persons camps in Allied zones of occupation. Those accused were Jews charged with having assisted the Germans or their accomplices in the persecution and murder of their own people—usually having been enticed by ghetto or concentration camp officials into positions of authority. While conducted outside the framework of municipal law, the proceedings often conformed to established principles of justice. Passionate testimony was heard for and against the accused; decisions were difficult and sometimes subject to appeal; and many of those charged were acquitted. Historian Isaiah Trunk, who reviewed records of such trials having to do with the Jewish Councils, or *Judenräte*, refers to the many-sided picture that emerged: "The trials exposed deep roots of human frailty and degradation, including the perfidy of the Nazi regime in the ghettos and camps in luring their collaborators. In addition to all this, the trials also revealed high moral standards and readiness to help Victims."[23]

A quite different version of these trials, some of them highly problematic for the communication of Holocaust history, occurred in Israel. Centering on particular ghettos and their Jewish policemen, several cases were brought to trial under the terms of a 1950 Israeli law for the punishment of Nazis and Nazi collaborators. Testimony at these trials characteristically also involved deep personal animosities within the community of victims, political vendettas, and an irrational urge for the irrational scapegoating of individuals. At least some of the judges who heard these highly emotional cases seem to have recognized that the judicial instruments were simply inappropriate for deciding crucial issues. In reversing a lower-court decision in the case of Hersz Bernblat, deputy chief of the Bedzin Ghetto police, the Israeli supreme court observed that "the historical and psychological criteria of this case [did not always] correspond to the legal criteria of the legislator." The study of the character of the Jewish leadership at the time, they concluded, "should be left to the historians."[24]

The most spectacular Israeli trial of this category centered upon a leader of Hungarian Jewry, Yisrael (Rudolf or Rezsö) Kasztner, reputed by some to have betrayed his fellow Jews in 1944 in conducting spurious rescue negotiations with the Germans. The proceedings began as a libel action in 1954 when Kasztner sued one of his accusers, the journalist Malkiel Grünwald. Tangled in questions of politics (the anti-Kasztner camp used the trial to stigmatize the Labor Party, with which he was identified), this libel trial became a national cause célèbre—revisited on Israeli television some years ago accompanied by intense controversy and partisanship. In the mid-1950s, in a climate of extraordinary vituperation, the results were utterly inconclusive: The trial judge concluded that Kasztner had "sold his soul to the devil" and had "paved the way for the murder of Hungarian Jewry"; the supreme court reversed this judgment and offered a more balanced interpretation, but not until after extremists had their say as well, assassinating Kasztner in a Tel Aviv street in 1957.[25]

A fifth set of Holocaust-related trials are third-party proceedings, actions taken against alleged war criminals identified in countries that were not directly involved in Nazi-sponsored wartime actions against Jews. These trials are often a response to public pressure in Western democracies, characteristically from Jewish groups, to move against perpetrators who have enjoyed refuge and anonymity for many years. The easing of cold war tensions, it has been pointed out, made it easier for some governments to respond to these appeals and to do something about this long-ignored problem. Governments have adopted various strategies intended to bring such criminals to justice, each of them involving important problems in the representation of historical issues.

The United States, as the first country to come to grips with this issue, established the Office of Special Investigation (OSI) in 1979, in the Criminal Division of the Department of Justice, to take action against particular individuals. Commonly acknowledged as the most sophisticated such unit in Western countries, the OSI has relied on civil suits seeking denaturalization and deportation rather than criminal proceedings, lacking the jurisdiction to file criminal charges against persons who have committed crimes outside the United

States against non-Americans. As a result, the trials brought by the OSI have often not been exhaustive examinations of particular incidents during the Holocaust but rather involve technical inquiries into the processes by which the alleged offenders immigrated to the United States and whether they did so fraudulently, hiding their wartime crimes or in some cases their association with other war criminals.[26] To be sure, such trials often do include full-dress examinations of historical questions related to the Holocaust, and with a standard of proof similar to that used in criminal cases. In almost twenty years of operation, the result has been the removal of a few dozen persons from the United States, including some who left voluntarily before the completion of such trials.

Another path, followed at various points by Canada, Australia, and Britain through the use of special legislation, has been to try alleged war criminals at home rather than deporting them. But this approach has proven even less satisfactory than the American, it is probably fair to say, and the success rate of prosecutions in such cases is very poor. With the passage of so much time, evidence is often hard to produce and authenticate; elementary historical circumstances of fifty years ago have become the object of intense debate during the course of the trials; the proceedings are regularly snarled in procedural and technical wrangles about the court's jurisdiction; and in the end, juries seem reluctant to vote for conviction. Discussing a particularly troublesome Canadian case, that of Imre Finta, a former Hungarian police officer accused of deporting Jews and stealing their valuables, historian Randolph Braham notes the paradox: Expert historians have no doubt whatever that Imre Finta facilitated the Final Solution; the Canadian court, however, set him free, a judgment that was subsequently upheld at two levels of appeal.[27]

A particular subset of third-party trials are the trials before Israeli courts of Adolf Eichmann in 1961 to 1962 and John Demjanjuk in 1987 to 1988. In each case, Israeli authorities claimed the right for the Jewish state to act on behalf of Jewish victims in bringing the accused to justice. They also hoped that the trials would deepen historical consciousness of the Holocaust. In each, but particularly with Demjanjuk, the pedagogic message had to fight for attention against other questions and other debates.

As we have noted, the Israeli leadership had an unabashedly didactic objective in launching proceedings against Adolf Eichmann in

1960. In particular, Ben-Gurion targeted "a generation of Israelis who have grown up since the holocaust." "It is necessary that our youth remember what happened to the Jewish people," he told the *New York Times Magazine.* "We want them to know the most tragic facts in our history, the most tragic facts in world history."[28] "Quite successful in accomplishing these objectives, the Eichmann trial undoubtedly contributed to the dissemination of knowledge and prompted new research into the destruction of European Jewry; this process was doubtless facilitated by the fact that the accused had Europe-wide responsibilities for the rounding up and deportation of Jews—for coordinating, in effect, an important part of the Final Solution. Yet the history was not entirely what Ben-Gurion had expected it to be. Unanticipated by the organizers of the trial, one of the most lasting historical results of the process was the debate sparked by Hannah Arendt's reportage of the trial for the *New Yorker* magazine; thirty-five years later, I would guess, what most people outside Israel knowledgeable about the Eichmann trial think about in this connection is the debate over Arendt's evaluation of Eichmann's character— the question of "the banality of evil." At the time, of course, attention focused not only on such Holocaust-related issues such as Jewish resistance (in which Hannah Arendt had quite a different view than that of the Israeli prosecution), but also on key legal matters, especially the jurisdiction of the Israeli court. Outside Israel, the legal aspects of the trial loomed much larger than in the Jewish state. To the American critic Susan Sontag, indeed, legal questions obstructed historical understanding. "The problem with the Eichmann Trial," in her view, "was . . . the contradiction between its juridical form and its dramatic function." She detected "a fundamental paradox" in the process, noting that "it was primarily a great act of commitment through memory and the renewal of grief, yet it clothed itself in the forms of legality and scientific objectivity."[29] The two, she felt, simply did not mix.

Technical and legal questions were much more prominent in the Demjanjuk case, to the point that they ultimately came to dominate public discussion worldwide. Demjanjuk, a Ukrainian-born auto worker living in the United States and accused of being "Ivan the Terrible," the operator of the gas chamber at Treblinka, was extradited to Israel in 1986, where he was tried and eventually convicted and sentenced to death. For a time, the trial apparently did serve historical interests, with terrible testimony about Treblinka being broadcast live on Israeli radio and television. Gradually, however, questions of procedure and, more important, the question of the identity of the accused himself (Demjanjuk insisted that he was not the man known as "Ivan the Terrible") became the main focus of his trial. In the end, as is well known, the Israeli supreme court overturned the conviction on the question of identification, thereby casting real doubt on some eyewitness testimony that had suggested otherwise. Whatever hand he may have had in the murder of Jews in Poland during the war, the prosecution of John Demjanjuk finished as a failure. That failure, and not the gassing of Jews in Treblinka, is probably what people remember most about the Israeli trial.[30]

Not all of the Holocaust-related trials involve war criminals. The sixth and final set of trials I wish to mention arise from the prosecution of what are commonly understood in some countries as hate crimes or "group libel"—the dissemination of material known to be historically false and which, as the relevant Canadian statute puts it, "causes or is likely to cause injury or mischief to a public interest." Overwhelmingly, these cases involve what has come to be called "Holocaust denial." In a sense, of course, these trials are very directly in the service of Holocaust history. Deborah Lipstadt's book on the Holocaust denial movement—for movement it has become—is appropriately subtitled *The Growing Assault on Truth and Memory,* and the trials to which I refer are intended to establish the truth and to set memory straight.[31] The real question is whether trials are equipped to do so, and what is the real effect of such trials.

From the standpoint of the grand history seminar to which Robert Kempner referred in relation to Nuremberg, Holocaust denial trials have provided their share of distractions. Most obvious are debates over the vexed issue, which arises in most jurisdictions, of whether it is wise or helpful to criminalize Holocaust denial at all. This serious question, upon which people of goodwill seriously disagree, continually challenges the very notion of such trials and in some cases becomes their dominant theme. This was certainly so in the 1985 and 1988 trials in Toronto of Ernst Zundel, a neo-Nazi publicist whose legal travails drew international attention.[32] In the second of Zundel's two trials, while the presiding judge took "judicial notice" of the Holocaust, accepting that it had indeed occurred, essential facts about the murder of European Jews were still at issue in

the courtroom because the prosecution turned on the accused's alleged bad faith when he claimed the killings were a hoax. Recognizing the uncertain legal basis in existing criminal codes for proceeding
against this and other Holocaust deniers, some have championed
special legislation for this purpose. However, drafting laws against
Holocaust denial which at the same time protect other interests and
satisfy diverse constituencies has proven to be highly difficult. Often
these controversies and difficulties, rather than Holocaust history or
Holocaust denial, have moved to the center of attention. In Germany, where there is a clear interest in banning Holocaust denial as
one element of Nazi recrudescence, debate over the 1985 law against
the *Auschwitzlüge,* or Auschwitz Lie, as Holocaust denial is called, was
intense, and the result may have diluted the focus on the Holocaust
as a result of a transparent political tradeoff.[33] Finally, such trials always run the risk of providing Holocaust deniers with a highly respected public platform, something which they value highly—"a
million dollars worth of publicity," as Ernst Zundel mentioned, referring to his own case. Debate continues, and the jury may be said
to be still out. Holocaust denial trials, however, seem to be a crude
caricature of a history seminar, rather than the real thing.

So far I have suggested that with each of the various kinds of Holocaust-related trials we find particular obstacles in the path of historical
representation. I want now to suggest that there are additional difficulties, inherent in the trial process itself, which often inhibit the capacity of trials to present the Holocaust historically. For historians, the
point may be a simple one. Historians are supposed to evaluate every
source with a view to its derivation, and since all sources are in some
sense "tainted," they can be fashioned into a historical account only
with the aid of extensive background knowledge, good sense, and perhaps a liberal dose of life experience as well. From this perspective, trials and their records should be thought of as sources, like any other.
The general public, however, may look at trials somewhat differently.
Unlike other sources, trials benefit from special prestige in most societies; attended with ceremony, they are widely considered in liberal,
democratic countries to be means by which the collectivity allocates
responsibility for criminal acts and registers its abhorrence of them.
(Here there is an important difference between the Anglo-American
legal system, which focuses on determining guilt or innocence, and
Continental models, which are more concerned with establishing the

truth about criminal events.) Moreover, the greater the wrong, the greater society's concern that representations of the past in trials be not only accurate but also complete. With Holocaust-related trials, particularly those with a high public profile, I have the sense of quite high expectations indeed. Hence it is commonly said that bringing perpetrators to justice will "open old wounds" or promote a "coming to terms with" or "mastering" the past. By these expressions people convey expectations that trials will reveal important, painful truths about how the Holocaust occurred and will assist a historical understanding of these events. Such anticipations may be quite unrealistic, however; in the case of the Holocaust, it seems to me they often are.

Perhaps the most obvious difference between what goes on at a trial and what conventionally occurs in historical expositions is that the account of the past which emerges in the former is the result of a contest between the prosecution and defense rather than the development of a narrative or the accumulation of evidence and argument that point in one direction. From the start, there is not one account of events, but two or more, depending, of course, on how many persons are on trial. At Nuremberg, with twenty-two defendants (including Martin Bormann, in absentia), the accused quite often disagreed among themselves in describing what had happened in Nazi Germany and reacted quite differently to accounts of the persecution and murder of European Jews. In the trial of Paul Touvier, in France, parties on the side of the prosecution differed sharply among themselves about the interpretation of events. Assuming that we are speaking of liberal jurisprudence, in which rules of fairness and civility are observed, and in which the defense and prosecution are allowed full range to present their versions of events, a trial's historical message is often blurred, difficult to discern, and accessible only with the aid of the most careful, even expert, attention. Those who hope for a coherent account, told in a clear voice, may well be disappointed. There is a "recurrent tension," Mark Osiel points out, "between the needs of persuasive storytelling and the normative requirements of liberal judgment."[34]

Such tensions are not always evident to historians drawing upon testimony, because they are more interested in gleaning evidence than in the working of liberal jurisprudence, with its elaborate network of rules that govern the conduct of trials. Having evolved as a way of protecting fairness and preserving impartiality, these rules help define the rhythm of trials, which for laypersons may perhaps be summed up in one word: slow. One very common reaction is boredom—a complaint that is hardly anticipated in Holocaust-related trials, which are supposed to probe some of the vital historical questions of our time. "Are liberal stories boring?" Osiel asks. Because of the rules of evidence and the requirements of judicial proof, he observes, the proceedings "are likely to dwell upon what many listeners regard as meaningless minutiae."[35] Novelist Rebecca West, who chronicled the trial of the major German war criminals at Nuremberg, found the courtroom "a citadel of boredom." And this was no ordinary monotony, she insisted, "this was boredom on a huge historic scale." Sitting through the sessions was painful. "All these people wanted to leave Nuremberg as urgently as a dental patient enduring the drill wants to up and leave the chair." While life in the ruined city was agreeable for her and her journalistic associates, their work was "the water-torture, boredom falling drop by drop on the same spot on the soul."[36]

Tensions between conventional historical representation and the "normative requirements of liberal judgment" burst through the surface in the two trials of Holocaust denier Ernst Zundel, whose counsel, Douglas Christie, an energetic and perverse nonconformist, deployed a wide array of legal arguments to challenge the court's acceptance of some basic facts about the Holocaust. The courtroom, he insisted, was not a place to establish historical truth. Testimony as to the facticity of the Holocaust by expert witnesses, notably Raul Hilberg in the first trial and Christopher Browning in the second, was "hearsay"; accounts by eyewitnesses were of dubious validity and were in any case unverifiable. In consequence, all history was opinion and susceptible to radically different interpretations. The prosecution confronted these challenges, and in the view of many, including the juries which in both trials found Zundel guilty, adequately exposed the defendant's deliberate mendacity. Nevertheless, some commentators were uneasy about the trial's representation of history and how this was publicly received. Historian Leonidas Hill, who whose evaluation of the trials is positive, has some disturbing observations about the popular reportage:

> Each day during the first trial, the newspapers simply reported some of whatever was said at the trial, however false or ludicrous it

was, and without correction. In some instances the corrections eventually appeared in a subsequent article, but casual and ignorant readers may have viewed the articles as merely one claim balanced against another. The newspapers in their summaries at the end of the trial did make value judgments about the substance of the arguments. They confirmed that the Holocaust was a fact after publishing reports for months that read as if they were not sure.[37]

Another observer, Lawrence Douglas, sums up why I think we should be skeptical about the role of the courts in such cases:

> At the same time that the law intervenes to protect the Holocaust from the charge that it is all falsehood, its evidentiary constraints and concerns with its own legitimacy may demand that it approach the past from a standpoint of formal agnosticism—a circumstance that may lead to the erosion of the very distinction between historical fact and falsehood that the law has been asked to support.[38]

Writers of history have long understood that in a liberal system of justice, courts are forbidden to hear evidence that is commonly used by historians, that indeed is vital in shaping historical opinion on issues great and small.[39] Hearsay, third-party accounts, inconsistent or fragmentary testimony, reports about the general atmosphere, the deeds of others or the tone set by leaders—these and other strands of evidence are woven into historical accounts to help "explain" how terrible events happen. But lawyers protest regularly against the inclusion of such evidence in trials, and judges, following the rules of evidence in particular systems, regularly accept their arguments. Commenting on the celebrated impeachment trial of Warren Hastings before the British House of Lords at the end of the eighteenth century, Lord Macaulay observed how trial practice, designed for ordinary crimes, decisively favored those accused of criminal activity far removed in time and place. The rules of evidence, Macaulay wrote, "save scores of culprits whom judges, jury and spectators, firmly believe to be guilty. [And] when those rules were rigidly applied to offenses committed many years before, at the distance of many thousand miles, conviction was, of course, out of the question."[40] Regularly, courts acquit persons accused of Holocaust-related crimes because of the exclusion of evidence commonly used in historical accounts, particularly by courts looking back to another era and an-

other continent. Indeed, with the passage of close to a half a century
or more, convictions may be now practically impossible in what we
have referred to previously as third-party trials.

As every historian knows, the narrative that emerges from his or
her pen depends directly upon the kinds of questions asked at the beginning. Among the difficulties with historical representation of the
Holocaust in trials is that the asking of questions is governed by a variety of factors—politics, the legal framework, the availability of evidence appropriate for use in court—that have little directly to do
with historical representation. How was the murder of European
Jews facilitated by anti-Semitic propaganda? At Nuremberg, this essential question was posed within the case of a specific defendant
whom prosecutors had decided to include on their list of major
German war criminals: Julius Streicher, editor of the pornographic
anti-Semitic newspaper *Der Stürmer.* Streicher, the indictment alleged—"the filthy Streicher," as Robert Jackson called him in his
summation—was a key figure in orchestrating crimes against humanity by inciting and directing others in the persecution of the
Jews.[41] The court, in the end, lent its authority to this quite dubious
interpretation in finding Streicher guilty of crimes against humanity
and sentencing him to death; Streicher's wartime role, as a result, has
become part of the legacy of the trial in terms of the historical representation of the Holocaust. A close look at the evidence presented at
the trial, however, suggests how inadequately the case of Streicher
addressed the question of incitement of mass murder. Under house
arrest for virtually the entire period of the Final Solution, Streicher
edited a paper with a circulation that fell steeply in wartime; especially during the war, Streicher was not taken seriously by any Nazi in
a serious position of authority. The prosecution of Streicher may have
helped illuminate some aspects of his career, and it certainly provided
insights into his loathsome character. It contributed little, however,
to an understanding of the Holocaust.

By the same token, the shape of the stories told in trials understandably follows the definition of the crimes with which the accused
are charged, rather than an impartial assessment of the events themselves. In France, "crimes against humanity" as understood by the
Cour de Cassation in 1985 (not subject to a statute of limitations and
hence the only crimes available in the prosecutors' arsenal in recent
times) was declared to involve "inhuman acts and persecutions com-

mitted in the name of a state practicing a politics of ideological hegemony." In the Touvier case, unfortunately, whereas the investigation of his crimes tended to show that he had acted so brutally on his own, the prosecution sought a conviction by showing that he had acted under orders from the authorities of the Vichy government. A Paris court set aside this charge against Touvier on the grounds that the Vichy government was not totalitarian and hence "practicing the politics of ideological hegemony." The result was much historical confusion, leaving many wondering whether, as one commentator has put it, "bad faith has triumphed over ignorance or the reverse."[42]

Historians pride themselves on how the questions they pose may force them into uncharted waters, broadening their understanding by utilizing hitherto unexplored source material. Often this involves making connections, linking the Holocaust to issues not previously associated with the Final Solution. For example, researchers have explored how the murder of Jews was prefigured in Nazi Germany by the so-called euthanasia campaign; how it meshed with anti-Semitic policies initiated in other countries; and how it was facilitated, and even in some places was encouraged, by collaborationist elements in occupied European countries. With each of these links, historians have enriched their appreciation of causation. But each of these involves a line of inquiry precluded by the trial format. Particularly in the immediate postwar period, judges forcefully refused to hear such contentions as a way of exculpating the accused. From the very start, trial organizers insisted that they were not conducting broad inquiries into wartime wrongdoing; they were trying particular Germans or particular collaborators.

Preparing for the trial of the major war criminals at Nuremberg, Allied negotiators feared that the trial might become a platform for neo-Nazi propaganda. More precisely, they worried that the accused would bring up embarrassing issues that might divert attention away from Nazi criminality in general and specific perpetrators in particular: matters such as the Soviet attack on Poland in 1939, the Anglo-American aerial bombardment of German cities, or anti-Semitism in Allied countries, for example. To forestall such allegations, the Allies added to the charter of the Nuremberg court a provision that the Tribunal should "take strict measures to prevent any action which will cause unreasonable delay, and rule out irrelevant issues and statements of any kind whatsoever."[43] Acting on this provision, the Tri-

234 • MICHAEL MARRUS

bunal rigorously blocked tu quoque arguments—claims that the accused should benefit from the fact that others were also guilty or that a general climate of opinion or practice supported their misdeeds. Subsequent trials simply followed this precedent. At the trial of Nazi doctors conducted in 1946–47, with defendants accused of terrible "experiments" conducted on Jews and others in concentration camps, defense lawyers did manage to describe experiments conducted in Allied countries on subjects who had not granted their consent. But these presentations were strictly limited and had no influence on the court.[44] None of this could have come as a surprise to defense counsel. Tu quoque argumentation is "more an argument addressed to the public at large and the future historian than a legal defense," observes Otto Kirchheimer.[45] Fair enough, but while justice may be served by its exclusion, history may be not.

Another example of the limitations imposed by the trial format is what happened in the trial of Klaus Barbie, defended by the brilliant iconoclast and political radical Jacques Vergès. In public pronouncements intended to shift attention from the accusation made by the prosecution—Barbie's commission of crimes against humanity—Vergès hammered away at French complicity in wartime and other crimes, raising tu quoque arguments referred to earlier. France itself was guilty, he claimed: its anticolonial wars, for example, were responsible for far more deaths than the Germans in their repression of the French resistance. "France officially had 200,000 deaths during the German occupation for 40 million inhabitants," he pointed out. "Algeria had during the French repression one million deaths for nine million inhabitants."[46] In the end, Vergès was prohibited from putting to the jury this "defense by deviation"; declared out of bounds for the Barbie trial, many of the disturbing questions Vergès raised about postwar French hypocrisy were nevertheless serious, whatever the motives behind them. "Vergès' arguments concerned the meaning of Nazism," writes Guyora Binder, "which was, after all, the central issue addressed by the prosecution and its legion of expert witnesses."[47] Excluding them may have facilitated justice in the case of Klaus Barbie. Whether it advanced historical understanding, however, is another matter.

In the judgments that they pronounce at the end of Holocaust-related trials, judges have often included extensive historical interpretation. Without heed to arguments for restraint such as we saw formulated by the Jerusalem court in the Eichmann case, judges thereby commit themselves to impossibly ambitious evaluations of history. For while the judgments of courts are fixed and cannot be revised except upon appeal, historiography moves, and most historians expect it to move. Invariably, our sense of historical events changes with the passage of time. New evidence, a broadening of context, a new generation of questions and questioners have their effect. "Recent generations of historians," writes Mark Osiel, "do not presume to provide the judgment of history. They uniformly disavow such aspirations as hubristic. To claim that one has written the definitive account, of a period or personage would today be to invite not merely immediate revision, but outright ridicule." But in casting their history in the mold of legal judgment, judges risk just that.[48] The International Military Tribunal at Nuremberg, for example, in finding many of the defendants guilty of a conspiracy charge, confirmed the prosecution's historical understanding and thereby established what has been called a "Nuremberg view" of Nazi policy, including the Holocaust. As most historians would agree, however, this interpretation has not withstood the research of a subsequent generation of scholars, whatever their differences among themselves. Few people now think of Nazism as a war-plotting conspiracy of high-ranking Nazis, who determined the course of history on their own. Given that the Nuremberg judgment was rendered within months of the end of the war, it is hardly surprising that we think differently about such historical questions now. But the illustration underscores why it is a mistake to dress such historical evaluations in the clothing of judicial pronouncements.

The conclusion I draw from these observations is that we should not look to trials to validate our general understanding of the Holocaust or to provide a special platform for historical interpretations. Sensing that the Eichmann trial was being used for just such purposes, Hannah Arendt protested forcefully. "The purpose of a trial is to render justice, and nothing else; even the noblest of ulterior purposes . . . can only distract from the law's main business: to weigh the charges brought against the accused, to render judgment, and to mete out punishment."[49] "Just as belief belongs in church, surely history belongs in school," writes Ian Buruma in a book on historical memories of the Second World War in Germany and Japan. And he goes on: "When the court of law is used for history lessons, then the risk of show trials cannot be far off."⁵⁰ That is a negative point, not the main argument made here, that trials and material from trials must be understood critically, and like all other sources with due regard to their significant limitations, in the formulation of historical accounts.

NOTES

1. Saul Friedländer, introduction to *Probing the Limits of Representation: Nazism and the "Final Solution,"* ed. Saul Friedländer (Cambridge: Harvard University Press, 1992), 23.

2. *Report of Robert H. Jackson United States Representative to the International Conference on Military Trials, London 1945* (Washington, D.C.: Department of State, 1949), 48.

3. International Military Tribunal, *Trial of the Major War Criminals before the International Military Tribunal, Nuremberg, 14 November 1945–1 October 1946,* 42 vols. (Nuremberg: International Military Tribunal, 1947), 3:92; hereinafter cited as IMT.

4. Quoted in Ian Buruma, *The Wages of Guilt: Memories of War in Germany and Japan* (New York: Meridian,1995), 144–45.

5. David Ben-Gurion, "The Eichmann Case as Seen by Ben-Gurion," *New York Times Magazine,* 18 December 1960, 61–62; Hannah Arendt, *Eichmann in Jerusalem: A Report on the Banality of Evil* (New York: Viking Press, 1965), 9.

6. Quoted in Tom Segev, *The Seventh Million: The Israelis and the Holocaust,* trans. Haim Watzman (New York: Hill and Wang, 1993), 333.

7. Gerald Tishler et al., "When Academic Freedom and Freedom of Speech Confront Holocaust Denial and Group Libel: Comparative Perspectives," *Boston College Third World Law Journal* 8 (1988): 70.

8. Ministry of Justice, State of Israel, *The Trial of Adolf Eichmann: Record of Proceedings in the District Court of Jerusalem,* 6 vols. (Jerusalem: n.p., 1994), 5:2082.

9. Henry L. Stimson, "Memorandum Opposing the Morgenthau Plan, September 9, 1944," *Foreign Relations of the United States: The Conference at Quebec, 1944* (Washington, D.C.: United States Government Printing Office, 1972), 125.

10. IMT, 1:186. On the background to the trial, see esp. Bradley F. Smith, *The Road to Nuremberg* (New York: Basic Books, 1981).

11. Lawrence Douglas, "The Memory of Judgment: The Law, the Holocaust, and Denial," *History and Memory* 7 (1996): 105.

12. Christopher Browning, "German Memory, Judicial Interrogation,

and Historical Reconstruction: Writing Perpetrator History from Postwar Testimony," in Friedlander, *Probing the Limits of Representation*, 26.

13. See *The Trial in the Case of the Atrocities Committed by the German Fascist Invaders and Their Accomplices in Krasnodar and Krasnodar Territory* (Moscow: Foreign Languages Publishing House, 1943); A. N. Trainin, *Hitlerite Responsibility under Criminal Law*, ed. A. Y. Vishinski, trans. A. Rothstein (London: Hutchinson and Co., 1945), 15–16; Tom Dower, *The Pledge Betrayed: America and Britain and the Denazification of Post-War Germany* (Garden City, N.Y.: Doubleday, 1982), 218.

14. Raul Hilberg, *The Destruction of the European Jews*, rev. ed. (New York: Holmes and Meier, 1985), 111, 1070.

15. United Nations War Crimes Commission, *History of the United Nations War Crimes Commission and the Development of the Laws of War* (London: United Nations War Crimes Commission, 1948), 107.

16. Otto Kirchheimer, *Political Justice: The Use of Legal Procedure for Political Ends* (Princeton, N.J.: Princeton University Press, 1961), 336.

17. Henry Rousso, *The Vichy Syndrome: History and Memory in France since 1944*, trans. Arthur Goldhammer (Cambridge: Harvard University Press, 1991), 61–62.

18. Adalbert Rückerl, *Die Strafverfolqung von NS Verbrechen 1945–1978: Eine Dokumentation* (Heidelberg: C. F. Müller, 1979), 39–41.

19. For a discussion of some difficulties by someone involved in these prosecutions, see Helge Grabitz, *NS Prozesse - Psychogramme der Beteiligten* (Heidelberg: C. F. Müller, 1986). Translation mine.

20. See Alfred Streim, *Die Behandlung sowietischer Kriegsgefangener im "Fall Barbarossa"* (Heidelberg: Müller Verlag, 1987), 74–93.

21. Hilberg, *Destruction of the European Jews*, 3:1086–90.

22. Michael Zylberberg, "The Trial of Alfred Nossig: Traitor or Victim?" *Wiener Library Bulletin* 23 (1969): 41–45.

23. Isaiah Trunk, *Judenrat: The Jewish Councils in Eastern Europe under Nazi Occupation* (New York: Macmillan, 1972), 556.

24. Ibid., 565.

25. See Segev, *Seventh Million*, 268–74, 278–89, and passim.

26. See Henry Friedlander and Earlean M. McCarrick, "Nazi Criminals in the United States: Denaturalization after Fedorenko," *Simon Wiesenthal Center Annual* 3 (1986): 47–85. In a recent case in Montreal, the tendency of such trials to involve guilt by association was frankly admitted by a lawyer acting for the Canadian government. Referring to the accused, an elderly man of Ukrainian background allegedly involved in killing units in Eastern Europe, the government attorney said, "It's difficult to say what his particular battalion would have actually done because it was just part of an operational task force. . . . All I can say is what the operational task force

would have done and it was basically involved in what you would call atrocities. We have no direct evidence that he actually did that. It's a question of inference." Nelson Wyatt, "Man Linked to Nazis Deserted Twice," *Globe and Mail,* 4 July 1998.

27. Randolph Braham, "Canada and the Perpetrators of the Holocaust: The Case of Regina v. Finta," *Holocaust and Genocide Studies* 9 (1995): 293–317.

28. Ben-Gurion, "Eichmann Case as Seen by Ben-Gurion," 62.

29. Quoted in Pnina Lahav, "The Eichmann Trial, the Jewish Question, and the American-Jewish Intelligentsia," *Boston University Law Review* 72 (1992): p. 559.

30. See for example, Willem A. Wagenaar, *Identifying Ivan: A Case Study in Legal Psychology* (New York: Harvester-Wheatsheaf, 1988); Gita Sereny, "John Demjanjuk and the Failure of Justice," *New York Review of Books,* 8 October 1992, 32–34.

31. Deborah Lipstadt, *Denying the Holocaust: The Growing Assault on Truth and Memory* (New York: Free Press, 1993).

32. Leonidas E. Hill, "The Trial of Ernst Zundel: Revisionism and the Law in Canada," *Simon Wiesenthal Center Annual* 6 (1989): 165–219.

33. Eric Stein, "History against Free Speech: The New German Law against the 'Auschwitz' and other 'Lies,'" *Michigan Law Review* 85 (1986–87), 278–324; and "Correspondence on the 'Auschwitz Lie,'" *Michigan Law Review* 87 (1988–89): 1026–32.

34. Mark Osiel, "Ever Again: Legal Remembrance of Administrative Massacre," *University of Pennsylvania Law Review* 144 (1995): 507.

35. Ibid., 529.

36. Rebecca West, *A Train of Powder* (New York: Viking Press, 1955), 3, 7, 11, 17.

37. Hill, "Trial of Ernst Zundel," 208.

38. Lawrence Douglas, "The Memory of Judgment: The Law, the Holocaust, and Denial," *History and Memory* 9 (1996): 112.

39. For a classic discussion of the differences between legal and historical analysis, see Paul Peeters, "Les aphorismes du droit dans la critique historique," in *Recherches d'histoire et de philologie orientales,* 2 vols. (Brussels: Société des Bollandistes, 1951), 1, 181, 209.

40. Lord Macaulay, *Critical and Historical Essays Contributed to the Edinburgh Review,* new ed. (London: Longmans, Green, Reader, and Dyer, 1877), 662.

41. Streicher, the indictment charged, "authorized, directed, and participated in the Crimes against Humanity set forth in the Count Four of the Indictment, including particularly the incitement of the persecution of the Jews" (IMT, 1:77).

42. Tzvetan Todorov, "The Touvier Affair," in *Memory, the Holocaust, and French Justice: The Bousquet and Touvier Affairs,* ed. Richard J. Goslan (Dartmouth, N.H.: University Press of New England, 1996), 119–20.

43. See the comments of Robert Jackson at the conference that drafted the charter of the International Military Tribunal in *Report of Jackson,* 306; IMT, 1:14.

44. For an account of the largely undeveloped context of medical ethics in the United States during the war, when experimentation without informed consent was not uncommon, see David J. Rothman, *Strangers at the Bedside: A History of How Law and Bioethics Transformed Medical Decision Making* (New York: Basic Books, 1991), 30. See also Michael A. Grodin, "Historical Origins of the Nuremberg Code," in *Nazi Doctors and the Nuremberg Code: Human Rights in Human Experimentation,* ed. George J. Annas and Michael A. Grodin (New York: Oxford University Press, 1992), 121–44.

45. Kirchheimer, *Political Justice,* 337.

46. Quoted in Guyora Binder, "Representing Nazism: Advocacy and Identity at the Trial of Klaus Barbie," *Yale Law Journal* 98 (1989): 1360.

47. Ibid., 1363.

48. Osiel, "Ever Again," 631.

49. Arendt, *Eichmann in Jerusalem,* 253.

50. Ian Buruma, *Wages of Guilt,* 142.

Robert O. Paxton

The Trials of Holocaust Perpetrators in France

IN FRANCE, TRIALS OF PERPETRATORS UNFOLDED IN THREE PHASES. THE first period began with the Liberation. General De Gaulle and the provisional government of France in Algiers decided well in advance to punish the collaborators as soon as the soil of France was liberated. This decision was intended not only in order to do justice but also to head off vigilantism. Even so, about 9,000 people were killed in direct settlement of scores, with little or no trial, during the Liberation period in 1944.

After the Liberation, France did conduct an authentic and extensive purge of collaborators. About 1,500 persons were executed after trial (proportionally far above the Netherlands), and almost 40,000 were sentenced to various prison terms (proportionally less than in the Netherlands). More than 100, 000 others were fired or demoted or lost civic rights ("national indignity") after a trial or administrative hearing.[1]

But the postwar purge had two problems. First, it was uneven. Writers and propagandists, whose collaboration had left written traces (along with police and militiamen notoriously involved in repressing the Resistance) were punished far more severely than administrators and businessmen, whose daily collaboration was more discreet and who were needed in 1945 for the reconstruction of France.

A second problem was that the Vichy French role in the arrest and deportation of Jews from France that began in the spring of 1942 was treated in a misleading fashion. Not that Vichy's anti-Jewish measures were absent from the trials. Raphael Alibert was sentenced to death (in absentia) for his role in drafting the first Jewish Statute in the fall of 1940, and it was clearly recognized in his trial that he had promoted such legislation at his own initiative, without direct German pressure. Louis Darquier de Pellepoix, the second commissioner for Jewish questions, in office after April 1942 and thus at the moment of the deportations of Jews from France, was also sentenced to death (in absentia). Xavier Vallat, the first commissioner for Jewish questions, whom the Germans had forced out of office for insufficient docility in spring 1942, was sentenced to ten years in prison. The Jewish issue came up in other trials as well.[2]

The problem, however, was that the trials of the Liberation period were conducted according to a narrative of treason (to employ Michael Marrus's formulation). Those brought to trial were accused of intelligence with the enemy (article 75 of the Penal Code). That perspective tended to attribute all initiatives to the Germans and thus to conceal Vichy's initiatives. If the defendant could claim that he had acted to obstruct those German initiatives, then he could sometimes receive very minor punishment.[3]

This was notoriously the case with René Bousquet, the Vichy chief of police. We know now that Bousquet was instrumental in making one of the most lethal decisions of any European country under German occupation, to deliver up Jews into Nazi hands from areas that were not occupied by any Germans troops. Bousquet was also responsible for police collaboration in the Occupied Zone, for he wanted to maintain the sovereign independence of the French police, even at the cost of taking actions against "the enemies of the Reich" (as the Bousquet-Oberg agreements put it). But even Bousquet was insufficiently helpful to please the Nazis, and they removed him from office in December 1943, soon thereafter transferring him and his father to house arrest in Germany. That helped Bousquet claim that he had obstructed German anti-Jewish measures. That claim (and inadequate documentation for his trial) allowed Bousquet to get off with five years of national indignity, immediately lifted for alleged actions favorable to the Resistance.[4]

The second phase comes with a major shift in the climate of opinion in France in the period from 1968 to the early 1970s. The shift had three components. First, a new generation emerged in 1968, skeptical of their elders' complacency and eager to ask their parents, "What did you do in the war?" Second, a new historiography (partly French, with scholars like Henry Michel; partly German, with Eberhard Jäckel's great work on Vichy's relations with Germany published in 1968; and partly American, with my own work published in France in 1973) put Vichy initiatives back at the center of the story. Finally, the Jewish victims themselves ended their postwar silence. Approaching the end of their lives, fearful of forgetfulness, they now wanted to tell their children and the public what it had been like. Beyond that, they wanted to obtain recognition from the French government and from French courts of the Vichy French role in facilitating the deportation of Jews from France.[5]

The third phase comes with a new round of trials in the altered climate since the 1970s. Far from refusing to talk about Vichy, many French people have become obsessed with finding out about Vichy. This late timing sets France quite apart from the other victims of Nazism. The statute of limitations had been removed from crimes against humanity in French law in 1964, with the intention of trying German perpetrators (the German statute of limitations was about to run out). That permitted the German Klaus Barbie to be prosecuted in France in 1986.

But, unexpectedly, beginning in the late 1970s, French citizens began to be charged with crimes against humanity by victims or their representatives, such as the French Nazi hunter Serge Klarsfeld. Among these was René Bousquet, against whom charges were brought by Klarsfeld in 1989. These legal proceedings worked their way very slowly through the indictment phase, obstructed by certain powerful figures who opposed such trials (notably by President François Mitterrand, who had his own reasons for not wanting intensive exploration of the Vichy past).[6]

The first French citizen actually sentenced for crimes against humanity was Paul Touvier in 1994. Touvier received a life sentence, the highest penalty available in French law. His case was relatively easy, for Touvier was a marginal figure without powerful friends: a militiaman (i.e., a member of the notorious supplementary police force) who was directly responsible for killings of resisters and Jews.[7]

Then came the trial of Maurice Papon. After a very long indictment stage that had proceeded off and on since 1981, it opened in Bordeaux on October 8, 1997, and ended on April 2, 1998. Papon was condemned to ten years' imprisonment for two charges (out of three) of complicity in crimes against humanity.[8]

This was a shocking outcome to many people, for Papon had been an important official of the Fifth French Republic, handpicked in 1945 by General De Gaulle's advisers as one of the civil servants who did not need to be purged. Subsequently he held many tough administrative assignments, including chief of police of Paris (1958–67) and minister of the budget (1977–81).[9]

The trial of Maurice Papon, it must be admitted, was not entirely satisfactory. It was tainted by the defendant's great age (eighty-seven) and ill health, the lapse of over fifty years since the incriminating acts, and unseemly political pressures on both sides during the indictment. The trial was also criticized for its great length, caused in part by the grandstanding of twenty-eight lawyers for the victims and their families and for these lawyers' efforts to make it serve pedagogical purposes.

Those purposes were served very imperfectly. The narrative this time was clearly focused by the prosecution on Vichy's complicity in the deportations, but the defense worked within the old narrative of overwhelming German pressure. Both points of view were thus aired equally in the trial, without any possibility for direct rebuttal.

Papon's trial had been pressed forward partly because Bousquet was murdered in June 1993 by an apparent publicity seeker, thus precluding the trial of the civil servant most centrally involved in the Vichy government's assistance to the Nazi deportation project. Papon claimed he was a scapegoat, and indeed he was, since he alone survived until history caught up with him. But the jury believed (correctly, in my opinion) that he was directly involved in the Vichy government's assistance to the deportation of Jews from Bordeaux.[10]

Despite the problematical nature of this trial, the judicial condemnation of Papon accomplished two important things. This trial judged a Vichy civil servant for actions he performed in the line of duty. Although his trial was legally the trial of one man, it clearly found that he had obeyed orders that were in themselves criminal. It thus constituted a legal recognition of Vichy's responsibility. Furthermore, the trial helped establish in French jurisprudence that a civil servant is responsible for his actions if he obeys criminal orders.

In any event, this was the last trial of a Vichy perpetrator. Other possible defendants are very few, and too old, and there is no heart left for another such ordeal. Pedagogy in France about the Holocaust depends henceforth on pedagogues, and that is perhaps as it should be.

NOTES

1. Henry Rousso, "L'Epuration en France; une histoire inachavée," *Vingtième siècle: revue d'histoire,* no. 33 (January–March 1992).

2. For the postwar trials in general see Peter Novick, *The Resistance versus Vichy* (New York: Columbia University Press, 1968) and Louis Noguères, *La Haute Cour de la Libération* (Paris: Editions de Minuit, 1965).

3. The methodological problems of using the trial records as a historical source are examined in Robert O. Paxton, *Vichy France: Old Guard and New Order,* rev. ed. (New York: Columbia University Press, 2001).

4. J.-P. Husson, "L'itinéraire d'un haut fonctionairre: René Bousquet" in Jean-Pierre Azéma et. al., *le Regime de Vichy et les francais* (Paris: Fayard, 1992); and Pascal Froment, *René Bousquet* (Paris: Fayard, 1994). For the Bousquet-Oberg agreement see Paxton, *Vichy France,* pp. 195–96.

5. Henry Michel, *Vichy: Année 1940* (Paris: R. Laffont, 1966); Eberhard Jäckel, *Frankreich in Hitlers Europa* (Stuttgart: Deutsche Verlagsanstalt, 1966). The best work on the evolution of opinion in France concering World War II is Henry Rousso, *The Vichy Syndrome* (Cambridge, Mass.: Harvard University Press, 1991). See also Eric Conan and Henry Rousso, *Vichy: An Ever-Present Past* (Hanover, N.H.: University Press of New England, 1998).

6. For these developments se Richard J. Golson, ed., *Memory, the Holocaust, and French Justice* (Hanover, N.H.: University Press of New England, 1996).

7. François Bédarida, *Touvier, Vichy, et le crime contre l'humanité* (Paris: Seuil, 1996).

8. See Robert O. Paxton, "The Trial of Maurice Papon," *New York Review of Books,* 46:20 (December 16, 1999), pp. 32–39; and Richard J. Golson, ed., *The Papon Affair* (London: Routledge, 2000).

9. Golson, *The Papon Affair,* pp. 256–60.

Therkel Straede

Inside the "Aussenlager"
Interpreting Survivors' Testimony of Jewish Slave Labor in German Industry

VOLKSWAGENWERK-FALLERSLEBEN, JUNE TO AUGUST 1944

THE CATTLE CARS STOPPED IN FRONT OF A HUGE REDBRICK BUILDING, which stretched for one mile along a canal with river cargo boats on it. Three hundred prisoners in striped pajamas were commanded down and into the factory. Through a labyrinth of doors and corridors they were led into a long, wide, low-ceilinged basement room. Electric bulbs lit the room, which had only one daylight window. The room was bright, because cream-colored tiles covered the walls and light-gray cement the floor. The place looked barren, but clean, with rows of new wooden bunk beds, each with a straw mattress and a blanket.

The yells and commands of the guards seemed somewhat feeble, and no one was being hit or beaten—a big difference from the camp from which the prisoners just came. There the guards were SS, here most were Wehrmacht, elderly gentlemen, quickly to be nicknamed the Bismarck Youth.

An unfamiliar deep and pounding sound was constantly heard from above. A whole indoor street of heavy-duty presses operated above their heads, its rhythmic booms seconded by the sharper sounds of numerous metal-punching machines. Whining and whizzling sounds of cutting, grinding, and welding devices were barely heard through the massive concrete ceiling.

Apart from a few, all these prisoners were trained metalworkers or engineers. But in Transylvania and the Carpathians where they came from, you would not have found a factory or machinery of such impressive dimensions. Actually, their Jewish—mostly middle-class—

parents would have liked to see them as doctors, lawyers, and accountants, but Hungarian anti-Semitic laws barred most Jews from higher education, so they had to do with a skilled worker's education instead. In May 1944 this turned out to be their luck. They were taken to Auschwitz with everybody else but selected to be slave laborers and, after passing a test of skills, transported to this factory.

Upon arrival, the same company official who had selected them in Auschwitz stood up in front of them and delivered a short speech. They had been chosen to perform important jobs in a top-secret production at this armaments factory, and if they worked hard, they would be fed and treated well. If not, they would be sent back to where they came from. "Meine Herren," he addressed them (as "gentlemen")—every one of them remaining today remembered this tremendous contrast to the Hungarian ghettos and Auschwitz, where they had just been *Saujuden* (dirty Jews) and *Dreck* (filth). Herr Schmiele—almost everyone remembered his name, too—even apologized for the meal not being ready yet. When it was served, car buffs immediately recognized the Volkswagen logo printed on the porcelain plates, obviously surplus stock from the factory canteen.

The next day, the 300 "specialists"—this was to become their label and identity in this and the following camps—were taken upstairs to the workshop, a confined area in the enormous production hall. They were assigned to workstations at an assembly line, on which passed not cars but metal shells the size and form of a torpedo, which were to be equipped and completed: the Fi 103 cruise missile, a weapon of mass destruction, known to the public as V1. This production process was impressively sophisticated, more so than anything they had ever seen, and so complicated that small acts of sabotage, organized by engineers from the prisoners' group, could be committed without the inspectors ever detecting it. The company eventually got into a lot of trouble, because low product quality caused the missiles to explode in midair before reaching their point of impact, and it lost the delivery contract without the true reason ever being discovered.

When hearing about this camp—Volkswagenwerk-Fallersleben—through survivors' testimony, one is struck by the seeming normality of the situation described. The prisoners did what they were expected to do, worked—not overly—hard, found the production highly interesting, and frequently discussed its technical aspects. The prisoners took interest in performing their respective tasks with accuracy and took pride in being seen as—and actually becoming—specialists of an unseen hi-tech production. When speaking about it decades later, they made drawings and reenacted work routines which had—as is the custom of Fordist/Taylorist work environments—become reflex movements, engraved into the body and subconscious.

The prisoners worked twelve-hour shifts. They are remarkably silent about the time they were "off duty"! Sleep, frequently interrupted by air-raid alerts and stays in the massive factory shelters next to the camp premises, dominated their accounts. Stories of interaction with other prisoners were scarce. The only episodes of violence reported were occasional blows, delivered with rifle butts, when nervous guards tried to speed up the movement in and out of the air-raid shelters.

The food was appreciated as simple and meager but not disgusting like in Auschwitz, and each prisoner had a plate and a spoon of his own. But it was clearly insufficient in quantity and quality. A cook, who managed to sneak into the group in Auschwitz, calculated the daily intake to be between 1,000 and 1,400 calories—that is, only half of the rations given to German nonworking women. These young and middle-aged men had lived a rather normal life in Hungary until few weeks before their deportation and had stayed in Auschwitz only a few days. Their bodies had not adjusted to starvation, so they suffered greatly.

The work and camp environment seemed predictable, however, and strategies—individual and collective—could be developed to save energy in order to preserve as much bodily strength as possible. Knowledge and skills from their ordinary wage-labor experience were highly instrumental, such as the ability of a workers' collective to informally regulate the pace of work and find the optimal compromise between the employer's demands and its own interest in long-term preservation of the ability to work.

The situation in the camp was stable, and—when remembered—not disastrous by any means. Transparency, predictability, and the feeling that you could—individually and collectively—influence your situation nourished the hope of survival.

Obviously, apart from the laborers being kept as prisoners and not being paid at all, in this camp slave labor was conducted very much in accordance with the procedures of normal, modern wage labor. Thus, the organization of the work process, as well as the developments and events of everyday life in the camp, appeared to be determined by a rationality that was familiar to every inmate on the basis of his earlier experience.

After two months, however, everything suddenly changed. Allied air bombardments devastated the factory and almost killed a number of prisoners, whose shelter had to be dug out from under tons of debris. The remains of the V1 production line were dismantled and transported to a safer place. The prisoners were commanded into cattle cars and taken away.

THE THIL VALLEY, AUGUST TO OCTOBER 1944

A two-day train ride took them to a region of low mountains and narrow green valleys. Blast furnaces, huge lift structures, and other mining facilities towered above petty workers' terraced houses. On a high railway dam they were ordered to get out of the railway cars. Guards—cursing and screaming, beating and kicking—forced them to descend, stumblingly, into the valley below. Here, they were led into an area fenced with barbed wire and divided into three precincts. In one, two rows of huts housed 500 prisoners who—they were soon to learn—had been with them in Auschwitz but failed to pass muster as metalworkers. These men had originally been on the same deportation transports from Hungary, so there were friends and acquaintances, even relatives among them.

A second precinct obviously was the area of the guards, who were Luftwaffe soldiers and a few SS. A third had nothing but a few tents. There were no sanitary facilities whatsoever in this part of the camp, and since neither food nor drink was offered until more than twenty-four hours after arrival, the prisoners had to dig a hole in the earth with spoons they had brought from the Volkswagenwerk and actually drink from this "well." During the following days, the 300 workers were commanded to carry big prefabricated wall and roof sections from the railway line down to the camp area and to build new huts. The guards, armed with sticks, whips, and fierce dogs, constantly tried to speed up the work pace by means of random violence.

A group of prisoners was selected to build an outdoor crematorium, the building materials for which had been taken from a nearby slaughterhouse. The prisoners had no idea where they were until they heard a funeral service at the neighboring parish churchyard being conducted in French. Only later did they find out that the place was Thil, in the district of Longwy, a traditional mining district in French Lorraine, the shafts of which were being turned into underground airplane factories by the Germans. Alongside their 500 fellow sufferers in the other camp precinct, they were taken to do excavation, construction, and refurbishing work in the galleries under truly horrible conditions. Food was scarce and irregularly served, and soup bowls had to be shared. Brutality prevailed from the German guards and foremen, and, when one prisoner managed to escape, *Stehappell* (roll call) was ordered as collective punishment for the rest, who were forced to stand at attention on the *Appellplatz* (mustering grounds) for twenty-four hours, with neither food nor drink, and were beaten up if they collapsed. It speaks eloquently of the ruthlessness of the camp regime that the SS randomly arrested a young Frenchman from the nearby village and incarcerated him in place of the escapee, so that the number of inmates would be correct. French civilian workers in the shafts and passersby, however, showed pity and now and then secretly supplied some bread, apples, and encouraging news on the Allied advance.

After some weeks, a number of the prisoners was assigned to unpack, mount, and degrease machinery in the shaft, and they recognized devices and German technicians from the Volkswagen main factory. The hope that they would soon again be employed as "specialists" in the V1 production helped them endure the hardship and unpredictable cruelty of the camp and building site. After less than two months, however, the camp was evacuated overnight, as the Allies closed in on the Lorraine iron and coalfields, and the prisoners were taken to a new camp in Germany much like Thil.

The descriptions of Thil in survivors' testimonies are by far not as detailed as the ones concerning Fallersleben. This may be ascribed to the fact that it was already the third camp, out of six, in which they were incarcerated over the course of just twelve months. Obviously, the prisoners in Thil experienced the most rapid deterioration in living conditions and soon found themselves in a desolate state of health, starved, and subject to cruelty, accidents, and harsh, alienating labor. The crematorium made the long-term perspective clear to them. That only one corpse was actually burned was due solely to the early evacuation of the camp. The threat of death was immediate in Thil, as it had been in Auschwitz, but not in Fallersleben.

THE VALUE OF SURVIVORS' NARRATIVES

I have described these two camps in order to make a point, which I believe is important when speaking about the establishment of "authority" in studies of the Holocaust. What I am groping for is an answer to the question: What can we use oral history for, and what not?

In *Writing and Rewriting the Holocaust,* James Young in 1988 expressed great skepticism concerning the usability of survivors' testimonies as sources of what happened during the period of the Holocaust: "The memoirist documents nothing more persuasively than his own existence after the Holocaust. The survivor's literature thus becomes testimony not so much to the deaths at Auschwitz but to his life after Auschwitz."[1]

With a basis in postmodernist literary theory, Young questioned whether survivors' testimonies also reveal the events that had been survived and how they actually occurred. For, can any text possibly represent anything but itself, and can meaning be justified anywhere else than in the intertextual space?

However, from his strong emphasis on the function of the narrative for the storytelling survivor in reestablishing a sense of personal life story continuity, Young more recently—in the 1997 article "Between History and Memory"—has shifted his focus to the information about the events and conditions which were actually survived that is contained in such narratives—and how to retrieve it.[2]

Remembrance and retelling of events by the survivors inevitably contain information that is contradicted by other material, that is, "mistakes." This fact has caused conventional historians to exclude these tales from the circle of credible sources: Survivors do not speak with authority, because they err! But in doing so, Young claims that historians have made themselves "blind . . . to the actual empirical value of such mistaken testimony." As mistaken information can be discovered in a chain of statements, the tale is clearly more than just a source for the narrative period and the narrator. It says something about the empirical field—and the period—that is the *subject* of the narrative. Thus, the survivors do not just contribute a personal nar-

rative about having survived. They actually pass on specific information about the past for us to use.

In his 1997 article, Young distances himself from Michel Foucault and the radical semiotic view to "return to the somewhat more
quaint notion of *history as a combination of events and their representations.*"[3] He now sees the relevance of the narrative as lying in narrative time *as well as* in time narrated. From a historian's point of view,
this must be applauded, because it opens for an establishment of tex-
tual authority which is not located in the intertextual sphere, in aesthetics alone. This will clearly ease the integration of survivors' testimonies into historians' narratives.

THE DOUBLING OF THE HOLOCAUST EXPERIENCE

In order to develop a strategy for "deep" reading of the texts, which
are created by survivors in interaction with oral historians, I turned
to Lawrence Langer's *Holocaust Testimonies: The Ruins of Memory,*[4]
but whereas this 1991 book should be valued for its heuristic qualities, I do not think that it brings us much closer to what the survivors
experienced and how. On the contrary, it blocks an understanding of
the events—at least, if we by "understanding" mean a rationalist
comprehension.

Langer distinguishes between five modes of telling about the
Holocaust and sees them as expressions of five types of selves, which
are different reactions to the same situation. But his assumption, that
"the Holocaust" was always a "same situation," one common experience for those subject to it, is a *most problematic* generalization, which
negates the specificity of the single event as well as the experience of
the individual human being. "Inside the Holocaust," everything has
one character, outside—before and after—another. "Inside" is chaos
and the distortion of all values. None of the specificities that constitute the modern personality, such as autonomy and freedom of
choice, are valid. The categories of normal life are distorted by instant
death, and "normal" properties and abilities lose their relevance, as do
the cultural codes and ethics of the outside world. Langer sees the survivors' universe as divided into a binary structure, of which one side
has a rational, discursive language and imposes upon the other, which
has not, a tyranny of literary, chronological narrative and romantic,
moralist closures not of the Holocaust but of "this" later world.

To Langer, the Holocaust was an undifferentiated "ordeal . . . [in which today's witnesses] were deprived of moral agency by their circumstances."[5] Whoever clung to the rationalist idea of being a sovereign individual in control of his destiny, or to the ethics of before, would limit his space for improvisation—and eventually the chance of survival. But—this would be my objection—which impulses does the improvising person follow, if not those implanted through socialization and earlier experience? The Nazi system and its agencies did not function outside of logic or *Zweckrationalität*, even if its victims could not fully see through it. Langer's reading marginalizes the calculable, rational elements, and thus the "modern" aspect of the persecution of the Jews, and leads to a one-sided description of the victims, who are effectively deprived of personal ability to demonstrate agency and moral choice. The attempt by—at least some—victims to detect meaning in the seemingly absurd situation that confronted and threatened to destroy them, and to act accordingly, is being marginalized. Despite his intentions, Langer's depiction of the Holocaust is in fact a new version of the Dan Diner thesis of the Holocaust as a "black hole" in history, inaccessible to rational(istic) perception.[6]

Langer's suppression of any "system" in "things" leads him to an appreciation of pragmatic, "unheroic" response as being *the* proper response.[7] The consequence is a dismissal of every demand to ethical behavior, and an almost Bettelheimian reduction of the victims to childish, will-less objects of a chaotic situation, an infantilization of the victims—exactly what the Nazis attempted to reduce their victims to. Active responses are judged romantic, heroic, and selfish as well as hopeless.

But the Holocaust was more than extermination camps; ghettos and forced labor camps were more than just a prelude to destruction, at least for some. The survivor clearly remembers everything in light of his knowledge of the meaningless death of so many others. But his testimony inevitably includes recollections not only of chasm but also of situations which he considers to be elements of life story continuity. His memory contains not only chaotic but also structured images, and these represent events and situations that were comprehended as—and in fact were—chaotic or structured when they occurred.

THE DIVERSITY OF THE SURVIVORS' EXPERIENCE

Most survivors did not *just* experience Auschwitz but were (like "my" 300 prisoners) dragged through a number of concentration camps— small and big. To demonstrate that life in various camps varied, and the experience of the *Häftlinge* (inmates) likewise, was my purpose in describing the experiences of the same group of prisoners in two very different camps, belonging to the same—late—phase of the camp system development and serving the same industrial enterprise. The situation in these camps was *neither* unstructured *nor* completely un-predictable. There was some maneuvering space for the prisoners' agency, although clearly not the same in both. Skills, socialization, and personal ethics did *not* lose their relevance but mattered to the development of both individual and collective strategies for survival.

After Auschwitz, the 300 "specialists" found themselves in a situation where survival again depended on individuality, personal effort, discipline, and productivity in a system, which they could compre-hend through an analytical effort by utilizing the technical and social qualifications achieved in earlier life. The life story narratives reflect the "order of productive life" in quite the same mode as when the wit-nesses talk about their earlier and later careers as working men. The shift to the chaotic, disorganized situation of an outdoor and under-ground construction project functioning under extreme time pres-sure leaves a different story, which contains humiliation and fear of death, not overview and professional pride, as leitmotiv *but still* re-flects ardent attempts to regain control by the proved means as well as new (such as bribery of the guards and foremen).

At first glance, my examples may seem to *strengthen* the Langer argument: even the "specialists" eventually ended up in hell. But the 300 could in principle have been taken *from* Thil *to* Fallersleben, just as they (and more than 200,000 other Jews) were taken *out of* the ex-termination camp and into industry. So *my* conclusion, which also implies a critique of Wolfgang Sofsky,[8] is that different *Aussenlager* (satellite camps)—like other concentration camps—had diverse, heterogeneous regimes and that they were experienced accordingly by the prisoners, who utilized a wide range of personal resources and neither surrendered themselves to the completely passive role of vic-tim nor gave up their right to moral judgment of their own and others' behavior. A reductionist description of the span of variations in life conditions and human reactions like Langer's hardly benefits historical enlightenment, and (maybe worse): It does *disqualify* the survivors' narratives, insofar as they speak as "normal" human beings.

In life story narratives of Holocaust survivors, both the experience of the large-scale *Stammlager* (base camp) and the smaller *Aussenlager* are represented. Thus, "trivial" everyday experience and the memory of incomprehensible violence and existential loss exist side by side in their memory and narratives—as they did in the Holocaust situation. One should not be allowed to marginalize either, just because we have come to consider death the ultimate authority.

NOTES

1. James E. Young, *Writing and Rewriting the Holocaust: Narrative and the Consequences of Interpretation* (Bloomington, 1988).

2. James E. Young, "Between History and Memory: The Uncanny Voices of the Historian and Survivor," *History and Memory* 1, no. 2 (1997). Young's article also appears as a chapter in Gulie Ne'eman Arad, ed., *Passing into History: Nazism and the Holocaust beyond Memory, In Honor of Saul Friedländer on His Sixty-Fifth Birthday.*

3. Ibid.

4. Lawrence L. Langer, *Holocaust Testimonies: The Ruins of Memory* (New Haven, 1991).

5. Ibid., 5.

6. Dan Diner, ed., *Ist der Nationalsozialismus Geschichte?* (Frankfurt am Main, 1988).

7. Langer, *Holocaust Testimonies.*

8. Wolfgang Sofsky, *Die Ordnung des Terrors: Das Konzentrationslager* (Frankfurt am Main, 1993); Wolfgang Sofsky, *The Order of Terror: The Concentration Camp,* trans. William Templer (Princeton, 1996).

Insa Eschebach

Interpreting Female Perpetrators
Ravensbrück Guards in the Courts of East Germany, 1946–1955

THE SOURCE MATERIAL THAT I SHOULD LIKE TO PRESENT IS NOT entirely straightforward: the files of East German courts dealing with former camp guards from the women's concentration camp at Ravensbrück (situated about 100 kilometers north of Berlin).[1] The problem is that these files reveal comparatively little about the camp itself, and even the profiles of the perpetrators seem strangely stereotyped.

This is mainly due to the high degree of political determination of East German trials, particularly during the Cold War.[2] Therefore, I should like to make clear at the start that this source material documents yet another chapter of postwar Germany's distorted approach toward dealing with National Socialism and genocide. While perpetrator status was downplayed in the immediate postwar period—and a similar attitude was displayed in West German trials of the time— from the beginnings of the 1950s, East German courts demonized perpetrators strictly for propagandistic purposes. The files contain very little evidence of the history of Ravensbrück. Because of this I had to limit myself to the question: *How* do the files report what happened? That is, which modes of reporting do they apply?

For this reason, my focus is not on the atrocities themselves nor on the broad range of cruelty, reaching from a grinding everyday neglect, scorn, and disdain to violent excesses. Rather, the emphasis is on the way the perpetrators are portrayed in East German files, that is, which images are used to describe them.[3]

From the current state of research, it would appear that after the war fifty people were prosecuted in East Germany for crimes committed in Ravensbrück and its satellite camps: forty-five former SS women guards, two SS men, and three female prisoner function-aries.[4] The conjecture which I should like to discuss is that both the indictments and the sentences in these trials utilize gender categories. While the behavior of the two accused men is interpreted within the context of their military careers,[5] the actions and motives of the women involved are viewed within the framework of their supposed nature.

The discourse on the nature of the women involved implies two possibilities. Either the action and motives of the accused women are interpreted in terms of traditional gender models—so that their SS activity appears as a mere mistake to be blamed on youth or political naïveté—or as representing behavior deviant from the traditional norm. In this case, the image is that of an updated version of a woman, reprehensible by virtue of her very gender, of a Megaera, a hyena, a beast.

I shall begin outlining a few examples from those trials in which the East German courts showed considerable leniency and then go on to discuss the image of the SS-Megaera.

In the immediate postwar period, there was at first no consensus on the question of whether the female SS personnel should be prose-cuted at all. While a total of thirty-seven women were in fact indicted in the Soviet zone of occupation before 1950, of these, eight were found not guilty or given suspended sentences. The majority received sentences of a few months of imprisonment.

During this period, three main devices were used in legal dis-course in order to exonerate those women indicted: first, the empha-sis was put on the youthfulness of the accused (most of the female SS guards trained in Ravensbrück were born around 1920); second, their activities were described as a moral lapse; and third—and here the particular nature of the legal texts of the Soviet zone becomes ap-parent—the working-class status of the accused was highlighted.

The youthful age of the accused is emphasized in the following manner: "In deciding the sentence, the fact that the accused . . . came into the concentration camp as a guard . . . at a young age was taken into account."[6] The expression "came into the concentration camp" sounds as if something unpleasant had happened to that young woman. In other judgments it is said that the accused was, "owing to her youth, not fully aware of the significance of her actions,"[7] or it is conceded that the accused learned "that she was dealing with innocent people only after having been appointed to the concentration camp."[8]

Entgleisung, or "moral lapse," is the key expression used in proceedings such as those against Marianne Eßmann, the SS camp leader of Rochlitz satellite camp, where about three hundred Jewish women prisoners from Poland and Hungary were forced to labor in an armaments factory. In 1948, Marianne Eßmann was given a suspended sentence on the grounds that in fulfilling her functions she had only been guilty of "a few moral lapses."[9] A similar situation may be seen in the case of the former SS guard Erika Schönleiter. The judgment, sentencing her to nine months of imprisonment, ends with the words: "The court is convinced that, despite her previous moral lapse, the accused can be won as a citizen of a democratic state."[10]

The third argument used is to place emphasis on the working-class status of many of the former women guards: "They simply were workers and had neither a definite political orientation nor a clear perception of the activities unreasonably demanded of them in the concentration camp."[11]

It becomes apparent that these patterns of interpretation regarding the service in concentration camps arise from a tradition of attribution. In this tradition, women are denied the capability of forming intentions of their own, that is, they are denied the status of subject. Their activity as camp guards is interpreted as a lapse, as youthful folly.

The willingness of East German courts to regard former camp guards as, in some ways, unfortunate victims of circumstance had a number of reasons. First, there was a lack of witnesses, who (if they survived at all) had returned to their home countries or emigrated to the United States or Israel. As a result, many of the early trials were based on the testimony of the accused themselves. Second, there was no pronounced desire on the part of the German people, nor within legal circles, to prosecute Nazi criminals. From 1948 on, a policy of integrating former National Socialists into society was practiced in the Soviet zone—a process which was also supported by the Soviet authorities by means of an enforced policy of granting amnesty.[12] Third, the leniency toward the female camp guards may also have been based on the perception of women's actions in the public domain as being relatively insignificant per se; in traditional career hierarchies, their positions are subordinate. Fourth comes a point made by Elizabeth Heinemann: "The notion that ordinary Germans were innocent victims of forces beyond their control was a familiar motif in post war representations of the Third Reich."[13] As far as I can see, these four reasons contributed to an unwillingness to realize that female perpetrators did form conscious decisions for which they were intellectually responsible.

There is another side to these traditional images of feminine innocence, however. Just as with the polarizations of wife and lover, mother and whore, saint and sinner, the innocently entangled female SS guard has her counterpart in the image of a woman, regarded as wicked by virtue of her gender, the SS-Megaera. Frequently, both images are projected onto the same woman. While the indictment describes her bad character, the judgments of this period tend to emphasize the topos of feminine innocence. Toward the end of the 1940s, and against the background of increasing politicization of criminal trials and their use for cold war propaganda purposes, the judgments became increasingly dominated by the negative image of the SS-beast and the SS-hyena. The severity of sentences increased drastically: five of the eight former women guards sentenced after 1950 received life imprisonment, and in one case the death penalty.

It appears probable that, from the beginning of the 1950s, the East German judicial system charged a number of those accused either with unproven crimes or with crimes that did not take place at the Ravensbrück concentration camp. At the very least, it can be said that some of the indictments and judgments contain a number of questionable statements: for example, in the death sentence passed on Christel Jankowsky by the Gera Regional Court on July 14, 1954. Among other things, she is found to have been "promoted to SS-Scharführerin because of her brutality." According to the current state of research, female concentration camp guards could not in fact attain this rank, SS-Scharführer being a position reserved for the male SS hierarchy. The judgment goes on to state that, in the course of their "marksmanship training" in Ravensbrück, female guards "used prisoners from the so-called penal section as living targets" and that Jankowsky had herself killed sixty people in this manner. This finding should also be viewed with caution; in none of the trials of Ravensbrück guards did the accusation that the women had used prisoners as targets during their marksmanship training ever play a role.

The judgment also states that Jankowsky had participated "about 6 or 7 times" in the gassing of prisoners, which, it is said, "took place 3 times daily in Ravensbrück." Now according to the records, Jankowsky was in Ravensbrück only in 1943, that is, at a time when there were no gas chambers at Ravensbrück. Today it is virtually certain that a gas chamber was established there only at the beginning of 1945.[14] The circumstance that the indictment lists only the "accused's own testimony" as evidence and that the judgment contains not a single reference to statements by witnesses should give further cause for thought.[15]

To return to the patterns of interpretation used in the indictments and judgments concerning the motives of the accused women: In one, for example, a description is given of an "infamous type of female concentration camp guard," a type "who literally forces her way into such positions in order to satisfy her sadistic desires and to enjoy the feeling of power over the helpless from the position of a superman."[16] In the words of another judgment, for women of this type, inhuman treatment of prisoners is "quite natural or even pleasurable."[17] According to one indictment, "the accused had a lot of sympathy for the SS"; it goes on to describe "the cowardice and baseness of these female SS-beasts" and "activity as an SS-beast."[18]

No longer is there any talk of the supposedly excusable mistakes of young women but rather of a negation and repudiation of the topos of feminine innocence. The formulations quoted are concerned with the emotions of the women involved. Their activity as SS guards is represented as being emotionally rooted, whereby in this context these emotions—sadistic desires, pleasure, or "having a lot of sympathy for the SS"—have to appear abnormal.

In addition, there is a second aspect: "After her training, the accused, a prostitute, who as a result of her way of life is of extreme ill-repute, entered into service as an SS-'Flintenweib,'"[19] an expression which perhaps can be best translated as an SS gun moll. Armed, and thus placed in a military context, the woman becomes a Flintenweib (gun moll). By the use of the key word "prostitute," the woman's body, militarized in this way, is given sexual connotations. Someone who transgresses gender boundaries is no longer part of humanity and becomes an animal, a beast. Such recourse to the animal world and to nature is, of course, well known from the history of constructions of femininity: the woman as a dangerous animal, incapable of controlling its own urges. Correspondingly, the legal texts repeatedly refer to "base instincts," to the "base character" of the accused who are at the same time described as "emotionally impoverished" and lacking in "feminine compassion." As animals or beasts, they are denied the status of subject; they are seen as servile creatures. The corresponding male counterpart is the Hitler gang. The following extract from the court examination of Christel Jankowsky presents the picture of this active group and the woman led astray by them:

> The accused is a primitive person who, for egoistical reasons, became the willing tool of the Hitler-gang, indeed as a result she became a beast.[20]

The accused is, it becomes apparent, neither independent nor self-motivated, but rather obedient, servile, and submissive both toward the Hitler gang and as regarding her own "most base instincts," her lusts and desires.

It is my impression that the legal texts of this period evoke images that are much older than National Socialism. The concept of Megaera, for instance, was used in ultraconservative *Freikorps* literature of the 1920s and 1930s when describing proletarian women who participated in the 1920 street fighting against the German Reichswehr. As Megaera—portrayed since Greek antiquity with a dog's head and snakes for hair—she is the epitome of the evil woman and emerges time and time again throughout the history of civilization, most recently as the rebellious female Communist and subsequent SS guard.

Through the use of the term *Flintenweib,* this woman is placed in a military context. Now weapons and uniforms are traditionally taken as representing the male preserve of martial conflict. To this field, women are only admitted in a twofold fantasy role: that of the sacred being to be defended and that of the prize to be gained in attack. Seen against this background, "the policewoman in uniform is," as Georg Seesslen noted, " a serious contradiction in the history of society."[21] The woman with weapons is a horror vision seen as existing only with the enemy. As a *Flintenweib,* she appears in the *Landserliteratur* (soldiers literature) of the two world wars. From a 1935 Nazi book: "These gun molls were cruel furies, such as could only be contrived by Bolshevism."[22]

It is, accordingly, precisely the uniform that up until today has dominated perceptions of the female SS personnel. Again and again the postwar legal texts take up the theme of the women's relationship to their clothing, as if the uniform and the boots formed part of a crime themselves. Throughout the history of culture, the image of a woman in uniform is nothing less than scandalous. Seen against this background, the SS women's uniforms doubly represent a break of taboo. This logic can be seen to be employed as recently as 1995, in the novel *The Reader* by Bernhard Schlink. The protagonist, a former camp guard, finds employment after the war as a tram conductor. Why? She "liked . . . the uniform."[23]

The attractive but vicious woman is a stereotype that has been transmitted throughout the history of culture and one which has seen a revival in postwar memory. The case of Ilse Koch is well suited to an analysis of the magnetism which this image seems to generate. Her fame is far greater than that of her husband, Karl Koch, who as commandant of Buchenwald was responsible for the crimes committed there. The national and international press coverage of Ilse Koch contributed substantially to the image of the attractive but vicious woman centrally representing Nazi crimes. In addition to the commandant's wife, two women guards, Irma Grese and Dorothea Binz, played a part in establishing this cliché. The press focused its attention on Irma Grese even before she was indicted. An English journalist interviewed her in prison and published an article about "The beautiful Nazi woman."[24] Grese, Binz, and Koch had much in common: blond hair, youthful age, and reputed brutality. The books and plays that have been written about them all dwell on the subject of their sexuality and bear titles such as *The Commandress* (*Die Kommandeuse*), *The Witch of Buchenwald* (*Die Hexe von Buchenwald*), *The Beast of Buchenwald* (*Die Bestie von Buchenwald*), and, about Irma Grese, *The Beautiful Beast*.[25]

Even though the attributions of sadistic lust, of emotional impoverishment, of being a *Flintenweib* or a beautiful beast may differ in details, they are nevertheless all merely different aspects of the same construction of femininity. The image is that of the woman who is abnormal and bad by virtue of gender. It becomes clear that this image is not an idiosyncratic product of East German courts but rather an established part of the imagery of popular culture. It is not even a unique product of the postwar period, but a topos rooted in various historic precursors.

The question arises of why the image of a woman driven by her instincts has proved so potent that it can encompass even a historically new phenomenon—that of the activity of women in concentration and death camps. Why are female SS guards seen as driven by their nature, as "servile" and "submissive," as the tools of both their superior officers and of their own urges? In the view of the texts examined, these women were not autonomous subjects; rather, their actions are seen as resulting from their (in part sexually connotated) emotions.

My suggestion is that this image has achieved such popularity precisely because it is so easy to distance oneself from it. The "dangerous beast" is seen as that which is completely alien. As Silke Wenk has observed within this meaning, "feminity becomes a metaphor for a bad past which has to be 'mastered,' 'controlled.'"[26] Emphasizing the abnormal nature of the SS woman reinforces the supposedly safe position from which we can view the "universe of the concentration camp." The idea of the female body as the "repository of sin and 'darkness'" which can always infect mankind is a long-established tradition within Christianity.[27] Evidently this image is seen as being so plausible that it can even explain completely the phenomenon of women perpetrators in the camps.

To sum up: In order to explain the participation of women in the crimes that took place in Ravensbrück and its satellite camps, the East German courts made use of two different patterns of interpretation. On the one hand, they used images of victimization: The women perpetrators were not really responsible for their actions. They are seen as young women, as young workers whose activity in the camps is described as an excusable mistake. Set against this image, on the other hand, is the image of the bad woman, whose actions are seen as being based in her female nature, in sadistic tendencies. As Megaera, beast and gun moll, she is no more capable of controlling her urges than is an animal; it is the urges that are responsible for the crimes.

The first interpretation is analogous to the policy of integrating former Nazis into postwar society. One was willing to forgive past mistakes on the condition that those concerned would participate in "building up a new Germany." The second interpretation, centered on the woman driven by instinct, became predominant from the end of the 1940s onward. In the context of the cold war, the demonization of individual perpetrators was used for propaganda purposes in order to legitimize East Germany as antifascist. Demonizing individuals had an additional advantage: The running of the camps was thus seen as caused by just a few individual beasts. In East Germany, National Socialism was not seen as a problem of the whole of society any more than it was in West Germany but rather as the work of a small fascist clique. The majority of German women was described in 1950s rhetoric as being "peace-loving women and mothers."[28] Through the public condemnation of a few female SS guards, this majority of German womanhood was exculpated.

Even though the texts examined contain little evidence, we know of atrocities in Ravensbrück from other sources: they have been described by survivors such as Germaine Tillion, Margarete Buber-Neumann, Isa Vermehren, Wanda Poltawska, and many others.[29] The problem as I see it is that these two images of female perpetrators, innocent woman or beautiful beast, cannot explain why thousands of women opted to serve in a dehumanizing system.[30] Neither of these images contributes to perpetrator theory as such—they have to be seen as canonized patterns of interpretation, fulfilling specific functions within the context of postwar memory.[31] Neither of these stereotypes answers what Jürgen Habermas once called the "fundamental question as to those dispositions determining miscarried normality."[32] It can therefore be said that the task of interpreting female perpetrators is only just beginning.

NOTES

This text summarizes the results of a research project conducted by the author at the Faculty of Political Science, Freie Universität Berlin, in 1996–97; the project was made possible by support from the Berlin Senate's program to promote women's research.

1. For the history of Ravensbrück, see, inter alia, Germaine Tillion, *Ravensbrück*, trans. Gerald Satterwhite (New York, 1975); Ino Arndt, "Das Frauenkonzentrationslager Ravensbrück," *Dachauer Hefte. Studien zur Geschichte der Konzentrationslager*, no. 3 (1987): 125–57; Claus Füllberg-Stolberg et al., eds., *Frauen in Konzentrationslagern. Bergen-Belsen, Ravensbrück* (Bremen, 1994); Gudrun Schwarz, "SS-Aufseherinnen in nationalsozialistischen Konzentrationslagern," *Dachauer Hefte. Studien zur Geschichte der Konzentrationslager*, no. 10 (1994): 32–49; Bernhard Strebel, "Ravensbrück—das zentrale Frauenkonzentrationslager," in *Die national-*

sozialistischen Konzentrationslager. Entwicklung und Struktur, vol. 1, ed. Ulrich Herbert et al. (Göttingen, 1998), 215–58.

2. See Falco Werkentin, *Politische Strafjustiz in der Ära Ulbricht* (Berlin, 1995); Karl Wilhelm Fricke, *Politik und Justiz in der DDR. Zur Geschichte der politischen Verfolgung 1945–1968* (Cologne, 1979).

3. "The present study does not inquire into the thematic representation of bloody horror, but into the narrative representation of events themselves. Rather than concentrating on the numbing shock evoked by the calculated murder of a people, this study asks precisely how historical memory, understanding, and meaning are constructed in Holocaust narrative." James Edward Young, *Writing and Rewriting the Holocaust: Narrative and the Consequences of Interpretation* (Bloomington, Ind., 1988), vii.

As to the question of gender-specific symbolizations in the discourse about National Socialism, see Silke Wenk, "Hin-Weg-Sehen oder: Faschismus, Normalität und Sexismus," in *Erbeutete Sinne. Nachträge zur Berliner Ausstellung "Inszenierung der Macht, Ästhetische Faszination im Faschismus,"* ed. Neue Gesellschaft für Bildende Kunst (Berlin, 1988), 17–32; Sigrid Weigel, "Erinnerung vor Gericht. Zum Opfer-Täter-Diskurs über den Nationalsozialismus in Helga Schuberts 'Judasfrauen' und ihren Gerichts-Quellen" and "Zur nationalen Funktion des Geschlechterdiskurses im Gedächtnis des Nationalsozialismus—Alfred Andersch 'Die Rote,'" in *Bilder des kulturellen Gedächtnisses. Beiträge zur Gegenwartsliteratur* (Dülmen-Hiddingsel, 1994), 198–231, 181–97; Kathrin Hoffmann-Curtius, "Feminisierung des Faschismus," in *Die Nacht hat zwölf Stunden, dann kommt schon der Tag. Antifaschismus, Geschichte und Neubewertung,* ed. Claudia Keller (Berlin, 1996), 45–69; Elizabeth Heinemann, "The Hour of the Woman: Memories of Germany's 'Crisis Years' and West German National Identity," *American Historical Review* 101, no. 2 (April 1996): 354–95; Dagmar Herzog, "Pleasure, Sex and Politics Belong Together: Post-Holocaust Memory and the Sexual Revolution in West Germany," *Critical Inquiry* (winter 1998): 393–444; Alexandra Przyrembel, "Transfixed by an Image: Ilse Koch, the 'Kommandeuse von Buchenwald,'" in *German History* 3 (2001), pp. 369–99.

4. See Insa Eschebach, "NS-Prozesse in der Sowjetischen Besatzungszone und der DDR. Einige Überlegungen zu den Strafverfahrensakten ehemaliger SS-Aufseherinnen des Frauenkonzentrationslagers Ravensbrück," *Beiträge zur Geschichte der nationalsozialistischen Verfolgung in Norddeutschland: Die frühen Nachkriegsprozesse,* no. 3 (1997): 65–74; Insa Eschebach, "'Ermittlungskomplex Ravensbrück.' Das Frauenkonzentrationslager in den Akten des Ministeriums für Staatssicherheit," in *Forschungsschwerpunkt Ravensbrück. Beiträge zur Geschichte des Frauen-Konzentrationslagers,* ed. Sigrid Jacobeit and Grit Philipp, Schriftenreihe

der Stiftung Brandenburgische Gedenkstätten 9 (Berlin, 1997), 94–114; Insa Eschebach, "Das Stigma des Asozialen. Drei Urteile der DDR-Justiz gegen ehemalige Funktionshäftlinge des Frauenkonzentrationslagers Ravensbrück," *Beiträge zur Geschichte der nationalsozialistischen Verfolgung in Norddeutschland: Abgeleitete Macht—Funktionshäftlinge zwischen Widerstand und Kollaboration,* no. 4 (1998): 69–81.

5. A common factor evident in both trials is the high degree of importance given to the reconstruction of the professional development of the two male accused. Even though in both trials *niedrige Motive* (base motives) of the accused are considered, the specific character of their crimes is primarily contextualized in regard to their respective positions within the concentration camp. The emotional dispositions of the accused or even their "nature" play a comparatively minor role. If and in what manner these specific patterns of interpretation influenced the outcome of these trials needs further investigation. See the case of Karl Theiner, Archiv des Bundesbeauftragten für die Unterlagen des Statssicherheitsdienstes der ehemaligen Deutschen Demokratischen Republik [hereafter cited as BstU] MfS ZA AU 531/58; and the case of Arnold Zöllner, BstU ZA ZUV 4. To my knowledge, there has not been any research on the use of gender imagery in West German prosecutions of Nazi crimes with the exception of Przyrembel, *Der Bann des ildes- Ilse Koch,* which focuses- on the use of negative sexual images in the case of Ilse Koch.

6. LG Potsdam [Potsdam Regional Court], Judgment in the case of Liehr, 23 July 1948; StKs 15/47; Bundesarchiv Zwischenarchiv Dahlwitz Hoppegarten [hereafter cited as BA DH] ZB 705 Obj. 4. All English translations in this chapter are mine unless noted otherwise.

7. LG Schwerin [Schwerin Regional Court], Judgment in the case of Schönleiter, 16 March 1949; StKs 359/48; BStU AST Schwerin 559/48.

8. LG Potsdam, Judgment in the case of Stiwitz, 23 July 1949; 7 StKs 14/47; BStU AST Pdm 7 StKs 15/47, p. 24.

9. LG Chemnitz [Chemnitz Regional Court], Judgment in the case of Eßmann, 12 April 1948; StKs 15/48; BA DH ZB 51 Obj. 14.

10. LG Schwerin, Schönleiter judgment, 16 March 1949.

11. LG Halle [Halle Regional Court], Judgment in the case of Rösch et al., 13 October 1949; 13a StKs 98/49; BA DH VgM 10041 A 17.

12. In a number of criminal proceedings from the years 1948–50 discussed here, Soviet Military Administration Order No. 43 of March 18, 1948, was applied. This order provided for the possibility of amnesty to mark the one hundredth anniversary of the 1848 revolution. The same is true for the law concerning the decree of repentance for former National Socialists and officers of the Wehrmacht, decided by the GDR parliament (Volkskammer) during its 5th Session on 9.11.1949 [*sic*]. To celebrate the

founding of the GDR in October 1949, amnesties were granted to those who had been sentenced to prison terms of less than six months. In the following years, a whole series of acts of clemency by the president of the GDR led to a number of former women camp guards being released before serving out their sentences. Regarding the question of amnesties in the GDR, see also Falco Werkentin, "Justizkorrekturen als permanenter Prozeß—Gnadenerweise und Strafamnestien in der Justizgeschichte der DDR," *Neue Justiz* 12 (1992): 1–7.

13. Heinemann, "Hour of the Woman," 359.

14. See Monika Herzog and Bernhard Strebel: "Das Frauenkonzentrationslager Ravensbrück," in Claus Füllberg-Stolberg et al., eds., *Frauen in Konzentrationslagern. Bergen-Belsen, Ravensbrück* (Bremen, 1994), 21.

15. BG Gera [Gera Regional Court] Judgment in the case of Jankowsky, 14 July 1954; 1 Ks 124/54; I-123/54; BA DH StVE K 219 A 5. Jankowsky's death sentence was commuted to one of penal servitude for life on July 11, 1955, by a clemency decision of the president of the GDR. Jankowsky, who had at this point already attempted suicide in the Brandenburg prison, died three hours after entering a prison hospital on May 12, 1956, at age thirty-seven. The records show the cause of death to have been a brain tumor.

16. LG Halle, Rösch et al. judgment, 13 October 1949.

17. LG Halle, Judgment in the case of Werner, 27 April 1948; 13a StKs 24/48; BStU AST Halle 6078, p. 8.

18. Polizeipräsidium Erfurt [President of Police Erfurt], Indictment against Gebhardt, 1 June 1949; BStU AST Erfurt 707/75 Bl. 54–55.

19. KKPA Dresden, Dept. of Investigation, Indictment against Nitzschner, 16 December 1948; BStU SV 5/78.

20. BG Gera, Court examination of Jankowsky, 14 July 1954; 1 Ks 124/54; Sammlungen der MGR/Stiftung Brandenburgische Gedenkstätten Bd. 22/250.

21. Georg Seesslen, "Die Wiederkehr der Kriegerinnen. Das Kino entdeckt einen neuen Heldentypus: Den weiblichen Körper als Kampfmaschine," *Die Zeit*, no. 12 (12 March 1998): 49.

22. Erich F. Behrendt, *Soldaten der Freiheit. Ein Parolebuch des Nationalsozialismus* (Berlin, 1935), 89, quoted in Waltraud Amberger, "Männer, Krieger, Abenteuer. Der Entwurf des "soldatischen Mannes," in *Kriegsromanen über den Ersten und Zweiten Weltkrieg* (Frankfurt am Main, 1984), 85. The idea that Bolshevism can transform women into *Flintenweiber,* making them masculine, can still be seen in the (West German) stereotype of women forced into performing men's work in the GDR.

23. Bernhard Schlink, *Der Vorleser* (Zurich, 1995), 40.

24. See Daniel Patrick Brown, *The Beautiful Beast: The Life and Crimes of SS-Aufseherin Irma Grese* (Ventura, Calif., 1996), 67f.

25. See ibid.; Pierre Durand, *Die Bestie von Buchenwald* (East Berlin, 1985); Arthur L. Smith Jr., *Die Hexe von Buchenwald. Der Fall Ilse Koch* (Weimar, 1994). For a critical reading, see Przyrembel, *Der Bann des ildes-Ilse Koch.*

26. "Rhetoriken der Pornographisierung. Rahmungen des Blicks auf die NS-Verbrechen" in Insa Eschbach, Sigrid Jacobeit, and Silke Wenk, eds., *Gedächtmis und Geschlecht. Dentungsmuster in Darstellungen des nationalsozialistischen Genzids* (Frankfurt, forthcoming).

27. See Christina von Braun, "Der Mythos der 'Unversehrtheit' in der Moderne. Zur Geschichte des Begriffs 'Die Intellektuellen,'" in *Theorie—Geschlecht—Fiktion,* ed. Nathalie Amstrutz and Martina Kuoni (Basel, 1994), 35. Alvin H. Rosenfeld talks of a "transposition of an old erotic type onto the new imaginative landscapes of slaughter." See A. H. Rosenfeld, *Imagining Hitler* (Bloomington, Ind., 1985), 52.

28. See Susanne Diemer, *Patriarchalismus in der DDR. Strukturelle, kulturelle und subjektive Dimensionen der Geschlechterpolarisierung* (Opladen, 1994).

29. Tillion, *Ravensbrück;* Margarete Buber-Neumann, *Als Gefangene bei Stalin und Hitler. Eine Welt im Dunkel* (Frankfurt am Main, 1993); Isa Vermehren, *Reise durch den letzten Akt. Ravensbrück, Buchenwald, Dachau: Eine Frau berichtet* (Reinbek, 1987); Wanda Poltawska, *Und ich fürchte meine Träume* (Abensberg, 1994).

30. In Ravensbrück alone, more than 3,500 women were trained as guards. See affidavit sworn by the former commandant of Ravensbrück concentration camp, Fritz Suhren, on March 19, 1946, concerning strength and composition of the camp personnel; IMT Nürnberg Document 746b-D.

31. It may be that the patterns of interpretation discussed here can be described as a form of antimemory; as Geoffrey H. Hartman explains, "forgetting on a collective scale can itself assume the guise of memory. . . . It constructs, that is, a highly selective story, focussed on what is basic for the community and turning away from everything else." Geoffrey H. Hartman, introduction to *Holocaust Remembrance: The Shapes of Memory,* ed. G. H. Hartman (Cambridge, Mass., 1994), 15.

32. Jürgen Habermas, "Was bedeutet 'Aufarbeitung der Vergangenheit' heute? Bemerkungen zur 'doppelten Vergangenheit,'" in *Die Moderne—ein unvollendetes Projekt. Philosophisch-politische Aufsätze 1977–1992* (Leipzig, 1992), 258f.

Andrew Ezergailis

The Holocaust's Soviet Legacies in Latvia

THOSE ORGANIZING AGENCIES THAT IN THE WEST DEFINED THE
Holocaust, such as the Nuremberg Trials, *Life* magazine's pictures of
the Nazi concentration and death camps, and Raul Hilberg's collection of documents, were absent in the Soviet Union. In a true sense,
the Holocaust experience within the Soviet realm was different—in
the Western sense almost nonexistent. On the Soviet side, until 1990
even the word "Holocaust" was missing. The major agency in the Soviet Union that processed the information on the Holocaust was the
KGB [*Komitet gosudarstvennoi bezopasnosti,* or State Security Com-
mittee] with its propaganda arm—the Agitprop. The Soviets have left
a contradictory legacy: on the one hand, they were engaged in truth
seeking in unraveling the Nazi "conspiracy"; on the other hand, they
simultaneously imposed a silence on the findings and created a "new"
Holocaust image that had little in common with the real one. While
the Soviet Union existed, the three legacies lived on separate tracks
that hardly ever met.

The three Soviet legacies or contributions to the Holocaust can
be outlined as follows:

I. The Silent Treatment, 1941–1990
II. Investigation Records, 1944–1960
  A. Extraordinary Commission Investigations, 1944–1946
  B. Trial Records, 1944–1966
III. Propaganda, 1946–1990
  A. Show Trials, 1960–1974
  B. Pamphlet War, 1961–1980

I. THE SILENT TREATMENT, 1941–90

The Soviet silence about the Holocaust began in 1941 and, if we exclude the "propaganda war" (silence in a new guise), continued until 1990. Even in the era of Gorbachev's glasnost, censorship about the Holocaust continued. Access to the Holocaust archives was among the last to become available.

In his speech of July 3, 1941, Stalin warned a variety of Soviet peoples—including those, such as Uzbeks, who were not in the direct path of the Nazi onslaught—but he failed not only to warn but even to mention the Jews as the people most directly and immediately threatened. Although thousands—perhaps as many as twenty thousand—Latvian Jews found refuge within the Soviet Union, thousands of others were blocked by NKVD [*Narodnyi komissariat vnutrennikh del*, or People's Commissariat of Internal Affairs] troops from crossing the Latvian-Soviet frontier and were pushed back into the guns of the Einsatzgruppe A commandos.

During the war, the situation did not improve much. The numerous wartime publications—newspapers, leaflets and handbills dropped from the air and pasted on the walls—do not talk about the fate of the Jews in Latvia. They talk about numerous Nazi crimes, but the killing of the Jews is not one of them. Although numerous Latvian Jews were fighting within the ranks of the Red Army, none were mobilized to expose the crimes against their people.

A slight crack in the monolith of silence occurred during late 1944, when the Red Army was returning and the Extraordinary Commission had begun to investigate Nazi crimes. During late 1944 and early 1945, there appeared occasional articles reporting about the work of the Extraordinary Commission in which the atrocity sites were described. But in April 1945, this "openness" was shut down for the next fifty years, allowing only occasional and calculated breaks.

The breaks in the silence, as few as they were, occurred mostly for propaganda purposes, and they were connected with the show trials. These show trials and the publicity surrounding them, loud as it was, added little to our knowledge about the Holocaust. To the contrary, they propagandized and sovietized the Holocaust and in many ways misled the world about the Nazi crimes in Latvia. In due time, some of the propaganda crept into Soviet "scholarly" works about World War II.[1]

II. INVESTIGATION RECORDS, 1944–1960

The results of the inquiries that were started in 1944 remained a dormant Soviet Holocaust legacy until the end of the USSR. Until very recently, this store of information was closed even to the most trusted Soviet scholars and KGB insiders. Only those operatives on special assignments could gain limited access to these sources. On a limited basis during the 1970s and 1980s, some selected documents were made available to foreigners.

There were two arms of the NKVD that even before the war had ended went to work on collecting information about the Nazi crimes: (1) the Extraordinary Commission to Investigate the Crimes of Fascism and (2) the Soviet courts, which were prosecuting cases against individuals. In addition, the NKVD also set up a special bureau that investigated the Arājs Commando alone. Their findings were cross-indexed and compiled into a twelve-volume compendium. What these volumes contain we do not know for sure, because the KGB in 1991 managed to evacuate eleven of the twelve to Russia. The one volume that was waylaid in Latvia shows the care with which the Soviets had approached the identification of the perpetrators and locating their whereabouts. It also contains a list of perpetrators who had become KGB informers.

A. Extraordinary Commission Investigations, 1944–1946

The Extraordinary Commission to Investigate the crimes of Fascism was the first to start its fact- finding assignment. In their footsteps followed Soviet military and NKVD courts, which were charged with the task of apprehending "collaborationists" and punishing them. The commission and the courts fulfilled their assignments less than perfectly, but they collected, perhaps inadvertently, a body of facts that can be used by the post-Soviet countries to reconstruct with some degree of accuracy the Nazi crimes in their lands, including Latvia. The importance of this database is that the information that can be drawn from it contradicts in all particulars the version of the Holocaust in Latvia that the KGB propaganda arm and the show trials developed in the 1960s.

The Extraordinary Commission's reports are especially good in documenting the basic fact of the killing operations: the locations of the grave sites and the time of the murders. They are less accurate on the personnel who participated in the killing actions because they fail to separate the guilty from the bystanders. The numbers of victims frequently are exaggerated by a factor of three or even four. The Extraordinary Commission was a hierarchical organization that first collected information at the grass roots and then abstracted it as it was processed up the steps to the all-republic level. The higher it climbed, the more abstracted and sovietized it became. Unfortunately, the grassroots reports are not available for all localities.

B. *Trial Records, 1944–1966*

Of the two sources, the trial records compose the more important one, because frequently the evidence is less formulaic and freer of Soviet ideologizing. From the Western point of view, the Soviet courts were ruthless, but they did not always skew the evidence, because the punishment did not depend on the evidence. It is superfluous to note that all witnesses were not equally good nor all interrogators equally thorough. No one witness nor any one trial will give enough information to reconstruct the killing of Jews in a town. The historian needs to labor as a master jigsaw-puzzle solver. The trial investigators and prosecutors seem to have been much more interested in the connections that the accused had with other accused or potentially accused than with forcing them to fill in a predesigned scenario. The NKVD interrogators needed more-or-less accurate information, because their assignment seems to have been to trap and punish all collaborationists. To be sure, many witnesses frequently attempted to wiggle out of giving evidence that would implicate them in crimes. But it needs to be remembered that the witnesses and the accused had none of the legal protections that would have been available to them had they been tried in a Western jurisdiction. We can also note that the witnesses frequently tried to please the interrogator by talking "too much."

These KGB trial records must be treated substantially as different from those that the same organization compiled for the show trials. For one, the Soviets treated them differently: these trial records, of which there were thousands, were held in seclusion until 1991, while those of the few show trials, especially abroad, received considerable publicity.[2]

III. PROPAGANDA, 1946–1990

The Soviets with their censor's iron hand first created a void in the knowledge of the Holocaust and then filled it with misinformation—in the best of cases, with half-truth. The show trials were intended for the purpose of filling the void left by censorship. The first of these show trials that received a considerable amount of publicity through Latvian newspapers and airwaves was the Fredrick Jeckeln one in 1946. Jeckeln, from November 1941 to the end of the war, served in Latvia as the highest SS and police leader in the Northern zone of occupation. At the end of the war, he was captured and brought to Riga to be tried. It was a show trial in the sense that the verdict was announced beforehand, that it took place in front of an audience that applauded the verdict, and that the execution by hanging was a public one. Although the trial took place in Riga, it had very little to do with Latvians. The point of the trial was to prove that Nazism was a criminal and murderous regime. It did not address the Latvian participation in the killing of the Jews.[3]

A. Show Trials, 1960–1974

The real "show trials" in Latvia began in early 1960s after Khrushchev commenced his war against the "nationalists." There were three major show trials: (1) the Eighteenth Police Battalion in 1961, (2) the Rezekne trial of Eichelis, Puntulis, Maikovskis, and others in 1965;[4] and (3) the series of Twenty-first Battalion trials, 1972 to 1974, of which there were six.

The three trials fully meet the aforementioned criteria for show trials. The similarity between these three cases was that they used the atrocities of the Nazi occupation as the basis of accusation and that immediately after the war, though all of the accused had already been tried and punished, the specific accusations for which they were tried in the show trials had not surfaced in the earlier investigations. There is no question that the crimes for which the people were tried had occurred, the question is whether the men accused in the show trials were the ones who committed those crimes or had played the kind of a role that was assigned to them. The verdicts were proclaimed before the trial, and there was no presumption of innocence, especially in the courts. The pretrial interrogations leave the impression that they were scripted, and the prosecutors, regardless of the evidence, drove the cases toward a predetermined conclusion. The verdicts, especially in the first and the third trials, were made on the basis of self-incriminations and the testimonies of witnesses who themselves, if they told the truth, must have been guilty of the same crimes as the accused. Yet these witnesses were never tried or suffered any punishment.

The first trial, that of the Eighteenth Battalion, took place in 1961. The Eighteenth Latvian Police Battalion was accused of murdering the Jews of Slonim in August 1942. Nine members of the unit were placed on trial, and five were sentenced to death. There is no question that the Jews of Slonim, from June 1941 to December 1942 when the Slonim ghetto was liquidated, were killed. It also appears that the Eighteenth Battalion was passing through Slonim when on August 20, 1942, one of the last and smaller massacres of Slonim Jews took place. The history of the murder of the Slonim Jews has been told by several Jewish authors, but none includes the participation of the Eighteenth Battalion. The men of the Eighteenth were convicted on the basis of "self-confessions" without any material evidence.

The peculiarity of the second, the Rezekne, trial was that along with four men living in Latvia, the Soviets also tried in absentia three former Rezekne police chiefs living abroad: Alberts Eichelis, living in Germany; Haralds Puntulis, living in Canada; and Boñeslavs Maikovskis, living in the United States. Rezekne was both the name of a city and of the district in which it was the capital. The case staged in 1965 revolved around the destruction of the Audriñi village that was razed in January 1942. The killing of the Jews in Rezekne district, though present, was peripheral to the case. The trial was held in a sizable auditorium and was accompanied by a large publicity hullabaloo.[5]

The three defenders from Latvia were Jåzeps Basankoviçs (born 1916), Jånis Krasovskis (1916), Péteris Vaiçuks (1919), and the three from abroad: Maikovskis (1909), Eichelis (1912), and Puntulis (1909).[6] All but Vaiçuks, who received 15 years, received death sentences.[7]

In 1972, the Soviet prosecutors planned to stage a huge Twenty-first Battalion case consisting of about twenty-four defendants. For reasons unknown, they decided to break it up into six cases. Though six they were, they differed from each other very little. The same accusations, the same documents, the same witnesses were cycled through all of them. Altogether, twenty-four men were charged with the murder of Liepāja Jews in massacres in September and December 1941 and February 1942. Of the twenty-four, seven were sentenced to death, and the rest received fifteen years of imprisonment. The falsity of the accusations is even more manifest than in the Eighteenth Battalion case. At the time of the September and December 1941 massacres, the Twenty-first Battalion did not exist, and while in February 1942 the battalion existed, the massacre was an imagined event that did not take place.[8]

B. Pamphlet War, 1961–1980

Simultaneously with the show trials, the pamphlet war commenced. Exaggerations, falsehoods, and half-truths formed their content. The assignment to write and publish the pamphlets was entrusted to a special KGB agency, the Committee of Cultural Relation with Latvians Abroad. The main pamphlets that the committee published were *Kas ir Daugavas vanagi?* (*Who Are the Daugavas vanagi?*), *Emigranti bez maskas (Emigrants without a Mask), Bez maskas (Without a Mask),* and *No SS un SD līdz. . . (From SS to SD. . .)*

The most influential of these pamphlets was the first one, *Kas ir Daugavas vanagi?* It was translated into English, German, and Swedish. Everything about the pamphlets was false; we do not know the full identity of the authors or the place of publication. The titles of these pamphlets never appeared on the lists of the publishing houses that purportedly published them, and they were not available in Latvia. One of the authors of the *Kas ir Daugavas vanagi?* was Paulis Ducmanis. He was a leftover of the Nazi times who had worked in the anti-Semitic press of the German occupation. These pamphlets projected a special Soviet point of view that was at variance with the Soviet earlier position on the Holocaust. The basic assertion of these pamphlets was that the Jews of Latvia were killed by Latvians. They contained the following three assertions: (1) that the Latvians killed a countless number of Jews before the Germans had arrived there, (2) that the Latvians were better killers of Jews than the Germans were, and (3) that Latvia was a fitting land for the killing of Jews and thus 200,000 Jews from Europe were brought to Latvia to be killed. The overarching premise of this literature was that the Holocaust in Latvia was Germanless.

In conclusion, we can note that the Soviet Holocaust's legacies in Latvia still continue to exist; and to a large measure they continue to exist in separate compartments. By and large, they are unmediated but have begun to merge. The tradition of silence has not as yet ended, although the airing of the archival information has begun. President Guntis Ulmanis has created a Historians Commission that among other matters will investigate the Holocaust in Latvia. The strongest tradition that still dominates in Latvia, especially within the non-Latvian community, is the propaganda one. The latent documentary tradition has as yet not fully come into its own as in the future it will and must. To be sure, if the country is to remain democratic, the Western views of the Holocaust will need to penetrate it more fully than they have after ten years of freedom.

NOTES

1. For an example of the internal use of propaganda, see Latvijas Zinåtñu Akadémija, Véstures Institüts, *Latviešu Tautas cîña Lielajå Tévijas karå* (Riga: Zinåtne, 1964), pp. 182–242.

2. The Historical Institute of Latvia has compiled an index of these trials; see Rudîte Vîksne and Kårlis Kangeris, eds., *No NKVD ldz KGB, 1940–1986: Noziegumos pret padomju valsti apsüdzéto Latvijas iedzîvotåju rådîtåjs* (Riga: Latvijas véstures institüts, 1999).

3. The records of the Jeckeln trial are found in Moscow. They have been transferred to microfilm and are also found at the U.S. Holocaust Memorial Museum's archives.

4. The fullest analysis of the Eichelis trial is by Ojårs, Jånis Rozîtis, "Justizfürmige Bearbeitung und offentliche Darstellungen in Lettland," *Juristische Zeitgeschichte*, vol. 4 (Düsseldorf: NS-Verbrechen und Justiz, 1996).

5. Representatives from the foreign press were invited, among them S. E. Nordlinger, who wrote his report for the *Baltimore Sun,* 12 October 1965. He expressed surprise that a court would operate and try people on the charge of murder under the conditions of such blaring publicity.

6. Riga Latvijas valsts vesturi kais archivs (The History Archive of Latvia, LVVA), case number 45038.

7. Whether or not any of the accused were guilty of any of the charges

cannot be adjudicated here, but from the tenor of the rhetoric, it is clear that truth was not the object of the Soviet prosecutors. There may have been a grain of truth behind the charges, but that does not expunge the show nature of the trial. The follow-up of the Rezekne case was a suit against Albert Eichelis in Germany and one against the Boñeslav Maikovskis in the United States. Albert Eichelis was convicted but died before the sentence was announced. Maikovskis was found deportable from the United States and then fled to Germany, where a suit was started against him. He died before the trial ended.

8. The cases are found at the Latvian State Historical Archives in Riga LVVA case numbers 45232, 45225, 45236, 45234, 45233, and 45230. In 1987, the Latvia state prosecutor's office asked its prosecutor Astra Leiçenko to examine the cases. She found them all to be falsifications and corruptions of justice. The prosecutorial office of Latvia as of yet has not made a final determination on these cases.

IV. M·E·M·O·R·Y A·N·D H·I·S·T·O·R·I·C·A·L P·E·R·S·P·E·C·T·I·V·E

Donald Schilling

Representing the Holocaust in the General Histories of World War II

INTRODUCTION

IN EARLY 1946, ROGER W. SHUGG AND HARVEY A. DEWEERD PUBLISHED one of the first general histories of the Second World War. In *World War II: A Concise History,* the authors aimed to help readers "understand what actually happened, when and where and how, in the greatest war in history, and to see it all in better perspective" and "to tell the whole truth so far as it can be told now in limited space and from public sources."[1] Despite these goals and brief references to the virulent anti-Semitism in the Nazi program and the general warning by the Allied leaders of the judgment to be rendered against those committing "monstrous crimes,"[2] this study did not discuss the destruction of the European Jews. This omission was neither unusual in the early general histories of the war nor just a function of the constraints of writing a concise history. Winston Churchill's massive six-volume tour de force, *The Second World War,* did no better. Except for a brief, rather oblique mention of the fate of Hungarian and certain rich Greek Jews in an appendix, Churchill was silent on the fate of the Jews.[3]

In contrast, Lucy Dawidowicz in *The War against the Jews, 1933– 1945* wrote of the National Socialists' "Final Solution of the Jewish Question":

> It was part of a salvational ideology that envisaged the attainment of Heaven by bringing Hell on earth. . . . To attain its heavenly Hell on earth the German dictatorship launched a war that engulfed the whole world. Over 35 million people were killed, 1 out of every 22 Russians were killed, 1 out of every 25 Germans, 1 out of every 150 Italians and Englishmen, and 1 out of every 200

Frenchmen. The human cost of 2,191 days of war surpassed the losses of any previous war in the world. That war brought death to nearly 6 million Jews, to 2 out of every 3 European Jews.[4]

While Dawidowicz offered a simplistic explanation of the war's causes, clearly for her the Holocaust was the essence of the Second World War. Yet in the rest of her book, the war itself remained an unexamined backdrop against which the Final Solution was ruthlessly implemented. The gulf between the historians of World War II and those of the Holocaust has often been vast, to the detriment of both.[5]

In this essay, however, it is my intention to focus on the former group in an attempt to understand several basic issues: (1) How long did the general histories of the war treat the fate of the Jews with silence? What factors might account for this silence? (2) When historians of the war began to recognize the Holocaust, how did they represent it? What were the strengths and weaknesses of these representations? (3) What is to be gained by overcoming what Gerhard Weinberg has characterized as a "[f]airly common tendency to write, talk, and teach about the Holocaust and about World War II as separate and only barely related events"?[6] I will explore these issues by examining general histories of the war published since 1945 in light of these questions and with the goal of defining the historiography of this issue.

TWO DECADES OF SILENCE

The year 1948 was an important one for general histories of the war. Not only did Churchill publish his first volume, but two distinguished British writers on World War I, Cyril Falls and F. J. C. Fuller, both accepted the challenge of giving historical definition to the recent war. Their aims were appropriately modest. Falls, in *The Second World War: A Short History*, the first of the venerated "short history" genre, attempted "a sketch of events,"[7] while Fuller, publishing three months later, eschewed a "full-dress history of the recent war . . . because . . . on the data as yet available it is [not] a practical undertaking."[8] If Falls wrote in a dry, factual style with little analysis or evaluation until the conclusion, Fuller's narrative bristled with judgments, thus etching the controversies of the war in acid. Falls never mentioned anti-Semitism or Jews, let alone that millions of them died in this war; in fact, he hardly ever mentioned Nazis or their racist policies in conquered territories.[9] Fuller, only slightly less guilty of this silence, did note in passing "the horrors of the concentration camps and gas chambers" but without ever specifying the victims. Further, Fuller made this reference only to emphasize that these horrors "will dim with the passing years," while "the ruined cities of Germany will stand as monuments to the barbarism of their conquerors . . . [and] will remain to beckon generation after generation of Germans to revenge."[10]. Extraordinarily critical of Allied saturation bombing, the Victorian Fuller believed these barbarities were caused by "the disappearance of the gentlemen—the man of honour and principle—as the backbone of the ruling class in England [for] political power rapidly passed into the hands of demagogues who . . . created a permanent war psychosis . . . to justify the massacre of civilian populations."[11]

Writing during the height of the cold war, the Australian journalist Chester Wilmot produced *The Struggle for Europe,* a masterful analysis of the war and grand strategy, primarily in Western Europe, from the Battle of Britain to the defeat of Germany. A single issue drove Wilmot's 1952 study, that being "how and why, in the process of crushing Nazi Germany and liberating Western Europe, they [the Western Allies] allowed the Soviet Union to gain control of Eastern Europe."[12] This approach and preoccupation offered no room for consideration of the Holocaust, and only once in his extensive text did Wilmot make reference to "the most bestial campaign of genocide that Europe had ever known."[13]

Fundamentally, the pattern of silence continued in the 1960s. If aspects of the Holocaust were mentioned at all, the references were cryptic and lacking any broader explanatory context. Writing in 1966, for example, Sandhurst historian Brigadier Peter Young noted in the course of his discussion of the Eastern Front in 1944 that "the extermination of the Jewish population [in Russia] was systematic" and cited a specific example from Alexander Werth, who "'saw the charred remains of some 2,000 Jews.'"[14] Similarly, Basil Collier, in his competent but traditional study, *The Second World War: A Military History,* wrote, "The Russian advance uncovered gruesome evidence of the wholesale slaughter of Jews and other persons obnoxious to the rulers of the Third Reich."[15] Then in the next sentence he seemed deliberately to balance the account by reporting on the Katyn massacre.

In 1970, one of the century's preeminent military historians, Basil H. Liddell Hart, completed his study of the war just before his death. A practitioner of traditional military history, Liddell Hart engaged many issues of historiographical controversy in a strong narrative based on the analysis of strategy and operations in all the major theaters of the war. In a perverse sense, this work was a fitting culmination of the historiographic trend I have just documented, for it is totally lacking any discussion of material directly or indirectly touching on the Holocaust.

What accounts for this deafening silence in the quarter century following the end of the war? Several possible explanations emerge. First, the traditional conception of and approach to military history put a premium on the analysis of strategy and operations to the exclusion of other topics. This form of history, most often written by the gentleman scholar, the military journalist, the antiquarian, the war buff, or the scholarly soldier, did not enjoy much status within the academy, especially within the United States, and remained isolated from many of the trends that moved the historical discipline beyond political and intellectual history. At their worst, these writers took a "drums and bugles" view of war as an adventurous and glorious crusade from which heroes and fools emerged larger than life. At their best, they provided a sober, clear analysis of strategy and operations in order to draw lessons from the past useful to the military leadership of the future. In neither case were they prompted to engage issues, such as the Holocaust, that lay outside of their conception of military history.[16]

Second, military historians shared the historical profession's more general blindness toward Jews and their history. Writing in 1981, Lucy Dawidowicz charged that "the frequency with which the Holocaust has been neglected or passed over, distorted or trivialized in history textbooks suggests that other factors besides professional competence are involved."[17] She went on to argue that anti-Semitism, the Jews' historic position as outsiders, and distortions in historical methodology helped account for Jewish invisibility.[18]

Third, the emergence of the cold war in the years immediately after 1945 was central to the transformation of Germans, especially those in the zones controlled by the Western allies, from "villains to victims."[19] To emphasize the Holocaust—with the profoundly troubling issues it raised about the society, culture, and people of Germany—would only complicate the redefinition of German identity and the transformation of West Germany to an ally in a divided Europe. For writers like Wilmot, as indicated earlier, the central task became to understand how the strategic decisions of the Western allies contributed to Soviet control of Eastern and Central Europe and thus fueled the cold war. In this context, the Holocaust, an unfortunate expression of Hitlerian excess, was best forgotten.

Fourth, the Holocaust was a raw wound, too painful and horrifying in its implications to confront in the aftermath of the war. How, for example, does one preserve the belief that killing on the battlefield is legitimate, essentially unrelated to murder, when central to the German war effort was a vast murder enterprise? Better to ignore it and treat the war as something entirely separate from the Holocaust.[20]

Fifth, scholarly work on the Holocaust, while not totally lacking, was not well developed at that time.[21] As Gerd Korman noted in 1972, "I have used 'Holocaust' in this article, but in 1949 [and presumably earlier], there was no 'Holocaust' in the English language, in the sense that the word is used today."[22] Scholars searched for language consonant with the magnitude of the disaster, but not until the 1960s did the term "Holocaust" acquire its specific meaning. Language reflected the development of the field. To be sure, information was available from an early date in the form of survivor accounts and initial scholarly investigation, but Raul Hilberg has recounted the many years he labored essentially alone and in obscurity on his massive, pathbreaking *Destruction of the European Jews,* published in 1961.[23] One can well imagine historians of the war regarding the challenges of writing their general histories with such trepidation that they had no desire to complicate the process further with the complex and insufficiently digested issues of the Holocaust. Since then, the point, however, is that the previous absence of readily available resources on the Holocaust reinforced the predilections of the writers of general histories of the war to ignore or skirt the subject.

INITIAL EFFORTS AT RE-PRESENTING THE HOLOCAUST

This pervasive silence began to end in the late 1960s. Four factors helped produce the change and reflected the overcoming of the limitations discussed previously. The first is obvious—the growing body of readily available material on the Holocaust, as work on the Holocaust gathered momentum and Holocaust studies emerged as a burgeoning and increasingly sophisticated field.[24]

The second factor is more subtle. Following the Cuban Missile Crisis of October 1962, the superpowers retreated from the intense and highly dangerous confrontations marking the height of the cold war, and its first phase came to an end. R. J. B. Bosworth has recently linked the ending of the "First Cold War" with the emergence of "what seemed a new atmosphere in which to pursue in a more scholarly and subtle fashion the historical explanations for 'Auschwitz' and 'Hiroshima.'"[25] Historians could now more easily approach the Second World War from new interpretive vantage points and redefine the range of topics appropriate for inclusion in its history.

Another historiographical shift informs the third factor. The 1960s not only witnessed the end the first phase of the cold war with its implications for the writing of history but also the blossoming of the "new social history." Social historians, initially very interested in history from "the bottom up," documented the experiences of those not traditionally recognized: the working class, women, African-Americans, and other minority groups.[26] This approach, coupled with a significant reduction in anti-Semitic attitudes in the English-speaking world, helped bring the historical experience of Jews, especially as revealed in the Holocaust, into the picture.

The fourth factor is more complicated but is also linked to shifts within the discipline. In 1956, Michael Howard began a long campaign to elevate the status and transform the nature of military history. Writing in *History,* he urged that military history become an accepted field of study for university faculty. This would require a shift in subject from "the technical aspects of combat and the lessons learned that could be applied to future operations" to the exploration of "its relevance to the nature and development of society as a whole."[27] Howard's critique, gradually reinforced by others in the field, contributed to such substantial growth in the "new" military history that Dennis Showalter could issue "A Modest Plea for Drums and Trumpets" in 1975.[28] More recently, Paul Kennedy, echoing Howard, articulated the challenge facing practitioners of the new military history:

No longer, it is argued, can a history of the war be confined to accounts of operations, generalship, and front-line combat. It must be widened to include the entire effort of the societies involved and thus to incorporate (among other things) the home fronts, political and propaganda aspects, ideology and race, social transformations, the changed position of women, culture, and art and literature. The historian taking this warfare-and-society approach is thus required to write what one might term *total* history [italics in the original].[29]

The redefining of military history in this manner made inclusion of phenomena such as the Holocaust much more likely as the general histories of the war moved toward the goal of total history.

In the late 1960s and early 1970s, three works emerged that took seriously the requirements of the new military history. The first was Gordon Wright's *The Ordeal of Total War, 1939–1945*, written in 1968 for the Rise of Modern Europe Series. This volume admirably fulfilled the mandate of the series, which was designed to provide the student and general reader with an "intelligent synthesis" and "a reliable survey of European history" that "went beyond a merely political-military narrative, . . . to lay stress upon social, economic, religious, scientific, and artistic development."[30] Wright defined an approach to the Holocaust (a term he did not use) characteristic of many subsequent works. He placed his brief, four-page discussion of the "repression and liquidation" of the European Jews, with emphasis on Nazi racial policy and the centers and methods of extermination, in the context of his treatment of German rule in occupied Europe.[31] His discussion was cursory and did little to probe the reciprocal connections between the Holocaust and the war, but it was a beginning—one reinforced by a substantive two-page bibliography on the topic.

The French military historian Henri Michel authored the second of these books, published in France in 1968 and available in English translation in 1975 as *The Second World War*. This book set the standard for the "heavyweight" category of general histories, that is, those tipping the scales at about five pounds and running to roughly one thousand pages in length. Michel, too, felt the time was right for a work of synthesis, and he brought to this project the benefit of his collaborative work as founder and general secretary of Le Comitè

Française de L'Histoire de la Deuxième Guerre Mondiale (the French Committee on the History of the Second World War), which had the goal of making known the total history of the war. Employing the concept of total war, Michel probed all its dimensions, from the key military campaigns to economic mobilization to German occupation policies and the destruction of the European Jews, which he examined in more depth than Wright did.[32]

The British team of Peter Calvocoressi and Guy Wint wrote the third piece of this breakthrough triad in 1972. Addressing a general audience, they wrestled with the question of how much war to include in a book on World War II and concluded, "[W]e did not want to write a military or campaign history and were not qualified to do so, but . . . we felt it was essential . . . to show why particular campaigns were fought, when, and where they were fought, and also what happened behind . . . 'the lines.'"[33] The result was an extremely readable book that gave substantial attention, as did Michel's, to all aspects of the total war. Although the heart of their examination of the destruction of European Jews occurred in their chapter "The New Order," Calvocoressi and Wint engaged the issues of causation, including the roles of religious and racial anti-Semitism in Hitler's weltanschauung; of implementation with particular attention to the nature, policies, and practices of the SS; of Jewish resistance; and of the responses of other countries to the Final Solution.[34] These three works represented an important step forward and established a pattern for treating the Holocaust emulated by many subsequent authors; however, this pattern emphasized the perpetrators and machinery of destruction to the exclusion of the victims and did not encourage integration of the Holocaust into a history of the war.

Following the spate of activity marking the twenty-fifth anniversary of World War II, general histories of the war appeared infrequently, but output dramatically increased in the period 1987 to 1990 as historians and others raced to capture the fiftieth-anniversary audience. By my count, ten substantive general histories of the war appeared in these years, and several volumes followed before the commemorative events had ended in 1995. Most of the writers of the short histories followed the pattern set by Wright, Michel, and Calvocoressi and Wint, falling between the former and the latter in the level of detail accorded to their discussions of the Holocaust.[35]

Writers of general histories of intermediate length might well have afforded more attention to the Holocaust, especially given the burgeoning literature in that field, yet H. C. Willmott, author of a provocative and engaging but more traditionally conceived military history, *The Great Crusade: A New Complete History of the Second World War,* treated it in less than one page of his 477-page narrative, belying the subtitle of his book.[36] John Ellis in *Brute Force* eschewed total history for an exploration of the connections between economic production and battlefield success and chose to exclude the Holocaust entirely.[37] Not to be outdone by his competitors, John Keegan adroitly presented the central strategic and operational issues of the war in *The Second World War.* Realizing that comprehensiveness was impossible, Keegan "decided from the outset to divide the story of the war into four topics—narrative, strategic analysis, battle piece and 'theme of war' and to use these four topics to carry the history of the six main sections into which the war falls."[38] Under the "theme of war," Keegan introduced such issues as production and supply, espionage and intelligence, resistance, and superweapons, and in this context he offered a passing nod to the Holocaust.[39] In short, the intermediate histories of the last few years, rather than presenting a more complete picture of the destruction of the European Jews, let alone beginning the process of truly integrating the Holocaust into the history of the war, instead retreated to the virtual silence of the immediate postwar decades.

Offering even greater potential for substantive consideration of the Holocaust are three lengthy recent volumes falling into the heavyweight division. One of these can be quickly dispatched: *Delivered from Evil: The Saga of World War II* by Robert Leckie. Leckie emphasized traditional military history supplemented by diplomacy and biographical sketches of the great men, all told in "a swiftly moving narrative" that at times degenerated into parody:[40] "His [Mussolini's] words ignited a train of gun powder that went flashing across the boot of Italy."[41] More troubling was Leckie's inability to discriminate among sources; he relied far too often on works lacking scholarly credibility. As a result, his chapter examining the Holocaust is marred by distortion and a crudeness of analysis. For Leckie, the brutalities of the Holocaust were largely explained by the character of SS men:

> Himmler's SS guards, like Heydrich's SD men, were the scum of the
> German earth: thieves, rapists, murderers, misfits, torturers, and

perverts, all of them deeply streaked with sadism. They took ghoul-
ish delight in contriving the vilest punishments for "capital" crimes
of attempting to escape, stealing a potato or smiling in the ranks.[42]

If Leckie saw the perpetrators as sadists, he explained the victims'
"unique submissiveness" in part "because they had become a migrant
people . . . no longer motivated by that territorial imperative which
impels all creatures—human beings included—to fight fiercest in defense of their own nest, lair or homeland."[43] Such explanations reveal
an ignorance of readily accessible recent literature and reduce the Holocaust to caricature. Silence on the subject would have been preferable.

The two remaining works, *The Second World War: A Complete
History* by Martin Gilbert and *A World at Arms: A Global History of
World War II* by Gerhard Weinberg, require more thorough examination. Gilbert, the author of a massive study of the Holocaust,
proved admirably sensitive to the fate of the European Jews in his
work.[44] Devoting substantially more space to the Holocaust than had
any other author, Gilbert broke out of the pattern of treating the
Holocaust with silence or in a self-contained section, which had the
effect of isolating it from the rest of the war, and instead interspersed
material on the Holocaust throughout his narrative. No readers of
Gilbert would conclude that the Holocaust had little or nothing to
do with the Second World War, but they would have to overcome
other liabilities. His "complete history" contained surprisingly "large
omissions."[45] Further, his narrative, based on an almost day-by-day
chronology, was strong on description but so weak on analysis that
general patterns disappeared. In the absence of a conceptual framework, readers drown in detail.

Gerhard Weinberg's monumental study, the third of the recent
histories in the heavyweight category, has come closer to realizing the
potential of total history than any single general history of the war.
Like Gilbert, Weinberg has been particularly effective in integrating
the Holocaust into the larger history of the war. Unlike Gilbert,
Weinberg wove this particular thread into a narrative possessing
comprehensive and comprehensible patterns. For Weinberg, the nature and course of the war in Europe could not be understood without explicit reference to Hitler's virulent anti-Semitic and social
Darwinist weltanschauung and its embodiment in the range of anti-

Jewish and racist policies leading to and encompassing the Final Solution. Weinberg probed its implications for Germany's home front; for the nature of the war, especially as it was waged in the East, where the army and much of its leadership were profoundly compromised; for Hitler's strategic thinking; for Germany's relations with its allies in Europe and treatment of occupied territories; and ultimately for our understanding of the human capacity for evil.

Given the constraints of space, let me offer just two examples of the insights yielded by Weinberg's approach. The first concerns grand strategy. Hitler's basic strategy in early 1944 was, according to Weinberg, "to hold the front in Italy as far south as possible and to hold as well as they could in the East but to concentrate on defeating the expected Allied invasion in the West."[46] Despite the urgings of the Japanese and Pierre Laval in France that he make peace with the Soviets to concentrate on driving the invasion forces into the sea, Hitler reaffirmed the strategy just identified, because, as Weinberg noted, "He was confident that it would succeed, in part because by this time he believed that the mass murder of the Jews and all opposed to the regime had . . . removed all possibility of problems at home. A Germany not subject to the stab in the back which he imagined responsible for defeat in 1918 could not be beaten this time."[47] The second example fell within Weinberg's examination of relationships within the wartime alliances. In exploring the strained relationship between Germany and Italy, Weinberg wrote,

> The divergence between the partners became ever more pronounced during the war. German initiation of the systematic killing of Jews was no more discussed with the Italian government than any other of their major political, military, or other initiatives, but the Italians were expected to participate fully. On the whole, in spite of Mussolini's willingness to go along, they mostly simply would not do so. In the Italian-occupied portions of France, Yugoslavia and Greece the local commanders, who knew perfectly well what the Germans were doing, refused to turn over the Jews to the Germans to be murdered, and endless arguments over this issue led to no agreement. The Italians were confirmed in their prior belief that the Germans were still barbarians and the Germans were reinforced in their view of the Italians as indifferent and incompetent allies.[48]

While in neither of these examples did Weinberg's inclusion of Holo-caust-related material result in a new interpretation, the reader comes away with a more sophisticated understanding of each case because of his approach.

CONCLUSION

As this review of a half century of writing general histories of World War II reveals, historians have largely been remiss in their incorpora-tion of the Holocaust into the history of the war. For the first two decades, they essentially ignored the Holocaust. They then began to include cursory discussions that largely isolated it from major war-time developments. Only with the recent histories of Gilbert—rather ineffectively—and Weinberg—with considerably more skill—did the Holocaust become integrated into the narrative in complex and stimulating ways.

Such integration adds an important explanatory element to our understanding of the war. Just a brief survey suggests that inclusion of the Holocaust is essential for sound analysis of (1) the origins and outbreak of the war and its expansion to include the Soviet Union in 1941; (2) the nature and conduct of the war, especially in Eastern Eu-rope; (3) the nature of German occupation policy and the degree of resistance it provoked; (4) certain of Hitler's key strategic decisions; (5) Germany's relations with its allies; (6) Germany's ability, or lack of it, to develop an atomic bomb; (7) the German allocation of scarce human and material resources in the war effort; and (8) certain of the decisions regarding the postwar treatment of Germany and its former leaders. This list is not exhaustive, but it suggests how imperative it is that historians of the war and of the Holocaust engage in productive dialogue. Both historians and their histories will be enriched thereby.

NOTES

1. Roger W. Shugg and Harvey A. Deweerd, *World War II: A Concise History* (Washington: Infantry Journal, 1946), p. v.
2. Ibid., 211.
3. Winston Churchill, *The Second World War,* vol. 6, *Triumph and Tragedy* (Boston: Houghton Mifflin, 1953), 693–95.

4. Lucy Dawidowicz, *The War against the Jews, 1933–1945* (New York: Bantam Books, 1976), xxii-xxiii.

5. Even the recently published comprehensive historiographical study of the vast literature of World War II—Loyd E. Lee, ed., *World War II in Europe, Africa, and the Americas, with General Sources: A Handbook of Literature and Research* (Westport, Conn.: Greenwood Press, 1997)—contains a chapter on the Holocaust by Richard Libowitz that, despite its solid review of Holocaust literature, fails to make any meaningful connection between the Holocaust and the war. This seems particularly ironic in this context.

6. Gerhard Weinberg, "The Holocaust and World War II: A Dilemma in Teaching," in *Lessons and Legacies II: Teaching the Holocaust in a Changing World*, ed. Donald G. Schilling (Evanston, IL: Northwestern University Press, 1998), 26.

7. Cyril Falls, *The Second World War* (London: Methuen, 1948), 285.

8. F. J. C. Fuller, *The Second World War, 1939–45: A Strategical and Tactical History* (New York: Meredith Press, 1948), 11.

9. The closest he comes occurs on page 107 when he writes, "The Nazis, in throwing Europe into war, had been fired by ambition: . . . to seek near their frontiers rich agricultural land in the hands of races which they ranked as inferior and in these territories plant settlements of their own people" (Falls, *Second World War*).

10. Fuller, *Second World War*, 408.

11. Ibid., 405.

12. Chester Wilmot, *The Struggle for Europe* (New York: Harper and Row, 1952), xi.

13. Ibid., 549. In Appendix A: A Note on Sources, Wilmot illustrated the meticulousness of German record keeping by noting the evidence recorded of victims killed at Mauthausen concentration camp (p. 719).

14. Brigadier Peter Young, *A Short History of World War II, 1939–1945* (New York: Thomas Crowell, 1966), 347.

15. Basil Collier, *The Second World War: A Military History* (New York: William Morrow, 1967), 384.

16. Basil Liddell Hart, *History of the Second World War* (London: Cassell, 1970). See discussion by Alan Millett, "The Study of American Military History in the United States," *Military Affairs* 41 (April 1977): 58–61; Peter Karsten, "Demilitarizing Military History: Servants of Power or Agents of Understanding," *Military Affairs* 36 (October 1972): 88–91. David A. Charters, Marc Milner, and J. Brent Wilson, eds., *Military History and the Military Profession* (Westport, Conn.: Praeger, 1992), part 2, provides extensive discussion of the linkages between military history and the military profession. A sophisticated analysis of the state of military his-

tory is also provided by Peter Paret, "The History of War," in *Historical Studies Today*, ed. Felix Gilbert and Stephen R. Graubard (New York: W. W. Norton, 1972), 372–92.

17. Lucy Dawidowicz, *The Holocaust and Historians* (Cambridge: Harvard University Press, 1981), 25.

18. Ibid., 26–34.

19. The phrase is taken from Petra Goedde, "From Villains to Victims: Fraternization and the Feminization of Germany, 1945–1947," *Diplomatic History* 23, no. 1 (winter 1999): 1–20. Goedde, who demonstrates that a variety of factors contributed to this transformation but emphasizes the role of fraternization between American soldiers and German women, concludes by noting, "With the onset of the Cold War and growing anticommunism in the United States, Americans conceived of Germans as victims, not only of material shortages but of a looming Communist takeover as well" (20).

20. Historians of the war in this period would not share the more recent assessment of John Shy, "The Cultural Approach to the History of War," *Journal of Military History* 57 (October 1993): 13–26, who wrote, "No need to rehearse the statistics, or stories; we can simply stipulate that, terrible as modern war had become by 1914, something far worse happened in the Second World War. At the center of our consciousness of the special horror of this war *of course* lies the Holocaust"(14, emphasis added).

21. Two general works on the Holocaust had appeared in the early 1950s, however: Gerald Reitlinger, *The Final Solution: The Attempt to Exterminate the Jews of Europe, 1939–45* (New York: A. S. Barnes, 1953); and Leon Poliakov, *Harvest of Hate: The Nazi Program for the Destruction of the Jews of Europe* (Philadelphia: Jewish Publication Society of America, 1954).

22. Gerd Korman, "The Holocaust in American Historical Writing," *Societas* 2 (summer 1972), as reprinted in John K. Roth and Michael Berenbaum, eds., *Holocaust: Religious and Philosophical Implications* (New York: Paragon House, 1989), 45.

23. Author's notes on Hilburg's remarks at the Second Lessons and Legacies Conference, 1987.

24. See, for example, Michael R. Marrus, *The Holocaust in History* (Hanover, N.H.: University Press of New England for Brandeis University Press, 1987).

25. R. J. B. Bosworth, *Explaining Auschwitz and Hiroshima: History Writing and the Second World War, 1945–1990* (London: Routledge, 1993), 27.

26. E. J. Hobsbawm, "From Social History to the History of Society," in *Historical Studies Today*, ed. Felix Gilbert and Stephen R. Graubard (New York: W. W. Norton, 1972), 1–26.

27. Michael Howard, "Military History as a University Study," *History* 41 (1956): 186. Just one indication of the significance of Howard's work is provided by Robert O'Neill: "In essence what Howard has done is to have raised the standing of the whole field of enquiry and expanded the thinking of most of those who can make a serious claim to know something about warfare and its impact in the nineteenth and twentieth centuries." Robert O'Neill, "In Appreciation of Michael Howard: Remarks Offered at the Modern History Faculty Farewell Dinner, 29 June 1989," in *War, Strategy, and International Politics: Essays in Honour of Sir Michael Howard*, ed. Lawrence Freedman, Paul Hayes, and Robert O'Neill (Oxford: Clarendon Press, 1992), 299.

28. Dennis Showalter, "A Modest Plea for Drums and Trumpets," *Military Affairs* 41 (April 1977): 71–74.

29. Paul Kennedy, review of *History* by Paul Howard, *New York Times Book Review*, 31 December 1989, 10.

30. Gordon Wright, *The Ordeal of Total War, 1939–1945*, Rise of Modern Europe Series (New York: Harper and Row, 1968), 11. Other authors whose treatment is similar to that of Wright are James Stokesbury, *A Short History of World War II* (New York: William Morrow, 1980), 197–99; M. K. Dziewanowski, *War at Any Price: World War II in Europe, 1939–1945*, 2d ed. (Englewood, Cliffs, N.J.: Prentice Hall, 1991), 261–67, including brief segments on the Allied response to the Holocaust and Jewish resistance; Michael J. Lyons, *World War II: A Short History*, 2d ed. (Englewood, Cliffs, N.J.: Prentice Hall, 1994), 126–29, 277–78; Martin Kitchen, *A World in Flames* (London: Longman, 1990), 194–206; R. A. C. Parker, *Struggle for Survival: The History of the Second World War* (Oxford: Oxford University Press, 1989), 264–80. In relative terms, Kitchen and Parker, the latter of whom was the only one to have a separate chapter on the subject, provided more substantive and insightful consideration of the Holocaust than did the others.

31. Wright, *Ordeal of Total War*, 123–28.

32. Henri Michel, *La Seconde guerre mondiale;* in English as *The Second World War*, trans. Douglas Parmée (New York: Praeger, 1975).

33. Peter Calvocoressi and Guy Wint, *Total War: Causes and Courses of the Second World War* (New York: Penguin Books, 1972), vii.

34. Ibid., 214–41.

35. See citations in note 30, above.

36. H. C. Willmott, *The Great Crusade: A New Complete History of the Second World War* (New York: Free Press, 1991), 444.

37. John Ellis, *Brute Force* (New York: Viking, 1990).

38. John Keegan, *The Second World War* (New York: Penguin Books, 1990), 5.

39. Ibid., 288–89.

40. Robert Leckie, *Delivered from Evil: The Saga of World War II* (New York: Harper Perennial, 1988), 947.

41. Ibid., 21.

42. Ibid., 913.

43. Ibid., 920.

44. Martin Gilbert, *The Second World War: A Complete History* (New York: Henry Holt, 1989); see, for example, index references to Jews, 812–13.

45. The term is Gordon Craig's, who notes that Gilbert "has nothing to say about the background and causes of the war . . . the details of battle or the performance of different kinds of weapons . . . the nature of the war experience and the vast difference between the home front's idealized view of it. . . . The reader will look in vain for an analysis of wartime diplomacy or even of strategic planning; there is no systematic account of economic warfare; there is virtually no assessment of military systems, civilian military relations in the belligerent countries, or . . . the performance of individual commanders." Gordon Craig, review of *The Second World War: A Complete History* by Martin Gilbert, *New York Times Book Review*, 26 November 1989, 16.

46. Gerhard Weinberg, *A World at Arms: A Global History of World War II* (Cambridge: Cambridge University Press, 1994), 665.

47. Ibid.

48. Ibid., 745.

Renée Poznanski

Jews and Non-Jews in France during World War II
A Daily Life Perspective

TWO CONCEPTS USUALLY SERVE AS POLES OF REFERENCES FOR AN analysis of the attitude of the French toward the Jews during the Second World War—anti-Semitism and rescue. These terms relate to distinct phenomena. The historical context of the former is the long term *(la longue durée)*—the evolution of French anti-Semitism. The ideological element is central to it. The second refers only to the period of the Occupation. Here the accent is on praxis.

Today, after the autonomous anti-Semitism of the French state has been conclusively established, studies of public opinion continue to reach divergent conclusions. Some depict the French as anti-Semites, receptive to the dominant ideology, accomplices in the application of the various measures of exclusion and dispossession. Later, they were at best indifferent, at worst content to see the Jews deported from France. For other scholars, on the contrary, the rescue operations made possible by the attitude of these same French people—civil society as opposed to the state—explain how three-quarters of the Jewish population of France managed to escape the fate the Germans intended for them.[1] These two perspectives have different chronological foci, too: the thesis of an anti-Semitic society is built chiefly on the first two years of the Occupation; that of a French population eager to save Jews ignores these two years and concentrates on the latter half of the war.

Yet it seems to me that neither of these two theses does justice to the complexity of the period we are studying, precisely because they are based on a confusion of these two phenomena—anti-Semitism and rescue—that are presented as mutually exclusive. Observing the issue through the prism of "daily life," however, leads to a reconsideration of the relations between ideological anti-Semitism and a social practice associated with a broader context. What is more, studies of the anti-Semitism–rescue pair generally concentrate on the Southern Zone, subject to the authority of Vichy, as if the presence of the Germans in Paris interfered with the analysis. Yet it is an essential element of the picture. If it is true that as the months passed, more and more Jews sought refuge in villages south of the demarcation line, one can understand what was going on there only by referring to what had happened, shortly earlier, in the Occupied Zone. There are two reasons for this: on the one hand, the mechanisms were often the same. On the other hand, rumors about events in the Occupied Zone constituted the pole of reference for the population of the Southern Zone.

The question that interests me here has to do with the nature of the relations that developed between French society and the Jews who were subject to anti-Semitic legislation, as well as the impact of these relations on the effectiveness of the anti-Jewish persecution.

Rather than attempt an exhaustive study of the entire period, and taking into account the complexity of the situation and the importance of sticking as close as possible to chronology, I will try to center my analysis on two examples: (1) Paris during the first months of the Occupation and the application of the anti-Semitic laws, and (2) the Southern Zone after the summer of 1942, at the height of the roundups of Jews who were arrested and deported to Auschwitz.

This type of study is facilitated by the existence of numerous documents from a variety of sources, which let us follow the evolution of French public opinion, despite the context of war and occupation, despite the heavy hand of an authoritarian regime that permitted no freedom for the expression of opinions other than those it implemented. On the one hand, Jewish activists of various prewar organizations endeavored to keep abreast of and describe these developments, in order to draw practical conclusions about the type of defensive strategy to adopt.[2] A number of diaries kept by Jews during this period belong in this category.[3] To this we may add bureaucratic and police documents. That the domestic intelligence service has left us precise studies of the evolution of public opinion is not astonishing—such sampling was the prime function of this bureau.[4] But the wide variety of documents available to us is richer still, because one of the "battles" that developed between the legal government in Vichy and the exiles who were organizing in London under General de Gaulle was from the very outset a struggle for legitimacy and thus a battle to win the support of the French people. Accordingly, Vichy employed various and sundry means to identify the slightest oscillations in public opinion, maintaining close surveillance of the mails and phone conversations in France and ordering monthly reports from regional prefects.[5] Across the Channel, the Free French intelligence office in London (the BCRA, or Bureau central de Renseignements et d'action militaires), too, undertook numerous opinion surveys, whose findings helped shape the propaganda broadcast on the French transmissions of the BBC.[6]

Taken together, these documents allow us to compose a fairly precise picture of French attitudes toward the Jews, placing it in the larger context of the various problems that engaged French public opinion during the war years. In this larger perspective, the trauma of the lightning defeat, which was total and unexpected, the constant apprehension spawned by the Occupation, the conditions of impoverishment, the shortage of food, the lack of coal during the long cold winters, the million-and-a-half prisoners of war, and then, starting in February 1943, the introduction of conscript labor service, and finally the quasi civil war during the last months of the Occupation all provide the background for the general indifference to the specific fate of the Jews, which was undoubtedly the attitude of the majority of the population. In the larger scheme of things that troubled the French people, the Jews occupied a marginal place, if any.[7] Here we shall inquire as to the contours, character, and limits of this indifference.

1. IN PARIS: A SENSE OF RELIEF FOR THE JEWS, A SENSE OF SATISFACTION FOR THE AUTHORITIES

In this respect, there was a clear difference between the two zones: in the north, and especially in Paris, the Germans were present, and everything must be measured against the yardstick of this presence. If from the outset a double anti-Semitic legislation applied there—that decreed by the government of Marshal Pétain and that imposed by the Nazi occupier, the most visible actions bore a German stamp. While the Parisians adopted, without too much strain, a behavior characterized by daily compromises and adapted to the presence of the Germans, they were from the beginning hostile to the occupier and devoted to an English victory.[8] "Paris is marked by its Ger-

manophobia," noted Report 24 of the Technical Control Department, dated May 6, 1941.[9] All other sources confirm the accuracy of
this observation.

It is in this perspective that we should interpret the sense of relief
expressed by the Jews in all the extant reports and testimonies from
this period. The journalist Jacques Biélinky, a valuable observer of
Jewish social life in prewar France, was alert to the slightest reactions
in the queues that stretched in front of the food shops and noted
them down in his diary meticulously. He rejoiced that he heard very
few anti-Semitic comments and observed that the shops marked with
a yellow sign, *Judisches Geschäft* (Jewish business), in accordance with
the German decree of September 27, 1940, had experienced no loss
of trade. He took comfort from the results of the inquiries that he
conducted from time to time on the streets of Paris to make sure that
the implant of anti-Semitism had not taken root among the population of the capital.[10] "It is noticeable that, during the period of the
yellow placards, Jewish businesses have seen their clientele swollen by
many French people who are thereby demonstrating their sympathy
for the victims of antisemitic Nazism," remarked another observer;[11]
he added that the "non-Jewish milieu" was becoming more favorable
to Jews as time passed. "You no longer hear antisemitic comments in
the queues (which are the public place where people talk the most).
The dominant tone is very anti-German," reported Léo Hamon in
April 1941.[12] Later he noted that "the people's sympathy for the persecuted Jew is a general phenomenon about which all observers concur. . . . All the Jews have kept their personal friendships, and it is
even said that they are in general warmer."[13] In this respect, then, we
find a general sense of relief in all Jewish circles in the capital.

Relief—first of all, because during the initial weeks of the Occupation, Paris had witnessed several outbreaks of violent anti-
Semitism. Starting in July 1940, no doubt persuaded of their immunity from punishment, ruffians affiliated with the collaborationist
movements came to hawk *Au Pilori*, "the weekly organ of the struggle
against Judeo-Masonry," in the Temple square, the heart of the Jewish quarter of the capital.[14] The first anti-Jewish propaganda posters
plastered on walls in Paris were noted by prefect Langeron on July
29.[15] August was marked by the proliferation of anti-Semitic incidents, on the Boulevard de Menilmontant and the Saint Ouen flea
market, in front of the Bouchara store, the Levitan buildings, and the

cafés in the Place de la République. These demonstrations hardly attracted more than fifty to a hundred participants each, but they were the only public demonstrations that disturbed the calm of Paris during the summer of 1940.[16] In addition, the weekly meetings of the new anti-Semitic groups seemed to be drawing a steadily increasing number of participants.[17] On August 20 and 21, for a period of two hours, young toughs assailed the windows of Jewish stores on the Champs Élysées, smashing them methodically.[18] But a month later, the climate seemed to have changed. The dreaded exponential increase in such violent acts did not occur. Popular anti-Semitism, in its violent forms, remained the province of the Germans and a handful of isolated fanatics.

Relief—with regard to the anxiety that followed the German entry into Paris. "We were not unaware of the Nazi vandalism against Jews in Germany, Austria, Czechoslovakia, and especially in Poland," wrote a Jewish activist.[19] At the start of the Occupation, the Jews dreaded that the scenes of popular violence which had erupted in the streets of Austria and Germany and the brutality of the anti-Jewish measures introduced in occupied Poland would be reproduced in Paris. But "things are not happening in Paris as in Warsaw."[20] Now, despite the relentless application of French anti-Semitic legislation and German decrees, the indifference of the majority of the population, the smiles of collusion displayed by some, and the continuation of personal relationships demonstrated for Jewish eyes the moral defeat of the occupier.

The most clear-sighted observer was certainly Léo Hamon, who also noted: "Naturally, this disapproval of anti-Semitism is passive, in the sense that it does not include any public manifestation; the cares of the hour mean that there is only a limited amount of time to devote to those of other people."[21] Then he adds, indirectly revealing the existence among the Parisians of anti-Semitic currents he had tried to deny, "If everyone condemns what has been done, we should not infer from this that everyone thinks that nothing should have been done. Many say that these measures are excessive, which leaves the implication that they are not totally unjustified."[22]

These two types of observation may contain the key. For the central fact remains that the implementation of the anti-Jewish laws did not encounter the least opposition on the part of the French public; the various professional guilds and government departments were quietly purged[23] or scrupulously applied the French- or German-originated instructions to exclude Jews. The Aryanization of Jewish property did not meet with any obstacle. The occupier found, first of all in the state but also in society, the means to attain his objectives. The gestures of personal sympathy permitted the Jews to endure the ordeal to which they were subjected. But as long as such gestures remained on the individual level only, as long as they were not transformed into public deeds, they could reassure the Jews and help them bear their lot, they could alleviate the effects of the law for some—but no more. This is the operative consequence of Léo Hamon's first observation about the passive character of what he called the "the disapproval of anti-Semitism."[24]

What is more, if we can note this dichotomy of the personal relations between Jews and non-Jews, which in general did not deteriorate, on the one hand, and the implacable application of exclusionary legislation, on the other, this is because the latter was perfectly compatible with the ideological anti-Semitism that was prevalent among the population. Unlike the inquiries conducted out on a daily basis by the Jews, the reports produced by the French bureaucracy and the summaries of the surveillance of the mails reflect public approval of the anti-Jewish laws promulgated by Vichy.[25] Ultimately this is an echo of Léo Hamon's second observation, an inkling of the deep-seated penetration of anti-Semitic propaganda. In the eyes of many French people, there was indeed a "Jewish problem." It was confounded in some fashion with the question of foreigners being indiscriminately incorporated into the French nation—a major theme of the 1930s; it was perceived as an overrepresentation in certain professions, to which appropriate remedies should be applied. This translated into the conviction that the presumed Jewish dominance of all spheres of political, economic, and cultural life should be ended. A majority of the public was more or less supportive of all or some of these ideas. Among their other consequences, the "deviations of the 1930s" had normalized anti-Semitism.[26] The new legislation, adopted by the very same circles who had helped propagate these ideas before they came to power under the auspices of the defeat, was viewed as an appropriate response to the various aspects of this "Jewish problem." With the parameters of the debate having been set in this fashion, the popular indifference—which the Jews interpreted as signaling the immunity of the French people to German anti-

Semitism—in fact represented support for the anti-Semitic policies of Vichy, whereas the individual gestures of sympathy underlined some vague solidarity against the despised occupier.

2. THE SOUTHERN ZONE: THE TURNABOUT IN PUBLIC OPINION, ENDURING ANTI-SEMITISM

In the Southern Zone, anti-Jewish policy could not be blamed on the Germans. It was the Vichy government that introduced exclusionary anti-Jewish laws; a special ministerial department to oversee their implementation, the Commissariat général aux Question juives (Commissariat General on the Jewish Question), was created on March 29, 1941. The full details of the measures adopted against the Jews were explained to the population. The state, whose head, Marshal Pétain, had broad support among the French people, codified, legitimated, and applied an anti-Semitic policy.[27] Indirectly, this grant of legitimacy by the French state—the only reference authority—clarifies to some extent the limited support for the Jews in the Paris region, noted earlier.

It certainly explains the echo of anti-Semitic themes among the population of the south, as noted by a Jewish observer of the period. Small communities seem to have been particularly receptive to government propaganda. In some large villages, there were cases where having the name Lévy or Weill was enough to get doors shut in your face: sometimes that of the only grocer in the village or of farmers in the surrounding countryside. Elsewhere, the rural policeman, with drumrolls on the public square, instructed the Jews to avoid any contact with the rest of the population.[28] Violent incidents that pitted a Jewish family, seated quietly at a table in a café or restaurant, against a passerby who suddenly took it into his head to insult them, seem not to have been rare. When an incident of this sort took place in Cannes or Toulouse, and no doubt elsewhere, indifference on the part of the other customers seems to have been the rule. Nobody dared get involved.[29] The atmosphere was so oppressive for the Jews in the "free" zone that a number of Jews who had run away from Paris observed that "here one can still move freely and doesn't have to be afraid of being arrested without warning. But as for the attitude of the French, it feels more like France in the occupied zone."[30]

This remained true until the summer of 1942, when a turnabout took place: the spectacle of the mass roundups of Jews provoked an outburst of indignation in French public opinion. Whereas the implementation of the legislative phase was practically complete and its application continued without incident, anti-Semitic policy in France had suddenly changed its nature. The German authorities had decided to deport the Jews of France as part of the Final Solution. Negotiations ensued with the French government to obtain its collaboration in the implementation of this policy. Pierre Laval, returned to power in April 1942, accepted the German demands about the Jews, first and foremost in order to obtain political gains on subjects to which he attached greater priority in the broader context of negotiations between Vichy and the occupiers. Thus the French government's collaboration in the deportation of the Jews of France followed a different pattern than that which prevailed over the adoption of anti-Semitic legislation during the earlier phase of the Occupation. There is no doubt that the xenophobic ideology of the ruling echelons facilitated this,[31] but no autonomous choice was at work here. It was rather a wholesale bargaining session in which the fate of the Jews carried a different weight for each negotiating partner. The result was the organization of the mass roundups in the summer of 1942, first in the north and then in the south—all of them carried out by the French police, using lists drawn up by French bureaucrats—and the arrest of thousands of Jews who were sent to Auschwitz. The popular support that the French government had heretofore been able to rely on when it confiscated Jewish property and redistributed it to non-Jewish French people vanished when French gendarmes began arresting Jews and detaining them in inhuman conditions. This was no longer an expression of traditional and long-consecrated French anti-Semitism, but of French submission to methods deemed barbarous and imposed by a country considered barbarian. This is the impression given by the monthly summaries of the surveillance of telegrams, phone conversions, and the mails, prepared for the French government.[32] In addition, twenty-four prefects in the Unoccupied Zone noted this outburst of public opinion in their reports.[33]

The spectacle of these roundups—beyond their astonishing brutality—starkly revealed the price that Vichy had to pay to maintain an appearance of sovereignty; the legitimacy of the regime was profoundly and permanently affected. The German occupation of the

Southern Zone in November 1942 merely confirmed what the French had already realized.[34]

From this time on, the evolution of public opinion with regard to various aspects of the anti-Semitic policy was intrinsically linked to the change in attitude toward Vichy and the Germans, which in turn largely depended on the military situation and expectations as to the outcome of the war. There was a clear interaction between these various levels. As long as a German victory seemed certain and the French government seemed to enjoy some measure of independence, its anti-Semitic policy was part of a reality that was not to be discussed. The summer of 1942 marked the first turning point. A year later, the situation had altered radically. The eventual outcome of the war was no longer a mystery for anyone; it was clear that an Allied victory was only a matter of time. This further highlighted the illegitimacy of the Vichy government as it sank deeper and deeper into collaboration with the Germans. Between the summer and fall of 1943, "the cause of the government [was] completely lost and definitively intertwined with that of Germany. Public opinion [reached] the stage of overt hostility."[35] Now all the government's actions, and especially those that bore a German trademark, were stained with illegitimacy. After the roundups of the summer of 1942, the policy of persecution was inextricably associated with the occupier.[36]

As an alternative society was thus emerging gradually in France, the Jews found it easier to locate allies to help them escape the roundups. The change was perceptible at all levels. Starting in the summer of 1942, Jews abandoned the cities where they traditionally lived and scattered to rural villages. Of course there were exceptional places where they benefited from the active complicity of the local population, especially in regions with a Huguenot majority. But even elsewhere, they were often able to live quietly without being denounced by their neighbors as Jews. As the gulf widened between the French people and French state, some agencies of the latter lost their effectiveness, because their officials had to take account of the population among whom they were active: thus, the very same gendarmes who in 1942 had had no compunctions about arresting Jews were a year later arranging to provide advance warning to those whose names appeared on their lists of potential victims. The activists of the Jewish organizations who were involved in rescue operations, who needed accomplices to help them produce false papers or hide threatened Jewish adults and children, found them in social organizations, religious institutions, and even in the French civil service.

This assistance was possible because an authority of another, spiritual order had taken over from the political authorities who had lost popular support; this new authority conferred the necessary legitimacy on this shift in public opinion. The break was initiated by Monsignor Saliège, the archbishop of Toulouse, who, ignoring the prefect's ban, had a pastoral letter that condemned in clear terms the anti-Jewish persecution read from the pulpit of the churches in his diocese on August 23, 1942. "There is a Christian morality, there is a human morality that imposes duties and recognizes rights," he wrote. "The Jews are men, the Jews are women. The strangers are men, the strangers are women. Not everything is permitted against them, against these men, against these women, against these fathers and mothers of families. They are part of the human race; they are our brothers like so many others. A Christian cannot forget this."[37]

Turning his back on the authorities, Monsignor Saliège addressed himself to Catholic society. Having this message read out from the pulpit guaranteed that it had a large circulation. Similar acts followed elsewhere. "I am sounding the indignant protest of the Christian conscience and I proclaim that all men, Aryans and non-Aryans, are brothers, because created by the same God; that all men, whatever their race or their religion, have the right to be respected by individuals and states. The current antisemitic measures are in contempt of human dignity, a violation of the most sacred rights of human beings." This is part of the pastoral letter read out from the pulpit on Sunday, August 30, 1942, at the instructions of Monsignor Théas, bishop of Montauban.[38] Other pastoral letters ensued, notably that by Cardinal Gerlier on September 6, which made several concessions to the consecrated rhetoric: admitting the existence of a Jewish question or insisting on the loyalty of their authors to the regime. In the name of the National Council of the Reformed Church, convened in emergency session on September 22, Pastor Boegner had read out from most Reformed pulpits a letter in which, aware of "the extreme complexity of the situations in which the national authorities find themselves" and repeating its objection to "any intrusion into the domain of politics," the Reformed church recalled that "divine law does not accept that families chosen by God should be broken apart, children separated from their mothers, the right of asylum and pity disregarded, respect for human beings transgressed, and defenseless persons be delivered to a tragic destiny," that "the Jews are the children in the flesh of the people among whom the Savior of the world was born, and that "these measures also strike non-Aryan Christians, members of Protestant parishes."[39]

They were many differences of nuance and weight from letter to letter, but their circulation—particularly that of the letters by Monsignors Saliège and Théas, as well as that by Pastor Boegner—extended far beyond ecclesiastical circles,[40] because they were reproduced in the underground press and read out on the Free French broadcasts over the BBC. The text was soon circulating throughout the Southern Zone.[41]

For its own part, the underground Resistance press, which with rare exceptions had been rather discreet about the fate of the Jews until then,[42] published clear condemnations of the anti-Semitic policy of Vichy during the of summer 1942.[43]

The disapproval was unanimous. Everywhere—even in the Communist press—it was based on the bishops' pastoral letters, frequently published in full. The same message echoed from London. "So France is becoming a land of pogroms, a land of shame?" André Labarthe asked rhetorically on August 8, 1942, in his evening broadcast over the BBC.[44] Between July 1 and September 15, the fate of the Jews in France was discussed seven times.[45] Thus, at the height of the roundups and for several weeks thereafter, there was a moment of unanimity among all the voices of the resistance, the largely loyalist clergy, and public opinion, which finally became aware of the subordination of the Vichy government to the German occupier and of the human price of this situation.[46]

Even though, during the last week of September, the author of the monthly summary of the postal surveillance department could note that calm had been restored,[47] and during subsequent months the subject disappeared from intercepted mail and prefects' reports about the state of public opinion, legitimacy had switched camps.

This switch explains, for example, the growing difficulties faced by the agents of the Commissariat général in recruiting temporary administrators or purchasers for Jewish property. The future for such deals seemed too uncertain. This uncertainty had the result of preventing some Aryanizations from being implemented. On September 15, 1942, Pierre Tissier, broadcasting over the BBC, issued a clear warning to those who might be tempted that by the lure of Jewish property. The sales of Jewish property "are invalid. The property involved will in principle be restored to their rightful owners. The purchasers may be assured in every case that they will be deprived of the property thus acquired and will generally forfeit, in addition, the purchase price."[48] As the military situation evolved, this threat took on much greater substance.

Starting from that date, there seemed to be a dichotomy between an unmistakably less enthusiastic application of the anti-Semitic laws and the emergence of silent complicity with the hunted Jews, on the one hand, and an intensification of the public's abstract ideological anti-Semitism, on the other.

This is the picture that emerges from all the reports about public opinion sent to London by Free French agents, without a single exception. A selection of extracts from these reports can help us grasp something of these deeper tendencies:

The persecution of the Jews has profoundly wounded the French in their humane principles; it has even, at times, made the Jews almost sympathetic. One cannot deny, however, that there is a Jewish question: the present circumstances have even helped plant it firmly. The Blum ministry, which was overflowing with Jewish elements, and the penetration of tens of thousands of foreign Jews into France provoked a defensive mechanism in France. People would pay any price not to see a similar invasion repeated. (February 1943)[49]

The persecutions directed against the Jews have not stopped stirring and angering the population. Public opinion is nevertheless somewhat suspicious of them. It is feared that after the war some leading professions (banking, broadcasting, journalism, cinema) will be invaded again and in some fashion controlled by the Jews. . . . Certainly, no one wants the Jews to be victimized and even less that they be molested. People sincerely want them to be as free as possible, in possession of their rights and their property. But no one wants them to be supreme in any domain. (March 1943)[50]

The French are revolted by the emergency measures taken against individuals. But they often find it congenial to unload some of their responsibilities on the Jews and the latter bear the weight of the excessively loud entourage of Léon Blum, of the excessive naturalizations, their rapid success, even their intellectual merit. They are feared or envied and many French people do not want to see them occupying a number of their former positions again. (October 1943)[51]

The French are not antisemitic. They despise racial persecution. They do not cry basely that the Jews must die so we can find our place in life. But they curse the Jewish banks (even while doing their best copy them!) and would like to get rid of the refugees from the ghetto who, everywhere set to flight, have invaded our country, with no hope of assimilation. (December 1943)[52]

There is not a single false note in these reports intended for General de Gaulle. All of them draw a fundamental distinction between popular anti-Semitism of an ideological nature, which seemed to be deeply rooted, and the genuine French indignation at the Nazi persecution of the Jews.

CONCLUSION

Thus, in Paris, the normalcy of those aspects of daily life that were a direct function of personal relations between Jews and non-Jews reassured the former. It even produced an illusory security, despite the unfettered application of legislation that inexorably reduced them to marginality and then to misery. Nonideological human relations could sweeten the pill, but the destiny of the Jews was determined by the ideological anti-Semitism rooted in the population and legitimized, codified, and applied by the various agencies of the French state. All the more so because no alternative authority—spiritual or intellectual—came out firmly against the anti-Jewish policy.

The persistence of ideological popular anti-Semitism in the Southern Zone, in conjunction with the fluctuations in public opinion about the anti-Semitic policy of the state, makes it possible to reevaluate the role of the ideological dimension in the various manifestations of anti-Semitism. When legitimized by the state, popular anti-Semitism could be expressed freely. But then the relations between state and society became the dominant factor in the people's attitude toward that same anti-Semitic policy. When a gulf opened up between the two, popular anti-Semitism lost its legitimacy, even when it survived as an ideological substrate. A survey conducted by the Commissariat général to sample French public opinion about the Jews and Vichy policy toward them paradoxically reinforces this thesis. Its findings confirm that the image of the Jews as exploiters and foreigners who could not be assimilated was firmly rooted among French anti-Semites, for all that they were hardly sensitive to the racial argument. They reveal that respondents who demonstrated some reticence about the anti-Semitic policy explained their reservations—or opposition—by means of backlash-derived arguments (because the Jews are victims of German measures, in counterreaction to fascism or the government).[53]

Vichy's participation in the Final Solution, which was based on this anti-Semitism but derived from a different logic, aroused French condemnation of the "barbarous," "German" forms of anti-Semitism henceforth practiced. Many Jews managed to escape arrest and deportation thanks to the general public's new attitude toward them. But popular anti-Semitism, whose roots went deeper and which had permitted the submissive application of the regime's anti-Semitic legislation, had not disappeared. It was this dichotomy that set the background for the relations between the Jews and the French in the immediate postwar period.

NOTES

1. Out of a community of about 330,000 in 1939, 76,000 French Jews were deported, and about 3,000 more perished in internment camps on French soil.

2. Some of these reports can be found in the archives of the Centre de Documentation Juive Contemporaine (Center for Jewish Documentation, CDJC) in Paris, France; the Collection of the Federation of Jewish Organizations in France; in the library of the Alliance Israélite Universelle [hereafter cited as AIU]; the Maurice Moch Central Consistory wartime collection [hereafter cited as CC]; and in various collections held by Institute for Jewish Research[hereafter cited as YIVO] in New York.

3. Particularly important is the diary of Jacques Biélinky, *Journal: juillet 1940–décembre 1942*, edited and annotated by Renée Poznanski (Paris: Cerf, 1992); that of Raymond-Raoul Lambert, *Carnet d'un témoin, 1940–1943*, edited and annotated by Richard Cohen (Paris: Fayard, 1985); and that of Léon Werth, *Déposition, Journal 1940–1944*, text established by Lucien Fevre, edited and annotated by Jean-Pierre Azéma (Paris: Viviane Hamy, 1992).

4. I rely chiefly on the reports entitled "Situation in Paris," drawn up by the intelligence branch of the Parisian police prefecture; every week until the summer of 1942, and thereafter every two weeks, a report of least a hundred pages provided details on every aspect of life in occupied Paris.

5. A special "technical control" department was responsible for this surveillance of the mails and telephone conversations. It produced both quantitative and qualitative reports about the subjects that were interesting or disturbing the French people, their reactions to every political or military development, and so on. Antoine Lefébure, *Les conversations secrètes des Français sous l'Occupation* (Paris: Plon, 1993), draws on these reports and analyzes a number of themes. See also Roger Austin, "Surveillance and Intelligence under the Vichy Regime: The Service du contrôle technique, 1939–1945," *Intelligence and National Security* 1 (January 1989). Note, too, that various departments within the German occupation authorities were also careful to keep their fingers on the pulse of public opinion.

6. The archives of the BCRA, held in the Archives National [hereafter cited as AN] in Paris, include documents copied directly from those of the Vichy intelligence services but also reports drawn up by agents dispatched by the Free French and others produced by the various internal resistance movements. On the battle for public opinion, see Jean-Louis Crémieux-Brilhac and Hélène Eck, "France," in *La guerre des ondes,* edited by Hélène Eck, prefaced by Jean-Noël Jeannency (Paris: Armand Colin, 1985), pp. 11–154.

7. Many documents attest to this, in particular diaries kept by non-Jews, from which the subject is almost absent, and the statistics collected by the Vichy "technical control" bureau, which include only infrequent allusions to the Jews in the tens of thousands of letters opened and read.

8. A report drafted by the Vichy Telephone Commission for the period from November 15 to December 1, 1940, noted the "pro English tendencies" of the Occupied Zone (AN, F7, 14,930). "The population is on the whole calm, on the whole accepting, but most of the time reserved, frequently unfriendly, and in part even hostile," notes a report of September 1940 produced in the armaments department of the Wehrmacht (the Wi.Rü.-Stab), cited by Philippe Burrin, *La France à l'heure allemande, 1940–1944* (Paris: Le Seuil, 1995). All English translations in this chapter are mine unless noted otherwise.

9. AN, F60, 502. On this subject, see also Denis Peschanski, "Le régime de Vichy a existé. Gouvernants et gouvernés dans la France de Vichy, Juillet 1940–avril 1942," in *Vichy 1940–1944, archives de guerre d'Angelo Tasco,* edited by Denis Peschanski (Paris and Milan: CNRS and Fondazione Giangiacomo Feltrinelli, 1986), pp. 41–49.

10. Biélinky, *Journal,* entries of October 25 and 31 and November 3, 1940; July 26, 1941; and others.

11. "Les Juifs à Paris sous l'occupation allemande," report by Ruven Grinberg, July 30, 1941, AIU, CC-4 and YIVO, Tcherikower collection, F.1,650.

12. Léo Hamon, "Etude sur la situation des Juifs en zone occupée," in "Avant les premières grandes rafles: Les Juifs à Paris sous l'Occupation (juin 1940–avril 1941)," by Léo Hamon and Renée Poznanski, *Cahier de l'Institut d'Histoire du Temps Présent* 22 (December 1992): 61.

13. Ibid., pp. 91–92.

14. Biélinky, *Journal*, pp. 41, 45, 47, and others.

15. Roger Langeron, *Paris, Juin 1940* (Paris: Flammarion, 1946), p. 134.

16. Archives of the prefecture of police [hereafter cited as PP], "Situation à Paris."

17. PP, "Situation à Paris," August 19, 1940.

18. Gérard Walter, *La vie à Paris sous l'occupation* (Paris: Armand Colin, 1960), pp. 177–78.

19. YIVO, *France during WWII*, 1–64, "Le Comité Amelot."

20. Hamon, "Etude sur la situation des Juifs," p. 78.

21. Ibid., p. 92.

22. Ibid., p. 95.

23. One of the most recent studies on this subject concerns the legal profession and courts: Richard H. Weisberg, *Vichy Law and the Holocaust in France* (New York: NYU Press, 1996).

24. In June 1942, when the Jews of the Occupied Zone were required to wear the yellow star, the same mechanism was reproduced, and even more clearly. It was a German measure that was largely disapproved of by the French, who sometimes demonstrated their individual sympathy but more often evinced an indifference interpreted by many Jews as refined squeamishness. As SS Hauptsturmführer Heinz Röthke, who was in charge of the Jewish Affairs bureau of the Gestapo, noted, "the demonstrations, processions, or expressions of sympathy that we expected at the beginning did not take place" (report dated June 10, 1942, cited by Serge Klarsfeld, *L'étoile des Juifs* [Paris: L'Archipel, 1992], pp. 106–7). On the yellow star in Paris and various reactions to it, see Renée Poznanski, "Porter l'étoile jaune à Paris," *Revue historique* 290, no. 1 (1995): 53–71.

25. Peschanski, "Le régime de Vichy a existé," p. 44.

26. Pierre Laborie, *L'Opinion française sous Vichy* (Paris: Le Seuil, 1990), pp. 273ff.

27. Michael R. Marrus and Robert O. Paxton, *Vichy et les Juifs* (Paris: Calmann-Lévy, 1981) remains the definitive work on this subject.

28. Henri Sinder, "La situation des Juifs depuis l'armistice en juin

1940," n.d., but certainly drawn up in November 1942, YIVO, *France during WWII,* 4–56.

29. Pierre Laborie, "The Jewish Statutes in Vichy France and Public Opinion," *Yad Vashem Studies* 22 (1992): 89–114.

30. Sinder, "La situation des Juifs."

31. "Reasons of state befouled by ideological connivance," to borrow the phrase from Burin, *La France à l'heure allemande,* p. 164.

32. AN, F7, 14,929, monthly summaries of the telegraph, telephone, and mail surveillance, summaries for July 10–August 10 and August 10–Sept. 10, 1942; AN, F7, 14,930, monthly report by the Central Postal Surveillance Commission, no. 44 (August 1942) and no. 45 (September 1942).

33. By contrast, only two prefects, those of Gers and of Indre, underlined the satisfaction of the local population with the departure of the Jews: located along the line of demarcation, the residents of these *départements* had viewed with a jaundiced eye the massive influx of Jews after the introduction of the yellow star in the Occupied Zone. Reactions were more restrained in five other *départements*—tourism centers and rural localities that were home to well-to-do foreign Jews in assigned residency. See Marrus and Paxton, *Vichy et les Juifs,* p. 256. Extracts from these reports of the prefects are reproduced in Serge Klarsfeld, *Vichy-Auschwitz,* vol. 1 (Paris: Fayard, 1983), pp. 305–7.

34. The relationship between the adoption of anti-Semitic measures and the public's attitude toward the Vichy regime is further confirmed in a report produced by the police: "The addition of the word 'Jew' to the identity cards of Jews went off without incident, but the population concur in considering this measure to be vexatious and see it as proof of a new German interference in government decisions. The impression is spreading more and more among the public that the government can exist and maintain itself only by subordinating itself to German needs" (AN, 3 AG 2/330, summary of monthly reports from the commanders of police units, January 1943).

35. Laborie, *L'Opinion française sous Vichy,* p. 286.

36. Among the posters observed by the domestic intelligence service on walls in Paris was the following (June 22, 1941): "To annoy Hitler, let us make common cause with the Jews" (PP, "Situation à Paris"). A similar phenomenon could be found in Belgium, where *La Libre Belgique* (no. 40 [August 1, 1942]) published the following call: "Belgians! Whether you are pro- or antisemitic, remember that the Jews are the victims of the Boches. Show them your sympathy! Greet them when they pass! Give them your seat in the tram! Protest against the barbarous measures taken against them! It will infuriate the Boches!!!"

37. AIU, CC-26; reproduced in Klarsfeld, *Vichy-Auschwitz*, p. 355.

38. AIU, CC-26, quoted by Marrus and Paxton, *Vichy et les Juifs*, p. 253.

39. Quoted by Marc Boegner, "Le combat de l'Eglise à Vichy," in *Les clandestins de Dieu: CIMADE, 1939–1944*, edited by Jeanne Merle d'Aubigné, Violette Mouchon, and Emile Fabre (Paris: Fayard, 1968), p. 25.

40. Evidently to Boegner's astonishment. See *Carnets du Pasteur Boegner, 1940–1945*, edited and annotated by Philippe Boegner (Paris: Fayard, 1992), p. 206.

41. "Some [activists] have four or five copies of the letter [by Msgr. Saliège] in their pocket, which they distribute," noted the (undated) testimony of a "neutral" investigator in France (AIU, CC-21).

42. Asher Cohen, "La presse clandestine face à la question juive de 1940 à 1942," *Le monde juif* 117, p. 5.

43. For examples, see Renée Poznanski, *Les Juifs en France pendant la seconde guerre mondiale* (Paris: Hachette, 1997), pp. 359–61.

44. Jean-Louis Crémieux-Brilhac, ed. *Les voix de la liberté: Ici Londres, 1940–1944*, vol. 2 (Paris: La documentation française, 1976).

45. On July 1; August 8, 23, and 31; and September 9, 12, and 15. See Crémieux-Brilhac, *Les voix de la liberté*, passim.

46. On this link between public opinion and the regime and how the roundups affected it, see Laborie, *L'opinion française sous Vichy*, p. 280.

47. AN, F78, 14,930, no. 45, September 1942.

48. Crémieux-Brilhac, *Les voix de la liberté*, p. 215.

49. AN, 3 AG 2/334, "Note sur l'état de l'opinion en France," February 1943; also cited, in slightly different form, in Archives of the Museum of the Resistance and Deportation, Champigny, May 3, 1943, 5,811; source: Fouquet.

50. AN, 3 AG 2/34, "Rapport de Lavergne," based on a report about Paris, March 2, 1943.

51. AN, 3 AG 2/34, "Note sur l'opinion française en matière de politique intérieure au debut de l'été 1943," drawn up on October 5, 1943.

52. Archives of the Museum of the Resistance and Deportation, Champigny, Inf: December 8, 1943, ref. 13,426.

53. Survey conducted in December 1942 of 3,150 persons, selected according to a predetermined socioprofessional and geographic distribution. For an analysis of this survey, see Poznanski, *Les Juifs en France*, pp. 454–59.

David Bankier

The Future of the Jews after Hitler

THIS ESSAY SEEKS TO DISCUSS THE VARIOUS PLANS DRAWN UP BY German anti-Nazi exiles to solve the Jewish question after Hitler's fall. We shall see that the Social Democrats' position on Nazi anti-Semitism formulated in 1934 never changed despite the new reality of Hitler's extermination policy. Not motivated by any loyalty to or belief in the concept of Jewish identity, assimilation was the favorite solution for Jews who would return to Germany. The schemes of conservative or right-wing anti-Nazi exiles in large measure reacted to Hitler's anti-Semitic policy, taking issue with the "otherness" of the Jews, who would or could not integrate themselves in postwar Europe. Surprisingly, Communist exiles modified their dogmatic approach and, alongside assimilation, saw in a national Jewish state one of the possible solutions for the survivors of the Holocaust.

A detailed examination of German Social Democrats' political literature indicates that the persecution of Jews was viewed as just another event in the extensive catalog of Nazi crimes. Only with the proliferation of news on Nazi extermination policy from late 1942 and with the mounting criticism by Jewish organizations of the exiles for avoiding the subject did the Social Democrats address the annihilation of European Jewry in public statements.

The official resolution of the national conference of German Social Democrats that met in New York in July 1943, for example, demanded that all those responsible for the Nazi crimes be punished. On the policy toward the Jews after the war, nothing was said.[1] There was a good reason for that. Since Social Democrats clung to the view that there was no radical difference between the persecution of Jews and the ill-treatment of other victims of the Third Reich, they reiterated that all they had in mind was the formal restoration of civil rights to German Jews after the war.

These declarations did not meet the expectations of Jewish organizations in Western countries. A case in point is the exchange between Leon Kubowitzky, head of the department of European Jewish Affairs of the World Jewish Congress, and Hans Vogel, chairman of the German Social Democratic Party in exile and head of the Union of German Socialist Organizations in the United Kingdom. When approached in November 1943 to issue a statement on the policy toward the Jews to be adopted by post-Hitler Germany, including the question of Palestine, Vogel replied that the attitude, in principle, of German Social Democrats to the Jewish question did not change as a result of the tragic events of the last decade. It was contained in the programmatic declaration of January 1934 and reaffirmed in the condemnation of the extermination issued in December 1942. After Hitler's fall, he said, a democratic Germany would revoke all forms of discrimination and compensate those who were persecuted on the grounds of their religion, political convictions, or racial origin. At the end of his letter, Vogel barely veiled the common stereotype in socialist circles that German Jews were nationalists and conservatives who had traditionally supported reactionary parties and added that "it would also depend on the conduct of the German Jews. When they return to Germany after the war they would have to show by their political stands and practical deeds that they feel themselves attached to the progressive and democratic forces of the German people."[2] This reply was deemed quite inadequate, because it purposely failed to address the Palestine issue.

While Jews in the West were gaining national consciousness and favored a Zionist solution to the Jewish question to guarantee a safe haven for the survivors of Holocaust, the leadership of the German Social Democrats persisted in its traditional distance toward Zionism. It is true that there were individuals in the party who sympathized with a national renaissance of Jews in Palestine, but the party preferred not to damage its relations with anti-Zionist Jewish socialist circles in Britain and the United States by making pro-Zionist declarations.

This explains, for instance, the disappointment of Zionist labor organizations with the German exiles. In January 1944, Haim Berman of the General Federation of Jewish Labor in Palestine approached Hans Vogel regarding the manifesto of the Union of German Socialist Organizations in the United Kingdom, "The International Policy of German Socialists," issued in October 1943.[3] Its four points had underscored the need for international cooperation and the destruction of the economic basis of fascism. Its third point stated inter alia: "We recognize it as a duty of honor for the coming free Germany to help with all her strength in the reparation of the injustices inflicted on other peoples by Nazi Germany." As a socialist, Berman said, he definitely agreed to the four points in the manifesto. As a Jew, however, he felt a fifth point was lacking. The statement that the future free Germany had a duty of honor to help in the reparation for injustices on other peoples by Hitler's Germany was utterly inadequate, since the annihilation of the Jewish people was more than just an "injustice." Berman emphasized that the property stolen from the Jews in Nazi-occupied Europe ought to be restored to the survivors. Since, however, only a very small minority of Jews would survive the war, he insisted that all such reparations be handed over to the Zionist movement to be used for the rehabilitation and reestablishment in Palestine of the remnants of the Jewish people.[4] Still, the executive committee refused to commit itself. In response to this letter, all that the executive committee of the German Social Democratic Party was ready to offer in this regard was a vague statement that "in the wake of the awful events of the last years, the Jewish question will need an international solution and this will be one of the most urgent problems that the international bodies of the workers movement will have to deal with and formulate concrete solutions."[5] In fact, of all the socialist emigrant organizations, the only ones that viewed in Zionism a possible solution to the Jewish question after Hitler were the small and barely influential Group of Independent Socialists exiled in Sweden, led by Willy Brandt, and the People's Socialists *(Volkssozialisten)*, headed by Hans Jäger.

Having realized to what horror anti-Semitism could lead, and spurred by Zionist circles in Stockholm, the Group of Independent Socialists issued a propitiative declaration in April 1944. In February 1945, Willy Brandt reiterated his support for the building of Palestine in an address delivered to the local German socialist group. On that occasion, he stated that the question of compensation to the German Jews and to the massively decimated Jewish population in Europe deserved special attention. He proposed that citizens of Jewish origin willing to return to Germany be placed on the same footing as all other Germans persecuted by the Nazis. As for those who would not be ready to return to their countries of origin, Brandt suggested the creation of a fund from confiscated Nazi property in order to help reconstruct their lives in a national home in Palestine.[6]

The People's Socialists suggested a similar solution but added another alternative: Jews as a national minority. After Hitler, surviving Jews could remain in Europe, either reintegrating into their countries of origin or becoming a national minority, or leaving Europe and building their national home in Palestine. Their party platform acknowledged the existence of a Jewish problem, which it attributed to the sociological composition of Jewish society and the function fulfilled by Jews in history. In their opinion, socioeconomic planning would enable the Jews to undergo vocational retraining, thus solving the problem of the surplus of Jewish intellectuals. As far as the Jews' status was concerned, the People's Socialists suggested that the problem be solved within the framework of a federation of nations to constitute the basis of Europe after Hitler. Those who so desired would come under the law on minorities, while the rest of the Jews would have to assimilate.[7]

The People's Socialists' perspective suggests certain interesting elements. First, their readiness to consider the Jews a nation is explained by the fact that they had broken with the dogmatic tradition of Marx and Kautsky and, under the influence of Belgian and French neosocialist thinkers, recognized the importance of the national factor. Second, notwithstanding the denunciation of anti-Semitism and the well-intended suggestions for a postwar arrangement, their planning is still constructed on accepted assumptions on Jewish "otherness" prevalent in the 1930s and 1940s, including in some socialist circles: that the number of Jews in the intellectual world is defined in negative terms as excessive and that Jews as a community cannot be absorbed in organic societies to which they are alien in some way. Consequently, if the Jews were not to disappear through assimilation and their reception is conditioned by improvement, then they should be segregated from national bodies and then either be considered as a minority or emigrate to Palestine.

The "otherness" of the Jews is also a central theme in the proposals for postwar solutions to the Jewish question contemplated by German conservative exiles. Unlike the socialists, conservative exiles intentionally avoided the Jewish question in their publications; yet the correspondence of individuals active in anti-Nazi conservative organizations, such as Joachim Schoeps, Albert Kluthe, and Hermann Rauschning, reveals their ideas on how to deal with the Jews after Hitler.

Schoeps defined himself as a conservative Prussian Jew, but his Judaism was incidental to his conservative worldview. Grounding his worldview in the writings of Friedrich Julius Stahl and Franz Rosenzweig, he maintained that Prussianism and the Jewish religion were based on common values. Schoeps held that, prior to Hitler's assumption of power, the Jews had been German nationalists and conservatives and they had been forced to turn to the Left only because of the misguided policy of the right-wing parties. Schoeps expected post-Nazi Germany to revoke all anti-Semitic legislation enacted since 1933, bring Jewish rights and duties into line with those of the rest of the German population, return all confiscated property, and grant German Jews full religious liberty.

In this he was no different from other exiles, yet he parted ways with them in his practical schemes on how to regulate the relationship between Jews and non-Jews after Hitler. According to Schoeps, in the event that post-Hitler Germany was to be a corporate state (*Ständestaat*), the establishment of a German Jewish branch (*Deutsche Judenschaft*) was to be considered. Here Schoeps in fact returns to the concept of the second or new emancipation, a theory developed in 1933 by certain circles of German Jews in a desperate attempt to adapt Judaism to the conditions created by the Third Reich. They believed that the proper integrational framework of German Jews was as a corporation in the Nazi state. When Schoeps spelled out practical measures, his proposals based the limitation of civil rights on the conviction shared by some Jews as well that the Jews and their anomalous socioeconomic behavior are the cause of anti-Semitism. After Hitler's defeat, he wrote, the Jews would become reintegrated, but their reintegration would be conditioned by the attitude of both parties: Jews should unequivocally affirm their adherence to the German nation to guarantee a friction-free symbiosis between Germans and Jews. This would not be enough, though, because Jews occupy relatively too high a place in German life. To eliminate the causes of anti-Semitism, it would be necessary to withhold rights from Jews and introduce a rigid *numerus clausus* (restricted entry). This policy would limit the participation of the Jews in public life to no more than double their percentage in the population.

The reimmigration of non-German Jews would depend on state interests, and the return of Jews forced to emigrate after 1933 would be regulated by a yearly quota, with priority being given to those able and willing to be artisans and farmers. Incentives would be offered for the returning immigrants to move to small cities, villages, and rural towns.

On the curtailment of Jewish rights, there was hardly a division of opinion between Schoeps and other conservative exiles. In one of his letters, Hans Albert Kluthe, one of the leaders of the German Freedom Party, noted that the German exiles ignored the Jewish question, believing that it would be automatically solved with the removal of Hitler. This attitude he considered both foolish and dangerous. He indeed declared his absolute opposition to racial prejudice but maintained that one must allow for the fact that Germans would remain anti-Semitic after Hitler. Therefore, if Jews could not be deterred from their quest for power, the solution will be to bar them from public office. He consequently also advocated the introduction of a *numerus clausus*. Though Kluthe hoped that it would be a temporary measure, its abolition would depend on the behavior of the Jews themselves.

It seems that the Kluthe opposition to anti-Semitism and support for pragmatic policies of discrimination were not necessarily mutually exclusive categories. A similar trail of reasoning was followed by Hermann Rauschning, who shared an intellectual kinship with exiles from the conservative Right and gained fame with his anti-Nazi publications *The Revolution of Nihilism* and *Hitler Speaks*. Unlike Schoeps and Kluthe, Rauschning rejected the imposition of discriminatory measures. He hoped, however, that Jews would be careful enough not to intrude into where they were unwanted. Thus, for example, writing to the exiled Bavarian Social Democrat Wilhelm Hoegner, Rauschning asserted that he saw no other solution but the absolute restitution of legal and economic equality to the returning Jews. He stated that the future German state would have to restore all civil rights and, as far as possible, compensate for destruction and confiscation of property.

However, he added, "it must remain to the Jews' self-discipline not to reach the economic and political influence they had in the Weimar Republic." Since Jews were not really Germans, but just admitted as such by the state, Rauschning hoped that the responsible circles among the Jews had learned from experience so that, at least in the first decades, Germany would not have to worry about Jews seeking power in senior economic and political positions.[8]

Schoeps's discriminatory scheme, Kluthe's readiness to impose a *numerus clausus*, albeit a temporary one, and Rauschning's hopes for Jewish self-restraint all fit aptly into the basic discourse of conservative exiles on the Jewish question. Their solutions for postwar German Jews are typical of those who understood that since the state was to be both Christian and constitutional, Jews who wished to be citizens and maintain their Judaism would have to accept an inferior status. To be sure, Kluthe and Rauschning were not crude anti-Semites. Yet, beneath their superficial formal opposition to Nazi anti-Semitism, they basically approved, on pragmatic grounds, legal discriminatory measures against the Jews. Sharing the image that in many fields of German life the number of Jews was much higher than their relative percentage in the population, they concluded that the real source of anti-Semitism was the Jews themselves, who foment animosity against themselves by seeking power and being too conspicuous.[9] Conservative exiles asserted that while the Jews certainly deserved state protection, the state must also protect itself from *Verjudung* (judified) and demanded of the Jews that they refrain from any act that would undermine the state's German character. As a safeguard against discriminatory legislation, the Jewish community would have to see to it that none of its members were active in the press, the arts, and the economy, so as not to compromise the German nature of the state.

What Schoeps, Kluthe, and Rauschning dared to confide only in their private correspondence, Otto Strasser, head of the Freies Deutschland Bewegung, or Free Germany movement, wrote openly.[10] It is clear from his private correspondence that Strasser disliked Jews. In many of his letters, he condemned "Jews and communists" in the same breath. And when he referred to a paper or group as "Jewish," the connotation was clearly derogatory, implying that its aims and methods could be neither honest nor decent. Nevertheless, whatever his personal views on Jews, in his political writings he also advocated a restricted Jewish participation in German life.

Strasser's general political doctrine is outlined in his *Aufbau des*

Deutschen Sozialismus (*Building German Socialism*), published in 1932.[11] All of his subsequent articles and books, written during his years of exile in Austria, Czechoslovakia, and Canada, are basically the development and elaboration of subjects discussed in this first work. His general political conception was based on a naive and eclectic theory according to which the era of liberalism was being replaced by a new era ruled by the principle of organic law, which emphasizes the differences between peoples and creates the need for their self-determination as national entities. Dissociating himself from Hitler's racial theory, with its emphasis on biological determinism, Strasser contends that the human spirit can surmount the obstacles created by the objective elements that define a nation and a race. Hence, the principle of self-determination accords to the individual the right to choose the collective entity to which he or she wishes to belong, even if he or she does not share the majority's historical and ethnic-racial qualities. The individual is thus able to assimilate into any national group, even that of a different race.

In keeping with this general view, Strasser suggests that all German residents whose racial origins differ from the those of the majority have three possible options: (1) they can be defined as foreigners; (2) they can be national minorities; or (3) they can be incorporated into the main body of the nation through assimilation. All three options, he says, are equally feasible, and every individual of a racial stock different from that of the majority has the right to decide which option to adopt.

His solution to the Jewish question builds on these principles. In his books, as well as in his periodical *Die Deutsche Revolution,*[12] Strasser sees the underlying cause of anti-Semitism not in racial, religious, or economic motives but in the problem of incorporating Jews into the state and into society, made difficult chiefly because of the obstinacy of the Jews in keeping apart and refusing to assimilate. In contrast to all the other peoples of Europe, Strasser says, the Jews have stubbornly resisted assimilating into European states or forming a state of their own. Hence, the solution to the problem of incorporating the Jewish people into the constitutional and social life of Europe after Hitler—and, he adds, of America, for sooner or later the problem would crop up there as well—should be pursued along two avenues: assimilation into the state majority and the development of a Jewish nation.

In the particular case of Germany, the Jews would be divided into three groups: *Nationaljuden, Volkstumsjuden,* and *Assimilanten.* The first group, the *Nationaljuden,* would be represented by the Zionist movement, which would provide some sort of framework until the establishment of a Jewish state. Legally, the Jews would enjoy the same status as other foreigners living outside of their homeland.

The second group, the *Volkstumsjuden,* would be considered a national minority and subject to the European laws governing minorities. This temporary solution was necessary, he believed, because it would be difficult for many European Jews—namely, the older generation—to choose either the category of emigrating to Palestine or that of assimilation. Moreover, such a framework would accommodate the Jewish communities that existed in Europe for hundreds of years and considered themselves attached to their host countries but were not prepared to relinquish their national religion or social identity. In post-Hitler Germany, the *Volkstumsjuden* would be state citizens *(Staatsbürger),* though not citizens enjoying full rights *(Reichsbürger),* as the state's political leadership, its institutions, and the military corps would all be entrusted solely to non-Jewish Germans.

Of the third group—*Assimilanten,* those willing to assimilate—Strasser demanded a declaration that they were no longer Jews and that they wished to cease to exist as an independent religious and social group. Whoever chose this solution would have to realize that his or her assimilation must be genuine, not merely formal. Jews would have to forcibly renounce their separateness and dissolve their organizational frameworks.[13]

We must be careful not to misconstrue this position. No matter how sincere Strasser was in his endeavor to solve the Jewish problem, and however fair his solutions may appear, his support for a German corporate state necessarily leads to an infringement of the civil rights of Jews. In the future Germany, the Jews would have to understand that the key positions in state leadership would be held exclusively by non-Jewish Germans, a policy which does not emanate from the introduction of the *numerus clausus* or from anti-Semitism but from the logical consistency of the translation of the idea of a Christian state into practice. Being unable to meet the objectives of a Christian state, the Jews would be relegated to positions that did not affect its essence. Strasser's support of a Zionist solution is thus consistent with these views. Strasser evaluated Jewish nationalism in a positive light because he doubted the workability of Jewish integration and denied the Jews the potential status of equal citizens in his proposed state.

Strasser's solutions are typical of those who ostensibly defended the Jews from Nazi anti-Semitism but ultimately negated any social space for them in the German body politic, whether by legally segregating the Jews and distancing them or by assimilating and absorbing them. Conservatives like Strasser saw Jews as aliens and demanded that if they wished to stay in Germany, they voluntarily renounce their group identity and vanish or be relegated to the status of second-class citizens.[14]

It is worth noting, though, that this rejection of Jews from postwar Germany is not unique to conservative exiles. A document composed by the Free Germany movement in Switzerland is of considerable significance to our topic, because it throws a bright light on the prevalent feelings toward Jews among German exiles right *after* the Holocaust. This movement comprised anti-Nazis of different political camps: Catholic exiles, followers of the famous Protestant theologian Karl Barth, former members of the German State Party, Social Democrats, Communists, and apoliticals.

In August 1945, the Free Germany movement drew up a memorandum for the solution of the Jewish question in postwar Europe and handed it over to the ambassadors of the United States, England, and France in Bern.[15] On the one hand, a vigorous anti-Nazi line runs through the whole document. In no uncertain terms, the memorandum denounces Nazi racial theory, with its stamp of vulgar materialism, and unequivocally repudiates the restriction of Jewish rights. The basic argument of this document, however, revolves around the concept that Jews are an alien element in Germany and in Europe. It admitted that Jews have unpleasant characteristics yet attributed them not to racial traits but to the Jewish dealings with money, which brought them to clash with the host nation. For that reason, it affirmed, the Nazis simply fueled preexisting anti-Semitic feelings and strengthened existing attitudes.

The anxiety of the exiles becomes apparent when they begin to deal with the question of the Jews returning to Germany. The memorandum demanded that, with the exception of a few unique cases of well-established Jewish families, Jews not be allowed to return to Germany, for a mass return would arouse a wave of anti-Semitism. Moreover, anti-Semitism should be considered a significant phenomenon even in countries in which it did not previously exist, including the United States. As a result, the conclusion of this memorandum is unambiguously plain: the survivors of the Holocaust must realize that anti-Semitism would not disappear overnight and, therefore, the Jews would have nowhere to return. The future League of Nations would have to commit itself to finding areas of settlement, especially in Latin America, which needed, so the memorandum argues, to strengthen the white component of its population.

If, despite all the efforts to discourage them, some Jewish families would insist on returning, then measures would have to be taken to prevent them from ascending to leadership positions. This arrangement would benefit the Jews as well, since their attempt to occupy places not meant for them would only encourage anti-Semitism. Thus, it was imperative to allow many years to pass before Jews were allowed to reach important posts. In addition, this solution would be combined with a demand that Jews with "Jewish-sounding" names change them to insure full assimilation. These measures, concludes the memorandum, would guarantee that in the future all that remained in Europe of the Jews would be a small national minority of Zionists and Orthodox. Upon reading this document, it is hard not to see the commonalities between the suggestions of anti-Nazi exiles of the Free Germany movement and the recommendations of the German opposition in the Third Reich formulated by Carl Goerdeler and by the economist Constantin von Dietze of the Freiburger Circle.[16]

For Goerdeler, the solution of the Jewish question after Hitler was to establish a Jewish state in parts of Canada or South America and grant German citizenship only to a small, elitist minority of Jews willing to assimilate completely. As to von Dietze, he made legal discrimination conditional upon the number of Jews returning to Germany and believed that discrimination was unnecessary because "the number of surviving returning Jews would be so small that they would pose no threat to the German people."

It is clear, then, that resisters and exiles were horrified by Hitler's extermination policy but that this did not influence their planning on the postwar solution of the Jewish question. For both anti-Nazi resisters and exiles, the Jews were a foreign body causing constant disturbance. Hence, both denied the possibility of reintegrating the Jews in a future German society and sought a territorial solution to the Jewish question outside the borders of Europe.

There is a temptation to take the facile point of view of imputing anti-Semitic motivation to the German exiles in their postwar suggestions vis-à-vis the Jewish question. Their social prejudices, however, have to be historicized and seen in the context in which the exiles operated. The formulations of the exiles were motivated chiefly by a desire to prevent a recurrence of the reality that preceded the Nazi assumption of power. Since the exiles assumed that there was a "Jewish question," they necessarily viewed it as one of the issues to be solved in the quest for a stable and desirable post-Hitler German society. They also realized that the Nazis had aroused anti-Semitism to such an extent that even if legal discrimination were revoked, Jews could not live in Germany for decades to come.

Finally, let us turn to postwar solutions formulated by German Communist exiles. It is well known that the general trend of Marxist interpretation of the Jewish question denied a unique place to anti-Semitism and depicted it as an epiphenomenon of fascist regimes' policies against all oppositionist elements. Since Communism predicted that Jews must sooner or later disappear through assimilation, it was especially harsh in the judgments it passed on Jewish nationalism and particularly so in its outright rejection of Zionism. Thus, Communist doctrine defined Zionism at the second congress of the Comintern in 1920 as "an utopian and reformist vision leading to counterrevolutionary consequences." Socialist Zionism was not excepted from this definition and was declared an ideology preaching race exclusiveness and race superiority blended with social demagoguery.

In their depictions of both Nazi anti-Semitism and Jewish nationalism, Communist German exiles were faithful followers of Moscow's line. Nazi anti-Semitic policy was pictured as serving the dictatorial pragmatic needs of German capitalism and, consequently, relegated by Communist German exiles to the periphery of their discussions. Also, keeping in line with the dictates from Moscow, the German Communist press in exile consistently portrayed the Zionist movement as a plot concocted by British colonialism and the Jewish bourgeoisie. Throughout the 1930s, whenever its exile literature referred to the problems in Palestine—the bad economic situation, the unemployment, and daily unrest, resulting in Jewish and Arab victims—it blamed Zionism's tendency to expand British imperialism. The British, Communist writings asserted, apply the principle of divide and conquer, inciting Jews and Arabs to clash in Palestine, and the Jewish bourgeoisie directly and actively participates in this policy. The German Communist press paid special attention to the Haavara treaty. This agreement on the transfer of Jewish property to Palestine, signed by Germany with the Zionist Organization, was for German Communists incontestable proof of how strong the bond between Nazism and Zionism was.

Considering this background, the entirely unexpected development that took place in the early 1940s in the attitudes of German Communist exiles vis-à-vis the Jewish question is startling.

To begin with, from October 1942 onward, German Communist Paul Merker—the ideological and political leader of the Freies Deutschland movement in Mexico—acknowledged the German nation's collective responsibility in the crimes committed against the Jews of Europe.[17] While the accepted Communist interpretation attached the blame to the reactionary classes of Junkers, monopolists, and Nazi hacks, Merker affirmed that the blame lay with anyone who did not ally himself against anti-Semitism to defend the Jews. Second, he recognized the uniqueness of the Jewish ordeal and regarded the Jews as a minority suffering from both national and economic oppression. Third, and most important, he argued that the Germany to rise after the war could not content itself with restoring to the Jews the citizenship of which they had been stripped but would have to recognize them as a minority. As such, it would have to accord them state protection and all the rights due to a national minority, including that of political expression. The peace conference to convene in the future, Merker added, would have to seriously consider the question of a Jewish state and the right of the Jews to immigrate to it. In December 1944, Merker again set down his position in clearer terms. After the war, German Jews would have the right to hold dual nationality: of Germany and of Palestine or Birobidjan. Furthermore, the new Germany should grant recognition of, and support for, the demands of the Zionist movement to establish a Jewish state in Palestine and help it do so.[18]

We are faced here with an apparent paradox, which requires clarification. Historians have noted this remarkable change in Merker's writings but interpreted it as an exceptional case among Communist exiles and attributed it to the personality of Merker, who, out of sympathy toward the suffering of the Jews, deviated from the normative

Communist line.[19] In my opinion, however, there is more than just
Merker's personality involved here, and the new approach is not exceptional. These declarations ought to be read in their functional
context as reflecting the instructions of Moscow, rather than independent humanitarian initiatives of Paul Merker. Moscow's change,
however, was not an ideological one; it was Stalin's political opportunism which dictated a temporary adoption of a pro–Jewish-
national tactic.

The popular front stratagem charted in 1935 is the key to understanding this new development. This policy, which became dominant after the German invasion of the Soviet Union in 1941 and
went on making considerable concessions on the Jewish question,
was the driving force behind the new positions of the German Communists in the West toward the Jewish question. To be sure, the basic theoretical assumptions regarding the Jewish problem and all that
Jewish nationalism entailed were not abandoned; the political tactic,
however, adapted to the new circumstances. In this context, the
Kremlin could simultaneously persecute Zionists in the Soviet Union
and support Jewish national aspirations abroad, so long as they served
its global interests.

The innovative attitudes were not limited to Merker's initiative in
Mexico. After the Free Germans' convention in 1943, this line became binding for other Latin American movements of Free Germans.
Free Germans' publications in Uruguay, Cuba, and Chile endorsed
Merker's views, which reaffirmed the movement's pro-Zionist position.[20] Similarly, in *Informaciones* and *Demokratisches Deutschland*,
both organs of the Ecuadorian Free Germany movement, Boby As-
tor, vice president of the Latin American Committee of Free Germans, not only praised the elimination of anti-Semitism in the Soviet
Union and the fact that Jews there achieved civil equality as well as
cultural and religious autonomy but also affirmed his positive attitude toward Zionism and saw in an independent Jewish state one of
the possible solutions to the Jewish question.[21] This change should
not be attributed to the unique authority of Merker in Latin America.
The chief theoretician of the American Communist Party, Alexander
Bittelman, expressed himself in a similar vein when he declared in
1943 that he viewed with favor "a new form of Jewish national existence for the Jews living in Palestine."[22]

Historians have also disregarded the fact that in the United Kingdom this shift can be detected even earlier. The declarations of cultural organizations under Communist direction and of Communist-led Free Germans throw light on this new development. In November 1942, representatives of the Communist-controlled Cultural Union of Free Germans participated in the official memorials of the British Jewish community. They not only lauded in their addresses the contribution of the Jews to the Red Army but also issued a declaration on the duties of a free Germany to compensate the Jews. In addition to the revocation of the anti-Semitic laws, rebuilding of destroyed synagogues, restitution of Jewish communal property, and reconstruction of Jewish life, these obligations included the "understanding that the persecution had strengthened the Jewish national consciousness and the Jews had therefore the right to establish their national and religious institutions to represent their interests."[23] Moreover, it is certainly striking that in an official statement, the German Communists supported the Zionist enterprise. The declaration stated that "the Free Germans support with sympathy the endeavors of part of the Jews to establish their own national state." These demands were reiterated by the Free Germans in the United Kingdom in May and June 1944.[24]

Two points are worth noting here. First, it is clear that Merker's initiative is not to be seen in isolation. The support for a national solution to the Jewish question, for those Jews willing to participate in it, is to be read as a reflection of Moscow's campaign to mobilize Jewish organizations into the general effort to support the Soviet Union in its fight against Hitler. Constantin Umansky, the Soviet ambassador in Washington, broadly intimated that his government's position on the question of Palestine would depend on the attitude of world Jewry toward the Soviet Union during the war. Second, in those years, Stalin was toying with the idea of destabilizing the British Middle East through the support of the Jewish endeavors in Palestine. This new policy is well illustrated by the contacts between Russian diplomats and Zionist leaders, such as the talks held in London by the Soviet envoy, Ivan Maiski, with David Ben-Gurion and Chaim Weizmann.[25]

Summing up, the solution of the Jewish question after Hitler envisioned by German exiles indicates that Hitler's anti-Semitic policy hardly changed their stands toward the Jewish issue. On the contrary, to the majority of Social Democrats, a formal restitution of citizen-

328 • DAVID BANKIER

ship after the war was enough. Conservatives formulated plans which echoed trends that developed in the Second Reich, demanding that emancipation in the sense perceived by the Jews be revoked as impractical. The Holocaust just strengthened their convictions that Jews had to either assimilate or leave Europe after the war. Convinced that Jewish particularism was very difficult to eradicate, some advocated a status of national minority for Jews in the postwar era, while others supported Zionism or other territorialist schemes to concentrate the Jews outside Europe.

The Communist position, by contrast, proved to be much more flexible. Despite its underlying dogmatism, it quickly accommodated to the political processes of those years. This accommodation, however, is not to be attributed to the independent initiatives of German Communists in exile but to Stalin's dictates from Moscow.

NOTES

1. *Aufbau*, July 7, 1943; Lewis J. Edinger, *German Exile Politics: The Social Democratic Executive Committee in the Nazi Era* (Berkeley, 1956), p. 232.

2. Hans Vogel to Leon Kubowitzki, London, January 6, 1944, Archiv der sozialen Demokratie der Friedrich Ebert Stiftung, Bonn [hereafter cited as AdsD], Sopade, Mappe 142. All English translations in this chapter are mine unless noted otherwise.

3. Ludwig Eiber, *Die Sozialdemokratie in der Emigration* (Bonn, 1998), pp. 296–98.

4. H. Berman to Hans Vogel, Tel Aviv, January 9, 1944, AdsD, Mappe 44.

5. Hans Vogel to the Executive Committee of the General Federation of Jewish Labour, London, April 26, 1944, AdsD, Sopade, Mappe 142; and cf. *Neue Volkszeitung*, 12 February 1944.

6. Willy Brandt, *Draussen* (Munich, 1976), p. 305. I am grateful to professor Einhart Lorenz for his information on Brandt's address to the SPD-Ortsgruppe Stockholm.

7. H. Jäger, *Diktatur Pogrom Krieg* (The Hague, 1939); H. Jäger, *Die Volkssozialisten und die Judenfrage. Ein Entwurf in sechs Thesen*, Wiener Library Archives, London/Tel Aviv, anti-Nazi pamphlets P 121.

8. Hermann Rauschning to Willy Hoegner, Paris, June 3, 1939, Institut für Zeitgeschichte, Munich, Nachlass Willy Hoegner, ED 120.

9. Albert Kluthe to Hans Schoeps, June 17, 1939, Bundesarchiv

Berlin, NL 162/27; Schoeps proposal and Kluthe's response, Bundesarchiv Berlin, NL 162/45.

10. See the many negative references to Jews in Strasser's correspondence, Institut für Zeitgeschichte, Munich, Nachlass Otto Strasser.

11. Otto Strasser, *Aufbau des deutschen Sozialismus* (Leipzig, 1932).

12. See, for example, the articles in Strasser's periodical *Die Deutsche Revolution:* "Die Eingliederung der Juden in das neue Deutschland," 19 November 1935; "Manifest über die Stellung der Juden in kommenden Deutschland," 9 August 1936.

13. For a detailed study of Strasser's attitude on the Jewish question, see David Bankier, "Otto Strasser und die Judenfrage," *Bulletin des Leo Baeck Instituts* 60 (1981): 320.

14. "Was ist Antisemitismus?" *Die Zeit,* 15 April 1938; cf. *Die Zeit,* 15 February 1939; "Wir und der Antisemitismus," *Die Zeit,* 15 October 1939.

15. Bewegung "Freies Deutschland" in der Schweiz, Betrifft, Judenfrage, August 1945, Nachlass Abegg-Gelpke, 90 Ab 1/26, Bundesarchiv Potsdam.

16. Goerdeler's position was articulated in Carl Goerdeler, *"Das Ziel,"* Beck und Goerdeler. Gemeinschaftsdokumente für den Frieden 1941–1944, ed. Wilhelm Ritter von Schramm (Munich, 1965), pp. 105–7; cf. Hans Mommsen, "Gesellschaftsbild und Verfassungspläne des deutschen Widerstandes," in Walter Schmitthenner and Hans Buchheim, eds., *Der deutsche Widerstand gegen Hitler. Vier historischkritische Studien* (Cologne, 1966), pp. 133, 266, 270; Christof Dipper, "Der 20. Juli und die 'Judenfrage,'" *Die Zeit,* 1 July 1994, p. 20. Von Dietze's recommendations were included in his memorandum, "The Polity: An Attempt at Self-Examination of the Christian Conscience in View of the Political Problems of Our Time." See Constantin von Dietze, "Vorschläge für eine Lösung der Judenfrage in Deutschland," in *In der Stunde Null. Die Denkschrift des Freiburger "BonhoefferKreises:" Politische Gemeinschaftsordnung. Ein Versuch zur Selbstbesinnung des christlichen Gewissens in den politischen Nöten unserer Zeit,* ed. P. von Bismarck, intro. H. Thielicke (Tübingen, 1979), pp. 146–151; Christof Dipper, "The German Resistance and the Jews," *Yad Vashem Studies* 16 (1984): 41–76.

17. "Das kommende Freie Deutschland und die Juden," *Freies Deutschland* of Uruguay, 25 July 1944. See the article of Merker, "Hitlers Antisernitismus und Wir," *Freies Deutschland* of Mexico, October 1942.

18. Rudolf Neumann, "Unser Kampf gegen Hitler. Protokoll des Ersten Landeskongresses der Bewegung," *Freies Deutschland* of Mexico, 1943, pp. 78–79; Leo Deutsch, "Zionismus, Freies Deutschland und Judenfrage," *Freies Deutschland,* 15 December 1943; "Brief an einen Freund, Die Bewegung Freies Deutschland und die Zukunft der Juden," *Freies Deutschland,*

April 1944, and the reactions in the issues of June, July, and August of that year.

19. Jeffrey Herf, *Divided Memory* (Cambridge, Mass., 1998); Fritz Pohle, *Das mexikanische Exil. Ein Beitrag zur Geschichte der politischkulturellen Emigration aus Deutschland, 1937–1941* (Stuttgart, 1986).

20. "Freie Deutsche und der Zionismus," *Freies Deutschland* of Uruguay, 6 April 1945, reproduced Merker's statement made in "Die Freien Deutschen und der Zionismus," *Demokratische Post*, 31 December 1944; "Zionismus und Freies Deutschland," in *Freies Deutschland* of Chile, April 1944; see as well the statements of the Comité Aleman Antifascista in Cuba in *Palabra Hebrea de Cuba*, 18 February and 14 June 1944.

21. Maria-Luise Kreuter, *Donde queda el Ecuador? Exilio en un pais desconocido desde 1938 hasta fines de los a os cincuentas*, Abya-Yala (Quito, 1997), pp. 250–51.

22. Cited in Simon Redlich, *Propaganda and Nationalism in Wartime Russia* (Boulder, 1982). Cf. the article of Schahno Epstein in *Einikait*, organ of the Jewish Antifascist Committee, on November 8, 1944, entitled "The Rebirth of a Nation." In it, Palestine is seen as a homeland for the Jews who wish to go there.

23. "Deklaration des Freien Deutschen Kulturbundes, November 15, 1942," in *Zur Frage der Wiedergutmachung des Unrechts an den Juden. Eine Erklärung Deutscher Antifaschisten* (London, 1943), p. 11. See also Ursula Adam, "Zur Geschichte des Freien Deutschen Kulturbundes in Grossbritanien (Ende 1938–Mai 1945)" (Ph.D. diss., Akademie der Wissenschaften der DDR, 1984), pp. 213–221.

24. Nachlass Fritz Eberhard, Institut für Zeitgeschichte, Munich, ED 117/8.

25. On these contacts, see particularly J. Hen-Tov, "Contacts between Soviet ambassador Maiski and Zionist Leaders during World War II," *Soviet Jewish Affairs* 8 (1978): 46–56; Y. Roi, "Soviet Contacts with the Jewish Community in Palestine and with Zionist leaders during World War II [June 1941–February 1945])," *Shalem* 1 (1974): 525–602.

Vojtech Blodig

Terezín and the Memory of the Holocaust in Czechoslovakia since 1945

ON MAY 6, 1947, TWO YEARS AFTER THE END OF THE MOST TERRIBLE war in human history, the government of the Czechoslovak Republic decided to set up a Memorial to National Suffering in Terezín, as a reminder of the fate of those who passed through it during the Nazi occupation. This memorial, later renamed the Terezín Memorial, was the only institution of this kind in the Czech lands. It was established on the site where the largest Nazi persecution facilities in the country operated.

In June 1940, in the Small Fortress of Terezín, a police prison of the Prague Gestapo was established, through which about 32,000 people, mostly political prisoners, passed. The prisoners (some of whom were Jewish) came from the Protectorate of Bohemia and Moravia as well as from many other countries. About 2,600 of the prisoners perished there, and another 5,500 of them perished after they were deported to other Nazi prisons, penitentiaries, and concentration camps. In the town of Terezín—the former Main Fortress—a Jewish ghetto was established in November 1941. More than 140,000 people passed through this concentration and transit camp until April 20, 1945. These prisoners came from the Czech lands as well as from Germany, Austria, Denmark, Holland, Slovakia, and Hungary. At the very end of the war, the evacuation transports carrying prisoners from concentration camps in the East and North which had been liquidated came to Terezín between April 20, 1945, and May 6, 1945. About 14,000 other prisoners from about thirty countries came with those transports. Some of them were former Terezín Ghetto prisoners who had survived forced labor after being selected for work in Auschwitz. Including them, the total number of the inmates of the

Terezín camp was more than 150,000. Approximately 35,000 of these inmates died in Terezín, and over 83,000 in other concentration camps and places of extermination. Half of this group perished in Auschwitz.

Toward the end of World War II, another concentration camp was established in nearby Litomerice, as a branch of the Flossenbürg concentration camp in Germany. It was situated in the vicinity of an underground plant with the code name Richard. From May 31, 1944, until May 4, 1945, about 18,000 prisoners passed through this camp and more than 4,500 perished there. A large number of prisoners in this camp were Jewish.

When the memorial was established, its staff sought to accent the fate of the Jewish victims in Terezín. Consequently, the Jewish cemetery and the crematorium in Terezín were included in the memorial. These decisions were made by the Jewish Religious Community in Prague between 1945 and 1947. The number of members of the community dropped rapidly after the Holocaust, and there were generally great problems reconstructing Jewish organizations in the country. The Jewish Religious Community hoped to solve the problem of maintaining the memorial sites connected with the victims of the so-called Final Solution of the Jewish question from the Czech lands, by taking part in the administration of the memorial. The negotiations between the representatives of the Czech Ministry of the Interior—under whose jurisdiction the memorial fell at that time—and the Jewish Religious Community in Prague took place on September 4, 1947, and an agreement was finally reached about taking over administration of the Jewish cemetery and crematorium by the memorial.[1]

At this time, there was a consensus among all the political parties that the memorial should be kept in its original state as a place of remembrance to all the victims of Terezín. Some publications about the Terezín persecution facilities appeared between the years 1945 and 1948, including the first survivor testimonies, many of which described details of life in the Terezín Ghetto. The most important of those publications was the testimony of Rabbi Richard Feder from Kolín, one of the great personalities of spiritual life in the ghetto.[2]

During this period, negotiations about Jewish property from Terezín also took place. This property had been brought to Terezín by its Jewish inmates, and a great amount of money was also spent on construction work in Terezín, which was necessary to enlarge the housing capacity of the town and realize other technical measures necessary for the functioning of the ghetto. The funds used for this came from the so-called emigration fund, controlled by the Gestapo and established from confiscated Jewish property. Jewish organizations asked that the Terezín property be restored to the Jewish communities as well as to help to support Czech Jewish people after the war. A special commission, with the representatives of several government ministries and different organizations, was established for solving this problem.[3] The demands made by the Jewish representatives in this commission were partly satisfied. However, at the beginning of 1948, the situation changed rapidly.

First, the Communist seizure of power in February 1948 stopped the negotiations concerning Jewish property. The bulk of Terezín property was confiscated by the state. In addition, ideas about the activities of the memorial began to change quickly. The attitude of the foreign policy of communist Czechoslovakia toward the State of Israel, following the instructions from Moscow, changed to a hostile one. This was reflected in the focus of the memorial's activities, because the development of the memorial was connected very closely with the orientation of the state's policy.

This situation was evident in the form and content of the first permanent exhibition of the memorial, opened in the Museum of the Small Fortress in June 1949.[4] The theme of this exhibition was the role of the Communist element of the Czech resistance movement against the Nazi occupation. The history of other groups of freedom fighters was minimized, as was information about the fate of the Jewish inmates of the Terezín Ghetto. It was not enough, however. By the beginning of the 1950s, the primitive stereotypes of class struggle had become permanent. The memorial was criticized in 1951 in the document "Terezín Yesterday and Today," which ideologically and contextually assessed the situation of the memorial. Commenting on the display about the suffering of Jewish inmates , the document says: "These are shattering documents of fascist murder of nations. But the most basic point is missing. The museum does not speak about class differences. It does not say that the SS and the Gestapo sowed class differences among citizens of Jewish origin and acted accordingly."[5] This brief excerpt indicates the obvious difficulty of precisely integrating this problem into the Communist propaganda system. Using the memorial as a "propaganda weapon" necessitated the concealment of a number of facts. This approach was characteristic of the entire 1950s and the first half of the 1960s.

By this time, practically any reminder of the existence of a Jewish ghetto in the town of Terezín had been expunged. On December 15, 1952, a proposal to set up an exhibition about the Terezín Ghetto in one of the houses in the town of Terezín was discussed in the committee in charge of the memorial and was ultimately rejected on the basis that information about the ghetto appears in the exhibition of the Museum of the Small Fortress.[6] It is quite significant that this discussion was held in the atmosphere of hysterical anti-Semitism around the Slánsky trial. At that time, many anti-Semitic groups were active. However, the democratic policy of prewar Czechoslovakia (connected mainly with the personality of former president T. G. Masaryk) was more powerful than the Communist propaganda as well as the former Nazi one on this topic. The great majority of the population did not take part in the campaign against the Jews. In spite of that, postwar history tarnished the reputation of Czechoslovakia.

This more direct anti-Semitism was replaced by anti-Zionism in middle of the 1950s. In the case of the Terezín Memorial, the consequences were the same, because everything related to Judaism and Jewish history was suspect to the authorities.

The first change in the activities of the memorial occurred in the first half of the1960s. It was decided that the memorial should change from a monument with one exhibition to a research center with its own collections of documents and objects, including the collections related to the former ghetto. Of course, this positive development still had its limitations. The activities of the memorial remained within the Communist ideological system, which put considerable restrictions on change. Positive shifts were possible only in the framework of a vast liberalization of the Communist Party and, subsequently, of the society as a whole.

The Prague Spring in 1968 made the conditions for work on the memorial more favorable. After a long period of silence, the need to establish a ghetto museum in the town of Terezín was stressed once again by the new leadership of the memorial. The future tasks of the memorial were discussed in a session of the Czechoslovak parliament on October 5, 1968: "In past years, the administration of the memorial and the bodies directly subordinate to the governing board did not correctly solve the question of the relation between anti-Jewish, racial Nazi theory and its reprisals against representatives of the organized antifascist resistance. Thus, it happened that individual positions were incorrectly assessed in relation to the overall antifascist struggle and were not explained in conformity with an objective evaluation of historical events. The overall influence of the memorial on public opinion was thereby reduced . . ."[7] At this time, the preparatory work began for the establishment of the ghetto museum as well as for work on the architecture of places of remembrance at the Terezín Memorial—the Jewish cemetery and crematorium, the national cemetery, the site at the Ohøe river (where ashes of Terezín Ghetto victims were thrown into the water) and the crematorium and surroundings of the former concentration camp in Litoměřice. This positive development continued even a few months after the invasion of Czechoslovakia by Warsaw Pact armies but was scaled down under the pressure of the occupation authorities. The Stalinists returned with the so-called normalization. Unfortunately, they brought with it a renewed anti-Semitic and anti-Zionist policy.

At this time, plans for establishing the ghetto museum were not terminated immediately, but the content had to be essentially changed. In a document from April 1973, one can read about the main tasks of the Terezín Memorial: "One of the greatest [tasks] is to build a ghetto museum, the need for which, in a period of rising Zionism whose aggression threatens world peace, is especially urgent. Yet, elsewhere in the world there is so much evidence proving that it is precisely imperialism which upholds racism and that it was the socialist order which stood in its way, that it was the Soviet Army which liberated Auschwitz and Terezín, as well as other places where Jews were liquidated. . . . In this spirit we are ready to set up a museum in one of the concentration camps which fascism established throughout the world. Nor will we forget the concentration camps in Vietnam and in Israel."[8] But not even this sufficed. Another exhibition was planned in the Small Fortress "showing the public how present-day Zionism learned nothing from the fate of Jews liquidated by the Nazis."[9] Instead of paying homage to the memory of the victims of the Terezín Ghetto, who perished directly in Terezín or in death camps in the East, the projected museum was to become an instrument of ideological propaganda. The last citation from a document of that time evaluated the content of the exhibition in the Museum of the Small Fortress:

"The museum exhibition at the time had shortcomings about the role of the Communists in the resistance and the liberating role of the Red Army. The activities of the memorial, on the contrary, gave excessive attention to the former Terezín Ghetto."[10] So after a very short period of liberalization in which the real story of the Holocaust was presented, a new period of regression began. The development of the Terezín Memorial was similar to that of the Jewish Museum in Prague. In the late 1950s, the names of the Jewish Holocaust victims from the Czech lands were written on the walls of the Pinkas Synagogue, which is a part of this museum, and became a famous and impressive monument to the memory of all who perished in the Holocaust. At the end of the 1960s, the synagogue was closed for "restoration of water-damaged walls"; in reality, all the names were expunged. This "restoration" remained in effect until the Velvet Revolution in 1989. It was necessary then to rewrite all of the names on the walls. The Pinkas Synagogue was reopened in 1996.

In Terezín, fortunately, the anti-Semitic projects for the museum and the mentioned anti-Semitic exhibition were not implemented. The building that was intended as a seat of the ghetto museum was transferred to the Ministry of Interior, and the Museum of the National Security and Revolutionary Traditions of Northern Bohemia—as it was called—was established there. To establish such a museum on a site connected with the memory of tens of thousands Jewish victims of the Holocaust was an indication of the arrogance of the regime. The new museum stood empty. No regular visitors, with the exception of organized groups, went to it. On the other hand, in the town of Terezín, every evidence of the former ghetto disappeared. The results of such a policy were dangerous. After so many years, many young people did not even know about the existence of the Terezín Ghetto. The Small Fortress was the only symbol of the history of Terezín in World War II.

It is necessary to mention that some positive changes in the work of the memorial remained from the late 1960s. The art collection gained many valuable works made in the ghetto as well as a great number of valuable modern artworks dealing with antiwar themes. Professional processing of archive documents also improved to a degree, and an archive of photographs was established and a collection of survivor testimonies recorded. Most important, the research of the history of the Terezín Ghetto and the Final Solution of the Jewish question did not completely stop, though it was not practically possible for the researchers to publish the results of their work. This situation was similar to that of researchers working in the Jewish Museum in Prague. After democratic changes in the country, however, this previously done work enabled the staff to establish the Ghetto Museum very quickly and to develop the presentation of the history of the Holocaust from good research. The anti-Zionist orientation of the regime in the 1980s continued. Despite that, events such as the unveiling of the memorial plaque for the Jewish transports in Terezín and the establishing of a small exhibition about the Holocaust in the crematorium at the Jewish cemetery in Terezín took place, and a scholarly conference about the mass murder of the prisoners of the Terezín family camp in Auschwitz was held in Terezín in March 1988. These events were the first signals of the coming changes.

The Velvet Revolution in November 1989 created a new situation in Czech society, including a new attitude toward Jews and Judaism as well as to the State of Israel. After forty years, the relations between the two states were normalized. Many former Terezín Ghetto survivors came to Czechoslovakia for the first time since 1948. Survivors from Czechoslovakia established Terezín Initiative, an organization supporting remembrance activities, research, and education on the Holocaust. From the beginning, Terezín Initiative supported the activities of the new leadership and staff of the Terezín Memorial in helping to establish the Ghetto Museum and developing research on the history of the Holocaust. These activities were also strongly supported by the new president of the Czechoslovak Republic, Václav Havel, who became a member of the board of directors of the new Ghetto Museum. Václav Havel addressed the Czech population several times, explaining the suffering of the Jewish people during the Holocaust, and he visited Terezín with Israeli presidents Herzog and Weizmann in 1991 and 1996, respectively.

The Ghetto Museum in Terezín was opened in October 1991 and together with the Pinkas Synagogue in Prague (which reopened a few years later) became the most important places of remembrance to the victims of the Holocaust in the Czech Republic. Also, a new exhibition about the mortality rate in the ghetto was established in the crematorium, and the memorial site on the Ohøe river where the ashes of the Ghetto victims were thrown to the water was redesigned. The main accent is on the development of research on the Holocaust and education about the Holocaust. Contacts were set up again with institutions and scholars abroad. International academic conferences about the history of the period of Nazi occupation have been held in Terezín every year since 1991. Almost all of those conferences were dedicated to the history of the Holocaust.

In 1993, the newly established Department of Education started its work. This work is oriented mainly on the history of the Holocaust because of the lack of information on this topic in existing schoolbooks. The main emphasis of the department was the education of teachers, but different programs were also prepared for groups of young people of various ages. In autumn 1997, a new meeting center was opened in the building of the former Magdeburg Barracks (which was the seat of the Jewish self-government in the ghetto). In this building, permanent exhibitions are established—also including a reconstruction of the dormitory of the ghetto prisoners and exhibitions about music, art, and literature in the Terezín Ghetto.

The emphasis on the memory of the Holocaust is permanent in the activities of the Terezín Memorial today. This topic has also achieved prominence in the Czech media. Interest is great among the public, and many young people are discovering more about this earlier unknown chapter of the history of their country. Some of them are even discovering their Jewish roots after a long period of forced assimilation. The number of the visitors of the Terezín Memorial has been increasing over the last few years. It is most important that the number of the Czech visitors has also been increasing (in 1996 and 1997 faster then that of the foreigners), because some people claim that the history of the Holocaust is emphasized too much in comparison to the history of the Czech resistance movement. According to an anonymous opinion poll in Terezín, however, made in the summer 1997, these opinions are in the minority, and negative responses about the memory of the Holocaust were rare. This finding has been confirmed by other polls. We hope that this positive attitude of the Czech population will grow as a result of new education and media influence. Yet the problem of racism is still present in our country and is connected with the Roma minority. Thus, learning from the memory of the Holocaust remains important not only for the memory of the victims but also for education about democracy and the danger of racism.

NOTES

1. Terezín Memorial Archives [hereafter cited as TMA], Inv. No. 24, K1/PA.
2. Richard Feder, *Židovská tragedie. Dejství poslední* (Kolín, 1947).
3. Vojtech Blodig, "Mìsto poznamenané tragédií. Pováleèny Terezín v letech 1945–1946," *Terezínské listy* 24 (1996): 7–34.
4. TMA, Inv. No. 26, K1/PA.
5. TMA, Inv. No. 38, K1/PA. English translations here and throughout the chapter are mine.
6. TMA, Inv. No. 61, K3/PA.
7. TMA, Inv. No. 35, K1/PA.
8. TMA, Inv. No. 85, K 14/PA.
9. TMA, Inv. No. 50, K 24/PA.
10. TMA, Inv. No. 85, K 14/PA.

V. T·H·E S·E·C·O·N·D G·E·N·E·R·A·T·I·O·N

Alan Berger

Second-Generation Jewish Identity and "Working Through" the Shoah
Helen Epstein's Journey from Children of the Holocaust *to* Where She Came From

REFERRING TO THE CONTINUING TRAUMA OF THE HOLOCAUST, Lawrence Langer observes, "Of course men go on living, even though some stains on the soul of history are indelible."[1] The question is: How does one live with this metaphysical stain? For survivors, the Shoah, as Elie Wiesel notes, continued after the war. Memory, unbidden and irrepressible, assumed a life of its own. For offspring of survivors, whom I term *Children of Job,* and some of whom were literally born in the shadow of death in various displaced-persons camps, the Holocaust is a great hovering presence that reveals manifold psychosocial and theological sequelae.[2] The second generation has the double burden of *mourning a past* that they never knew but which shapes their lives while, at the same time, seeking to *shape* this elusive memory for their own children and for future generations.

The *indelible stain* on the soul of history is felt in an intensely personal way by the second generation. They seek to achieve what Freud termed a "working through" traumatic memory and mourning. While much has been learned since Freud about working through, and the concept itself has undergone various changes, it remains vital for understanding an important dimension of second-generation writing and cinematic discourse. For example, Saul Friedländer notes that *"Working through means confronting the individual voice* in a field dominated by political decisions and administrative decrees which neutralize the concreteness of despair and death."[3] Dominick LaCapra, for his part, understands working through as the process of making "ever more explicit what was lost and to feel, again, the anguish of losing."[4] For LaCapra, in order to master the traumatic past, we must be prepared to "read scars." That which is "not confronted critically," LaCapra writes, "does not disappear; it tends to return as the repressed."[5]

Working through does not mean "getting over" the Holocaust. Rather, it is appropriate to understand working through in the *therapeutic* sense of the term. Here, one revisits the source of pain by speaking about it, analyzing its impact on an individual's perception of psychosocial life, her or his life, and her or his view of the non-Jewish world. In the process, one seeks to detoxify the issues involved in order that further exploration and understanding can occur without the various psychic barriers that can block self-understanding. In contrast to reading scars, this way of working through enables one to be in touch with the past without being paralyzed by its legacy. Commenting on LaCapra's terminology, Helen Epstein observes, "Scars are covers that have become dry and static over wounds."[6] For Epstein, working through means having achieved the capacity for dealing with the Shoah while at the same time placing the catastrophe within the broader perspective of Jewish history.

But working through is a multidimensional phenomenon for the second generation. The question needs to be asked what the offspring do with their inherited memory. Emmanuel Levinas's insight concerning the nature of memory provides a useful clue. He writes:

> It is not memory itself which is essential but the reading, the interpretation of the facts of memory. The work of memory consists not at all of plunging into the past, but of renewing the past through new experiences, new circumstances, new wonders or horrors of real life. And from this point of view, it is the future that is important and not purely the past. . . . The essential is to always find the actuality of the lessons of the Holocaust.[7]

Levinas's call for each generation to interpret *and* renew the "facts of memory" combines elements of the Passover Haggadah and the autonomy of the individual. With the Haggadah, each generation is called upon to experience a foundational event in history. Like much of the modern, and postmodern, world, Levinas invests individuals with the responsibility for reading, for example, shaping the experience. In the words of Ellen Fine, "each individual must read the past and relate to it from the perspective of his or her own circumstances in the present."[8]

The Shoah has already undergone various stages of "reading." Initially, only a few survivors wrote and spoke about their experience. For approximately twenty years after the Holocaust, however, a "curtain of silence" seemed to have dropped on speaking about the event. The trial of Eichmann in 1961 broke this silence. In the 1970s, there was a veritable eruption of literary works, films, and courses dealing with the Shoah. Beginning in the mid-1980s, literary and cinematic "texts" of survivor offspring began to appear. These texts provide a different angle of vision concerning the "reading" of the Holocaust and its continuing impact on second-generation witnesses. This generation, attests Nadine Fresco, "are like people who have had a *hand amputated that they never had. It is a phantom pain, in which amnesia takes the place of memory.*"[9]

In this essay, I discuss Helen Epstein's reflections on working through the Holocaust and the nature of second-generation memory. How does she work through her legacy, and what lessons does she derive from the Holocaust? I focus on two of her writings, the pioneering study *Children of the Holocaust: Conversations with Sons and Daughters of Survivors* (1979) and her recent memoir *Where She Came From: A Daughter's Search for Her Mother's History* (1997),[10] which was published nearly a decade after her mother's death. I contend that Epstein's work exemplifies a type of working through that involves a process of "repair or mending" (*tikkun atzmi*) of the post-Auschwitz self, insofar as this is possible in light of the "indelible stain" that the Holocaust has left on the soul of history. Three questions help reveal what is involved in Epstein's journey of post-Holocaust Jewish self-discovery and self-mending. First, what does she understand by "working through" the Holocaust? Another way of phrasing this question is: How does she work through the Shoah's impact on the Epstein family? What does the second generation remember? Next, I discuss her understanding of post-Auschwitz Jewish identity. The second question is: What is the impact of the indelible historical stain on this identity? Or, in Levinas's terms, what does Epstein see as the "actuality of the lessons of the Holocaust"? How does she "read" the Holocaust through the prism of the second generation? Third, what is the role of pilgrimage to parents' European birthplace among the second generation? Underlying the paper is the role of gender and the mother-daughter relationship in Epstein's quest for her proper relationship to the Shoah and to Jewish history. I contend that Epstein's work reveals a two-stage process of "working through" the Shoah, revealing how the psychological impact of her Holocaust legacy serves as stimulus to historical inquiry.

A BRIEF HISTORICAL NOTE

Epstein is the eldest of three children, and the only daughter, born to Frances (Franci) and Kurt Epstein, survivors of Theresienstadt and Auschwitz. A prolific writer and former journalism professor, Epstein through her odyssey sheds a threefold light on reading second-generation Holocaust memory: she illumines issues and perspectives of survivor offspring; her books reveal a heightened cultural awareness of this generation and its mission; and her own "working through" brings about a search for a *tikkun* of the self and a quest for understanding her relationship to her mother and to Jewish history. Yet her journey did not have an auspicious beginning. Over two decades ago, when Epstein first attempted to publish an article on the second generation, she was told by the *New York Times* that there was no indication that such a group existed.

It is informative to compare the time frame in which each of Epstein's books was published. This comparison reveals a sea change in the reception of the Shoah by American culture. To cite Epstein on this matter:

> When *Children of the Holocaust* was published, there were a dozen professional articles on the second generation world-wide. The book was cutting edge journalism. The idea of psychological "sequaelae" was new. I had to put forth a thesis, define a group of people and have my thesis substantiated by "experts" who were mental health professionals. The group experience had to be "proven" by putting forth a variety of [second-generation members] from all backgrounds and all over the world.[11]

Epstein notes an additional initial cultural barrier in writing about the second generation. Addressing the issue of the relationship between genre and credibility, she attests that she would have "*preferred* to write a personal memoir rather than a reportage but did not feel I could credibly do so. I had to establish the existence of the group phenomenon and in doing so I feel I lost a literary opportunity."[12] Much has changed since then, in no small measure due to her own pioneering study *Children of the Holocaust: Conversations with Sons and Daughters of Survivors.*

Epstein's book greatly facilitated American discourse about the children of survivors and about the role they play as witnesses of the Holocaust's continuing impact. Many referred to it as the *bible* of the second generation. Deborah Lipstadt terms the book a "turning point in the evolution of children of survivors as a communal, emotional, and political entity."[13] Among Epstein's findings is that her "family tree had been burnt to a stump." "Whole branches," she writes, "great networks of leaves had disappeared into the sky and ground" (11). Yet she also found a second, nonbiological, family. The second generation comprises "an invisible silent family scattered about the world" (13). Her conversations with this family revealed certain shared experiences. For example, the second generation is united in its experience of inherited trauma, such as the pervasiveness of Holocaust imagery and unusual photographs. "The Seventh Avenue local," she recalls, "became a train of cattle cars on its way to Poland" (10). Photographs of murdered relatives were, writes Epstein, "documents, evidence of our part in a history so powerful that whenever I tried to read about it in the books my father gave me or see it in the films he took me to, I could not take it in" (11).

At this point, it is helpful to recall the distinction among voices in the post-Holocaust generation that Ellen Fine makes. Fine notes that the inherited memory of this generation eventuates either in an affirmation of their role as part of history or in suffering from the weight of the past. In the latter case, daughters and sons of survivors "are unable to come to terms with [their] anguished legacy."[14] While this distinction is perhaps too rigidly drawn and does not take into account the fluidity of both positions, it is suggestive. Fine views Epstein as an articulate formulator of the second type of response. And indeed Epstein writes of an "iron box" entombed deep within her, so deep that she herself was "never sure just what it was" (9). The box contained, in Epstein's words, "unprocessed, undigested *material*" which she would have to work through. She described its unknown yet omnipotent contents as "slippery, combustible things more secret than sex and more dangerous than any shadow or ghosts" (9). Inchoate yet omnipresent, the content of her "iron box" was "so potent that words crumble before they describe" (9).

WORKING THROUGH THE HOLOCAUST

But *Children of the Holocaust* is only the first step Epstein took in dealing with her Holocaust legacy. The book bears witness to a crucial fact about the second generation. They are not writing about the Holocaust per se but about their own experience of growing up in a survivor household. For Epstein, this experience included her mother's periodic depression and suicidal states; her parents rejection of a God who permitted Auschwitz; the realization that her parents did not fit the American mold; and listening to bits and pieces of their Holocaust stories. She also reports feeling at times that "my life seemed to be not my own. Hundreds of people lived through me, lives that had been cut short in the war" (170). Consequently, Epstein notes the psychological bind of many in the second generation who are laden with expectations impossible to achieve. "It made me special, important and precious but it deprived me of carelessness, the carelessness of childhood" (170). Yet, Epstein attests, "Once one works through the issues involved in being a child of survivors, it is then possible to study what happened prior to the *Shoah* and immerse oneself in the richness and diversity of Jewish history."[15] Fine's argument to the contrary notwithstanding, Epstein's second stage of working through reveals a quest for Jewish history that permits her not only to come to terms with her "anguished legacy" but to "affirm [her] role as part of history."

MEMOIR, POST-AUSCHWITZ IDENTITY, AND LEVINAS

Where She Came From is both memoir and a search for a usable past. Epstein herself comments on the different cultural milieu into which her two Holocaust books were born. Appearing nearly twenty years after *Children of the Holocaust, Where She Came From* was published at a time when "there were nearly 400 *professional articles about the second generation*—not to mention novels, plays, films, rock, etc."[16] Epstein notes that this time she "didn't have to establish the validity of [her] subject and was free to play with literary forms." The author hopes that *Where She Came From* will be "read not as journalism but literary nonfiction." Furthermore, there is a crucial difference between her two Holocaust books: "the first is about rupture, the second about connection."

Commenting on the genre issue, Susan Suleiman terms the book "an interesting new genre of memoir: the reconstruction by writers born after the war (or during the war, but too late to have any actual memory of it) of the world their parents knew and lost as a result of Nazi persecution."[17] Other examples of this genre include Julie Salamon's *The Net of Dreams: A Family's Search for a Rightful Place,* Anne Karpf's *The War After: Living with the Holocaust,* and Elaine Kalman Nayes's *Journey to Vaja.* Epstein herself attests that the memoir is an attempt, "*on the personal level,* to create a family, while *on the tribal level,* she seeks to connect with Judaism."[18] Thus, one of the readings Epstein takes from her Holocaust legacy is the importance of knowing about Jewish history, *which is where she came from.*

Commenting on the relationship of the second generation to their legacy of anguish, she distinguishes between *remembering* and *doing.* "Remembering the Holocaust is not an issue for us," she writes, "we are, in our parents' minds, the answer to the Holocaust."[19] But there is a difference between survivors and their offspring. "We are, in our own minds," attests Epstein, "the guardians of a problematic, unique and volatile legacy. We do *not* need to be reminded of it" (emphasis mine).[20] The task of the second generation lies elsewhere. Working through is in effect a work of translation. In Epstein's words, "we need to find a way of best utilizing it [our legacy]. We need to learn how to translate our consciousness of evil, our skepticism, our sense of outrage into constructive action."[21] For Epstein, this constructive action involved defining her relationship to her mother and her quest to educate herself as a Jew.

Epstein's memoir is based on her mother's twelve-page family history, written at Helen's request, in the early 1970s. The author's relationship with Franci is intense. In fact, the epigraph for *Where She Came From* is taken from Virginia Woolf's observation: "We think back through our mothers if we are women." Franci Epstein was a dressmaker, fluent in four languages, resourceful, and full of self-blame over the Holocaust. Helen recalls the intensity of the bond between herself and her mother: "I was never sure what belonged to whom, where I ended, and she began" (10). Although their relationship was not a seamless web of tranquillity, Epstein observes that she always viewed her mother as a "heroine more compelling than any in the Bible, any novel or myth" (11). The world of the fashion salon, which was the world of both her grandmother and her mother, was a women's world. "It was," writes Epstein, "along with the convent, the brothel, the birthing room, and the all-girls school, a feminine realm, where women could speak" (118).

It was in her mother's workroom, Epstein confides, "that I fell in love with the dead women in my mother's family" (13). Distinguishing her task from that of the girls who "swept up and threw out threads and scraps of cloth," at the end of the working day, Epstein recalls that she "collected threads and scraps of stories, hoarding them, mulling them over" (13). These story threads, unlike the clothes that her mother so skillfully made, contained no seams, only wide gaps in the fabric. "My mother," writes Epstein, "would never have made a dress the way she told these [Holocaust] stories. There was something wrong in their proportions and some disturbance in her telling that prevented them from making a whole" (13). A perfect seamstress, Franci Epstein "never fixed the way she told her past. The parts never fit. . . . Those disjunctures fascinated me" (13).

Epstein becomes an archaeologist of Jewish memory. Her "dig" does not, however, involve collecting shards of pottery or sifting through broken artifacts. Rather, by reading through volumes in Czech, English, and German, Epstein began feeling that she "was picking up pieces of narrative" (16). She refers to Franci's twelve-page chronicle as a "map to my mother's world." Like many in the second generation, Epstein notes the "annihilation of the past," which led to a deformation of the present. The results of this annihilation are seen in a variety of ways: no grandparents; very few—if any—extended family; a lack of, or only very few, photographs of relatives, family heirlooms, old recipe books, prayer books, and so on. Perhaps most crucial, however, is the lack of a family story. This adds to the difficulty of both working through and reading the Shoah. Far from the multiple versions of the family story in large families, Epstein notes the difficulty of constructing even a *single* version in survivor families. Too few relatives possess too few documents. The narratives that are told frequently obscure more than they reveal.

Epstein's memoir is a vivid and moving account of three generations of secular Czech women: her great-grandmother Theresa

Furcht, who committed suicide in Vienna following the death of her seventeen-year-old son; Pepi Rabinek, Theresa's daughter and Epstein's grandmother, murdered by the Nazis in a forest near Riga; and Franci, Pepi's daughter, survivor of Theresienstadt, Auschwitz, Hamburg, and Bergen-Belsen, and Epstein's mother. Underlying this is the author's desire to write a secular version of what observant Czech Jews of the seventeenth and eighteenth centuries called *megillot mishpachah* (family scrolls). "I liked the idea of taking my mother's twelve page chronicle," writes Epstein, "and bringing three generations of increasingly secular women to life in an old Jewish literary form" (18). Like her mother before her, Epstein is fluent in several languages, including Czech. She utilizes a variety of sources—including novels, history books, ledgers, political speeches, and her own imagination—in reconstructing two centuries of Czechoslovakian Jewish history prior to the Holocaust. The memoir genre enables Epstein to read the Holocaust in her own voice. She can put flesh on the bones of the few remaining photographs.

Much of *Where She Came From* is, however, focused on the life of Epstein's grandmother Pepi, who, before the memoir took shape, was a figure in a photograph hanging above her mother's workbench. Both her mother and her grandmother were "strong, liberated women who supported the family *and* kept house." Consequently, Epstein recalls thinking in the 1970s with the advent of the women's liberation movement, "Whats the big deal?"[22] Epstein sees in Pepi's life the Jewish experience in Central Europe. Pepi was raised by her Orthodox Aunt Rose, whose strictures against involvement in the Gentile world focused on the omnipresent danger of seduction, both in the literal and metaphorical senses. Aunt Rose's rigorous advocacy of adherence to halakha had a profound experience on Pepi; Jewish teachings remained ingrained in Pepi even while she joined herself to the larger, secular and non-Jewish, world. Moving to cosmopolitan Prague from the small Bohemian town of Koln, she abandons formal adherence to Judaism, marries, and works—obtaining a job as a seamstress in a dress salon by demanding to see the boss. She divorces her husband—a difficult step to take in those times—when she discovers he has syphilis. Pepi carries on a ten-year affair with the baptized Emil Rabinek, whom she eventually marries. Rabinek shares none of Pepi's concerns about the Jewish refugees flooding into Prague. The couple argue about everything, using "traditional gendered gestures to reinforce their words: Emil has angry outbursts and brandishes an old army revolver. Pepi sheds tears." When Frances was born, Rabinek insisted on having her baptized so that she would have no civic liability.

Not surprisingly, Pepi and Emil differed radically on the nature of the Nazi threat. She was greatly concerned. He dismissed it. Throughout her discussion of Emil, Epstein underscores his illusions about social standing, acceptance by Catholics, and the unimportance of being Jewish. In the end, she writes, "Emil and Pepi were simply two elderly Jews loaded on a transport and murdered." This comment assumes increasing significance when she recalls her own mother's response to the tightening of the Nazi noose around the neck of Prague Jewry: "The imposition of a Jewish form on [her] identit[y] felt like a punishment dreamed up by a lunatic." Epstein's mother had not known where *she* came from, never having "set foot inside a synagogue nor said a Jewish prayer." As was the case with many lapsed or secular Jews, the Shoah proved their entry into Jewish identity.

Writing *Where She Came From* enabled Epstein to form a better understanding of her mother and to continue their relationship. For example, the daughter comes to understand her mother's frequent bouts of depression. "I realized," writes Epstein, "her years in the camps had transformed a normal, happy, adolescence into something shameful"(165). Franci had both "discredited" her teenage years and "buried" her memories of those times. Consequently, "shame" accounted for her silence in place of stories. One of the many paradoxes engendered by the Holocaust is that it is the *victims who feel guilty.* For example, when Franci and her parents had been arrested by the Gestapo in 1942, she returned home and discovered pills in her father's desk. Fearing for her parents, she took the pills to a pharmacist, who replaced the poison pills with saccharin. At the moment of their deportation to Riga, Franci realized, "*Instead of being protective, I had deprived my father of the last possibility to decide his fate as a free man*" (237). Moreover, the Judaically innocent Franci does seem to have inherited—as if by osmosis—the rabbinic notion that misfortune is a result of sin.

It is the act of writing, however, which both unites and distinguishes mother and daughter. Epstein confides that writing *Children of the Holocaust,* in her mid-twenties, was "an effort to separate what was mine from what was hers" (234). At that point, Epstein did not want her mother's book, *Roundtrip.* "It was," writes Helen, "her story, not mine." Yet Franci had decided in her mid-fifties to write her own Holocaust memoir for her children, whose generation "seem to me almost as troubled or even more than I was at their age." Seeking her own second-generation voice, Epstein attests that it was "far easier to reread *Roundtrip* after my mother's death." Only then could she look at it "with my own eyes in a way that would have seemed to me disloyal while she was alive."

Furthermore, the resourceful Franci, who saves her own life during the Shoah by falsely claiming to be an electrician—there were too many dressmakers—engages in an *act of writing as self-rescue.* Stealing a notebook from the commandant's desk, she keeps a diary in which she writes and fantasizes about Pepi. When the diary is discovered, Franci is forced to burn the text. Helen's memoir, for its part, neither fantasizes nor idealizes Franci. Quite the contrary is the case. The second-generation memoir "supplements" her mother's nostalgic memories and provides a cultural and historical context of the Jewish experience in Moravia and Bohemia.

Epstein's memoir refines her understanding of the Jewish historical experience in central Europe while simultaneously avoiding sentimentality. She distinguishes between the typically benign view of Judaism held by Czech Protestantism and the vastly different perspective of their German brethren. Yet, she also uncovers the swirls and eddies of philo-Semitism and anti-Semitism in Czechoslovakia. History is not simply the task of "apportion[ing] good and evil along ethnic lines" (47). Her investigation also reveals significant, if little-known, information about historically important Jewish families. For example, the Langer family was outraged when their son Jiri studied, and wrote about, Hasidism. The family's Christian maid was the one who kept them kosher. She also discovers an antifeminist letter written by Herzel. The founder of political Zionism writes of what he terms "girl snakes." This phrase refers to three daughters of a local physician, whom Herzel describes as "three debt-free but ugly daughters whom he *permits* to roam about freely without regard to people's aesthetic sensibility." There are as well other historically significant Jewish voices, such as the playwright Arthur Schnitzler and the psychiatrist Otto Rank, who embraced a "reductionist view of women."

Epstein's memoir provides much in the way of detail about the acculturation of the Jews of Moravia and Bohemia. She cites Kafka's letter to his father in which the tormented writer comments on the increasing irrelevance of traditional Judaism for many Jews who had abandoned rural living and flocked to the cities. Similarly, the "stock exchange Jews" would ultimately be "blamed" for capitalism and the transition from an agrarian economy.

SECOND-GENERATION IDENTITY

The issue of second-generation Jewish identity is complex. Epstein notes this complexity in distinguishing between identity and praxis. She writes in *Children of the Holocaust:*

> Those many survivors who had lost their faith in the war did not know what to pass on to their children. The Holocaust had become a touchstone of their identities as Jews and it became a touchstone for their children as well. The trouble was that while it conferred an identity, it provided no structure, no clue to a way of life. (260)

This Jewish cluelessness was a feature of Epstein's experience. While she certainly knew about her parents' Holocaust experience, she knew next to nothing about their life prior to the war. The picture is further clouded because, as secularists, her parents knew little of Jewish history. In one sense, Epstein's experience is a mimesis of that of secular Jews during the Shoah. For example, her search for the Jewish past takes Epstein, her husband, and their young sons to Czechoslovakia. In a Prague washroom, a young bride exclaims, "You're my *first* Jews!" Epstein writes of feeling confused. "I grew up in New York City," she confides, "where being Jewish was about as remarkable as being a farmer in Kansas. Here [in Prague] I was a representative 'of the *now extinct community of Jews*'" (67, emphasis mine).

Epstein's search for a content to her Jewish identity occurs through both a series of interviews and a pilgrimage to Czechoslovakia. She seeks to connect to Judaism on the *personal* level by interviewing her few surviving relatives. Epstein recounts the time that Franci read a *New York Times* book review of Ilse Achinger's *Herod's Children*, recognized the story, and got in touch with the author. This led to a reunion with some relatives whom she thought lost in the Holocaust. Epstein's own interviews help fill in some of the missing pieces of her mother's Holocaust experiences. Yet she astutely observes the large number of variables that comprise the reminiscences of her mother's three surviving Czech cousins: their personalities, relation to her mother, and also the way Nazism, Communism, and emigration affected their lives, their memory, and their outlook.

For example, one relative, age ninety-nine, denied that there was ever anti-Semitism in Vienna. She regarded Helen's interest in Jewish history as an "unpleasant, unwelcome preoccupation." Another relative, who left Czechoslovakia shortly before Munich, helped her parents financially but seemed to be trying to forget the past. After Franci's death, he begins the process of retrieving that past. Still another cousin was not at all interested in family history. A fourth source, Kitty—who survived the Holocaust with Franci—was the most willing to speak of the two cousins' wartime experience.

PILGRIMAGE TO PARENTAL BIRTHPLACE

Pilgrimage to parental birthplace has assumed the role of ritual among the second generation. One thinks here of Art Spiegelman, Julie Salamon, Thane Rosenbaum, and Melvin Bukiet, among others. The journey "back there" where life began and, for so many millions, ended serves as an entry into the landscape of Jewish history. It is, as Eva Fogelman notes, a way that the second generation mourns their losses. It is also a means of better connecting to their parents and to Jewish history before the Shoah. Epstein recounts that physically being in the Czech lands enables her to imaginatively re-create—and identify with—the pre-Holocaust history of her great-grandmother, her grandmother, and her own mother. This journey is a pilgrimage because it is undertaken with ritual intensity. Moreover, like a pilgrimage, the journey evokes a change in the individual sojourner; she or he goes from ignorance to more complete knowledge—even if this knowledge means awareness of the unmasterable nature of the Holocaust trauma.

Working through, as noted earlier, does not mean wiping the slate clean. Near the end of her memoir, Epstein goes to Vienna and visits the grave of her great-grandmother Theresa Furcht. There she plants a pot of heather. But the city itself is a place of pain. Citing her cousin Ilse Achinger, Epstein refers to Vienna as a mixture of "brutality and charm." Epstein writes that she "acted out" in the city. For example, entering hotels where, as she poignantly notes, Jews would have been denied entrance half a century earlier, she refuses to speak

German and wears T-shirts and sneakers in the elegant breakfast room. She befriends people from China and Japan; "fighting for distance," Epstein notes. "The further removed anyone was from Europe the better" (307).

CONCLUSION

Where She Came From is a second-generation act of working through the Shoah that involves a *tikkun* of the self and a reading of survivor experience. While she speaks for the second generation in attesting that the Holocaust is clearly her point of entry into Jewish history, Epstein moves beyond this initial entry without, however, abandoning her legacy. Jewish history prior to the Shoah, and Jewish Studies as a discipline, form the context of Epstein's contemporary reading of the Holocaust. Epstein is a daughter of Job whose mission is to excavate the past in order to properly remember the Holocaust.

Her memoir emphasizes three things: the hideous psychic wounding suffered by survivors; the anguished legacy inherited by the second generation; and the offspring's determination to continue Jewish history. Furthermore, this memoir and others like it have important implications for post-Auschwitz Jewish expression. Three of the more important of these implications seem to me to be the following. First, her memoir sheds light on the meaning of secular Jewish identity and indicates that this identity may be an untapped resource for Jews for whom the Sinai covenant is only a dim echo. Epstein's account exemplifies the contention of Yosef Hayim Yerushalmi that "history becomes what it had never been before—the faith of fallen Jews."[23] Second, the notion of a pilgrimage to Europe as an irreducible part of post-Auschwitz ritual that impacts strongly on Jewish identity should encourage further study of sources, including the history and languages, of Jewish life in Europe *prior* to the Holocaust. Third, this memoir emphasizes the significance of the *tikkun* of bearing witness to both the Holocaust and the richness and diversity of Jewish history. Moving beyond the Shoah, Epstein's work points to the significance of knowing one's origins. The difference between mother and daughter is twofold. One is a survivor and the other a nonwitness, yet it is the daughter—unlike her mother—who discovers where she comes from.

NOTES

1. Lawrence L. Langer, *Versions of Survival: The Holocaust and the Human Spirit* (Albany: SUNY Press, 1982), 57.

2. Alan L. Berger, *Children of Job: American Second Generation Witnesses to the Holocaust* (Albany: SUNY Press, 1997).

3. Saul Friedländer, "Trauma, Transference, and 'Working Through' in Writing the History of the *Shoah,*" *History and Memory* 4, no. 1 (1992): 53.

4. LaCapra is quoted by Janet Burstein in "Traumatic Memory and American Jewish Writers: One Generation after the Holocaust" (paper presented at the annual meeting of the American Literature Association, Boca Raton, Florida, 23 October 1998), 2.

5. Ibid.

6. Helen Epstein, letter to author, 25 November 1998 [hereafter cited as Epstein letter].

7. Levinas is quoted by Ellen Fine, "Transmission of Memory: The Post-Holocaust Generation in the Diaspora," in *Breaking Crystal: Writing and Memory after Auschwitz,* ed. Efraim Sicher (Urbana: University of Illinois Press, 1998), 185–86.

8. Ibid., 186.

9. Nadine Fresco, "Remembering the Unknown," *International Review of Psycho-Analysis* 11, no. 4 (1984): 419.

10. Helen Epstein, *Children of the Holocaust: Conversations with Sons and Daughters of Survivors* (New York: Penguin Books, 1979), and *Where She Came From: A Daughter's Search for her Mother's History* (Boston: Little, Brown, 1997). All page citations are from these editions and appear in parentheses in the text.

11. Epstein letter.

12. Ibid.

13. Deborah Lipstadt, "Children of Jewish Survivors of the Holocaust: The Evolution Of a New-Found Consciousness," in *Encyclopedia Judaica Year Book* (Jerusalem: Keter, 1988–89), 141.

14. Fine, "Transmission of Memory," 189.

15. Helen Epstein, discussion in Eva Fogelman's film *Breaking the Silence* (1980).

16. Epstein letter.

17. Susan Rubin Suleiman, "Fashioning a Narrative from the Fragments of History," review of *Where She Came From* by Helen Epstein, *Forward,* 28 November 1997, 11. Mention should also be made here of Professor Suleiman's own memoir, *Budapest Diary: In Search of the Motherbook* (Lincoln: University of Nebraska Press, 1996).

18. Helen Epstein, lecture "Where She Came From" (Florida Atlantic University, November 1997) [hereafter cited as Epstein lecture]. Julie Solomon, *The Net of Dreams: A Family's Search for a Rightful Place* (New York: Random House, 1986). Anne Korpf, *The War After: Livig with the Holocaust* (London: Minerva, 1996). Elaine Kalman Nayes, *Journey to Vaja: Reconstituting the World of a Hungarian-Jewish Family* (Montreal: McGill-Queens, 1996).

19. Helen Epstein, "Guardians of the Legacy," *Jerusalem Post Supplement–Holocaust Survivors Gathering,* 14 June 1981, 7.

20. Ibid.

21. Ibid.

22. Epstein lecture.

23. Yosef Hayim Yerushalmi, *Zakhor: Jewish History and Jewish Memory* (Seattle: University of Washington Press, 1983), 86.

Rachel Feldhay Brenner

The Second Generation and the
Problematics of *Tikkun*
A Reading of Alan Berger's Children of Job

I WOULD LIKE TO PREFACE MY DISCUSSION OF THE SECOND-generation Holocaust literature with some comments on the problematics of literary representation as encountered by the first-generation Holocaust writers. Although the injunction to consign the memory to silence has not been heeded even by those who proclaimed it, the literature of the Holocaust by writer-survivors continues to raise the critical issue of the Shoah and the aesthetics of its representation. Fictional work deeply grounded in its author's experience of unimaginable horror has posited a conceptual as well as an emotional challenge for scholars of Holocaust literature, such as Langer, Rosenfeld, and Ezrahi.

In particular, I would like to mention Sarah Horowitz's recently published profound study of Holocaust fiction. Her *Voicing the Void* focuses on "the trope of muteness and its multiple functions in Holocaust fiction. . . . The trope of muteness functions as an index of trauma, which both compels and disables the testimony . . . it connects with the author's search for a credible, authentic voice, and for sheer, unmediated representation."[1] It is then both the overpowering need to tell the experience as it was and the fear of not being able to do it that underlie the muteness of the writer-survivor.

Drawing upon Horowitz's observation, I suggest that the writer struggles with muteness not only because the experience is too painful to be expressed but also, and probably foremost, because the recipient of the story is not equipped to understand it. Ida Fink's story-memoir "Scrap of Time" is a text which Horowitz analyzes in her final chapter and which I always discuss in my course on Holocaust testimonies.

Fink's text tells of the difficulty of transmitting the experience. "This time," Fink recalls, "was measured not in months but in a word—we no longer said 'in the beautiful month of May,' but 'after the first action, or the second, or right before the third.' We had different measures of time, we different ones, always different, always with that mark of difference that moved some of us to pride and others to humility."[2] What follows is a narrative which, Fink demonstrates, in fact teaches what "action" meant *then*.

The need to explain and exemplify what "action" was signals the intended reader of the story. It is certainly not the fellow survivor, who has no need for explanations of that kind. The trope of muteness, to recall Horowitz, has multiple functions. Directed to a fellow survivor, it would have been a sign of solidarity, perhaps a "choking" sense of communion, but not lack of common language. The reader or the listener who needs to learn the concrete actual meaning of the "difference" of the Jews in the Holocaust is, for the most part, a member of the postwar second and even third generation of Jews and non-Jews alike.

Thus, it is important to note that, to a large extent, the painful struggle against muteness amounts to a persevering search for an aesthetic to "translate" the story for the uninitiated. The process indicates an overriding urgency to tell the "innocent." There are of course many possible reasons for the survivor's motivation to share her past with those who were not there, and I cannot discuss them in this essay. What the testimonies have in common, however, is the wish to impart the knowledge of this past. The personal story is a window to this "another planet," whose horrific reality the second generation must learn, even if only from a muted voice reaching from behind the glass pane.

As we know, some stories never end but rather evolve by teaching and thus transforming the audience. Holocaust has been a transforming story. Nobody doubts that. But what is the nature of its transformative effect on the uninitiated? This is the question that needs further investigation. Has the story turned its recipients into cynical disbelievers in the values of kindness and justice or rather instilled in them the urgency to seek *tikkun* in a daunting effort to mend the world?

In a recently published essay, Zygmunt Bauman turns passionately against some recipients of the story. He castigates those members of the second generation who have reduced the lesson of the Holocaust to belief in physical survival as the ultimate value and objective of Jewish life. Assuming the identity of the "hereditary victims," these "children-pretenders," as Bauman calls them, sanctify physical survival, thereby cynically rendering insignificant the "dignity and ethical value of life."[3] These "children-pretenders" exploit the Holocaust memory of their parents to claim exemption from moral responsibilities and to affirm the right to hate the world which, they claim, continues to hate them.

At the other end of the spectrum, Rachel Altman, a daughter of Nazi camp survivors, writes in her memoir that "hatred cannot be the lesson." Having contemplated her parents' life experience, Altman struggles to discover the way their story has affected her life. "It is," she says, "the bigger [not just personal] questions that compel me. What are my obligations as a daughter of victims of oppression in its most extreme form? What are my obligations, as a woman and as a Jew, to others of the disadvantaged and oppressed?"[4]

Bauman's "hereditary victims" learn from the Holocaust story that in this evil world, they have the obligation to preserve their lives at any cost. This is a simplistic and dangerous argument whose sophistry justifies oppression and victimization of others in the name of survival. In contrast, others, such as Altman, take a different course. I call this group the "questioning and questing" children of the Holocaust victims. These second-generation Jews learn that the story imposes upon them the obligation to fight evil and to reassess the meaning of life in light of this obligation. These children see in the story of the destruction not only an injunction to live but also an imperative to quest for a constructive ethics of existence in the post-Holocaust world.

In his study, *Children of Job,* Alan Berger explores the pole of "questioning and questing" in the second-generation responses to the Holocaust. A very important contribution of this study lies in its overarching argument of the difficulty of this quest. Practically all the discussions of the second-generation responses, even the most uplifting, which deal with the stories of the rescuers, demonstrate that there are no easy and painless ways to reconstruct the values of humanistic ethics in the post-Holocaust world. The study concurs with scholars of Holocaust literature, such as Lawrence Langer, who in a recent article reiterated that the Holocaust "permanently disrupted" the "normal momentum of human experience." In a very real sense, Berger's study reconfirms Langer's claim that "[t]he national habit of transforming European nightmares to reinforce the American dream does not work with the mass murder of the European Jewry, although efforts to achieve this conversion do not abate."[5]

Indeed, prominent examples of popular second-generation recent rereading of the Holocaust point to the tendency to offer easy and optimistic solutions that would make all of us feel good and obligation-free. Such, I would claim, is Spielberg's *Schindler's List*, whose characterization of the rescuer as a heroic John Wayne–like "good guy"—or rather, "good goy"—reaffirms that values of generosity and altruism will always prevail, even under the terror of the Final Solution. Such is also Goldhagen's *Hitler's Willing Executioners*, a study that exonerates everybody through a categorical indictment of the German people. Subsequently, the author gets the Germans "off the hook" as well by claiming that today they are different people. And so, we are lulled into the belief that redemption is always possible.

The reductive treatments of the Holocaust and of the world after intend to appease our anxieties and make us feel complacent about ourselves and the world. This certainly is not the intention of Berger's book. His critical treatment of short stories, novels, documentaries, and docudramas by "second-generation witnesses," as he calls the children of the Holocaust survivors, intends to expose the disturbing aspects of post-Holocaust reality to us, whether we are Jewish or not. The book speaks to every reader, regardless of religious affiliation or ethnic roots, precisely because it probes Holocaust consciousness, which, while remaining particularly Jewish, has in a very real sense become universal.

The children of survivors, whose works are considered in Berger's study, strive to define their place in their community and in society at large as Jews, as well as citizens of a free society. As Berger sees it, "These second-generation witnesses live in the dawn of 'a broken world' while simultaneously attempting to seek a *tikkun* of both the self and the world." However, as Berger emphasizes, "the readers need to understand that this *tikkun* does not lead to resolution of the *Shoah*." While the artists "articulate the legacy and lessons of the *Shoah,* they do so always against the background of the disaster."[6] This important statement defines the peculiar dilemma that places the second-generation witnesses in a paradoxical situation of being obligated to seek mending for a world that can no longer be mended.

To comprehend the complexity of the problem that faces the second-generation witness, we should first recall that, to a significant extent, Jewish religious tradition defines the chosenness of the Jewish people as a particular obligation to strive for the spiritual improvement of the self and of the community in order to become "light to the nations." According to sages, rabbis, and scholars, such as Rabbi Yehuda Halevy, Ha-Rambam, Ha-Maharal, and Rabbi Kook, among others, the special position of Jewish people among the nations does not alienate them from other nations but rather impels love and concern for humanity, because, as the Talmudic rabbis declared, all humanity descends from Adam and Eve.[7] In a sense, therefore, the responsibility of the second-generation witnesses to witness the parental story of the Holocaust does not deviate from a very important concept in the Jewish tradition. Their subsequent retelling of the story and its implications to the the world is meant to bring forth *tikkun olam* (mending the world).

In the post-Holocaust situation, however, the striving for the *tikkun* of self and others becomes a contradiction in terms because, in effect, no *tikkun* of the Holocaust is possible, and no salutary action can bring forth a resolution of the Shoah. The Final Solution has disrupted, to recall Langer, the pre-Holocaust understanding of humanity and humanism. The second-generation witnesses, and, for that matter, all post-Holocaust Jews, are alive by pure luck or a historical coincidence. The consciousness of accidental survival transmitted to all postwar generations precludes putting the shards of the "broken world" back together and pretending that all is well. The impossibility of restoring the validity of ethical values invalidates the chosenness of the people whose chosenness in history was manifested in the reception and the guardianship of these values. In an unspeakable tragic irony, the eternal covenant with God determined the Nazi choice of the Jewish people for total destruction. Never before in the history of Israel had the abandonment of the divine been so indefensible; never before was it so definitive.

The distance from God who was not there when the children were burning therefore calls in question the proposition of the *tikkun*. For how is it possible to establish some sense of completeness in the "broken world," without restoring a sense of the eternity of Israel? Yet, how is it possible to restore faith in the eternity of Israel with the relentless consciousness of these so horribly abandoned children? The second generation seems to be trapped in an impossible situation whereby the injunction of *tikkun* clashes with the imperative never to forget. The poignant metaphor of Berger's title, *Children of Job,* suggests the predicament of the second-generation witnesses as accidental inheritors of the burned children.

"Of whose 'children of Job' is it about?" asks Elie Wiesel in the foreword to the book. "There used to be many. Those before the misfortune and those after it. The first ones were taken by a premature and sudden death. The second ones were born after their parents' 'reconciliation' with life and perhaps also with God. It is the latter ones that [the book] deals with."[8] According to Wiesel, the book is about the second set of children whose birth signifies the survivor's coming to terms with life and with God. However, the quotation marks around "reconciliation" and the modifier "perhaps" disclose Wiesel's hesitation. I would venture that these are signs of Wiesel's "muteness," to recall Horowitz, when he searches for proper words to describe the survivors' capability for a second parenthood.

What do these hesitations mean? Do they communicate an "as if," a *kh'vyakchol* reconciliation with Jewish life, which at a certain point had became the decree of death, and a reconciliation with a God who abandoned his people? Do they communicate the doubt as well as the need of the survivor to believe that some partial and imperfect, or even a make-believe, *tikkun* had to take place before the replacement children were born? Is it the unwillingness to accept that in begetting children the survivors followed only the instinct to procreate, rather than some kind of spiritual, religious, or ethical motivation?

The raison d'être in its literal sense, that is, the reason to be, to exist as meaningfully as possible after the Holocaust, depends on asking these questions. Perhaps it is this uncertainty and the hesitation about the reality into which the postwar children were born that leads to a new understanding of the essence of the Holocaust legacy. In the Jewish tradition, the notion of the continuity of life is of central importance; here we confront the shocking notion of replacement of life. To what extent were the "children of Job" meant as replicas of the tragically lost first children? To what extent is their existence a reaffirmation of life and faith in the wake of this loss? And if their existence constitutes both the memory of the loss and the tenuous hope for the new, where is the possibility of a resolution?

The resolution, always partial, never definitive, lies in the second-generation witnesses' "questioning and questing" for the sense of a life that is a replacement of another life, destroyed in the Holocaust. If such a replacing of life is meant to be a *tikkun,* then the *tikkun* that this life represents impels questioning, searching of meaning in a world in which continuity has been replaced by coincidence and randomness. The parents who leave with their children the "mute," unspeakable story of the circumstances of their birth, assign to them the search for a redefinition of Jewish identity. For what kind of a Jew is a "replaced" Jew? How does the consciousness of replacement connect this Jew to the Jewish people?

Even more fundamental questions regarding the continuity of chosenness arise in the *Children of Job:* How can accidental parents and replacement children reconstruct the covenant? What kind of covenant will it be?

The story of the survivor has undermined the covenant itself, because it has transformed the identity of the partners. Now it is the absent God and the Jew alive by accident who need to reconnect. Thus, it is appropriate to "question mark" the survivor's reconciliation with God, as Wiesel does it, because reconciliation with God after the Holocaust does not connote the same meaning as before the destruction. Reconnection with God in the framework of the old covenant is no longer possible. As Berger shows in his examination of four post-Holocaust thinkers, a rewriting, or at least a reediting, of the covenant is necessary. He discusses Richard Rubenstein's difficult struggle with the notions of implausibility of the covenant and the unreliability of its divine composer. He examines the problematics of Emile Fackenheim's idea of the "Commanding Voice of Auschwitz," which adds the "614th Commandment" to remain faithful to Judaism after the Holocaust.

In particular, Berger emphasizes the theological thought of Elie Wiesel and Irving Greenberg. These two thinkers suggest neither an annulment nor an emendation of the covenant. Rather, each proposes a sequel to the original contract. In the spirit of the classic Jewish scholarly tradition, their commentary reinterprets the text and thus shifts its meaning. Elie Wiesel's "additional covenant" speaks of the importance of solidarity, witnessing, and sanctification of life in the post-Holocaust world. We note that Wiesel's addition, in fact, is a matter of emphasis, since it places in relief aspects of Jewish life and law that have maintained the Jewish people for centuries. Now these aspects come to the fore as the hypostases of Jewish post-Holocaust identity. In a similar way, Greenberg's "voluntary covenant" uses the traditional notion of partnership between God and Israel. The shift in the proportions in the partnership, whereby Israel becomes the prominent partner vis-à-vis the inactive God, redefine the identity and the role of the Jew.

I would suggest that the redefined identity of the Jew that emerges in both the additional and the voluntary covenants focuses on the responsibility of the human being for the *tikkun* in the post-Holocaust world. In this world, a consciousness of unfamiliar and frightening spiritual alienation invades the post-Holocaust Jew and non-Jew alike. Whereas at Mount Sinai the children of Israel witnessed a revelation that promised redemption to them and to the world, the second generation witnesses in the parental story the "muteness" of a horrible absence, a "black hole." The consciousness of an emptiness, which has eclipsed pre-Holocaust ethics and faith, raises the specter of despair. At the same time, it communicates the extent of the second-generation witness's responsibility to work toward redemption.

Berger shows clearly that the triumph of redemptive forces is by no means assured. The ethics of the post-Holocaust world is predicated upon, on the one hand, the consciousness of unmitigated evil and, on the other hand, the awareness that evil must be prevented from defeating hope and faith. This awareness enjoins the human partner in the covenant to assume active responsibility for mending the world; at the same time, it does not eliminate the pervasive and persisting doubt whether mending is still possible. We recall Altman, who ponders her obligation as a Jew and a woman toward the Jewish world and toward the world at large. Is it still possible to revive the sense of vitality as a Jew? Is it still possible to restore validity to humanistic ethics? Can we regain the fear and trembling of faith in universal values?

In his penetrating analyses of the works of the second-generation witnesses, Berger delineates attempts to confront these questions. He identifies the trajectories of the individual's responsibility toward *klal Israel,* the Jewish community, and toward the world at large. These trajectories follow the patterns of *tikkun atzmi,* mending the self, and *tikkun olam,* mending the world.

The artists who struggle with the notion of *tikkun atzmi,* self-mending, highlight the particularity of the Jewish world in post-Holocaust reality. Their works demonstrate the struggle to understand oneself in the context of the traumatic legacy of parental past. Perhaps the best-known example of this struggle is Spiegelman's *Maus,* a comic book attempt to assimilate the memory of parental past. Spiegelman, who claims that *Maus* is an autobiography rather than fiction, depicts, in both his drawings and his text, the process whereby his father's biography has become part of his autobiography. It is important to note that while assimilating the father's story, which reshapes his self-understanding, the artist reshapes the father's story through his artistic sensibilities.

What *Maus* seems to suggest is that no matter how complex and embittered the relationships between the parents and the children are, both generations are inextricably interconnected. However powerful the parents' experience, for it to be known, its "muteness" must be shared with the child and then retold by the child. In the act of telling, the accidental survival of the Holocaust victim gains a measure of continuity; in the act of retelling, the child-witness-artist discovers a measure of meaning in his or her replacement. The story shaped through art affirms both the voluntary and the additional covenant. In telling the story of the victim, the second-generation witness undertakes a role of a "senior" covenantal partner by bearing witness to the past and taking responsibility for the memory of future generations.

The other trajectory is that of *tikkun olam,* mending the world. Works that highlight *tikkun olam* struggle for a better world, free of subjugation, inequality, and racial hatred. Here both covenants assume the universal dimension that emerges from the particular. In other words, works of art that emphasize the value of *tikkun olam* suggest that the lessons of the Holocaust need to be considered not only by Jews but by all human beings. The best examples of the trajectory of *tikkun* that encompasses the whole world are documentary films about the rescuers of the Jews in the Holocaust. These stories on film affirm the existence of goodness and raise questions that each of us must ponder. As Berger insightfully notes, the crimes of the perpetrators "do not challenge us. The deeds of the righteous do. Uncomfortable questions, accusations really, present themselves when watching and listening to these people."⁹

I would suggest that this challenge, these uncomfortable questions that face the listener or the viewer of the rescue story, open a tentative possibility of *tikkun*. The *tikkun* in the wake of the Holocaust is challenging and uncomfortable and does not promise a happy ending. On the contrary, as I was attempting to show all along, the *tikkun*, the mending, lies in the consciousness of the Hebrew expression *lo takkin*. The expression *lo takkin* describes a condition that fails to meet the standards, which does not work, which is out order. The "questioning and questing" second-generation children, as the reflection of the lost children, demonstrate the extent to which the world has been "out of order." But the reflection that the second-generation witnesses see in the eyes of the rescuers posits a question that "saves" them from becoming, to recall Bauman, the "hereditary victims," who mind only their own survival. This is the question that concludes Altman's memoir. "If it were happening now, here," she asks, "would I risk my life—and the life of my family—to save another? Would you?"¹⁰

This question, which, we all hope, will never have to be answered, is hypothetical yet very real. The story of the rescuers confronts Jews and non-Jews alike with the responsibility to work for the *tikkun* of the world with the knowledge that this world will remain *lo takkin* forever. The rescuers who saved human beings in a world condemned to destruction present us with an unsurpassable model of ethical behavior. The scarcity of their numbers teaches a chilling lesson about humanity, but their story contains the difficult message of the possibility, indeed the responsibility, of leaving a mark of goodness on this world that has been irreparably broken.

NOTES

1. Sara R. Horowitz, *Voicing the Void: Muteness and Memory in Holocaust Fiction* (Albany: State University of New York Press, 1997), 29, 30.

2. Ida Fink, "A Scrap of Time," in *Different Voices: Women and the Holocaust,* ed. Carol Rittner and John K. Roth (New York: Paragon House, 1991), 40.

3. Zygmunt Bauman, "Hereditary Victimhood: The Holocaust's Life as a Ghost," *Tikkun,* July–August 1998, 33–38.

4. Rachel Altman, "Fragments of a Broken Past," in *Different Voices,* ed. Carol Rittner and John K. Roth (New York: Paragon House, 1991), 371.

5. Lawrence L. Langer, "Moralizing the Holocaust," *Dimensions* 12, no. 1 (1998): 6.

6. Alan L. Berger, *Children of Job: American Second Generation Witnesses to the Holocaust* (Albany: State University of New York Press, 1997), 11.

7. See the articles on the chosenness of Israel by Rav Dr. Tzvi A. Yehuda in *Hadoar* 76, no. 19 (7 August 1998): 7–8; *Hadoar* 77, no. 20 (21 August 1998): 7–8; and *Hadoar* 78, no. 21 (4 September 1998): 6–7.

8. Elie Wiesel, foreword to *Children of Job: American Second-Generation Witnesses to the Holocaust,* by Alan L. Berger (Albany: State University of New York Press, 1997), vii.

9. Berger, *Children of Job,* 161.

10. Altman, "Fragments," 371.

Sara R. Horowitz

Filming the Generations
Holocaust Survivors and Their Children

ALMOST IMMEDIATELY AFTER THE LIBERATION OF THE NAZI concentration camps, film emerged as an important vehicle for documenting the Holocaust and conveying the shock of extreme atrocity. Whether they rely on original film footage or later shots of the concentration camps, personal interviews, or photographs and other artifacts, documentary films dealing with the Nazi genocide have tended to be self-consciously testimonial, public documents. Even when the focus is on an individual's experiences, the films take pains to present "objective history" alongside the survivor's recollections. These films present the Holocaust in historical perspective, as an event of great magnitude involving and affecting large numbers of people. As much as they document the past, they also emerge out of the political environment and zeitgeist of the filmmaker. Whether explicitly acknowledged or not, the past serves as a warning or justification for or explanation of the present. The past decade or so, however, has introduced a number of intimate films by children of Holocaust survivors, in Israel, in North America, and elsewhere, focusing on their own families. These films are at once biographical and autobiographical, in that each recounts the story of the filmmaker's parent (or parents), and also reflect upon the filmmaker's own relationship to the parent's past.

Part of a larger trend of children of survivors working in a variety of media and disciplines, these intimate films share some of the qualities of home movies and of historical documentation. Dealing, often for the first time, with the complicated relationship to the parents and the impact of the parents' experiences on subsequent generations, the burgeoning collection of works by children of survivors has both a public and a private dimension. As the horrors of the Holocaust recede from current or personally remembered events to a past that Primo Levi refers to, sadly, as "distant, blurred, 'historical,'"[1] works by children of survivors take on a metaphorical importance, a significance beyond the biographical. The film artists, who are literally children of Holocaust survivors, appear in their own films as themselves. At the same time, they represent the viewer, those of us who come after, struggling to understand and absorb the implications of the Holocaust in our own lives, our own world. Like the filmmakers grappling with a past at once their own and not their own, the viewer, too, belatedly tries to commemorate an event we ourselves cannot remember but whose presence infiltrates our culture.

The testimonial work of three filmmakers serves to illustrate the dynamics of these intimate films dealing with the residue of Nazi atrocity: *Ha-Behira ve-hagoral* (*Choice and Destiny*) by Israeli filmmaker Tsipi Reibenbach; *Half-Sister* and *Everything's for You*, two films by New England filmmaker Abraham Ravett; and *Punch Me in the Stomach*, a joint project of New Zealand–born performance artist Deb Filler and Canadian director Francine Zuckerman. Reibenbach's film is the most conventional aesthetically. In a straightforward chronological movement, she interviews both of her parents in their Israeli apartment. Ravett's two avant-garde films mix interviews with his parents, old photographs, brief film clips from the Nazi era, and images of the New England countryside in a surrealistic film montage. Filler performs a one-woman show, where she performs her father and other members of her extended family. The performance, a comedy, culminates her reenactment of a "whirlwind tour of Eastern European concentration camps," a trip with her father to Eastern Europe, to see the places where he had been imprisoned.

Like Art Spiegelman's now-famous *Maus*,[2] these films reveal a double story—biography and autobiography intertwined. They probe, uncover, and retell the story of the parent's past. They also explore the adult child's history of living with—and yet, in some ways, apart from—the parent. These are complicated relationships, fraught with tensions. In making public these intimate sets of stories, the films connect individual with collective memory. The adult child serves as an intermediary between the parent's world, on the one hand, and the world and culture of the child's present, on the other. The adult child is both the representative of that culture in the film—

a stand-in for the viewer—and also—bodily—a part of the parent's world. In exploring the parental legacy, the films also implicate the Holocaust in the construction of postwar Jewish identity. In different ways, these films reflect a sense of cultural identity secure enough to allow for the unpredictability of survivor testimony, which may be psychologically unsettling and may challenge convention and ideologically safe understandings of the Holocaust. As utilized in these films, survivor testimony opens up a multiplicity of memories and viewpoints, often in conflict with official and public interpretations of the Holocaust.

While these films depict vastly different experiences during and after the war, and different sets of family dynamics, the films share certain important elements. First, in each film, the survivor-parent authorizes the adult child to tell the story. After all, a child of survivors—like anyone else born later or elsewhere—cannot rely on personal experience and eyewitnessing to authenticate the stories told about the Holocaust. This authorization is integral to the film; it is asserted simply and directly, by virtue of the parent's presence in the film. Reibenbach interviews both of her parents inside their apartment. The camera follows them as they perform quotidian domestic chores, even enters the privacy of their bedroom. Ravett, too, films his parents in private spaces, in their home and his. His mother reads aloud the captions on the back of family photos for him and recites other lines at his request. Such intimate filming unequivocally implies the willing participation of the parents in the film project. In *Punch Me in the Stomach*, Filler triply affirms this authorization. In role as her father, Filler repeatedly interrupts herself in her role as herself, Deb, asking with mounting urgency, "Did you tell them yet?" In addition, the "father" validates her comic approach. After narrating his remembrance of his first night in Auschwitz as grotesquely absurd, he concludes, "We laughed the whole first night. What else could we do?" Finally, the real father makes a cameo appearance after the daughter performs his memories. Although he quibbles with a particular mortality figure she has mentioned, he expresses his approval of her performance and the accuracy of her accounts. By securing the parent's consent to the child's representation of the past, each of these films anticipates and tries to navigate what Lori Lefkovitz has referred to as "the ethics of ventriloquism"[3]—the problematic appropriation of the parent's experiences by the child.[4]

REPERCUSSIONS OF THE PAST

Second, the films reveal the repercussions of the parent's past on the child. Interpolated in Ravett's *Everything's for You* are two animation sequences, both emerging from Ravett's memory of growing up with his father and focusing on their troubled interaction. The first of these begins with the voice of Ravett's mother as she repeats several times, at her son's request, a line in Yiddish. Her voice is heard over multiple animated representations of a man beating a boy with a strap. The boy cringes on the ground until a woman restrains the man. A door closes on the three of them, with an old-fashioned skeleton key flying from the lock. The subtitle, "Henyek control yourself," appears. After a short take of the filmmaker's aging father sitting in a darkened New York apartment, the animation resumes. The skeleton key now dominates the screen, dwarfing a house in the background. The key grows smaller until it fits the keyhole, unlocking the front door and beginning the action that ensues. An apparently loving family—the same three figures seen moments earlier—emerges through the doorway. The boy happily leaps through the hole in the head of the key, which has now grown large again, to join a group of children at play. From this point until the end of the sequence, the filmmaker's voice can be heard in Yiddish, from offscreen: "Ich hob gebrochen die shloss, Pop. For vos hot mich azoy geshlangen? Zog mir, for vos?" The round key head now becomes a frame through which we see first the boy and his parents, then an old-fashioned floor clock. Finally, we see once again the beating sequence shown moments earlier. Now, in context, it becomes the clear that the father is beating his son in anger, as punishment. Only then, on a blackened screen, appears a translation of the filmmaker's words: "I broke the lock, Pop. Why did you beat me so hard? Tell me why!"

Central to this episode is the father's anger and the broken key that motivates that anger. The key fits the family's front door but at the same time also connotes a broken key to the father's past. The animation format allows Ravett to articulate a painful memory, particularly one that is critical of his father. By preceding the animation with the repeated takes of his mother's voice reading the script prepared by the filmmaker—something normally edited out of a final production—Ravett reveals this segment to be his own subjective reconstruction of the past. The use of Yiddish in the sequence is significant, as well. Here and throughout the film when he speaks with or of his father, it functions as an intimate tongue, a "papa losh'n" if you will, the language of his father's memory and of his own memory of his father. While the animation plays on-screen, the non-Yiddish-speaking viewer can only surmise what the filmmaker is saying. The struggle to understand a foreign tongue, and the belatedness of the translation, mirror Ravett's own difficulty understanding his father's past, and the belatedness and imperfection of whatever understanding he possesses.

In *Punch Me in the Stomach,* Filler attributes her origins as a performance artist to her early attempts to diffuse her father's anger. As a young child, she recalls, when she sensed her father's anger, she would begin to imitate his gestures and other idiosyncrasies. She was then already performing him, and he would laugh instead of erupting. In one short sketch, Filler acts out a telephone conversation between two daughters of survivors, one of whom is preparing to pick up the other at the airport. Their elaborately detailed contingency plans give evidence of their internalized knowledge that things can go horribly wrong at any instant. In *Ha-Behira ve- hagoral,* Reibenbach's father tells her that he wishes that the man who had saved his life had died before he had the opportunity to do so. The early death of Reibenbach's father, he explains to his daughter, would not have been a catastrophe. "You would not have been born," he concedes, "but I would have suffered less." The daughter listens, as her father contemplates undoing her existence.

PARENT-CHILD RECONCILIATION

Third, the films enact a reconciliation between the child and the parent, or the child's memory of the parent, or the child's imagining of the parent. This occurs because the adult child is now able to see the parent not only as his or her parent—that is, from the perspective of a child. An adult him- or herself, the filmmaker sees the parent also as an individual, horribly traumatized by atrocity. Frequently, in some measure, this shift in perception comes about because the adult child has become a parent. For example, Ravett's *Everything's for You* explores the Holocaust memories of Ravett's father and the ghost presence of the filmmaker's siblings who died during the Nazi genocide, of whose existence Ravett has only recently learned. Ravett focuses on the personal impact of these events—memories he cannot himself recollect but must recover from others. Through conversations with his father, Chaim, Ravett explores the dimensions of his father's past in his own life. Father-son conflicts become comprehensible and ultimately resolved and forgiven in light of the father's traumatic experiences and deep bereavement. The son learns belatedly that his father had a wife and children before the war, a family that perished under the Nazi genocide. The filmmaker struggles to imagine what it was like for his father to lose a wife and two children in the Nazi genocide.

Interspersed with conversations with his father and animated reconstructions of their troubled past interactions are scenes showing Ravett and his own young son, a toddler whom he diapers, entertains, and cares for. Ravett's son is named Chaim, after his grandfather, who died before the film project was brought to completion. One segment shows Ravett and his toddler son showering together. The scene thus suggests an intimate connection between both sets of fathers and sons—Ravett and his father and Ravett and his child— and the father's role in teaching his son what it means to be "a man." The man and child showering together conveys also a sense of acute vulnerability and cannot help but evoke for the viewer an afterimage of the false showers of the gas chambers. Thus, in this scene, Nazi atrocity is shown to mediate between father and son, to insert itself in this most intimate and formative relationship. Becoming a parent, then, awakens Ravett to the dimensions of his father's experience during the Holocaust as father. Perhaps thinking of his own small children, Ravett focuses on his father's murdered family. As Ravett's film shows original film footage of Jews in a European ghetto, Ravett's voice repeatedly questions his father—who by now is no longer alive. Ravett wonders about the elder Chaim's two small children, left behind in the ghetto while their father worked on a labor detail: "Vos hat dein kinder getin, Pop?" (What did your children do, Pop?). As in the animation sequences and elsewhere in the film, the diasporic Yiddish is the language of the Jewish past and also the intimate language between father and son. The language links the son with his father but always implies the presence of anguished memory enfolded in their relationship.

In depicting himself with both Chaims—his father and his son— Ravett's film communicates a loving father-son relationship as implicated in a complicated, composite sense of identity—as a Jew, as a man, as an American, as an artist. In contrast to most earlier films about Holocaust meaning and Jewish American identity, Ravett's film engages issues in a private, rather than a public, discourse. Representative of a generation of Jewish Americans that has been characterized as the first to be able to choose whether or not to be Jewish, and to choose from an array of Jewish possibilities, Ravett personalizes Holocaust memory as a family affair, not a focalizing point for Jewish destiny, Jewish community, or Jewish survival.[5] Although Holocaust commemoration has been referred to frequently as a the "civic religion" of secular American Jews, Ravett's films do not depict it as such. For example, Ravett's father expresses his preference that his son marry a Jewish woman. Chaim casts this desire in terms of compatibility through shared culture (someone who is "like" Abraham), but he does not invoke the Nazi genocide to buttress his argument.[6]

Reibenbach's film, too, relies on the presence of the third generation—the grandchildren of the survivor—to enable the adult child to engage with the parents' story of survival.[7] Reibenbach's parents' story unfolds in the presence of their Israeli grandchildren. And, just as Ravett breaks with popular American ways of viewing the Holocaust, Reibenbach challenges Israeli visions. Reibenbach's film intersperses contemporary domestic scenes—survivors cooking and baking bread and cakes for their grandchildren—with the father's description of gruesome aspects of the struggle to survive conditions of atrocity: drinking urine when thirsty or cannibalizing bodies from the Mauthausen gas chamber if any flesh remained on them. These ghastly details prevent survival from being construed as glorious and heroic. The film thus breaks with the convention of official Israeli narratives of the past wherein the new Israeli Jew sees himself in the exceptional Shoah hero rather than in the victim.

Throughout the film, Reibenbach's mother silently busies herself with cooking and cleaning chores while the father speaks. Bursting with emotions and memories that she wants to reveal but cannot, she is visibly in internal conflict. Only at the film's end does she speak up. She tells her daughter that she cannot stop the flow of memories, the resurfacing of losses. Since the filming has begun, the mother cannot fall asleep. When alone, she walks around the apartment calling the dead by name. All these years, she explains, she had not wanted to speak about her experiences. But now, suddenly, she finds herself compelled to do so. The entire family, especially the Israeli- born grandchildren, watch her emotional outburst. In essence, this film is not only about the memory of European-born Shoah survivors but about the younger generation of Israelis seeking and accepting the history of their elders. The mother's long-deferred speech takes place in a room full of young Israelis; their willingness to listen to unbridled testimony makes her act of witnessing possible. Like the father's detailed description of atrocity—and his admission that he would have preferred death to survival, even at the cost of his daughter's existence—the mother's long-deferred speech in the presence of her grandchildren interrupts a theological-political discourse which sees the suffering of European Jews redeemed by the birth of the State of Israel. Implied in the film is a rejection of the more ideologically determined narratives of *Shoah ve-gevurah*—destruction and heroism. The willingness of the Israeli family to listen to the grandparents' story represents the willingness of contemporary Israel to look anew at the Jewish past. The film depicts the listening posture of the family as the necessary catalyst for the parents' reexamination of the past. Indeed, one might say that the film could be made (the family was ready to listen) because the narrative of heroism had already begun to unravel.

In different ways, both Reibenbach and Ravett utilize in their films the trope of the third generation as facilitator of memory and reconciliation. *Punch Me in the Stomach,* too, invokes this trope, but only to subvert it. *Punch* contrasts the single, childless state of Deb with her younger sister Estelle's redemptive fertility—a concept the film mocks. Estelle boasts that she is "very, very fertile," noting the pleasure her parents derive from grandchildren that she alone provides. However, Estelle's motherhood has not brought her an understanding of her father's trauma and its effect on her generation. Instead, as Filler portrays her—and Filler plays all the roles in the film—Estelle reenacts her parents' trauma. Speaking with Deb and her offscreen film crew, Estelle compulsively wipes and rewipes the kitchen counter, giggling nervously. In their presence, she telephones her husband several times. On each occasion, having waited a nanosecond for him to answer the phone, she blurts out, "What took you so long to pick up?" Filler's brother-in-law, an Israeli immigrant to New Zealand, runs a home security business, installing burglar alarms. "New Zealand is a very dangerous place," we hear him telling a potential customer on his cell phone. "Six alarms is the minimum you need in one house." Estelle's anxieties suggest the return of the repressed trauma passed whole cloth to yet another generation. By contrast, Deb—the childless sister—travels to Eastern Europe with her father and becomes the witness to her father's memory. This journey brings the two closer, and the film ends with the image of the real father and his performer daughter leaving the theater after her performance, their arms around one another. The performance we have just seen turns out to have been staged for him; after Filler's closing monologue, she breathes a deep sigh, and the camera pans the interior of a theater. The theater is empty, except for her father.

IMPOSSIBILITY OF KNOWING

Perhaps most disturbingly, each of the films admits the ultimate unknowability of the parent's past, despite the child's best efforts. In Reibenbach's *Ha-Behira ve-hagoral,* the father touches on ghastly memories and a despair that only hints at what he experienced. The film closes with the mother's declaration that she is ready to speak to her family about her experiences, but what she says remains undisclosed.[8]

Ravett struggles, in both *Half-Sister* and *Everything's for You,* with the impossibility of knowing the half siblings who perished during the war—his father's two children, his mother's daughter. In an early sequence in *Half-Sister,* the camera closes in on a photograph of Ravett's long-dead half sister. This photograph, belatedly arriving into Ravett's life, is the only trace of his mother's murdered daughter. The camera comes in closer and closer, as if somehow to penetrate the image in the photograph and touch the essence of this lost sibling. But as the camera closes in, the photograph reveals no secrets, only the texture of the paper, the shadings of ink. Significantly, at several points the film rolls silently as the mother is shown speaking. The soundlessness acknowledges her profound bereavement as unspeakable, unknowable.

The trip to Eastern Europe in *Punch Me in the Stomach* serves only to reinforce the sense that Filler ultimately cannot bridge the distance between herself and her father. In the scene that opens her reenactment of this trip, Deb and her father drive through the Polish countryside. As Deb admires the bucolic beauty of a field of corn, her father tells her that he once saw a French woman shot in the head in that field. The disparity between what each sees demonstrates to Filler that she cannot fathom her father's past, despite her sense that "in a way, it was my Holocaust, too." The car sequence ends with Deb telling her father about a children-of-survivors group she attended in New York. Her father reacts incredulously to the idea that such people might have personal problems. "What? What are you telling me? Their parents are survivors and they have those problems? Drugs? Prostitution? Attempted suicide? No. . ." Her father then turns to his daughter and asks, "You never had any problems, did you, darling?" When she does not respond immediately he repeats, "Did you?" indicating that his question is not merely rhetorical but demands a response. After a pause, she offers an answer containing the reassurance he seeks but which the rest of the film gives the lie to: "No, Dad." Her father's need to see her as "happy" precludes his understanding the effects of the Shoah on her. And, although she believes the war to be "her" Holocaust, too, once in Eastern Europe she realizes that she does not possess these memories, only their afterimage. Moreover, since she does not know which particular field was once a place of atrocity, which market square a killing ground, she can never be certain that any spot was not.

Finally, each of the films deliberately discomfits the viewer, disturbing the viewer's assumptions about and ways of living with the Holocaust past. In Reibenbach's film, the father's ghastly memories and regrets about surviving interrupt certain staples of Israeli Holocaust remembrance—heroism and martyrdom—and unravel the more ideologically determined narratives. Ravett's avant-garde style unsettles the viewer, who cannot be certain of seeing what is there, of understanding the film, much less the Holocaust. Filler's use of transgressive humor and performativity sets the viewer on edge.

While these new and intimate ways of examining the resonances of the Holocaust have not displaced the more communal, historical representations, they exist alongside them in a growing compendium of cinematic representations of Holocaust memories and meanings. The range of these Holocaust representations enriches and deepens our understanding of the Holocaust past and the shaping and reshaping of Jewish identity.

NOTES

1. Primo Levi, *The Drowned and the Saved,* trans. Raymond Rosenthal (New York: Summit, 1986).

2. Art Spiegelman, *Maus I, A Survivor's Tale: My Father Bleeds History* (New York: Pantheon, 1986); Art Spiegelman, *Maus II, A Survivor's Tale: And Here My Troubles Began* (New York: Pantheon, 1991).

3. Lori Lefkovitz, "Inherited Holocaust Memory and the Ethics of Ventriloquism," *Kenyon Review* 29 (Winter 1997): 34–43.

4. In *Maus,* Spiegelman depicts his father telling his story while the son takes notes or runs a tape recorder. The comix even depicts Art showing his father portions of the work in progress.

5. While Joel Brandt's earlier film *Kaddish,* about the relationship between Yossi Klein and his father, a Holocaust survivor, contains much of this personal element, *Kaddish* contemplates the competing meanings of the Holocaust for the Boro Park community that Klein's family inhabits and for the radicalized Jewish American youths of the 1960s. Here, the conflicts of Jewish American identity are resolved for Yossi by *aliyah* (emigration to Israel).

6. Marriage to a non-Jewish wife as a means of redeeming or reversing the inherited trauma is a recurrent trope in European and North American writing by and about sons of Holocaust survivors, and sometimes male survivors themselves. In an insightful essay, Froma Zeitlin has observed, "Both [Isaac Bashevis] Singer and [Art] Spiegelman . . . also equate the tainted and death-centered past with the Jewish feminine, a past that can only be overcome through the generative power of the Gentile wife." Froma Zeitlin, "The Vicarious Witness: Belated Memory and Authorial Presence in Recent Holocaust Literature," *History and Memory* 10, no. 2 (1998): 34.

7. The trope of the third generation figures also in the second volume of *Maus,* which contains a photo portrait of a child as a frontispiece, bearing a dedication to memory of Richieu, the author's half-brother who was murdered during the Holocaust, as well as to Nadia (literally, Hope), Spiegelman's first child. In fact, since the name of one child is on top of the photo and the name of the other beneath it, there is some ambiguity about whose photograph we are actually seeing.

8. A later Reibenbach film focuses on her mother.

Robert Melson

False Papers
*The Tension between Testimony and Story
in a Holocaust Memoir*

STORY AND TESTIMONY

ON OCTOBER 12, 1941, MOST OF THE JEWS OF STANISLAWOW, A MIDSIZE
town in Polish Galicia, were massacred by units of the SS and the Order Police under the command of Hans Krueger. My parents and I
survived because, mistrusting the Germans' motives, we had refused
to go to the place of assembly and went into hiding. Later, my mother
was able to acquire false papers of identity that enabled us to imper-
sonate a Polish Catholic family until the end of the war. Most other
Jews were less lucky. My grandfather, my father's father, committed
suicide before his arrest by the Gestapo. My other grandparents, my
mother's parents, were first interned in the Warsaw Ghetto and then
killed in the Treblinka death camp. After the war, I heard about many
other relatives who had been murdered, but either I did not know
them or could not remember them.

In 1978, thirty-three years after the war, I finally had the courage
and enough background knowledge about the war to interview my
parents and to begin to shape the story of our survival. Most of the
story is based on seventeen hours of taped interviews that I conducted
in separate sessions with my mother and father and on my own recollections and re-creations of the past. Then for fifteen years I set the
interviews aside, and it wasn't until I had written a book on the history of the Holocaust and the Armenian genocide, and my parents
had passed away, that I returned to my interviews with them and
completed a memoir entitled *False Papers*.[1]

The interviews with my mother were conducted in Polish, her

mother tongue, which I later translated into English. Those with my father were conducted in English, although he would have felt more comfortable speaking German, the language of his birth. Much of the story I knew already, from having lived it with my parents and from having heard them tell their versions many times before, but some of the details were a surprise even now, many years later. I was two when the war started and eight when it ended. I have my own childhood snatches of memory of that time, which start out rather dimly but become clearer near the end of the war as I was getting older.

We conducted the interviews in my parents' apartment in Cambridge, Massachusetts, off Central Square, in a decaying part of town. They had been living with my younger brother Richard—he was born after the war—for a number of years, ever since my father's business had failed. That same year, my father underwent open-heart surgery and discovered that he had cancer. Earlier my mother had suffered a severe depression, which left her speechless and nearly immobilized until she received electroshock therapy. Neither was in good health, and they were in strained economic circumstances.

Given their situation at the time of the interviews, and our awful memories of the war, one would think that our sessions would have been permeated with gloom, but they were not. At some moments we recalled the past with sorrow, but at others we dissolved in laughter at the recollection of some ridiculous event. The interviews transported my parents, Willy and Nina, to a terrible era, but also to a time when they were young, attractive, strong, and resourceful enough to outwit Hitler and his Nazi killers.

Since I am a survivor and the son of survivors, in writing about our experiences, I felt a special responsibility to be true to my parents' and my own memory of the events. I felt like I was a witness at a supremely important trial. My testimony had to be pure and true, out of respect for the memory of those who could no longer speak for themselves and for the deliberations of future generations. Yet, I also wanted to tell a compelling story that would bring our experiences to life. The result was that I felt uneasy about being both a son—privy to his family's secrets—and a chronicler of his family's history, a witness and a storyteller.

I tried to be truthful by neither denying nor embellishing my parents' exploits nor suppressing incriminating or embarrassing moments. My parents showed extraordinary courage, resourcefulness, and kindness during the war. Indeed, they managed to save not only our immediate family but also my uncle and three Jewish women, chance acquaintances, one of whom became my aunt. It was risky business to include such strangers in our charade, since at any moment we might have been betrayed for being Jews trying to pass as so-called Aryans. However, neither Nina nor Willy, nor I, for that matter, were candidates for sainthood.

At one point in the interview, when she recalled being a young woman in prewar Poland, Nina said that she had rejected a suitor because, "He looked too Jewish." "I despised that look," she added for good measure. (I should add that she fell head over heels in love with my father, who was quite handsome and distinctly "Jewish-looking" in a blond and blue-eyed Polish context.) At another juncture, Willy discussed his wartime affair with a Czech woman as if it were inconsequential. In each of these instances, as their son and memoirist, I was tempted to suppress the incriminating evidence. I was startled that my mother, whom I adored, had a streak of Jewish self-hatred, and I worried that my father's wartime exploits, during which he saved all our lives many times over, would somehow dim because of his propensity to womanize. But I left these things in on purpose.

I wished to pit our very bodies, our quirky, sexy, funny, wicked, frail, and ordinary selves against the totalizing, flattening, unrelenting, undifferentiating, and grotesque fantasy concerning race and the "Jewish world conspiracy" that had Germany and so much of Christian Europe in its grip during the war. Let our faults stick out, I thought, they only make us real.

I was determined to commemorate my parents not as martyrs and heroes but as the authentic people I knew. It was after all not caricatures but living human beings, with their light and dark sides, their strengths and their weaknesses, their goodness and their badness, who perished. And it was real people like my parents and me who survived. As I. B. Singer, writing of the Polish Jewish generation preceding the war, put it in *Shosha*, "The generations that will come after us . . . will consider all of us holy martyrs. They will recite kaddish after us and 'God Full of Mercy.' Actually everyone of us will die with the same passions he lived with." My family, I know, lived and died with many passions.

The original interviews with my parents took the conventional question-and-answer format, with my posing the question and their responding, but the final product is a continuous manuscript based on their interviews but not the protocols of the interviews themselves. I wished to be as truthful as I could; however, unlike testimony at a trial, the structure of a narrative creates its own demands for continuity, pacing, color, all the elements that make for a "good story." I supplied historical information that they didn't know, details that they had left out. In some places, I had one say things that were said by the other. In sum, I shaped these interviews into a narrative somewhat in the manner of a novelist. And that's why I felt additional unease between being a credible witness and a good storyteller.

The remainder of this essay is the voice of my mother telling how she got the false papers of identity that enabled us to survive the war.

NINA

The morning of October 12, 1941, I woke up toward dawn. I'd had a disturbing dream and was drenched in sweat.

"Let's get out right now," I said to Willy. "We don't even have time to wash up."

I was getting dressed, as Willy examined me with the dumb look of someone just woken out of deep sleep.

"I am certain the Gestapo will come this morning to arrest us. We'll be killed. We've got to leave immediately."

"You're insane," Willy said.

I usually go along with him, but I knew we were in grave danger, and I had to get us out of the house.

"Let's take Sylvio and let's get out now!" I pulled the child out of bed and started to dress him. Sylvio was confused and kept falling back asleep in my arms. He smelled sweet like newly mowed hay.

Ever so grudgingly, Willy got out of bed.

"What makes you think we're in danger?" He slipped a black ski parka over his head.

"Last night I had a dream: My father stood in the middle of a town square. He was surrounded by a bright light, and was holding up a placard with the number 12 printed on it over his head. He then waved me over. When I approached him, he said, 'Take care, you're in grave danger! You're in grave danger!' I tried to touch him, but he turned away and faced a blank wall. That's when I woke up. Today is October 12—something terrible is going to happen . . .'"

Without further questions, the three of us fled to friends who lived out of town. The Offenbergers, Jews who had converted to Catholicism, knew the Mendelsohn family from before the war. We walked for three hours. Sylvio was cranky, so Willy and I took turns carrying him part of the way.

When we arrived, we simply said that we feared for our lives. Could they help? During the war no long explanations were necessary. I didn't tell them about my dream, I was too embarrassed. They'd think I was hysterical, but they didn't question us further.

"Of course," they said. "First let's have lunch, and then we'll show you where you can stay."

They were a middle-aged couple, possibly in their forties. He wore glasses and had thinning blond hair, while she was short and plump and looked very Jewish to me. In every room of their two-story house there hung a crucifix, which made me feel uneasy because I still thought of them as Jews. Willy told me that they had become Catholics way before the war, not because of any advantage it might bring them but because they were genuine believers. That made no difference to me. All I cared was that they were kind and brave. Everyone knew that they could be killed for hiding Jews.

After a midday dinner of hot vegetable barley soup and baked pigeons with potatoes—luxuries during the war—they took us downstairs to a cellar filled with straw and told us to make ourselves at home.

I heard some scurrying and scratching under all that straw. I'm terrified of mice and rats, but I was so relieved to be out of Hela's house and in a safe place that I stretched out with great pleasure. Willy lay down next to me, and Sylvio, having jumped up and down in the pile of straw, crawled in between us and fell asleep. Willy and I said very little. What was there to discuss? We listened to the sounds of the Offenbergers moving above us, but somehow I found that comforting, and I fell into a deep sleep.

While we slept the Jews of Stanislawow were being killed. Preparations had started in July 1941 when the German army had marched into the city. Willy's hometown had a population of about sixty thousand people, half of whom were Jews. First the Germans established a *Judenrat,* a Jewish council, that was supposed to help them in running the Jewish community. Then they rounded up other Jews who might have become opposition leaders—teachers, doctors, lawyers, journalists—and so on. The victims were told to bring their books and to assemble at Gestapo headquarters. Among this early group were photographers, I suppose because the killers were afraid of photographic evidence.

When he first heard the announcement, Willy wanted to go. Reminded me that he had a diploma from the Handelshochschule, a business school in Berlin. Since he spoke perfect German, perhaps he could make himself useful, like under the Russians. But I told him to forget about it. That was the first time he had trusted my intuition. One of Willy's uncles went. He was never heard from again. None of the men who went ever returned.

On October 12, 1941, after posting placards in public, the Germans ordered the Jews to assemble in the center of town. Thousands of people showed up, with all their pathetic belongings. Some even brought their pets! They were loaded onto trucks and driven to the new Jewish cemetery where they found SS, German police units, and Ukrainian militia waiting. They were first told to undress and to line up in front of previously dug ditches; then they were machine-gunned to death.

Hans Krueger, the commander in charge of the operation, had brought a picnic with him. He picked people off at random and shot them in the head with his service revolver in his right hand while he munched on a sandwich with his left. Later the bodies were covered over with earth by Ukrainian laborers. The killing lasted from 11 a.m. to 7:30 p.m. The *Judenrat,* standing stark naked with the rest, was made to watch the proceedings. Shooting was halted by darkness, although it continued for a while under the headlights of trucks.

A few people, including one of Willy's high school girlfriends, escaped by feigning death until nightfall. They managed to dig themselves out from among the bodies in the ditches and to climb over the 2–3 meter high wall of the cemetery. Other Jews like us survived because they had refused to go to the original roundup. Willy told me that after the *Aktion,* Krueger sent his blood-stained tunic to the *Judenrat* for cleaning.

The next morning, after thanking the Offenbergers, we went back to Hela's.[2] We didn't want to overstay our welcome and endanger them. By the time we got home in the evening, we had heard about the massacre. When we opened the door, there was a party. Hela, wearing my favorite red dress, which was much too tight on her, was surrounded by her Ukrainian friends who were singing and drinking vodka. I asked Willy to stay in the hall. They would see a man, and there would be trouble. When I walked in, Hela was dumbfounded.

"Madame is still alive?"

"You see, I'm still alive."

"I feel real bad that I'm wearing your dress."

We exchanged looks, she turned away. Then she chased all her Ukrainian friends out of the house, took off the dress, and got right back to work. She washed Sylvio and prepared dinner for us as if nothing had happened. Hela was no angel, but she stood by us when we needed her.

The next day I went to the *Gmina,* the seat of the Jewish council, to find out more about what had happened. The few Jewish acquaintances that I ran into seemed like shadows. They would sidle up, whisper a few words, and quickly move on. I found it all very bizarre. No one grieved or showed any emotion whatsoever. People would mention that their wives or husbands or children or parents had been shot, but they did so without expression, almost as if it were distant news. I was no different. I, too, spoke in the same impersonal tone of voice. My body was chilled. Half the time I was trembling, and my vocal chords seemed paralyzed.

At first, Willy stayed home because he was afraid of being recognized. Later he was able to get a hold of a railroad worker's uniform, including an official-looking cap that allowed him to get out at dusk. On one of his walks he had seen a small crowd surrounding two elderly religious Jews, still dressed in their long black caftans, being humiliated by German troopers.

The two old men were on their hands and knees while two grinning Germans were straddling their backs as if they were riding horses. A race was on, and the old Jews, their beards mostly cut off or pulled off, were being whipped about their bloody faces and buttocks to "gallop" as fast as they could. Other troopers, laughing and shouting, were placing bets as to which of the two "riders" would come in first.

Willy tore himself from the crowd and ran blindly home. He told me the story without looking at me, as if he were addressing the air. I could sense his rage and grief. But when I asked him what we should do, he replied simply, "I don't know."

For a while Willy thought that we could save ourselves by getting converted like the Offenbergers. He went to a priest for help. The priest, an elderly man, totally bald, dressed in a black cassock, with a heavy cross dangling from his neck, was very cheerful about the whole thing. He told Willy that it might take six months of heartfelt study and dedication to get converted. When Willy pointed out that he didn't have six months, the priest shrugged, and announced that it was impossible. As Willy left, the good man urged him to take an apple from a bowl on his desk.

Willy didn't realize that conversion wouldn't have helped anyway. The Offenbergers, whom we had envied for their foresight, were later murdered with all the others when the Jews of Stanislawow were shipped off to the Belzec extermination camp. But that came later.

Soon after the massacre of October 12, the Germans blocked off a few streets and ordered the surviving Jews to move into a ghetto. The Carpens, friends of ours who owned a bakery, came to visit and proposed that the two families look together for a place to stay. I agreed. I liked them because, although they had been reduced to being humble bakers, they were charming, good-looking, and had a great sense of humor. He looked like Leslie Howard, the actor in *Gone with the Wind*. I always preferred Clark Gable, but Leslie Howard was sweet.

"Let's do it, Willy, " I pleaded. "We must, and it will be nice living together." I tried to make it seem almost cozy to cheer us all up. But Willy, who had been silent while we were discussing plans, would have none of it. "Never!" he shouted. "I'm not going into any ghetto. If they're going to kill me, let them kill me here!"

"But you're endangering yourself, Willy," said Carpen.

"No, you are. Don't you understand that in the ghetto we'll all be killed? Outside we have a slim chance."

The Carpens left shaking their heads.

The night we were supposed to move into the ghetto, Willy and I stayed up to discuss what to do. We figured that our time at Hela's was running out. Every day she reported that friends were asking her about her strange guests. We had a child, which under the circumstances made things more difficult. We had very little money, only some junk to barter—an old typewriter, Willy's bicycle, a sewing machine, a few good dresses and suits. Meanwhile, we were all condemned to death simply for being Jews. We had to find some way of passing as "Aryans," and we had to get out of Stanislawow, but how? Toward morning Willy and I decided that our only chance was the Zamojskis. When we finally went to bed that night we slept restlessly, listening to strange sounds from the street and the creak of floorboards on the stairs.

We had met the Zamojskis by chance one evening a few months before the war at the Unionka, a café and "dancing." The place was crowded and smoke-filled. An orchestra was playing a set of chardash Gypsy music, and then it switched to tangos and fox-trots so that people could dance. The proprietor, who knew us, apologized, but there were no empty tables, would we mind sitting with another couple? He then led us to a corner table where we met the Zamojskis.

Jan Zamojski stood up, clicked his heels, and pulled out a chair. He was tall, bony, sandy-haired, wore glasses, and was dressed in a somewhat worn double-breasted tailor-made flannel suit. Janina Zamojski was rather plain looking. She was a fleshy blond with watery-blue eyes, but she was well educated and well spoken. After the introductions, Willy and I realized that we had been seated next to descendants of Polish aristocrats who bore an illustrious name. The family Zamojski was old-time nobility. They had been state builders and prime ministers. In Poland the name was as famous as Copernicus, Mickiewic, and Radziwill. When we introduced ourselves as "Mendelsohn," Jan and Janina Zamojski did not let on that it made a difference, but they plainly realized that, charming or not, we were Jews.

The two couples danced, exchanged partners, chatted and flirted. Even Janina and I hit it off when we discovered that we both had little boys nearly the same age. I was especially pleased to make their acquaintance. To speak frankly, I found most of the people I had met in Stanislawov before the war dull and boring. They were rather primitive, even the Jews. I missed Warsaw, its cafés, theaters, films, and nightlife. Now, by pure chance, Willy and I had met another young, urbane couple, named Zamojski, no less. Willy, ever the cynic, remarked later when we got to know them better that though he may have been well educated and had a famous name, Jan Zamojski was a petty clerk in the town's administration. The Zamojskis of Stanislawow had no castles, no horses, and no lands. But I was beaming!

We met quite frequently before the war and during the Soviet occupation. We didn't invite each other home. Jews and Gentiles didn't do such things, but we agreed to meet at the Unionka or at some other restaurant. By the time of the German occupation, we were not exactly close friends, but we were acquaintances who were fond of each other.

One afternoon, a few weeks after the formation of the ghetto, I decided to go to the Zamojskis to ask for help. When I knocked, Janina opened the door and seemed startled to see me, but she quickly recovered. This was the first time that either one of us had visited the other at home.

"Nacia! How nice. Come in."

I was relieved by the cordial reception. She hadn't thrown me out or called me a lousy Jew. Still, I was disappointed by their rather shabby apartment. In my mind I had built up the Zamojskis as rich and powerful and had hoped for something more grand than a nondescript living room, a kitchen, and a bedroom, with a few portraits of the family hanging on the walls.

Boguslaw (Bobi) Zamojski, their little towheaded, blue-eyed kid, was playing with blocks on the floor while Jan Zamojski came out of the kitchen smiling and wiping his hands on a towel. They served tea and some homemade cookies. After the usual banalities, I came quickly to the point.

"You know what's been happening under the Germans. The Jews are sentenced to death. Willy, Sylvio, and I are in hiding. We don't know what to do. I've come here to ask for your for help. You're our last chance."

Jan Zamojski looked sympathetic but confused. "Us? How can we help you?"

"You could let us have your papers of identification, especially your birth certificates. Willy, Sylvio, and I would leave Stanislawow and make a life for ourselves somewhere else. Meanwhile, you could go to church and get new birth certificates. You could tell the priest that you had lost your documents or that the Soviets had confiscated them from you. It's our only chance."

I had rehearsed that speech with Willy, but now I realized how bizarre the proposal must sound.

Jan and Janina listened silently, observing me over the rim of their teacups. When I finished, Janina stood up, picked up her little boy, and signaled Jan to accompany her. The three Zamojskis disappeared into the bedroom. I could hear the little boy protesting being put to bed. Then I heard some whispering. Finally Jan and Janina came out to face me in the living room. They looked uncomfortable and embarrassed standing in front of me, while I was seated.

"I'm sorry," said Jan, his eyes downcast. "We realize what a difficult situation you're in, but so are we all. We can't just hand over our birth certificates. If the Germans got wind of it, we'd all be killed . . ." he paused, allowing that thought to sink in. "As you can see from where we live," he gestured vaguely to take in their flat, "we are in very difficult straits. After the Russians and the Germans got through with us, we've got nothing left. We have no money and live from day to day. . ." Here he paused again, while my heart skipped a beat. "Willy comes from a well-to-do family . . . There must be some money left . . . Perhaps for twenty thousand Zlotys, about five thousand dollars, we could let you have the documents . . ."

"It's true," added Janina with finality. "We could get us new birth certificates at the church. In the meanwhile, of course, you'd have to leave Stanislawow."

"So it's a simple business proposition!" exclaimed Willy with anger, clenching his jaw. "Our lives for twenty thousand Zlotys. And where are we supposed to find this treasure? Maybe we can sell the bicycle and the sewing machine, we'll throw my suits and your dresses into the bargain, and then we'll have about five hundred Zlotys! What the hell are we supposed to do, take Sylvio by his sweaty little hand while he drags his potty behind him and start marching down the road in winter?" He ran his hands through his long, unkempt hair, which seemed like a gesture of despair.

I started to cry. The Zamojskis were our last chance. Now that was gone. We were sentenced to death. We didn't know why, and we didn't know where next to turn.

That night I couldn't sleep. I had taken a few drops of valerian, hoping that it would help, but all it did was to increase my restlessness. The next morning I got up with a desperate plan: I would go back to the Zamojskis. I didn't tell Willy, because I didn't want to disappoint him should my scheme fail, and I was afraid that he would stop me from going. I left in the afternoon, after making a lame excuse that I needed to go shopping.

When I knocked on their door, the Zamojskis were in a good mood. They may have assumed that I was bringing the money and that their economic problems were over. Once again the three of us sat in the living room. Bobi was asleep in the bedroom, and Janina served bitter-tasting phony ersatz coffee. You couldn't get real coffee during the war.

"My dear friends," I started. "I spoke to Willy about your proposal. He thinks the price is a bit steep, but he can raise the money. There is no problem from our end. In the meanwhile, I've come to inspect the 'merchandise,' you understand. I need to see what your birth certificates and other documents look like. I hope you don't mind." I smiled. I tried to exude calm and confidence.

The Zamojskis looked disappointed. They exchanged knowing glances, but after a moment's hesitation, he said, "You'll have to excuse us for a few minutes." Then they both disappeared into the bedroom. A few minutes later they came out with the documents. There were birth certificates and wedding certificates. These were passes to life. How I envied their being Polish and not Jewish! But I tried to look as nonchalant as possible as I inspected the merchandise. While the Zamojskis left me alone and busied themselves in the kitchen, I tried to memorize the pertinent information: names, dates, places. I scratched whatever facts I could on the flap of my worn brown leather shoulder bag, breaking a nail in the process.

After a few minutes they returned with a bottle of schnapps and some glasses, which I refused because I needed to keep a clear head. As I left I told them that I'd be back with the money in a few days.

"It's a large sum," I said, "but Willy will manage to raise it. Don't you worry."

When I heard the door of their apartment close behind me, I descended to the ground floor. I sat on their pitch-dark staircase, and by the light of matches I wrote furiously into a child's small lined notebook that I had brought with me just for this purpose. I copied whatever facts I could remember and make out from the scratches on my pocketbook: Jan Ferdynand Zamojski, Boguslaw Marian Zamojski, Janina Victoria Zamojska, born in Lvov on such and such a date, baptized in Stanislawow at the church of so and so. Good.

The next morning around eleven, again I gave Willy a lame excuse about needing to go out to barter for food. I wore pale rose lipstick that suited me, I covered my hair in a blue silk babushka in a rose flower pattern, I pulled on a pair of prewar, fur-lined black leather winter boots, and I wore my black woolen coat, which was starting to look ratty, belted at the waist. I did the best I could to look presentable. I knew I looked like a hundred Polish young women all boiled into one, and I spoke the Polish of the upper classes. Thus armed, I proceeded to the church where all the Zamojskis had been baptized.

The tall black iron-wrought gates of the church were open. I felt giddy as I proceeded toward the priest's outer office. The place was very busy with clerks and parishioners; nevertheless, a young man stood up and gave me his seat. Polish men are very polite, especially when it comes to a pretty woman.

"Perhaps, Madame would like a teensy smoke?" The clerk offered me a cigarette. He used the cute and polite form of the diminutive when speaking to me. The thought that, despite everything, I still had my appeal gave me confidence.

I sat down, lit up, grateful for the cigarette, and realized to my surprise that I was as calm as a rock. I decided to treat the whole experience like a performance at the Adria. I recalled fat Moskowitz and how he had tried to kiss me, and I smiled to myself.[3] Finally I was ushered into the priest's study. He was an elderly man, perhaps seventy, tall, totally bald, dressed in a black cassock, a huge cross dangling from his neck. He had been standing, paging through a book, but he sat down behind his desk without offering me a seat. I realized with a start that he was the same priest who had refused to give Willy the conversion documents. In front of me was the bowl of apples that he had once offered Willy. But when I looked again, I thought he had a plain but sympathetic face and a cheerful disposition; suddenly, I was prepared to like him.

"How can I help you, Madame?" he asked.

I smiled and answered him in the most disarming way I could, "But Father, don't you remember me?"

The good father looked bewildered. There is a Yiddish expression that goes: *Haben dem Fisch bei der Schwontz*. Holding the fish by its tail. I knew he couldn't possibly remember me. So I repeated the question:

"Father, don't you remember me?"

"There's been so many people here today. It's hard to remember everyone."

"I'm Countess Zamojska! Janina Zamojska!"

For a moment he looked like he was going to faint. He stood up and started bustling about. The Zamojski name had produced its magic.

"My dear countess! Your excellency! Please have a seat! How about some tea or a little glass of wine?"

"No. Thank you. I never drink in the morning." For some reason I thought of Willy back at Hela's and what he might make of this scene.

"My dear Father, I've come here to ask you for a huge favor . . . The Russians before they left confiscated all our documents. They were about to arrest us and deport us, but then the Germans came. The Russians, the Germans, may the cholera take them both away! In any case, we don't have a single piece of identification. Should the Gestapo ask for our papers, we have nothing to show them, and we're likely to be in a lot of trouble. Perhaps, dear Father, you can help me in this matter. I was baptized here. So was my husband. So was my little boy. I need birth certificates for the three of us." I needed his help, but I didn't want to look pitiful, so I gave him my most radiant smile.

"There is no problem, my dear countess," he said. "Let me just jot down a few details."

He took a pad of paper and a pen and began to question me:

"Your full name. Your date of birth. Your place of birth. Your mother's name. Your father's name. Your husband's full name. His date of birth. His place of birth. His father's name. His mother's name. Your son's name. His date of birth. His place of birth . . ."

I had been a quick study back at the Adria. I was prepared, and I never faltered.

He rose and excused himself. "Why don't you just wait a few minutes and have a cigarette. My clerk will type out the birth certificates for you, and I'll keep a copy. They might be of use at a later date."

I thought I had stepped through the screen into a movie. At any moment the director would come into the room and tell me that I was acting in a silly comedy and that I should go home. I also thought how impressed Willy would be with my chutzpah.

A few minutes later the good father returned with the documents. I glanced at them and stuck them nonchalantly in my purse.

As I got up to leave, the priest came from behind his desk and kissed my hand.

"We'll be in touch," I smiled and waved gaily at him as I left.

On the way home, I stopped every few minutes to look into my purse to make sure that the documents were still there. I felt I'd burst like a balloon. I had pulled it off! Now we had a slim chance.

When I got home, I took Willy aside. "Willushu, darling," I whispered, "I've got the papers."

"What?" He almost shouted. "What papers?"

"Willy, dear, here's your new birth certificate. You're now 'Count Jan Ferdynand Zamojski.' I'm 'Countess Janina Zamojska.' You can call me 'Nina' from now on. And Sylvio is little 'Count Boguslaw 'Bobi' Zamojski.'"

Willy took the documents to the window and for a few minutes studied them carefully. Then he hugged me gently to him, and like a small child I started to bawl.

From now on we were Jan, Janina, and Boguslaw (Bobi) Zamojski. Sylvio was four years old and had learned his name, but Willy and I tried to impress on him how important it was that he be "Bobi Zamojski" instead of "Sylvio Mendelsohn." He was a smart little kid and must have sensed that we were living in dangerous times. I don't know how, but he soon responded to being called "Bobi," and it was just as well that in time he forgot he had ever been Sylvio.

NOTES

1. See Robert Melson, *Revolution and Genocide: On the Origins of the Armenian Genocide and the Holocaust* (University of Chicago Press, 1992); Robert Melson, *False Papers* (Urbana: University of Illinois Press, 2000).

2. Hela was a young Ukrainian woman who had been our cook before the war. During the Soviet occupation, we moved in with her. Under the Nazis, she shielded us from both the Germans and their Ukrainian collaborators. She was one of the "righteous Gentiles" in our family history who enabled us to survive the war.

3. The Adria was a nightclub in prewar Warsaw where Nina had once performed as a singer. Moskowitz had been the owner-proprietor.

Notes on Contributors

MICHAEL ALLEN is an associate professor of European history and the history of technology at the Georgia Institute of Technology in Atlanta. His publications include *The Business of Genocide*.

DAVID BANKIER is a professor of Holocaust studies at the Institute of Contemporary Jewry, Hebrew University of Jerusalem and the head of the International Institute for Holocaust Research at Yad Vashem. He is the author and editor of books and essays on modern anti-Semitism and the Holocaust, among them *The Germans and the Final Solution* and *Probing the Depths of German Antisemitism*.

OMER BARTOV is the John P. Birkelund Distinguished Professor of European History at Brown University. He has written widely on Nazi Germany, interwar France, and the Holocaust. His books include, most recently, *Mirrors of Destruction* and the forthcoming *Germany's War and the Holocaust*.

ALAN BERGER occupies the Raddock Eminent Scholar Chair of Holocaust Studies and directs the Center for the Study of Values and Violence after Auschwitz at Florida Atlantic University. Among his books are *Children of Job*, *Second Generation Voices* (coedited with his wife, Naomi), and *The Continuing Agony* (as coeditor).

PETER BLACK is the senior historian at the United States Holocaust Memorial Museum. He previously served as the chief historian at the United States Justice Department's Office of Special Investigations, which is charged with investigating and prosecuting alleged Nazi offenders residing in the United States. He is the author of *Ernst*

Kaltenbrunner, Ideological Soldier of the Third Reich as well as several recent articles relating to SS and police officers and the use of police auxiliaries in German-occupied Poland.

VOJTECH BLODIG is the resident historian and deputy director of the Terezín Memorial in the Czech Republic. He has published several books and essays on the topic of the genocide of the Czech Jews in the period of Nazi occupation.

RACHEL FELDHAY BRENNER is a professor of modern Hebrew literature at the University of Wisconsin-Madison. She is the author of *Writing as Resistance* and has written numerous essays on literary responses to the Holocaust.

INSA ESCHEBACH is a historian at the memorial site and museum Neuengamme in Hamburg, Germany. She has published on the field of postwar memory and gender images and is the coeditor of the book *Gedaechtnis und Geschlecht.*

ANDREW EZERGAILIS is a professor of history at Ithaca College in New York. He is the author of *The 1917 Revolution in Latvia, The Latvian Impact on the Bolshevik Revolution,* and *The Holocaust in Latvia, 1941–1944.* He continues to write on the Holocaust.

HENRY FRIEDLANDER is a professor emeritus at the City University of New York. He is the author of *The German Revolution of 1918* and *The Origins of Nazi Genocide* and the coeditor (with Sybil Milton) of *Archives of the Holocaust.*

SAUL FRIEDLÄNDER is a professor of history at the University of California at Berkeley and Tel Aviv University (retired).

PETER HAYES is a professor of history and German and the Theodore Z. Weiss Professor of Holocaust Studies at Northwestern University. He is the author of the prizewinning *Industry and Ideology* and the editor of volumes 1 and 3 in the Lessons and Legacies series. His contribution to this volume represents a portion of the findings in his forthcoming book, *From Cooperation to Complicity.*

HANNES HEER has worked as a historian, film director, and research fellow at the Hamburg Institute for Social Research. He is the author of *Burgfrieden oder Klassenkampf, Ernst Thälmann in Selbstzeugnissen und Bilddokumenten*, and *Tote Zonen* and the editor (with Klaus Naumann) of *Vernichtungskrieg* and *War of Extermination*. He was the director of the exhibition *Vernichtungskrieg: Verbrechen der Wehrmacht 1941 bis 1944*. He is writing a book on the Wehrmacht and the Holocaust.

SARA R. HOROWITZ is the associate director of the Centre for Jewish Studies and an associate professor in the Division of Humanities at York University. She is the author of *Voicing the Void*, which received the *Choice* Award for Outstanding Academic Book. She also served as the editor for fiction of *Jewish American Women Writers*, which received the Association of Jewish Libraries Award for Outstanding Judaica Reference Book, and is the coeditor of the journal *KEREM: Creative Explorations in Judaism*.

MICHAEL R. MARRUS is the Chancellor Rose and Ray Wolfe Professor of Holocaust Studies and the dean of the graduate school at the University of Toronto. He is the author of *Vichy France and the Jews* (with Robert O. Paxton) and *The Holocaust in History*, among other works. He was a member of the recently concluded International Catholic-Jewish Historical Commission to examine the role of the Vatican during the Holocaust.

ROBERT MELSON is a professor of political science at Purdue University and the former codirector of the Jewish studies program there. He is the author of a family memoir, *False Papers*, and the prizewinning *Revolution and Genocide*.

SYBIL MILTON (1941–2000) served as chief historian of the United States Holocaust Memorial Museum until 1997. She is the coauthor (with Janet Blatter and Lori Stein) of *Art of the Holocaust*, author of *In Fitting Memory*, and coeditor (with Henry Friedlander) of *Archives of the Holocaust*. At the time of her death she was the vice president of the Independent Experts Commission: Switzerland–World War II.

ROBERT O. PAXTON is a professor emeritus of history at Columbia University. He is the author of several works about Vichy France, including (with Michael Marrus) *Vichy France and the Jews*.

RENÉE POZNANSKI is a professor of contemporary history in the Department of Politics and Government at Ben Gurion University, Beer Sheva, Israel. She is the author of *Jews in France during World War II*.

ALVIN ROSENFELD is a professor of English and the director of the Borns Jewish Studies Program at Indiana University. He is the author of *A Double Dying, Imagining Hitler*, and numerous other publications on the literature of the Holocaust.

DONALD SCHILLING is a professor of history and the dean of first-year students at Denison University, where he regularly teaches a seminar on the Holocaust. He is the editor of *Lessons and Legacies II* and has recently published a review essay on books on World War II in the *Journal of Contemporary History*.

GITTA SERENY has written several books on the Third Reich: *Into That Darkness, Albert Speer*, and most recently *The Healing Wound* (also known as *The German Trauma*), a collection of her articles about Germany from 1938 to the present.

RONALD SMELSER is a professor of history at the University of Utah in Salt Lake City. He is the author of *The Sudeten Problem, 1933–1938* and *Robert Ley*. He is the editor or coeditor of six books, including *The Nazi Elite* and *Learning about the Holocaust*, as well as the author of numerous articles. Smelser is also the past president of the German Studies Association.

THERKEL STRAEDE is a professor of contemporary German history at the University of Southern Denmark at Odense and the producer of the traveling exhibition *A Human Wall*, about the rescue of the Jews of Denmark in October 1943. He is the coauthor (with Hans Mommsen et al.) of *Das Volkswagenwerk und seine Arbeiter im Dritten Reich* and is researching Jewish slave labor in the Nazi armaments industry.